Inculturation Theology of the Jerusalem Council in Acts 15:
An Inspiration for the Igbo Church Today

European University Studies

Europäische Hochschulschriften
Publications Universitaires Européennes

Series XXIII
Theology

Reihe XXIII   Série XXIII
Theologie
Théologie

Vol./Bd. 520

PETER LANG
Frankfurt am Main · Berlin · Bern · New York · Paris · Wien

Mbachu Hilary

Inculturation Theology of the Jerusalem Council in Acts 15:

An Inspiration for the Igbo Church Today

PETER LANG

Europäischer Verlag der Wissenschaften

Die Deutsche Bibliothek - CIP-Einheitsaufnahme

Hilary, Mbachu:

Inculturation theology of the Jersualem Council in Acts 15 : an inspiration for the Igbo church today / Mbachu Hilary. - Frankfurt am Main ; Berlin ; Bern ; New York ; Paris ; Wien : Lang, 1995
  (European university studies : Series 23, Theology ; Vol. 520)
  Zugl.: Vallendar, Univ., Diss., 1994
  ISBN 3-631-48005-9

NE: Europäische Hochschulschriften / 23

ISSN 0721-3409
ISBN 3-631-48005-9
© Peter Lang GmbH
Europäischer Verlag der Wissenschaften
Frankfurt am Main 1995

Printed in Germany 1 2   4 5 6 7

Dedication

to:
the Blessed Trinity;
the Apostolic People;
the Jews and Gentiles;
Pope John Paul II;
the Society of Jesus;
Inculturators in Africa.

Deep Gratitude

Any dissertation requires many hands, ideas, a vast field of contacts, material and moral support, and above all intensive work to bring it to fruition. So is this work. My gratitude is so deep that I would have burst into *an open and unbridled extensive euology* of all who contributed to its successful completion.

But reading through the Scriptures and remembering the words of the Lord Jesus who said, *"when you give me alms, your left hand must not know what your right is doing; your alms must be in secret, and your Father who sees all that is done in secret will reward you"* (Mt 6,3-4), I am constrained not to reveal the names of all those who have in any way contributed to this work.

Again "remembering the words of the Lord Jesus, who himself said, *'there is more happiness in giving than in receiving'"* (Ac 20,35), I must continue to pray for the happiness of all who helped me in any form or shape to the accomplishment of this project.

Yes we are *"unprofitable servants: we have done no more than our duty"* (Lk 17,10). But may the Father in heaven, who sees in secret, reward abundantly each one of my helpers, benefactors and benefactresses in the way his divine providence sees it best.

However, the obligation of our academic protocol, urges me to express my special gratitude *openly* to Prof. Dr. Alfons Weiser (SAC) who moderated this thesis.

"Blessed be the God and Father of our Lord Jesus Christ, the merciful Father and the God of every encouragement; he supports us in every hardship, so that we are able to come to the support of others, in every hardship of theirs because of the encouragement that we ourselves receive from God..." (2 Co 1,3-4f).

"The Lord is my shepherd, there is nothing I shall want" (Ps 23). "My soul mangifies the Lord and my spirit rejoices in God my Saviour..." (Lk 1,46ff). "Only Luke is with me... But the Lord stood by me and gave me power, so that through me the message might be fully proclaimed for all the gentiles to hear; and so I was *saved from the lion´s mouth.* The Lord will rescue me from all evil attempts on me, and bring me safely to his heavenly kingdom. To him be glory for ever and ever, Amen" (2 Tm 4,11-18)

Hilary Mbachu

Germany, *Bonus Pastor* Sunday, April 24, 1994

Table of Contents

Chapter Three:No Salvation Without mosaic Law and Customs (15,1-5).

Chapter Four: Formal Assembly and Peter's Speech: Salvation for Jews
And Gentiles Alike (15,6-11).

Appendix

Bibliography.

Abbreviations

Abbreviations for the books of the Bible are not included here. They are basically taken from the New Jerusalem Bible (NJB) version. Variant abbreviations from other bible versions are retained in the citations from authors.

AA	Apostolicam Actuositatem.
AAS	Acta Apostolicae Sedis.
ABR	Australian Biblical Review.
AD	Anno Domini.
AECAWA	Association of Episcopal Conferences of Anglophone West Africa.
AFER	African Ecclesial Review.
AG	Ad Gentes.
AIC	African Independent Churches.
AMACEA	Association of Member Episcopal Conferences in East Africa.
AnBib	Analecta Biblica.
ANIM	Anambra-Imo.
Apg	Apostelgeschichte.
Art(s).	Article(s).
ATJ	African Theological Journal.
AUSS	Andrews University Seminary Studies.
BARC	Bulletin of African Religion and Culture.
BC	Before Christian Era.
BETL	Bibliotheca Ephemeridum Theologicarum Lovaniensium.
Bhash	Biblebhashyam.
Bib.	Biblica.
BiKi	Bibel und Kirche.
BiTrans	The Bible Translator.
BTB	Biblical Theology Bulletin.
BTS	Bigard Theological Studies.
BWANT	Beiträge zur Wissenschaft vom Alten und Neuen Testament.
BZ	Biblische Zeitschrift.
BZNW	Beihefte zur Zeitschrift fur die Neuentestamentliche Wissenschaft.
CATHAN	Catholic Theological Association of Nigeria.
CBQ	The Catholic Biblical Quarterly.

CBCN	Catholic Bishops Conference of Nigeria.
CBECSN	Catholic Bishops of East Central State of Nigeria.
CBOEP	Catholic Bishops of Onitsha Ecclesiastical Province.
CD	Christus Dominus.
Cf/cf.	Confer.
CGT	A Concordance to the Greek Testament.
Ch/ch.	Chapter.
Chaps.	Chapters.
CFL	Christifideles Laici.
CIC	Codex Iuris Canonici.
CIDJAP	Catholic Institute for Development Justice and Peace.
CIWA	Catholic Institute of West Africa.
CJ	Concordia Journal.
Conc	Concilium.
CMS	Catholic Missionary Society.
CPC	Convention of Protestant Citizens.
CSN	Catholic Secretariat of Nigeria.
CT	Catechesi Tradendae.
CWO	Catholic Women Organization.
DH	Dignitatis Humanae.
ECS	East Central State.
(Ed.)	Edited by.
ed.	edition.
EdR	Enciclopedia delle Religione.
e.g.	exampla gratia.
EN	Evangelii Nuntiandi.
ENCC	Eastern Nigeria Catholic Council.
Engl. ed.	English edition.
EP	Evangelii Praecones.
EpR	Epworth Review.
ER	Encyclopedia of Religion.
ERE	Encyclopedia of Religion and Ethics.
ETL	Ephemerides Theologicae Lovanienses.
ET	The Expository Times.
etc.	Et cetera.
EvQ	Evangelical Quarterly.
EWNT	Exegetisches Wörterbuch zum Neuen Testament.
FABC	Federation of Asian Bishop's Conference.
FC	Familiaris Consortio.
FD	Fidei Donum.
F.I.U.C.	Federation Internationale des Universités Catholiques.

Fr.	Father (Reverend).
genl. Ed.	General Editor.
GS	Gaudium et Spes.
HarvTR	Harvard Theological Review.
HALAT	Hebräisches und Aramäisches Lexikon zum Alten Testament.
HeyJ	The Heythrop Journal.
Hrsg.	Herausgegeben (Edited) or Herausgeber (Editor).
Ibid.	Ibidem (the same work or page or place).
Id.	Idem (the same author or work).
IRM	International Review of Mission.
IrTQ	The Irish Theological Quarterly.
ISMIC	Imo State Ministry of Information and Culture.
JAAR	Journal of the American Academy of Religion.
JBL	Journal of Biblical Literature.
JC	Jerusalem Council.
JETS	Journal of the Evangelical Theological Society.
Jr.	Junior.
JRA	Journal of Religion in Africa.
JSNT	Journal for the Study of the New Testament.
JSNTS	JSNT Supplement Series.
JSOT	Journal for the Study of the Old Testament.
JSOTS	JSOT Supplement Series.
JTS	Journal of Theological Studies.
KSM	Knight of St. Mulumba.
L.G.A,	Local Government Area.
LG	Lumen Gentium.
LS	Louvain Studies.
LebZeu	Lebendiges Zeugnis.
Loc. cit.	Locus citatus.
MD	Mulieris Dignitatem.
MI	Maximum Illud.
NA	Nostra Aetate.
NACATH	National Association of Catholic Theology Students.
NCE	New Catholic Encyclopedia.
NECN	National Episcopal Conference of Nigeria.
NEE	New Era of Evangelisation.
NJB	The New Jerusalem Bible.
NJBC	The New Jerome Biblical Commentary.
NJT	The Nigerian Journal of Theology.
NRT	Nouvelle Revue Théologique.
NT	Novum Testamentum / New Testament.

NTSuppl	Supplements to Novum Testamentum.
NTA	New Testament Abstracts.
NTS	New Testament Studies.
NUT	Nigerian Union of Teachers.
NZMw	Neue Zeitschrift für Missionswissenschaft.
L'OssRom	L'Osservatore Romano.
Opt.Tot.	Optatam Totius.
OT	Old Testament.
PACT	Pan African Conference of Theologians.
PalCl	Palestra del Clero.
par.	paragraph.
PBC	Pontifical Bibilical Commission.
PCID	Pontifical Council for Interreligious Dialogue.
PG	Patrologia Graeca.
PL	Patrologia Latina.
p(p).	Page(s).
PO	Presbyterorum Ordinis.
PP.	Pope.
PrinPa	Princeps Pastorum.
PRS	Perspectives in Religious Studies.
RAT	Revue Africaine de Théologie.
RB	Revue Biblique.
RCI	Revista del Clero Italiano.
RCM	Roman Catholic Mission.
RE	Rerum Ecclesiae.
REx	The Review and Expositor
RM	Redemptoris Missio.
RNC	Royal Niger Company.
RQ	Restoration Quarterly.
RSR	Recherches de Science Religieuses.
SA	Slavorum Apostoli.
SBL	Society of Biblical Literature.
SC	Sacrosanctum Concilium.
SCC	Sacred Congregation for the Clergy.
SCCE	Sacred Congrgation for Catholic Education.
SCPF	Sacred Congregation for the Propagation of the Faith.
SD	Studiorum Ducem.
SECAM	Symposium of Episcopal Conferences of Africa and Madagasca.
SEDOS	Servizio di Documentazione e Studi.
SJ	Society of Jesus.
SLA	Studies in Luke-Acts.

SP	Summi Pontificatus.
SPUC	Secretariat for the Promotion of the Unity of Christians.
SRS	Sollicitudo Rei Socialis.
SS.	Saints.
St.	Saint.
ST	Studia Theologica.
STE	Studi di Teologia Evangelico.
SVC	Second Vatican Council.
SWJT	Southwestern Journal of Theology.
TBNT	Theologisches Begriffslexikon zum Neuen Testament.
TLZ	Theologische Literaturzeitung.
TR	Theologische Revue.
TRu	Theologische Rundschau.
TS	Theological Studies.
TWAT	Theologisches Wörterbuch zum Alten Testament.
TWNT	Theologisches Wörterbuch zum Neuen Testament.
UBS	Bulletin of the United Bible Societies.
UNESCO	United Nations Educational, Scientific and Cultural Organization.
UPE	Universal Primary Education.
UR	Unitatis Redintegratio.
V(v).	Verse(s), in capital or small letters.
VKGNT	Vollständige Konkordanz zum Griechischen Neuen Testament.
Vol(s).	Volume(s), in capital or small letters.
VoxEv	Vox Evangelica.
VS	Veritatis Splendor.
WAJES	West African Journal of Ecclesial Studies.
ZNW	Zeitschrift für die Neutestamentliche Wissenschaft.
ZDP	Zeitschrift des Deutschen Palästinavereins.
ZTK	Zeitschrift für Theologie und Kirche.

General Introduction

The convocation of the early Church in Jerusalem (Ac 15,1-35) or the Jerusalem Council (**JC**) to resolve the faith-culture conflicts caused by the Judaizing Christians of the sect of the Pharisees should provide a veritable inspiration for the resolution of faith-culture conflicts in the local Churches of our times and in the future.

Scope of Study.

The positive or negative evangelical and missionary activities of the "*dramatis personae*" of the Council story and their respective contributions to the resolution of the faith-culture conflict in the apostolic Church constitute the inculturation theology of the JC. The study proposes to use the JC theology as a basis for the resolution of a similar faith-culture conflict for the current Igbo Church.

It aims at inspiring the Igbo Catholic Church to emulate the example of the apostolic Church and to evangelise as the apostolic people did so that Christ's message may be fully rooted or inculturated in every aspect of Igbo Christian life. It also aims at the use of the JC theology as an inspiration for the insertion of the Gospel message in the contemporary Igbo Church so that the native believers can freely worship God and gain salvation without being subjected to the yoke (*zugos*) or burden (*baros*) of the foreign Euro-American cultures through which the Gospel was transmitted to them.

Just as the Graeco-Roman Gentiles were not obliged by the JC to become Jews first or to adopt Jewish life style in order to become Christians and be saved, so also should the modern Igbo Gentile Christians not be obliged to live like the Graeco-Romans or like Europeans and Americans in order to become Christians and be saved. Rather by following the wise counsels of the JC, the salvation of all peoples, white or black, rich or poor, young or old, should be achieved through a pastoral inculturation of the Good News in their lives.

Inculturated Evangelisation.

"Inculturation", though a theological "*neologism*"[1] is in fact an old evangelical reality as is evident from the biblical revelation in OT and NT. Coined and promoted in Jesuit circles more than thirty years ago and introduced in 1979 into papal teachings and documents by Pope John Paul II, inculturation has not only become a household word in the Church's life and ministry but has become the current method of ecclesial evangelisation[2] in order to establish an unbroken dialogue and encounter between "the salvific message of the Gospel and the multiplicity of cultures"[3] for the salvation of all peoples.

Inculturation has become a prime task of the missionary Church and the preferred method of evangelisation. Therefore it is not just a task for the Blacks or for "the black continent of Africa" (*für den schwarzen Kontinent*) nor is it a theology which the Black Africans must learn from the white Euro-American missionaries and theologians. Rather "evangelisation through inculturation"[4] is a task for the whole People of God (white or black, red or yellow) scattered throughout the four winds of the earth (cf. Ac 1,8; Rv 5,9).

If inculturation is a neologism, and if modern scholars have accepted Luke-Acts as "a storm centre in contemporary scholarship"[5], the inculturation study of the Acts as a basis for inculturated ministry in the local Churches is still the "storm centre" in the missionary inculturation theology and *praxis* of the Church. This is because while Luke-Acts is a narrative unit[6] of how the Lord Jesus and the apostolic people inculturated the faith in the Jewish and Greaco-Roman environments, the study of the inculturation theology of Acts continues to bring the early apostolic mission of the Acts narrative into the limelight of contemporary missiology, pastoral theology and inculturated evangelisation especially in the "young Churches" of Africa[7].

And if the whole Acts now occupies a pride of place in the theology and practice of inculturated apostolate, the apostolic Council in Acts 15 is even drawing more attention from scholars and pastors as the basic text ("*texte fondamental*")[8] for inculturation in the local Churches. This is a basic reason for my choice of the study of the inculturation theology of Acts 15 as an inspiration for the contemporary Igbo Church.

---

1   John Paul II, CT, no. 53.
2   Cf. Id., RM, 53-54.
3   Id., Epistula, in: AAS (74) (1982) 686.
4   Cf. CBCN, Nigerian Church: Evangelisation through Inculturation (1991), passim.
5   Van Unnik, Luke-Acts, A Storm Centre, in: SLA, 15-32.
6   Cf. Tannehill, Narrative Unity, the two volumes.
7   Cf. Amewowo et al., Les Actes des Apotres et les Jeunes Eglises (1990), passim
8   Pasinya, L' Inculturation, in Amewowo et alii, Les Actes, 126.

Now it must be pointed out that, despite the ecclesial and scholarly recognition of the inculturation value of Acts, not many books have been devoted to a *systematic thematic treatment* of inculturation theology based solely on the inspiration drawn from the ministry of the apostolic people in general or from Acts 15 in particular.

But two works deserve special mention in this regard. They are: M. Dumais' twenty two-page article on *"The Church of the Apostles: A Model of Inculturation"*[9]; and a series of eleven articles and responses to them in *"Les Actes des Apotres et les jeunes Eglises"*[10] by the participants at the Second Congress of African Biblical Scholars. This fewness of *systematized theses or volumes* on the inculturation value of the Acts makes our study an original contribution to the theology and practice of inculturated evangelisation today.

If an *ordinary study* of "inculturation theology" is already a worthwhile and a very commendable project, more noble still is such a study from the biblical perspective because the Holy Scripture is regarded as "the soul of all theology"[11]. This fact also lends more weight to the importance and significance of our work based on the inculturation phenomena in Acts 15.

Motivation.

The project is particularly motivated by the longing to provide some possible solutions to the problems posed by the Euro-American acculturated Gospel among the Igbo. The mode in which the white missionaries at times presented the Good News has often led the local people to despise their *God-given* cultural values. This cultural apathy or lethargy resulted in creating numerous dichotomies in the Igbo way of life[12].

By making a strict distinction between the sacred and the secular/profane, the christian Good News shattered and dichotomised the originally monistic Igbo world view, attacked the Igbo spirit and even alienated their souls from their authentic cultural and traditional values[13]. The Igbo person thus "fell apart"[14] at the onslaught of a Christian message presented to him/her in strange Western spirituality, theological and philosphical categories and thoughts[15].

---

9   Dumais, in: Crollius, Inculturation, 10, 3-24.
10   Amewowo et alii, op. cit., passim.
11   Vatican II, Optatam Totius, 16.
12   Cf. Ojukwu, Because I am Involved, 2.
13   Cf. Agu, Secularization, 257ff; 295ff.
14   Cf. Achebe, Things Fall Apart (1962), passim.
15   Cf. Agu, op. cit., 296f.

The consequence is very grave and painful. Now clergy, religious and laity are caught in the dilemma of how to reconcile the dichotomy or the "rift"[16] between the Gospel in Euro-American cultural garb and authentic Igbo cultural values. Against this background, this study is hoped to be a *"vade mecum"* in trying to bridge the split between the Good News and Igbo culture and in promoting a reciprocal reconciliation of the Igbo way of life with the Good News.

Division of Work.

The Greek Text of Acts 15,1-35 form the basis of the study which is being organized within a framework of *Three Parts* consisting of *Ten Chapters.*

Part One is an excursus on preliminary issues and consists of the first two chapters. Chapter one shall try to clarify the fundamental notions of the title of the work. Chapter two is devoted to a brief survey of the fruitful insights gained from the Acts-research since 1826 and the methods being employed for our study.

Part Two consits of six chapters (chapters three to eight) and shall focus on the narrative-inculturation, exegetical study of Acts 15,1-35. The exegesis shall seek to spotlight and highlight the inculturation phenomena patent or deducible from the Council proceedings.

Part Three consists of chapters nine and ten and is devoted to inculturation theological evaluation of the JC and its correlation to the Igbo Church. Chapter nine shall discuss the theological import of the exegetical study of the JC proceedings and shall seek to draw from it a missionary message for a given local Church. The *hermeneutical* correlation in chapter ten shall try to show how the JC's provisions can be employed in the resolution of faith-culture conflict in the contemporary Igbo Church.

The conclusion shall emphasize the appropriateness of drawing inspiration from the JC teaching for the inculturation of the faith in the Igbo Church today.

Methodological Procedure.

Using the narrative-inculturation exegetical method[17], Acts 15 shall be studied as a plot of resolution and as a *theological* story of faith-culture conflict and

---

16   Cf. Paul VI, EN, no. 18.
17   "A method is a particular way of doing something" (Sinclair et al., Pons Dictionary, 910). Hence here "methods" should be understood in the comprehensive sense of the

its resolution. Such a study is expected to act as an inspiration for the resolution of faith-culture conflict in the Igbo Church or in any other local Church willing to learn and benefit from the theology of the JC.

The import of each method and the reason for the choice of a combination of the two methods shall be explained in chapter two. While the exegetical study is to be basically conducted on the *synchronic* (narrative) level, the historical-critical method which is basically *diachronic* furnishes the scientific basis for the synchronic method. Also inculturation study is basically diachronic. This means that our narrative-inculturation study is synchronic with a diachronic tinge.

The narrative-inculturation exegetical study is a difficult attempt at marrying scientific exegesis and theology with christian pastoral practice in the socio-cultural context of a People of God. For me, it is a personal response and contribution to the Second Vatican Council's (SVC's) clarion call on theologians to seek out, "within the methods and limits of the science of theology", "more efficient ways of presenting their teaching to the modern man"[18].

Sources of Study.

The sources of our study are based mainly on library research on Acts 15, Acts theology, and allied works on the Holy Scriptures, the Fathers of the Church, papal and ecclesial documents, literature on inculturation theology and on the Igbo, Nigeria and Africa. My traditional life as an Igbo, the long years of personal contacts with peoples of Nigeria, Africa, America, Asia and Europe and my special experiences as Editor of "The Leader", pastor, tutor, student of the Pontifical Bibilical Institute (Rome) and of the Hebrew University (Jerusalem), and as lecturer in the Catholic Institute of West Africa (CIWA), are all integrated in this exegetico-theological inculturation research and reflection.

On a Hopeful Note.

I must add that this work is appearing at an opportune time - indeed "*at the fullness of time*" (Ga 4,4) during which the Vatican City (the headquarters of the Catholic Church) establishes diplomatic and friendly relationship with Je-

---

"more efficient ways" by which theologians and exegetes seek to present "their teaching to modern man" in accordance with the exhortation of the SVC (cf. GS, 62).

18   SVC, GS, ibid.

rusalem (the headquarters of the State of Israel or the Jewish nation)[19] and the Synod of Bishops from African Catholic Churches is taking place in the Vatican City[20].

These two events are indicative of the fruitful results that can be achieved or reaped from a continual, friendly and mutual dialogue between the carrier-culture of the Gospel and the culture of the receiving audience. They also add colour to my proposal of using the *Jerusalem Council* that took place in the Jewish country/Israel in the first Christian century as an inspiration for a hermeneutical inculturation of the faith in the Igbo Gentile Church (or any other local Church) in the approach of the third Christian millenium.

It is hoped that as the Universal Gentile Church tries to end her conflicts with the Jewish nation/Israel and Judaism, the Igbo Church basing herself on the teaching and provisions of the Jerusalem Council should also seek to bring an end to the faith-culture conflicts between Euro-American acculturated Christian message and the Igbo culture.

---

19 Cf. Holy See and Israel, in: L'Osservatore Romano, N. 1 (1322), (5 January 1994), p. 9; Konferenz von Christen und Juden in Jerusalem, in: Deutsche Tagespost, 47/14, (3. February 1994), p. 1.

20 The Synod begins on Low Sunday, April 10, 1994.

Part One.

Excursus on Preliminary Issues.

This part consists of chapters one and two. Chapter one shall make an exposition of the concepts contained or implied in the title. Chapter two shall make a brief review of the main direction of the Acts-research with a special focus on Acts 15 and expose the selected methods for the study.

1. Chapter One.

Exposition of the Title of Our Study.

This expositon is necessary in order to finetune meanings and ensure that the reader understands what the theme is all about. The concepts and notions included in the title of the work are theology, culture, inculturation, Acts 15, inspiration, Nigeria, Igbo and Church.

1.1 Theology.

Theology should be understood both in the scholastic sense of "faith seeking for understanding" and from the import of its Greek etymology "*theos-logos*" as the knowledge or wisdom or discussion about God or divinities. "Basically, theology is no more than *theo-logia*, a speaking about God or the gods"[1] . The focus in this work is on Catholic inculturation theology. Inculturation theology is the God-talk which takes into account the cultures, socio-religious beliefs and practices of a people and tries to come to terms with them. It is a theology that recognises and respects cultural pluralism[2] and engages in inter-religious dialogue[3] with all peoples, cultural groups and their world views[4] .

1.2 Culture.

Culture is the root word for inculturation. Originally culture was understood either in terms of the level of one's cultivation, civilization or sophistication, or in terms of one's intellectual enlightenment, classic education, and artistic refinement[5] . But from the later part of the 19th century it began to connote the characteristic mode of human life equiperated with civilization.

---

1   Shorter, African Christian Theology, 27.
2   Cf. Onaiyekan, Nigerian Theology, 6f.
3   PCID, Bulletin 82 [(1993) XXVIII/1], 6 passim; Id., Bulletin 84 [(1993) XXVIII/3], 223 passim.
4   Cf. Hesselgrave, Communicating Christ, 121ff.
5   Cf. Carrier, Understanding Culture, 13; Lang, Culture, 522. Cf. Kroeber/Kluckhohn, Culture, 149.

Culture or civiization is that complex whole which includes knowledge, belief, art, morals, law, custom, and any other capabilities and habits acquired by man as a member of the society[6].

In our times culture embraces the "sum total of what an individual acquires from his society"[7]. Culture is

a plan consisting of a set of norms, standards, and associated notions and beliefs for coping with the various demands of life, shared by a group, learned by the individual from the society, and organized into a dynamic system of control[8].

The Second Vatican Council (SVC), teaches that "the word 'culture' in general refers to all those things which go to the refining and developing of man's diverse mental and physical endowments"[9] such as human labour, family and community life, customs, institutions, spiritual experiences, religious practice, laws and juridical institutions, science, arts and aesthetics. All these are the components of culture which should be related to christian faith and life[10].

The theological notion of culture was later popularised by Pope Paul VI whose teaching laid much emphasis on the "evangelisation of cultures"[11]. The present Pope John Paul II equally laid and continues to lay stress on "the apostolic dialogue of the Church with cultures"[12], because "true culture" is "humanisation... development carried out in all fields of reality in which man is situated and takes his place: in his spirituality and corporeality, in the universe, in human and divine society"[13]. Furthermore,

culture is the life of the spirit, it is the key which gives access to the deepest and most jealously guarded secrets of the life of peoples; it is the fundamental and unifying expression of their existence... In a word, to say 'culture' is to express in a single word, the national identity which constitutes the life of these peoples and which survives despite the adverse conditions and trials of every kind, the historical or natural cataclysms, while remaining one and compact across the centuries[14].

---

6   Tylor, Primitive Culture, I, 1.
7   Lowie, History of Ethnological Theory, 3. Cf. Kroeber, Anthropology, 8; Kluckhorn, Mirror, 17; Keesing, Anthropology, 18.
8   Luzbetak, Church, 156 (cf. p. 74). Cf. Onwuejeogwu, Evolutionary Trends, 6.
9   Vatican II, GS, no. 53.
10 Id., GS, nos. 57-58.
11 Paul VI, EN, no. 20.
12 John Paul II, CT, no. 54.
13 Id., To Men of Culture, AAS 72 (1980) 848.
14 Id., To Diplomatic Corps, AAS (1981) 188-189. Cf. To UNESCO, AAS 72 (1980) 738; To Scholars, AAS 73 (1981) 422-423.

In sum, culture is the totality of the mode of human existence from the most insignifcant things of life to the highest moral and spiritual values from birth to death. It embraces a people's worldview; the way they think, decide, act, speak or talk; the way they organize themselves, interact, communicate, and celebrate; the way they work, pray, and worship; the way they eat, drink, play, dance and rest until death comes[15].

1.3   A History of the Term "Inculturation".

While culture is primarily an anthropological concept before being introduced into theological literature, inculturation is basically a theological concept coined by Churchmen and Theologians in order to express the inter-relationship between the Christian faith and human cultures. The exact time of its origin or coinage is not easy to point out.

In 1988 Hervé Carrier of the Society of Jesus (SJ) stated that inculturation had been employed in the Catholic circles for more than fifty years[16]. Crollius (SJ) seemed to trace the origin of the term to J. Masson (SJ), who in 1962 wrote an article in which he made useful suggestions for an "inculturated" catholic Christianity[17]. This article titled "*L'Église Ouverte sur le Monde*" was historic since it coincided with the beginnings of the reforms and renewals of the SVC. Alyward Shorter stated that Masson was the first to employ the term in a theological tract as the SVC was about to commence. Masson then wrote that,

aujourd'hui, alors que, tout justement, l'exigence se fait plus urgente d'un catholicisme inculturé d'une facon polymorphe[18] (Today there is a more urgent need for a catholicism that is inculturated in a variety of forms).

Masson's reason for his "thesis" was that by 1962, there was already an un-precedented cultural awareness among peoples. The great cultural groups had begun to feel, appreciate and defend their cultural origins, their customs and characteristics, their language, art, symbols etiquettes, their general world view and way of life[19].

---

15   Cf. Fitzpatrick, One Church, 27-48.
16   Cf. Carrier, Inculturation, 4; Id., Evangélisation, 83.
17   Cf. Crollius, So New About, 722.
18   L'Eglise, 1038. The English translation is mine.
19   Ibid. The french original of this paraphrase reads: "*Jamais sans doute autant que de nos jours, les grands groupes culturels de l'humanité n'ont senti, apprécié et voulu défendre leur originalité culturelle, leur sol avec ses caractères propres, leur langue,*

In 1973 a protestant missionary, G. L. Barney, used the term inculturation as he made proposals on how to intermarry faith and culture[20]. Then in 1974 the Federation of Asian Bishop's Conference (FABC) issued a document in which they hoped for "a Church" that is both "indigenous and inculturated"[21].

Between December 1974 and April 1975, the Society of Jesus spent much of their 32nd General Congregation on the theme of inculturation. One sees the frequent use of the term in the fourth, fifth, and sixth "decrees" of the Congregation. The fifth decree itself was devoted to the theme of "Promoting the Work of Inculturation of Faith and Christian Life"[22]. Then in October 1975 the Dominican priest, Yves congar, wrote that inculturation was coined in Japan as a modification for "acculturation"[23].

At the 1977 Synod of Bishops on Catechesis, the then Jesuit General Superior, Fr. Arrupe, used the term in his own interventions and stressed the need for a balanced cultural pluralism in the Church. At the close of the Synod in November 1977, the Bishops made a vital pronouncement on catechesis as "an instrument of inculturation".

> The Christian Message must find its roots in human cultures and must also transform these cultures. In this sense we can say that catechesis is an instrument of inculturation[24].

The Synod pronouncement constitutes a landmark in the Church's awareness and use of the term, since it was probably the first time the word occurred in a message addressed to the Universal Church. Sequel to these events, Fr. Arrupe, on April 15, 1978, addressed a letter on inculturation to all the Jesuits. This was followed by seminars on inculturation held in the Gregorian University, Rome[25]. In the same 1978 J. O. Buswell attributed the coinage of the term to G. L Barney and went on to cite the latter's viewpoint on the implications of the supracultural elements for missions:

---

leur art, leur symbolique, leur étiquette, leur **svadharma** indien, leur **Weltanschauung** ou leur négritude, jadis honteuse, mais maintenant brandie comme un fier drapeau".

20 Cf. De Napoli, Inculturation, 71.

21 FABC, His Gospel, 322.

22 Cf. Crollius, op. cit., 722; Shorter, op. cit., 10.

23 Cf. Christianisme, 100. But Congar did not furnish us with his sources information about the Japanese coinage/origin of the term.

24 Synod, Relatio Finalis, II, D, 4. In this latin text of the Message, "inculturatio" stands for inculturation.

25 Cf. Shorter, op. cit., 10.

the essential nature of these supracultural components should neither be lost nor distorted but rather secured and interpreted clearly through the guidance of the Holy Spirit inculturating them in these cultures[26].

Inculturation appeared for the first time in a Papal document on April 26, 1979 in the address of John Paul II to the members of the Pontifical Biblical Commission gathered in Rome to study the subject of the "cultural integration of revelation"[27]. The term occurred again in the Pope's "*Catechesi Tradendae*" (CT, no. 53) of October the same year.

So in the history of papal documents, inculturation appeared for the first time, not in the missiological or catechetical context, as some authors may lead us to believe[28], but in a *biblical* context. This fact gives the ecclesial teaching on inculturation a specifically strong biblical basis and perspective. The term also appeared in the teaching of the Pope in the "*Familiaris Consortio*" of November 1981 in which he exhorted the whole People of God to a

"greater pastoral diligence so that this 'inculturation' (*cultus humani inductio*) of the Christian faith may come about ever more extensively in the context of marriage and family as well as in other fields[29].

From 1980 upwards inculturation became the frequent theme of John Paul II during his "Pastoral Visits to the young Churches"[30] of Africa. In my own country Nigeria, his inculturation teaching in February 1982 introduced and stimulated a "new era of evangelisation"[31].

Among the Jesuits, more seminars on inculturation were organized first in Jerusalem (1981) then in Yogyakarta (1983) and again in Jerusalem (1985)[32]. In a message to the participants of the 1981 Jerusalem Seminar, Fr. Arrupe noted the particular devotion of the Jesuits to the inculturation question and also pointed out the significance of that first *interdisciplinary* Seminar:

So much had been spoken and written in recent years about inculturation - particularly by the Jesuits, and by myself since the 32nd General Congregation. The great amount of material that has appeared in print serves rather to show how much has still to be done, and

---

26   Buswell, Contextualization, 90.
27   To PBC. AAS 71 (1971) 606.
28   Cf. CT, no. 53. Some scholars regard CT 53 as the first official time "inculturation" appeared in a papal document (cf. Shorter, Toward A theology, 10; 16). But in actual fact, the term occurred for the first time in the Pope's Address to members of the PBC.
29   John Paul II, FC, no. 10.
30   Id., RM, no. 52.
31   NECN, Papal Message, 38; CBCN, New Era, 1. More will be said on this papal visit in chapter ten.
32   Cf. Crollius, Inculturation, vol. 3, ix; vo. 8, ix.

the need to do it well... It is significant that the seminar takes place in Jerusalem, where at the very beginning of her history the Church faced up to the question of what is the proper expression of the faith in daily life and activity[33].

What emerges from this survey of the origin and evolution of the term "inculturation" is that it has been coined, introduced into theological language and popularised particularly among the Jesuits. But this affirmation of the "*Jesuit* origin" of the word does not in any way detract from the positive contributions of other renowned Churchmen, missionaries and scholars to the coinage, usage, and popularisation of the term in their Writings. After the impact of the teachings of the *Catechesi Tradendae* and the Jesuits' Seminars, inculturation became a vogue-word in biblical science, theology, missiology, in the pastoral ministry and in the contemporary Christian life[34].

1.4 What is Inculturation?

Though a 'neologism,' inculturation has evoked many descriptions and definitions which are basically reducible to the reality of the "insertion of the Gospel" or the divine word in human culture(s). It is in general a reciprocal exchange between the Gospel values and a people's way of life. It is a dialogue between the greater and more sublime (the Christian Faith or Gospel) and the lesser or less sublime (culture), in which the Faith or the Gospel becomes the authoritative norm because the Good News transcends every culture. It is a dialogal evangelisation of cultures. In a letter to "All Jesuits", Fr. Pedro Arrupe defines it as

> the incarnation of Christian life and of Christian message in a particular culture context, in such a way that this experience not only finds expression through elements proper to the culture in question, but becomes a principle that animates, directs, and unifies the culture, transforming and remaking it so as to bring about "a new creation"[35].

Crollius modifies this definition by adding the element of mutual enrichment of Church and culture as the result of inculturation. Inculturation is meant "to create a new unity and communion, not only within the culture in question, but also as an enrichment of the Church Universal"[36].

---

33 Message, in Crollius, vol. 1, xi.
34 Cf. Onwubiko, Theory, 1-11, for similar informations on the "*genesis of the term inculturation*".
35 Arrupe, Letter, 9.
36 Crollius, So New About, 735.

Pope John Paul II, in his very first employment of the term, used it inter-changeably with "acculturation"[37] and based the reality on the analogy of the incarnation of Jesus Christ.

The term "acculturation", or "inculturation" may well be a neologism, but it expresses very well one of the great mystery of the incarnation... The same divine word had previously become human language assuming the ways of expression of the different cultures, which from Abraham to the seer of the Apocalypse, offered the adorable mystery of God's salvific love the possibility of becoming accessible and understandable for successive generations in spite of the multiple diversity of their historical situations[38].

Right from the post-apostolic period through the Medieval times up to our own era, the history of the Church is replete with theoretical teachings and practical efforts by the Church Fathers, theologians, missionaries, and the Church Magisterium to insert the Gospel among every people and culture in accordance with the mandate of Christ (Ac 1,8)[39].

---

37   In 1935 the Social Science Research of America defined *acculturation* as that which "comprehends those phenomena which result when groups of individuals having different cultures come into continuous first hand contact, with subsequent changes in the original cultural patterns of either or both groups".(Cited by Herskovits, Man, 523). It differs from **enculturation** which refers to "the aspects of the learning experience which mark off man from other creatures, and by means of which, initially, and in later life, he achieves competence in his culture". (Herskovits, Man, 39).

38   To PBC. AAS 71 (1979) 606; cf. CT, 53. Here the Pope considers "acculturation" as being synonymous with "inculturation", but both concepts do not have identical meanings. Generally, however, they connote a cross-cultural contact: acculturation in the *anthroplogical* sense and context; inculturation in the *theologico-missiological* sense and context.

39   For some examples of the seminal teachings and the practice of inculturation: **1.** Among the **FATHERS**, cf.: Ad Diognetum, 5-6; St. Justin Martyr, Apologia, 1,44 & 46; 2,10 & 13; Clement of Alexandria, Stromata, 1,5; Eusebius of Caesarea, Historia, 1,4; St Irenaeus, Adversus Haereses, III, 18,1 & IV, 6.7; Tertullian, Apologeticus, 27. These Fathers did not use the term "inculturation", but the reality it signifies is contained in their teachings. **2.** Among **THEOLOGIANS**, cf.: *St. Augustine of Hippo*, De Civitate Dei, 10,29; De Trinitate, 13.19.24; Enarationes in Ps. 130.9-12; Epistola, 118.4.23; Sermones, 266-269; Du Roy, Augustine, 1041-1058; Also cf. *St. Thomas Aquinas*, In Ethic. 1.2-3; ST 1a 3.4 ad 2; ST 1a 2ae 94.2; Wallace/Weisheipl, Aquinas, 102-115. St. Augustine (also one of the Fathers) and St. Thomas distinguished themselves in their ability to intermarry and integrate pagan Greek or non-christian philosophies with the Christian Faith. While the Second Vatican Council copiously cited the works of Augustine, the Church had institutionalized Aquinas since the 1918 Code of Canon Law, and has now taken him as a "model" of all Priest and Theologians (cf. 1918 CIC, 1366; 589.1; Opt. Tot., 16; Pius XII, To Seminarians, 247; Paul VI, In Gregorian University, 365; To Thomistic Congress, 788-792; Schineller, Life, 18-33. **3.** Among the **MISSIONARIES** were Cyril and Methodius, the

1.4.1 Perspectives of Inculturation.

The meaning of inculturation indicates that the reality can be understood from different perspectives expressed with different, and more or less adequate, terminologies. It can be understood from the local, cultural, domestical, social, personal, liturgical, and theological points of view. A brief overview of each of these may throw more light on the meaning of "inculturation".

From the perspective of the *Locale*, inculturation is a universal phenomenon and takes on a meaning from the place where it is practised or from the people who practise it. It can assume continental, national, and ethnical connotations. In this sense one can speak of inculturation as the Americanisation, or Europeanisation, or Asiatisation, or Africanisation, etc of the Church; or as the Germanisation, Italianisation, Nigerianisation, etc of Christianity; or of making the Church English, French, Bavarian, Prussian, Hausa, Yoruba, Igbo[40] and so on.

"Apostles of the Slavs"; cf. John Paul II, SA. AAS (1985) 779-813; Devos, Cyril, 579; Fitzpatrick, One Church, 54-61. So also was the Italian Jesuit, Matteo Ricci; cf. Rouleau, Ricci, 470-472; Fitzpatrick, One church, 61-91; Hering, Evangelisierung, 19-20; Rosso, Conficius, 156-165. Another Italian Jesuit, De Nobili was noted for his inculturation efforts in India; cf. Cronin, Nobili, 477-478; Metzler, Memoria Rerum, vol. 3/2,702-703; Griffiths, Vedanta, 584; Id., Vedas, 584. **4.** For the teachings of the **MAGISTERIUM** on Faith and cultures, cf. Gregory the Great, Ad Mellitum, 1215-1217; Collectanea S.C.P.F., vol. 1, no. 2 pp. 1-2; no 3 pp. 3-4; no. 135, p.42; Metzler, Memoria Rerum, vol.1/1, 28-30; 3/2 784-789; Benedict XV, MI. AAS 11 (1919) 445-448; Pius XI, RE. AAS 18 (1926) 74-77; Pius XII, SP. AAS (1939) 429; Message. AAS 38 (1946) 18; EP. AAS 43 (1951) 521-524; John XXIII, PP. AAS 51 (1959) 836-846. Pope John inaugurated the Second Vatican Council which made the relationship between Faith and culture one of its principal pastoral themes: cf. for example, SC, 37. AAS 56 (1964) 110; LG, 1-17. AAS 57 (1965) 5-21; AG, 10-22. AAS 58 (1966) 959-974; *GS, 53-62. AAS 58 (1966) 1075-1084.* All these passages teach on the insertion of the Gospel in cultures. But consult in a special way,-Paul VI, EN. AAS 68 (1976) 1-96; John Paul II, CT. AAS 71 (1979) 1277-1340; SA. AAS 77 (1985) 779-813; RM. AAS 83 (1991) 249-340 as the "new magnae cartae" on evangelisation, catechesis, misson, and inculturation of the Gospel. **5. MONOGRAPHS** (among so many taken together) may provide the reader with a sufficient history of inculturation reality and process from the Biblical to modern times. They are: Wilson, Gentiles; Shorter, Theology; Schineller, Handbook; Fitzpatrick, One Church, Onwubiko, Theory and Practice. **6. SPECIAL ARTICLES ON INCULTURATION** are found in Okure/Van Thiel et al., 32 Articles Evaluating Inculturation; in AFER 22/6 (1980) passim and AFER 36/1 (1994) passim.

40   The Hausa, the Igbo and the Yoruba peoples constitute the three major ethnic and language groups of Nigeria in which are found more than 250 ethnic groups and languages (cf. Newswatch, March 20, 1989, pp. 13-18).

This must have led Pope John Paul II in his address to the Zairean Bishops to speak of "inculturation of the Gospel" among Africans as "the Africanisation of the Church"[41]. And from the perspective of the evangeliser in any of these local contexts, Hervé Carrier says that

> inculturation is the effort to inject Christ's message into a given socio-cultural milieu, thereby summoning that milieu to grow in accordance with its values so long as the latter can be reconciled with the Gospel message. Inculturation seeks to naturalize the Church in every country, region, and social sector, while fully respecting the native genius and character of each human collectivity[42].

Culturally inculturation is the integration of the Christian faith with every culture and language. Here readily comes to mind the Pentecost event in which Jewish peoples "from every nation under heaven" heard "the marvels of God in their own native languages and were converted to the faith (Ac 2,1-12). This means a "cross-culturation" of the Good News whereby the Gospel meets cultures, and the cultures interact with the Gospel and with themselves via the medium of the Good News proclaimed to the peoples. The result is the mutual enrichment of both Gospel and culture(s). This is why some have preferred to talk about inculturation in terms of "interculturation" of the Christian Faith[43].

Socially inculturation is the insertion of the Gospel into all the strata of the human community (cf. EN, 18) in accordance with the mandate of the risen Christ to "go out to the whole world" and "proclaim the Gospel to all creation" (Mk 16,15). The social dimension of inculturation is bound up with the missionary task of the universal Church[44]. Of special importance in this social insertion are the

> basic Ecclesial Communities confessing and celebrating the Gospel, Communities of Faith socially involved, or Communities of Solidarity between peoples of different faiths or differing opinions.... Inculturation of the Gospel remains always the responsibility of the Christian community, of which the missionary is a part[45].

Domestically inculturation is the rooting of the Gospel in every home and among all the members of a family since the family is the domestic Church, and "the Church is a home and family for everyone"[46].

---

41   To Bishops of Zaire, 223.
42   Inculturation, 6; cf. Evangelisation, 87-88.
43   Blomjous, Development, 393.
44   Cf. Katechismus, nos. 849-856.
45   SEDOS, Seminar, 377-378.
46   John Paul II, FC, 85.

Individually inculturation is the incarnation of the Christian message into the life of a human person in such a way that this message takes place in the person, renews, and transforms the one into a true follower of Christ, making him/her "a new creation"[47]. From this point of view,

> inculturation calls for a special **kenosis** in the missionary who disposes himself or herself for a change and participation in the creative inculturation undertaken by the whole christian Community in a particular place[48].

Liturgically inculturation involves the employment of local elements and symbols as "the matter and form" of sacramental rites and Christian worship. It connotes the use of the local "fruit of the earth and the work of human hands" in the worship of God taught by the SVC[49]. It includes the accomodation of sound cultural elements in the liturgy[50].

Theologically inculturation is basically incarnational since "it expresses very well one factor of the great mystery of the incarnation" (CT, 53) and it is "a reflection of the Incarnation of the Word" (Christ) who is the embodiment of the "divinity in all its fullness" (Col 2,9). Although inculturation is radically incarnational and christology is basic to inculturation[51], it would be incomplete to understand inculturation only on the analogy of the Incarnation or of Christology.

Inculturation is equally, if not moreso, Trinitarian and *"Trinitological"*. It means the insertion of the trinitarian life of the Triune God into the life style of every person and people and into every stratum of the human life and existence and vice-versa. It is the perennial rooting of the Gospel among all nations and peoples "in the name of the Father, and of the Son, and of the Holy Spirit" (Mt 28,19f).

While "inculturation has its source and inspiration in the mystery of the incarnation" and may in infact be another way to describe Christian mission, while it really sees that "mission in the perspective of the flesh, or the concrete embodiment, which the Word assumes in a particular individual, institution or culture"[52], nevertheless it is the Triune God, (not solely Christ or the Holy Spirit) who is responsible for the inculturation of the Good News in every place and in all persons because,

---

47 Cf. 2 Cor 5,17; Gal 6,15.
48 SEDOS, op. cit., 378.
49 Cf. SVC, SC, nos. 39-40.
50 See the summary teaching of the "Katechismus" on "Liturgy and Cultures", nos. 1204-1209.
51 Cf. Shorter, Theology, 75-88; Hearne, Christology, 89-96.
52 SEDOS, op. cit., 377.

there are many different gifts, but is always the same Spirit; there are many different ways of serving, but it is always the same Lord. There are many different forms of activity, but in everybody it is the same God who is at work in them all (1 Cor 12,4-6).

Theologically inculturation is based on the universal and provident love of God for all his children who live and move and die in the Trinity[53]. To them the Triune God has revealed Himself through Jesus Christ and has offered His Grace and salvation to all without exception[54]. The reality of inculturation depends on the equal and corporate operation of the Trinity. While using the analogy of the incarnation mystery of Chrtist to express and explain it, inculturation has its firm basis on the mystery of the Triune God[55].

In sum, inculturation is inspired, initiated, directed, and executed by the activity of the Three persons in one God through pastoral agents. That is why the leaders of the early Church, gathered together at the Jerusalem Council (JC) to resolve the problem of faith-culture conflict could boldly and confidently assert that they were working in union with the Holy Spirit (cf. Ac 15,28), the Father's promise through Jesus Christ (cf. Ac 1,8; Jn 14,26).

1.4.2   Essential Components of Inculturation.

The essential components of inculturation deal with the who, the what, the why, the scope, the levels, the demands and the how of inculturation[56]. They are also of immense help in understanding the meaning of inculturation.

WHO inculturates? The whole Church is responsible for the inculturation of the Good News. It is the missionary task of every disciple of Christ[57] "from every nation under heaven".

---

53   Cf. Ac 17,28; Rm 14,11. So much emphasis has been laid on either the *incarnational* or the *Christological* basis of inculturation. That is proper, for "the subject matter of inculturation is Jesus Christ himself" (Shorter. op. cit., 75). But the argument here is that such an emphasis should not be oblivious of the active role and power of God the Father and the Holy Spirit in the whole process of inculturation. An attentive reading, for example, of the Acts bears this out. A one-sided emphasis on the christological basis of inculturation will not be true to the *biblical/theological foundations* of the reality of inculturation, and may eventually result in a *truncated form* of inculturation. But a *veritable inculturation* should be based upon the dynamic operations of God the Father, Son, and Holy Spirit manifested in the incarnation of the Son among human beings.

54   Cf. Is 9,1-2; Mt 4,14-16; Ac 10,34-35.

55   Cf. Jn 16,13; I Co 12,3-11; 2 Co 13,13; Ga 4,4-7.

56   Cf. Schineller, Handbook, 8-13; 61-73; Müller, Accommodation, 358-360.

57   Cf. Mt 28,19; Ac 1,8; SVC, AG, no. 15.

WHAT does one inculturate? It is the Christian message, the Good News of salvation, the inspired word of God, the incarnate Word of God or Christ Himself.

WHY does one inculturate? Its purpose is to make Christ incarnate in all cultures, peoples and families and in every individual so that the fullness of his Godhead can be felt every time and everywhere (cf. Col 1,15f).

What is the *scope* of Inculturation? To what extent should one inculturate the Good News? The scope of inculturation is the whole world and its peoples since among all of them, the "Seed of the divine Logos" is very operative either vividly or in shadows and images[58].

What are the *levels* of inculturation? It involves the personal, interpersonal, socio-political and theological dimensions of human existence because each of these areas require purification and sanctification by the Gospel. Inculturation involves the transformation of all levels of human life into "a more effective witness and agent of God's love for the world, for communities, and for each person"[59].

What are the *demands* of inculturation? The inculturator requires natural, intellectual and spiritual talents in order to execute his evangelical and pastoral tasks. Inculturation "requires a great deal of theological lucidity, spiritual discernment, wisdom and prudence, and also time"[60]. A deep faith, solid spirituality and the guidance of the Holy Spirit are necessary requirements for an effective insertion of the Gospel in cultures[61]. The inculturator should humbly acknowledge his/her capabilities and limitations, knowing very well that each pastoral agent carries the immense "treasure" of inculturation "in pots of earthenware" (2 Co 4,7). He/she should humbly accept the daily trials of the apostolate with equanimity (cf. 2 Co 4-6)[62].

How should one carry out the difficult process of inculturation? *What method* should one adopt? Since inculturation is a slow process requiring patience and study, the inculturator must then approach it with a cautious discernment of what should inculturated. It is therefore imperative that he/she

---

58 Cf. Vatican II, AG, 22; LG, 13 & 16; DV, 2-6.

59 Dorr, Integral Spirituality, 8.

60 John Paul II, To Bishops of Zaire, AFER 22/4 (1980) 224. Papal teachings on inculturation have always stressed this patient, slow, gradual, cautious, but steady approach to its realisation (cf. Paul VI, To SECAM, AFER 11/4 (1969) 402-405; John Paul II, RM, 52-54).

61 The role of the Holy Spirit in the spread and insertion of the Gospel in cultures is self-evident from the Acts of the Apostles. (cf. 1,8; 8,29-39; 15,28; 16,6-8 etc. Also Bruce, Holy Spirit, 166-183; Wong, Holy Spirit, 57-95, Hesselgrave, Communicating, 53-56; 286).

62 Cf. Luzbetak, Church, 6; Schineller, Handbook, 69.

should have adequate self-knowledge, sufficient knowledge of the Good News of Christ and a basic understanding of the culture of one's audience.

This is known as the **three-pole** or the **three-culture** model for inculturation, which comprises the minister or the pastoral agent, the Christian message, and the situation of the people. In other words, it comprises the missionary's culture, the Bible culture and the people's culture[63].

The tripolar culture-model is a "culture-bound experience" approach which proceeds from anthropological phenomena (cultural forms and expressions, social relationship and thought-patterns) to theological issues or questions about faith and culture[64]. It is a method that dates back to the Prophets, to Jesus, to the apostles and their companions although certain ecclesial epochs had failed to apply it to their audiences. It is a method that requires teamwork from all groups in each Christian Community[65]. In his "*Redemptoris Missio*", John Paul II approved the tripolar culture-model as a standard method for missionary inculturation[66].

In *principle* inculturation begins with the one who inculturates because every attempt to evangelize others begins first with self-evangelization or the witness of true Christian life (cf. Mt 5,13-48)[67]. But in *practice* the inculturator begins with the analysis of the socio-cultural situation of his audience and then brings the Christian message via biblical culture to this situation along with the informations and experiences religiously learnt and gleaned from one's socio-cultural background.

1.4.3 Terminologies for Inculturation.

Different terminologies have been used to describe or represent the reality of inculturation more or less adequately[68]. Among these are translation, implantation, adaptation, accommodation, indigenisation, acculturation, contextuali-

---

63 Cf. Nida, Message, 33-58; Hesselgrave, op. cit., 72-78; Schineller, op. cit., 62-73.

64 Cf. Wilfred, Inculturation, 185-189; Hesselgrave, Communicating, 82-86; Crollius, So New About, 733-734: The tripolar/triculture method also involves respectively the three moments of the *translation* of the message and culture, the *assimilation* of the message and culture, and the *transformation* of the message and culture in the entire process of inculturation (733).

65 Cf. Shorter, Theology, 261-270.

66 Cf. John Paul II, RM, nos. 53-54.

67 Cf. Paul VI, EN, no. 21.

68 Cf. Luzbetak, Church, 64-84; Crollius, So New About; 721-737; Shorter, Theology, 3-16; Schineller, Handbook, 14-17; Azevedo, Inculturation, 6.8; Muller, Accommodation, 347-349; Hering, Evangelisierung, 15-30.

sation, interculturation, and incarnation. However inadequate or inappropriate some of these terms may be, there is no gainsaying it that upon closer examination, each of them has tried to express the same reality either "darkly" or clearly. This fact becomes a "*caveat*" to anyone who may outrightly reject any of those representative concepts as totally inadequate. Rather each of those descriptions can help the inculturator gain more insight into the meaning, the facets and the implications of inculturation[69].

1.4.4   Inculturation, Catechesis and Evangelisation.

In the context of *catechesis and evangelisation*[70] Pope John Paul II teaches that the purpose of inculturation is to embody the Gospel message in the culture of every people in such a manner that both Gospel and culture are mutually enriched. But when the Gospel and culture come into contact, it is the culture, not the Gospel, that has to change lest the Gospel be emptied of its power (cf. I Cor 1,17) because "the power of the Gospel everywhere transforms and regenerates. When that power enters into a culture, it is no surprise that it rectifies many of its elements"[71]. This is an echo of Pope Paul VI who taught that,

the Gospel and, therefore, evangelisation cannot be put in the same category with any culture. They are above cultures... the Gospel and evangelisation are not specially related to any culture but they are not necessarily incompatible with them. On the contrary, they can penetrate any culture while being subservient to none[72].

Thus the Good News is the authoritative norm for what is good or bad in a culture. Yet Paul VI lamented the dramatic "rift between the Gospel and cul-

---

69   In the same vein, one talks about the Americanisation, or Europeanisation or Africanisation, etc, of Christianity.

70   (a) In the context of pastoral activity, the General Catechetical Directory of April 11, 1971 (*Ad Normam Decreti*) defines Catechesis as "that ecclesial activity which leads the community and individual Christians to maturity of faith" (no. 21); it takes on various forms (no. 19), and presupposes a total acceptance of the Gospel of Christ put forward by the Church (no. 18). (b) "Evangelisation means the carrying forth of the Good News to every sector of the human race so that by its strength it may enter into the hearts of men and renew the human race" (EN, 18. AAS 68 (1976) 17). Inculturation thus becomes very meaningful in the contexts of catechesis and evangelisation.

71   John Paul II, CT, no. 53.

72   Paul VI, EN, no. 20.

ture" and then urged all to devote their resources and efforts to a "sedulous evangelisation" and regeneration of the various human cultures[73].

In the *Slavorum Apostoli* Pope John Paul II defines inculturation as the insertion of the Gospel message into an autochthonous (native) culture and also as the introduction of this very culture into the life of the Church[74]. It is through inculturation that the Church becomes "a more intelligible sign of what she is, and a more effective instrument of mission"[75].

The process of the Church's insertion into peoples' cultures is a lengthy one. It is not a matter of purely external adaptation, for inculturation "means the intimate transformation of authentic cultural values through their integration in Christianity and the insertion of Christianity in the various cultures[76].

In the reality of inculturation is a mutual harmonious embrace between the Church and cultures, between Christ the head of the Church and peoples of every culture.

It is by means of inculturation that one proceeds towards the full restoration of the covenant with the Wisdom of God, which is Christ himself. The whole Church will be enriched also by the cultures, which though lacking in technology, abound in human wisdom and are enlivened by the profound moral values[77].

1.4.5   Inculturation an Old but New Reality.

Inculturation is nothing new in the Church's mission[78]. What is rather new, as Crollius notes, is "the *status questionis*".

---

73 Cf. Ibid.
74 Cf. John Paul II, SA, no. 21. AAS 77 (1985) 802. The full latin text of this definition reads:"*In evangelizationis opere, quod - uti praecusores in regione a Slavicis populis habitata exegerunt - simul illius rei exemplum invenitur, quae nomen hodie prae se fert "animi culturae inductionis" - nempe insertionis Evangelii in humanum autochthonum cultum - atque simul inductionis in Ecclesiae vitam ipsius illius cultus humani*".
75 Id., RM, no. 52. Cf. Paul VI, EN, no. 20; Synod of Bishops, Lineamenta, no. 47.
76 John Paul II, RM, 52. Cf. footnotes to this section of the RM for a catalogue of the Pope's numerous teachings on inculturation, especially during his pastoral visits to Africa. They are found on p. 90 of the "*Libreria Editrice Vaticana*" of the RM.
77 Id., FC, no. 10.
78 Cf. Id., RM, 52.

The way the problem is envisaged, is new. Evidently this is the consequence of a new historical situation. The "state of the question" corresponds to the "state of those who ask the question"[79].

The historical situation has changed because all peoples have come to realize and appreciate their own cultural values. The changed situation is brought about by the Church's new awareness of the cultural plurality of mankind[80]. The Church does not take away whatever is good from the temporal welfare of any people but rather she respects, fosters, purifies, stregthens and elevates them[81].

The time is forgone when certain countries, nations or peoples would try to arrogate to themselves the monopoply of culture or make their own way of life the "*exemplar*" *culture* for fellow human beings. It is now clear that no person is *culture-less*[82]. Inculturation requires that "whoever is to go among another people must hold their inheritance, language and way of life in great esteem"[83]. Therefore,

if the missiological literature after *Catechesi Tradendae* took up the new phraseology so eagerly, the reason may well be that the word 'inculturation' expressed an idea with which mission theology was for a long time engaged and which resolved the dichotomy on which the past so much suffered. It is an idea which "*Gaudium et Spes*" had paraphrased with numerous excellent words: inculturation, the much sought-for unity of the secular and the divine[84].

As the unifying term for the sacred and the secular, inculturation has now become for the Church the *explanatory term* for the reality which she had for ages taught and practised but lacked adequate words to express it[85].

1.4.6   A Holisitc View of Inculturation.

Negatively inculturation forbids and condemns every form of cultural iconoclasm. *Positively* it orders and obliges everyone to give due respect to all cultural values in harmony with the Gospel values. *Technically* it is a harmonious

---

79   Crollius, So New About, 721.
80   Cf. Vatican II, GS, 53-62; AG 10; 11.
81   Id., LG, 13.
82   Adelakun, Concept, 5. Cf. Legrand, L'Evangelisation, 500-518; Eyt, L'Assemblee, 481-499.
83   Vatican II, AG, 26.
84   Muller, Accommodation, 352.
85   Cf. Hering, Evangelisierung, 15ff. Schineller, Handbook, 14ff; 24f.

indissoluble union of Cultural Anthropology and Theology, a union of human life with divine life. *Holistically* it is a harmonious synthesis of faith and cultures, an ongoing "apostolic dialogue" in which faith, as the authoritative norm, confronts culture. It involves the whole person and all the strata of the human society.

Inculturation is the insertion of the Good News into cultures in such a way that it brings about both the transformation of cultures and a mutual enrichment of faith and culture. It is a transforming encounter between Gospel and culture, a Gospel renewal of culture from within, an interpenetration of Christian faith and culture[86]. It is the expression of divine word and Christian life in cultures. It addresses itself to a people's way of life which seeks to give cultural expression to the life and teaching of Christ[87].

Inculturation teaches that Jesus is the "*light of revelation for Gentiles and glory for* (God's) *people Israel*" (Lk 2,32). It emphasizes that in Jesus Christ all peoples are united equally without any distinction of persons or favouritism (cf.Ac 10,34-35). In an inculturated faith, all peoples and cultures are reconciled because the walls of hostility are broken down by the faith and new life in Christ[88].

Inculturation is the possession of every culture for Christ in Christ and by Christ in the unity of God the Father and the Holy Spirit[89]. It is a trinitarian event because it is founded upon, and springs from, the salvific action of the triune God among all peoples. Inculturation invites all nations and peoples to extol God's name (cf. Ps 117). It invites every being to praise God (cf. Pss. 100; 150). It calls upon all the earth to acclaim God and sing hymns to the glory of his name (cf. Ps 64,4) as the *pantokrator* and saviour of all through Christ the Lamb (cf. Rv 4-5).

Inculturation issues out the glad tidings that "all humanity shall see the salvation of God" (Lk 3,6), and consequently obliges "every knee" to bend before God and Christ (cf. Is 45,23; Ph 2,19) and to acknowledge Jesus Christ as Lord to the glory of God the Father (cf. Ph 2,11). It commands all to respect everyone as God's own image and likeness (Gn 1,26f) created to know him, love him, serve, worship and glorify him every time and everywhere[90].

Inculturation represents the efforts of Christians in particular places to understand and celebrate their christian faith in a way peculiar to those contexts. While sharing in the one,

---

86   Cf. Carrier, Evangelisation, 87-88.
87   Cf. Id., 89-95.
88   Cf. Ep 2,14-22; Ga 3,26-28; Rm 10,12-13.
89   Cf. Schineller, Handbook, 6f.
90   Cf. Ex 20,1ff; Dt 5,1f; Mt 19,16ff; Mk 10,17ff; 12,28f; Lk 10,25f; 18,18ff etc.

holy, catholic, apostolic Church, they search for the particular ways in which this faith must be lived in their situations[91].

"What inculturation means, in a word, is being fully and truly Christian in a particular, cultural context or situation"[92].

1.5 What is the Acts?

The Acts is *an account of the exploits of heroic men and women* who committed themselves to the spread of the Good News of Christ in the early Church. The Greek title of the Book is *"Praxeis Apostolon"* - Deeds or Actions of Apostolic People - without the corresponding plural Greek definite article *"hai"*[93]. "The Acts of the Apostles" is not therefore an accurate translation of the title of the book, but a generic characterization of the missionary activities of the apostles and the apostolic Christians, most of whom saw Jesus or worked with the apostles and bore witness to his deeds and words (cf. Acts 1,21-22)[94].

This generic title is made obvious by the contents of the Book itself. Of the apostles mentioned in Acts 1,12-13, only Peter, James, and John his brother appear later in the body of the narrative. What we know of James is only his execution narrated in one sentence (12,2), while John appears as the silent companion of Peter in their ministry (3; 4; 8,14-25). Peter himself remains the head of the apostles in the early section of the Acts (chs. 1-12), disappears awhile from the scene after his arrest and miraculous deliverance (12) and re-appears at the Council of Jerusalem (15). And just as Peter's ministry dominates the apostolic scene in the early section of the Acts, so also does the ministry of Paul, commissioned by the risen Christ (9), dominate the later part of the Acts (13-28). Nevertheless the ministries of these two prominent figures, interpolated with the activities of their co-evangelizers, represent the evangelizing mission of the apostles of Jesus and can be taken as a starting point by, and for, succesive Christian evangelizers.

---

91   Sarpong, Evangelisation, 2.

92   Schineller, op. cit., 122.

93   Nestle-Aland, Novum Testamentum, 320.

94   Cf. Brown, Churches, 64; Barclay, Acts, 1; Weiser, Apg, 1, 26. Pesch, Apg, 22f. The German title *"Die Apostelgeschichte"* (The History of Apostles) is equally not an accurate, but a "free" translation, of "Praxeis Apostolon".

1.6 Inspiration.

The meaning of inspiration can be traced back to the Latin verb "*inspirare*" which means "to blow" (of wind), "to breathe in/upon". Its Greek equivalent is "*pnein*"[95]. Inspiration thus implies the existence of a breath (*spiritus*) that is breathed into a soul and puts life into it.

In the religious sphere, it is "a spiritual influence that occurs spontaneously and renders a person capable of thinking, speaking or acting in ways that transcend ordinary human capacities"[96]. In the secular sphere it imports an empowering stimulation to do something spectacular[97].

Thus an inspiration for a "particular piece of work theory, etc is the thing that provides new ideas and acts as a model for the work"[98]. It can also signify the state or quality of being filled with creative powers, of being full of the spirit that leads to outstanding achievements[99].

So when Acts 15 is taken as an inspiration for the Igbo Church, the word "inspiration" should be understood in terms of an "empowering stimulation" that has both secular and religious imports and implications. It is a stimulation empowered by the Holy Spirit, which can also provide the Igbo Church with creative, divine and human insights for harmonious integration of culture into the Christian faith.

1.7 Church (*Ekklesia*).

"Church" is the English (bible) translation for the Greek word "*ekklesia*" which in the NT means a *regularly covened assembly*[100]. *Ekklesia* itself is the Greek Septuagint (LXX) translation of the hebrew word "*qahal*" which means "an assembly called together". Among the OT Jews *Qehal Yahweh* refers to both Israel and the eschatological People of God who will be revealed at the

---

95 Cf. 2 Tim 3,16.
96 Carpenter, Inspiration, 256; Cf. Dei Verbum, nos 11-13.
97 The German word *Anregung* can very well explain the meaning of inspiration in terms of "stimulation".
98 Sinclair et al., Dictionary, 755.
99 Cf. Cowie, Dictionary, 648-649.
100 In the NT, *ekklesia* is both used in secular and religious contexts (cf. Matt 16,18; 18,17; Acts 19,32.39-40). In the secular sense ekklesia is to "those who have been called out", the gathering of "those who have been summoned together", that is, a political meeting of the people. In the religous sense ekklesia is a cultic community convoked and gathered by God (cf. Kung, Church, 82).

gathering up of the scattered children of Israel. The OT frequently uses *qahal* to designate the community of the chosen people[101].

Qahal or *ekklesia* or church thus means the assembly or community of the (chosen) people of God. In Greek "*qehal Yahweh*" is translated as *ekklesia tou Theou*. In the NT Jesus promised to build his *ekklesia* on Peter (Mt 16,18). This signifies that Peter would be the foundation for the "assembly of Christ" or the Christians. This *ekklesia* now known as the "Church" thus becomes a gathering of the community of Christ (*ekklesia Christou*, Ga 1,22; Phm 2) united with Him as a body.

The NT *ekklesia* itself carries three significations: a congregation gathered for divine worship; the local Christian community; the universal Church which arises through the mutual interaction and communion of the local Churches and is realized in, and through, the local Churches (cf. LG, 13)[102]. *Ekklesia* has now become an assembly whose membership is based not on tribe or tongue or colour but on divine election and faith in Christ. The *ekklesia* is at one and the same time the *ekklesia* tou *Theou* and *ekklesia tou Christou*. *Ekklesia* continues to mean the congregation, the assembly, the community, the Church of[103] God in Jesus Christ the Lord.

In this work *ekklesia* is to be understood in its ecclesial and biblical meanings as "institution", "hierarchy" and "People of God" while the context will determine the proper meaning of its usage.

1.8 The Term "Igbo".

The term is spelt as "*I-g-b-o*" but the *anglicized* Igbo authors and non-Igbo writers unable to pronounce the double implosive consonant "*gb*" have unfortunately preferred to spell it as "*I-b-o*". Other corrupt forms of the term by colonialists and foreign anthroplogists include "Eboe", "Hebos", "Ebus"[104]. This accounts for the differences of orthography in Igbo literature.

The term "Igbo" represents the culture area, the people, and their language. It can be used as a *noun* or as an *adjective*, depending on the context. Hence one can talk about Igboland, Igbo People, Igbo Language[105]. In this work I am

---

101 Cf. Dt 4,9-14; 9,10; 18,16 etc. Schmidt, Ekklesia, 502-539; Qahal, 530-534; Koehler/Baumgartner, Qahal, 829.

102 Cf. Zerwick/Grosvenor, Grammatical Analysis, 52.

103 Cf. LG, 6-9.

104 Cf. Horten, West African Countries, 171; Echiegu, Sacral Igbo, 125; Agu, Secularization, 209; Nwoga, Focus of Igbo, 1984 Ahiajoku Lecture, 2.

105 Cf. Uchendu, Igbo of Southeast, 3; Echiegu, Sacral Igbo, 7.

using the correct "*I-g-b-o*" spelling. But for the sake of fidelity to original texts or works, I shall retain the "strange" spellings of the word in citations[106].

1.8.1 Who Are the Igbo?.

Simply put, the Igbo constitute one of the three major ethnic groups[107] of Nigeria who speak the Igbo Language and are the natural sons and daughters of Igboland.

Their language is one of Nigeria's three official local languages. In the 1991 census the Igbo numbered about 18 million or 20 per cent of Nigeria's 89.5 million people. They are a race to be reckoned with and are noted for their proverbial *ubiquity and great enterprise* in politics, social life, religion, technology, science, business, education and sport. No field of life or learning escapes their special attention and/or involvement[108].

In recent years several hypotheses/theories have been put forward about the origin of the Igbo. One hypothesis links them culturally with the biblical Jews[109] but it fails to win a popular acclamation among Igbo anthropologists[110]. What is rather gaining more acceptance is the theory of both their *outside and inside origins*. It proposes that the Igbo originated from the beginning from within the territory which they now inhabit, with possible movements and migrations due to both internal conflicts and natural disasters[111].

Other peoples also migrated from other parts of Nigeria, especially from the western enclave and mixed up with them. The Igbo people at last became a mixed race of the majority-traditional folk (the *Nwadiala*)[112] and a small group of immigrants that have been enculturated within the society of the original traditional folk.

The majority of the contemporary Igbo is Christian. Almost all christian denominations and sects, including the teeming number of African Independent Churches, can be found scattered throughout the length and breath of the

---

106 Cf. Edeh, Towards an Igbo Metaphysics, 14.
107 Two other major ethnic groups are the Hausa-Fulani, and the Yoruba.
108 The other two languages are Hausa and Yoruba. Along with English all three can, in principle, be used in some Houses of Assembly and in teaching in schools and some universities.
109 Cf. Basden, Niger Ibos, 411-422; Id., Among the Ibos, 31; Uchendu, op. cit., 3.
110 Cf. Afigbo, Prolegomena, 50; Edeh, Igbo Metaphysics, 11f.
111 Cf. Afigbo, op. cit., 5; Edeh, op. cit., 12f.
112 Cf. Onwuejeogwu, Trends, Ahiajoku (1987) 7-17; Echiegu, Sacral Igbo, 9.

present Igbo culture area[113]. A smaller number have converted to Islam motivated rather by financial gains than by any conviction of/with Islamic teachings and beliefs. However the Catholic Church has a pride of place in Igboland.

1.8.2 Igbo Culture Area in Nigeria.

Nigeria is a country of about 250 ethnic groups now divided into thirty States patterned on those of the U.S.A. The country is located in the bowel of the West African Coast, with its northern border touching the countries of Niger and Chad; on the East is Cameroon and on the West is Benin. Stretching from the Atlantic Ocean up to the brink of the Sahara Desert, and with a population of 89.5 million in 1991, Nigeria becomes the most populous and unique country of Africa[114].

The Igbo culture area (Igboland) occupies a large section of Southeastern Nigeria and a strip of land west of the River Niger from which Nigeria derived its name. Measured geographically, the Igbo enclave falls between latitudes 5 and 7 degrees North, and longitudes 60 and 80 degrees East, within the equatorial rainforest region[115]. Because of this locale, authors have variously referred to the Igbo as "the Ibos of Nigeria"[116], the "Niger Ibos"[117], "the Igbo of Southeast Nigeria"[118], or one of the "tribes" of "the Lower Niger"[119]. Each of them is correct, differing only in their specifications or perspectives.

But currently it is more specific and more exact to state that Igboland lies in the hinterland of Southeastern Nigeria in which are now located Abia, Imo, Anambra and Enugu States of Nigeria. The strip of land between the west bank of the Niger and the Ancient Kingdom of Benin is inhabited by the West Niger Igbo who, along with several other ethnic groups, make up the present Delta State. Some other Igbo people in the Etche, Ikwerre, and Opobo areas also share the Rivers State with other ethnic groups[120].

---

113 Cf. Ndiokwere, Prophecy, 56-134.
114 Cf. Ojukwu, Because I am Involved, 20-21.
115 Cf. Uchendu, Igbo of Southeast, 1.
116 Cf. Basden, Among the Ibos of Nigeria passim.
117 Cf. Id., Niger Ibos, passim.
118 Cf. Uchendu, op. cit., passim.
119 Cf. Leonard, The Lower Niger and its Tribes, passim.
120 Ifemesia in: Southeastern Nigeria, 9, has divided Igboland into six zones that correspond to six major sub-cultural and language groups. Cf. Echiegu, Sacral Igbo, 7-8.

It is to this culture area which dominates the former Onitsha Ecclesiastical Province[121] that the inculturation study of Acts 15 shall be correlated. Next comes a survey of the Acts-research as a prelude to the exegetical study of Acts 15.

---

121 On March 31, 1994 six new Ecclesiastical Provinces were created out of the former three Ecclesiastical Provinces of Nigeria. They are: Abuja and Jos from Kaduna Province (North); Benin and Ibadan from Lagos (West); Calabar and Owerri from Onitsha (East). Onitsha and Owerri Provinces are entirely Igbo. Calabar is a mixture of many ethnic groups including the Igbo. Several million Igbo are found in the Province of Benin [cf. Vatican Bulletin, Ecclesiastical Provinces, in: L'Osservatore Romano, Weekly Edition in English (6 April 1994), p. 8].

2. Chapter Two.

Survey and Method.

Preamble: Scope of Survey and Method.

The survey is from the outset limited in scope since it shall not embark on a detailed and fullscale examination of the forest of literature on the Acts-research[1]. Rather it seeks to give a summary of the main direction and results of the critical study of Acts since 1826[2] in order to sharpen the focus of the present study. Special attention shall be focused on the results of the studies of Acts 15,1-35 and on the reasons for its choice as a paradigm for inculturated evangelisation in the Igbo Church today. This shall be followed by a discussion of the study of the whole Acts with the narrative and inculturation methods selected for the exegetical theological study. Since there is no presuppositionless exegesis, what follows shall constitute my presuppositions for the study of Acts 15,1-35.

2.0 Tendenz-Kritik and Acts-Research (1826-1897).

In 1826 F. C. Baur, the head of the influential Tübingen School and the man who "raised NT criticism to a truly scientific level"[3], initiated a critical study of the Acts with his *Tendenz-kritik* (tendency criticism) which dwelt more on the authorship and purpose of the Acts. *Tendenz-kritik* is

the study of a New Testament Writing in terms of its special theological point of view in the context of the history of primitive Christianity[4].

Baur's thesis based on the four factious Church groups of the *First* Corinthians (1,11) forcefully stated that the early Church was characterized by a severe conflict between two Christian factions: a Petrine (Jewish) party and a

---

1   For a summary of NT Critcism in general, cf. Kselman-Witherup, Modern NT Criticism, in: NJBC, 70: 1-84, pp. 1130-1145
2   The year 1826 is generally regarded by scholars of the Acts as a turning-point in the critical study of the book. Cf. Gasque, Historical Value, 68-88; Mcgiffert, Historical Criticism, 368-395.
3   Kselman/Witherup, op. cit., 7, p. 1132.
4   Gasque, Historical Value, 74.

Pauline (Gentile) party. Baur was convinced that the Acts and indeed most of the NT Writings could be studied and understood in terms of this factious dichotomy.

In this way this basic dichotomy between Petrine and Pauline Christianity, between the *Urapostel* and Paul, becomes the basic assumption of the Tübingen conception of the Acts[5].

The Tübingen Schoolmen held that a Pauline disciple wrote the Acts as an apologetic attempt to reconcile the factions in the Church and to defend Paul against his Judaistic opponents. For Baur this special purpose or *tendency* is crucial for the resolution of the critical and historical questions about the Acts. By regarding the Acts as a second century Writing, the *Tendenz-kritik* robbed the book of its historical validity in the 19th century[6] and also exercised a lot of influence on subsequent scholarship.

But the theory of the *Tendenz-kritik* did not go unchallenged even by some of Baur's students and colleagues who insisted that the Acts was neither a conciliatory apologetic for petrine and Pauline factions nor a creative immagination of the author influenced by his theological tendencies and much concern for a good graphic narration. Rather the Acts is an expression of a *Gentile Chrisitanity* and a reliable source for the history of the early Church even if its historical validity may not be homogeneous in all its parts[7].

In spite of its long and enduring influence on the Acts-research, the *Tendenz-kritik* could not withstand the onslaught of the critical orthodoxy of the time. By the end of the 19th century it gradually fell into oblivion. Infact it fell silent with the work of Johannes Weiss (1897) as the last *Tendenz-kritiker*[8]. However the strong opposition of critical orthodoxy was unable to stem the mounting tide of skepticism over the historical reliabilty of the Acts. The basic

---

5   Id., 77.

6   For more details on *Tendenz-kritik* confer, Windisch, Case Against, 298-348. Windisch regards as "untenable" the theory "that a special purpose, of furthering the plans of a definite party, controlled the pen of the author, and led him to revise what he knew to be a reliable tradition" (348).

7   Cf. Gasque, op. cit., 81-82.

8   Cf. Haenchen, Acts, 24. Prominent among those who worked hard for the demise of *Tendenz-Kritik* are Bruno Bauer, Franz Overbeck, and Paul W. Schmiedel. Though in some ways more radical than their predecessors, "they rejected Baur's conception of Acts a conciliatory writing" (Gasque, Historical Value, 81). They were later joined by W. M. Ramsay, A. von Harnack, and the three famous Cambridge (British) Scholars: J. B. Lightfoot, B. F. Westcott, F. J. A. Hort (cf. Hunkin, British Work, 418-431; Kselman/Witherup, NT Criticism, 8-12, 1132-1133; Bruce, Acts Today, 37).

thesis of the *Tendenzg-kritik* namely, *the assumed dichotomy between the Petrine and Pauline parties*, continued to be topical in the 20th century.

The eventual demise of *Tedenz-kritik* ushered in the use of the other historical critical and literary[9] critical methods for the study of the Acts and the whole of NT[10]. The employment of these methods in the Acts-research has yielded some fruitful results and insights into the nature and message of the book.

2.1 Fruitful Insights Into the Whole Acts.

Inspite of differences of opinion, scholars have attained a considerable amount of consensus about the sources, the plan, the purpose and author of the Acts. There is also a general acceptance of the hermeneutical, theological, evangelistic, and missionary importance of the book and of its historical, literary and cultural value. Hence the Acts can be studied from the point of view of biblical exegesis, theology, history and literature. This fact has drawn for the author of the book the four titles of Evangelist, Theologian, Historian, and Writer[11].

2.1.1 Authorship of the Acts.

The world of NT tradition and scholarship has accepted the Lukan authorship of Luke-Acts as testified in their prologues addressed to the same "Excellent Theophilus" (Lk 1,1-4; Ac, 1,1-3)[12]. But there is a lot of controversy about the personal identity of the author. Church tradition holds that the author is Luke,

---

9   Here "'Literary criticism' is used as it is in the field of literature, not as it has been used in the biblical field, where it refers to the exploration of such historical issues as author, time and place of composition, nature and provenance of sources and socio-religious implications of literary forms" (Brown-Schneiders, Hermeneutics, in: NJBC 71:55, p. 1158).

10   Other historical critical methods include source criticism, form criticism, tradition criticism, redaction criticism, and the current cultural critical or inculturation method. The literary critical method includes structural criticism, canonical criticism, rhetorical criticism and the more recent narrative criticism. Cf. Suezler-Kselman, Modern OT Criticism, in: NJBC, 69: 1-80, pp. 1113-1129; Kselman-Witherup, op. cit., passim; Brown-Schneiders, op. cit., 71:53-74, pp. 1158-1162.

11   Cf. Haenchen, Acts, 90-112; Graßer, Apg., (1960), 107; Richard, Luke - Writer, 3-15; Marshall, Luke - Historian; Dillon, Acts, in: NJBC, 44:2-4, p. 722-723.

12   Cf. Barrett, Third Gospel as a Preface, 1451-1464; Beck, Common Authorship, 346-352; NJB, Acts, 1793.

a native of Syrian Antioch, a medical doctor (cf. Col 4,14), a Gentile convert and a missionary companion of Paul[13], who was with him in prison (cf. Phlm 24; 2 Tim 4,11)[14]. While some writers uphold the traditional teaching, others, on the basis of their critical research, would not identify the author as a missionary companion of Paul or as his prison companion[15].

2.1.2   Date and Place of Composition.

Acts-research proposes that the book was probably written between 80-100 A. D. but not before 80 A.D. Macedonia, Asia Minor, Caesarea, Rome, Antioch and Achaia respectively have been proposed as the likely places of its composition. But the early Christian tradition favours Achaia more than the other localities[16].

2.1.3   Purpose of the Acts.

Why did Luke write the Acts? What were his main concerns in writing the Acts? Many theories have been put forward with and without sufficient proofs or evidence. But agreement is somehow reached on Luke's "primary" and "secondary" aims[17]. His secondary concerns include political and ecclesial apologetic and the edification of Christians. But his primary aims are found in the two prologues (Lk 1,1-4 & Ac 1,1-3). In them Luke asserts his serious historical intention and his allegiance to Christ. Then he goes on to narrate the salvific plan of God, the activity of Christ and his special mission to the poor, the weak and the despised.

This mission is continued in the Acts through the apostolic witnessing beginning from Jerusalem and reaching out to the whole Gentile world as programmed in Ac 1,8[18]. Witnessing to Christ before all peoples and a 'history' or

---

13   Cf. Eusebius, Historia Ecclesiastica, 3, 4.6; Acts 16,10-15; 20,7-78; 21,1-20; 27,1-28,16.

14   Cf. Bruce, Acts (1952), 1-8; Williams, Acts, 1-7; Haenchen, Acts, 3-14; Marshall, Luke, 13-20; 223-235; Id., Acts, 44-46; Barclay, Acts, 1-2; Fahy, Council of Jerusalem, 232.

15   Cf. Weiser, Apg, 1, 39f; Pesch, Apg, 25-27.

16   Cf. Bruce, Acts, 10-14. Weiser, op. cit., 38-41; Williams, Acts, 13-15. Marshall, Acts, 46-49; Pesch, op. cit.,28; NJB, Acts, p.1794.

17   Cf. O'Toole, Why Did Luke, 66-76; Cassidy, Society, 145-170.

18   Cf. Du Plooy, Design of God, 1-6.

story of that witnessing can therefore be regarded as the principal and central purpose of the Acts[19].

2.1.4   Structure and Plan of the Acts.

The book consists of three major parts structured around the bearing of witness to Christ in Jerusalem, Judea, Samaria and their surroundings up to the utmost ends of the earth (1,8). The three-part division is prefaced by the introductory chapter (1,1-26) of which vv. 1-5 is the prologue. Then comes part one: witnessing in Jerusalem (2,1-8,3); part two: witnessing in Samaria, Judea, Antioch, Asia Minor (8,4-15,35); part three: witnessing up to Rome symbolically representing "the ends of the earth" (15,36-28,31). Thus the end of the Acts leaves it "openended" and makes it a book that is ever valid for all generations of readers, students, scholars and missionaries until the witnessing to Christ reaches to the *real* "ends of the earth"[20].

2.1.5   Sources of the Acts.

There are opinions galore and much guess-work about the sources of the Acts. It includes a wide variety of hypotheses and theories that compel the researcher to try to establish a network of criteria in order to arrive at some approximation of its sources of composition. But A. von Harnack's three-source theory modified by other scholars seems to have gained a wider acceptance in the Acts-research[21].

Today it is generally assumed or supposed that Luke used many sources to compose the Acts. They include Jerusalem, Caesarean, Antiochian, story cycle or legendary and itinerary sources plus his own personal knowledge and contacts especially in the second section of the book. As a historian and writer, Luke is believed to have drawn from extensive and manifold traditional materials from the records of the local Churches and cycle stories about the promi-

---

19   Cf. Weiser, Apg, 34-39; Bovon, Luc, 19-21; 81-84.
20   Cf. Talbert, Literary Patterns; Weiser, Apg., 26-28; Taylor, Making of Acts, 504-524; Gasque, Fruitful Field, 122-123; NJB, Acts, p. 1796.
21   Cf. Von Harnack, Acts, 131; Mcgiffert, Historical Criticism, 385-395; Haenchen, Acts, 24-34; Dillon, Acts, 10, p. 725; Graßer, Acta-Forschung TRu 41 (1976) 186-194; Hengel, Acts, 61-66; Weiser, Apg., 1, 36-38; Ludemann, Paul, 23-43; Schneider, Apg, 1, 90-91; Plumacher, Acta-Forschung, 12--128; Dupont, Les Sources, passim.

nent personages of the Acts (cf. Lk 1,1-4). All these he artistically processed, reworked and pieced together with redactional formulas[22].

2.1.6 Literary Form or Genre of the Acts.

Luke has been described as "an artist in his words" and his combined work is regarded as "the most literary part of the NT"[23]. He is also said to have employed the style of early biblical-Jewish and hellenistic-Roman historians and writers. But he differs from the ordinary secular historians because his own is a religious history. The Lucan literary form is a versatile combination of ancient literary genres[24].

> For the type of audience Luke apparently addressed, the edifying historical novel was then the genre most appropriate to his purposes and most available... When the content of the Acts, with its high proportion of exciting episodes, legendary presentations, and brief speeches, is taken into account, the scale tilts even more sharply toward the historical novel[25].

2.1.7 Historical Reliability of the Acts.

The redactional activities of Luke notwithstanding, recent scholars have come to affirm the historical reliability of the Acts. His editorial creativity or ingenuity may account for the re-arrangement of materials that do not follow the historical order or sequence of events narrated in the book. This may also account for certain reduplications in the text, yet this in no way calls into question the historical validity of the Acts story[26].

A creative writer, historian, evangelist and theologian of Luke's calibre did exercise some freedom of style and plan in his composition in order to highlight his overall missionary purpose. Luke is a historical theologian who wrote history, "but history that had a message for his contemporaries"[27].

---

22 The redactional formulas are: Ac 2,47; 6,7; 9,31; 12,24; 16,15; 19,20; 28,31. Cf. Bruce, Acts, 21-26; Haenchen, Acts, 81-90; Barclay, Acts, 6; Williams, Acts, 7-13. Dillon, Acts, 44:10, p. 725.
23 Bruce, Acts, 26.
24 Haenchen, op. cit., 77-88; Weiser, Apg, 29-32; Dillon, op. cit., 44:5, p.723; van Unnik, Luke's Second Book, 37-60.
25 Pervo, Profit, 137.
26 Cf. Gasque, Historical Value, 68-88.
27 Wilson, Gentiles, 266.

While it would be naive to accept uncritically everything Luke says, it remains true that for the careful and critical reader Acts contains an immense amount that is of great historical value[28].

That is why the Acts itself is comparable to the works of classical ancient historians[29] because "Luke is no less trustworthy than other historians of antiquity"[30].

History here is the vehicle of kerygmatic art, not art in its modern expression the chic pastime of a jaded bourgeoisie but art in service of the conversion and sanctification of the church.[31]

2.1.8   Theological Contribution of the Acts.

The pivotal theme of the Acts is witnessing[32] to Christ, and the Acts-research has unconvered the various aspects and riches of this witnessing. These include the salvific will or design of God, christology or the messianic question, pneumatology, soteriology, ecclesiology, missiology, homiletics (preaching), socio-political theology, apologetics, the Jewish/Gentile question or the racial problem of the apostolic Church[33]. Around these revolve the two axes of Acts theology of "the triumph of God who will not allow the Gospel to be overcome *and* the rejection of the gospel and the persecution of its apostles"[34].

It is usually agreed that the speeches in Acts provide a main clue to Luke's understanding of Christian theology. Different assumptions may be made about them, however. Are they Luke's compositions? Do they reflect accurately the tradition of the common teaching of early mission preachers? Do they represent the words used by Peter, Stephen, and Paul? Yet the fact cannot be denied that Luke incorporated the speeches in Acts, presumably to show his readers what the Christian faith was[35].

---

28   Id., 267. Cf. Graßer, Acta-Forschung (1977), 58; Marshall, Luke, 225-227.
29   Cf. Sterling, Luke-Acts, 326-342; Balch, Comments, 343-361; Jones, Lukes' Unique Interest, 378-387.
30   Hengel, Acts, 60; Cf. Marshall, op. cit., 225.
31   Willimon, Eyewitnesses, 158.
32   Cf. Bassey, Witnessing in the Acts, passim.
33   Cf. Bovon, Luc passim; Id., De Vocatione; Wilson, Gentiles, passim; Marshall, Luke, 77-215; Id., Present State, 54-57; Tyson, Emerging Church, passim; Gasque, Fruitful Field, 123-128; Gaventa, Toward a Theology, 146ff.
34   Gaventa, op. cit., 157.
35   Williams, Acts, 36. Cf. Cadbury, Speeches in Acts, 404ff.

Through their preaching the apostolic missionaries handled these theological themes and motifs as they bore witness to the risen Lord and Son of God. Preaching as typified in the speeches was a chief means of evangelisation[36].

2.1.9 Textual Traditions of the Acts.

Since the early second century the Acts was perhaps transmitted in two text types: the Egyptian or Alexandrian text found in its purest form in the Codex Vaticanus (**B**), and the Western text mainly witnessed to by the Codex Bezae (**D**), the African Latin version, and the Harclean Syriac (*apparatus*). Twentieth century criticism favours the Egyptian text as more consistent with its original authograph[37].

2.1.10 Acts, Culture and Inculturation.

As the Church currently emphasizes the rooting of the Gospel in the cultures of people, scholars are considering the apostolic mission of the Acts as an "archetype" of the insertion of Gospel in the Graeco-Roman cultures.

Under the auspices of the 1985 Jerusalem seminar on inculturation organized by the Jesuits, M. Dumais asks whether the Church of the Acts cannot be a model of inculturation[38]. Dumais first considers the encounter between Christian faith and the ethnic groups in the Acts. By observing how the apostolic people proclaimed the Gospel to Jews and Gentiles, he demonstrates how the author of the Acts tried to forge a harmony between faith and cultures.

Respect for Jewish and non-Jewish cultures and the non-imposition of circumcision and the law on converts from paganism no doubt indicate the situation of the Church at the end of the first century when Luke drafted his text... Luke writes for his Church and calls it to live out a difficult pluralism as a Church composed of a majority made up of converts from paganism who hold firm to their cultural values and an active minority of Jews who have become Christians and remain faithful to the customs of Judaism[39].

In this way Dumais shows that the Acts is a privileged witness to the encounter between faith and cultures, and that "the problem of the inculturation

---

36   Cf. Willimon, Eyewitnesses, 158-170.
37   Cf. Bruce, Acts, 40-49; Haenchen, Acts, 50-60; Williams, Acts, 48-53. Wilcox, Luke, 447-455; Dillon, Acts, in: NJBC, 44:11, p.725.
38   Cf. Church of the Acts, 3-24.
39   Dumais, Church of the Acts, 12.

of the Gospel and the Christian faith was sharply felt in the primitive Church"[40]. The way the first Christians handled that problem should also serve as an inspiration and a model for Christians today.

In line with Dumais, Pathrapankal proposes in a six-page article that the Church of the Acts can serve as "a model for our times". He argues that the growth of the Church in the Acts can be a model for the growth of today's Church. In the footsteps of the apostolic people under the inspired Leaders who tried to resolve the problems of the culture-clash in a multi-racial Christian community (cf. Ac 15,6ff), the Leaders of the Church today can in a similar manner strive to resolve the crises facing the "World Church" in a multi-racial and pluralistic religious culture[41].

But the eleven papers of the 1984 Congress of the African Biblicists remain in my opinion a blueprint in the study of the Church of the Acts as an inspiration for the Local Churches of Africa[42]. The scholars tried to demonstrate that the mission theology of the Acts offers a "model" for an inculturated evangelisation in the "young Churches"[43].

Nous sommes convaincu que les résultats de ce Congrès inspireront tous ceux qui militent pour la maturation des jeunes Eglises[44]. (We are convinced that the results of this Congress will inspire those who work hard for the maturity of the young Churches[45]).

Archbishop L. Monsegwo Pasinya's study of "*L'inculturation dans les Actes des Apotres*"[46] seems to me to be the most inspiring of all because it deals precisely with the *inculturation theology* of the Acts. His three-part exegetical study examines texts that refer obliquely to inculturation; the texts which are an application of inculturation; and the basic text on inculturation. He concludes that the theology of inculturation is found in different ways in the Acts[47]. While several texts show that the principle of inculturation is there in the transmission of the Good News, the author of Acts applies these principles notably in the missionary speeches addressed to the Gentiles[48].

---

40   Id., 4.
41   Cf. Pathrapankal, Church, 19-24. Pathrapankal represents the Indian (Asian) voice and contributions to the study of the Acts from the Inculturation perspective.
42   Cf. Amewowo et al., Les Actes, passim.
43   Cf. Ibid.
44   Id., 1.
45   Translation in brackets is mine.
46   Cf. L'inculturation, 120-133. Monsegwo is the current Archbishop of Kinshasa, Zaire in Central Africa.
47   Cf. Id., 131.
48   Cf. Ac 13,15ff; 17,22ff; 20,18ff; 24,10ff.

Generally Acts teaches a gradual emancipation of Christianity from Judaism and this is constant with the primary intention of the book to Theophilus (Ac 1,8). In this way the theology of the Acts can be an exemplar for all the Gentiles and especially for the young (African) Churches seeking to inculturate the Christian message in their various socio-cultural contexts[49].

2.1.11 Why Acts as a Paradigm of Inculturation?

Already described by Van Unnik as a "storm centre in contemporary scholarship"[50], there are many cogent reasons for taking the Acts (and not any other biblical work) as a paradigm for inculturation in our times:

Firstly, the Acts narrative constitutes a *direct link* between the Gospel narratives and the immediate and post resurrection disciples of Jesus. The force of this linkage is strengthened by the acceptance of the common authorship of Luke-Acts[51] by Christian tradition and modern scholarship (see 2.1). They are addressed to the same noble Theophilus whom Luke wanted to give an orderly account about Jesus and his eye-witnesses (cf. Lk 1,1-4; Ac 1,1-5). The intimate connection between the Gospel tradition and the Acts makes the latter a *mediator* of the Gospel message for the modern man and a veritable inspiration for all engaged in bearing witness to Christ in the manner of his early disciples.

Secondly, besides the Pauline Letters, the Acts is the *chief source of our information* on early Christianity[52]. Despite its historical lacunae and deficiences, it furnishes us with a progressive narrative of the spread of the Good News from Jerusalem to Rome (cf. 1,8; 28,14). This exciting account of "the beginnings of Christianity" makes it a unique canonical NT book to be read, studied and treasured by all who seek to evangelize as Jesus and the early Christians did[53].

Thirdly, Acts clearly demonstrates that the apsotolic kerygma or evangelism[54] is centred on faith in Christ. The kerygma involves the theological growth of the Church and its geographical spread from Jerusalem to Rome

---

49 Cf. Tyson, Luke-Acts, passim. This book contains eight critical articles that more or less treat question of the Jewish/Gentile relationship in the Acts and helps the researcher or reader understand and appreciate the cultural teachings of the whole Acts.

50 Cf. Van Unnik, Luke-Acts, 15-32.

51 Cf. Weiser, Apg, 1, 39; Beck, Authorship, 346-352; Dillion, Acts, 722-723; O'Toole, Unity (the whole book).

52 Cf. Haenchen, Acts, 90-103.

53 Cf. Galilea, The Beatitudes: To Evangelise as Jesus Did (1984), Chapter 5 passim.

54 Cf. Fackre, Evangelism, 73-89.

during which she gradually passes from a predominantly Jewish messianic community to a predominantly Gentile Church. The coming together of Jews and Gentiles as one Christian *ekklesia* raised theological and social questions on the interaction of both groups. How the Acts narrative presents the apostolic efforts to resolve those burning issues under the continuous guidance of the Holy Spirit[55] cannot but become a paradigm of evangelisation for modern Christians.

Fourthly, the evangelistic method and the mission theology of the Acts have a great respect for every nation and culture[56]. Right from the day of the Pentecost God revealed through the Holy Spirit that the Good News is not for the Jews alone, but for "every nation under heaven" (2,5) because Jews from all nations gathered in Jerusalem to celebrate the feast could hear in their own local or native tongues the marvels of the Lord proclaimed by the native Galilean Apostles (2,7-12). Through the narration of the events, the Acts demonstrates that the Christian faith is not a special possession of any group or race but for all peoples[57] beginning from Jerusalem unto the ends of the earth (Ac 1,8). So the theologico-evangelistic approach of the Acts was from the start *inculturational* and directed to all peoples and cultures. The Christian preachers did cross the barriers of races and cultures and proclaimed the Good News effectively to the Jewish and Graeco-Roman peoples (Ac 13-28). This fact also motivates the modern Christian to take the Acts as an inspiration for inculturation in our times.

Fifthly, besides being an inspiration for a local Church, the missionary stance of the Acts presents a big challenge to contemporary pastoral agents. It can act as a disturbing factor to the "Establishment Church" which may not always follow the examples of the apostolic people but is quite content to adopt and promote the comfortable but the Gospel opposed status quo[58]. It can also act as an awakening and catalyzing factor to a Church which is gradually falling into a deep spiritual slumber or whose faith is withering away due to inordinate quest for an unusual convenience and comfort in pastoral life and religious practice.

A comfort-seeking local Church is a contradiction to the discipleship of Christ (Lk 9,23-26) and it cannot face up to the challenges presented to her by the missionary evangelism of the Acts: the challenge of conflict with established secular and religious authorities, the possibility of martyrdom[59], and

---

55   Cf. Ac 1,8; 2,1ff; 4,8.31; 5,3.9; 6,5.10; 7,55; 8,15f.29; 9,18; 10,19.44f; 13,2f; etc.
56   Cf. Rutledge, Methods, 35-47.
57   Cf. Ac 10,34f; 13,44f; 15,7f.
58   Cf. Tannehill, Narrative Unity, 2,1.
59   Cf. Ac 4,5-22; 5,17-42; 7,55-8,1; 12,1-19.

above all the challenge of the new religious experience under the inspiration of the Holy Spirit[60].

Sixthly, in the Church of the Acts God opens "the door of faith to the gentiles" (14,27). The latter account of the Acts (chaps. 16-28) can be regarded as a story of the Gentile Church. The cultural issues and realities of this part of Acts are nearer to us (Gentiles) than those of the Jewish acculturated Gospel tradition. Furthermore the "Church" of the Acts refers to the local Churches and not to the "mystical" churches that are typical of the letters to the Colossians and Ephesians or the hierarchical Church of the the Pastoral Letters and their like.

The author has been acclaimed as the theologian par excellence of the one, holy, catholic, and apostolic church, since every one of those features marks the Christian life he describes[61].

This is again the pressing reason for taking the Acts and not any of the four Gospels as a paradigm for inculturation in a catholic Gentile (Igbo) Church[62].

Finally, the universalism of the Acts[63], its inclusive vision and scope, commands the reader's respect and admiration. R. E. Brown has given us some insight into the ecclesiologies of the seven NT witnesses addressed to the Churches that came into being after the death of the apostles who had seen the risen Christ. He studied and evaluated their "strengths and weaknesses" and related them to the local Churches today.

Despite its "triumphalistic" attitude[64], the Church of the Acts is in my view the most tolerant and the most accomodating of all the seven Churches depicted by R. E. Brown because this Church emphasizes its "continuity from Israel through Jesus to Peter and Paul", the free inclusion of the Gentiles in the

---

60 Cf. Ac 4,8-12.23-31; 5,32-33; 6,8-7,60. Cf., Cassidy, Society and Politics, passim.
61 Brown, Churches, 63.
62 Cf. Wilson, Gentiles, 219-238. This affirmation holds despite Jesus' openess to the Gentiles (1-28). But the Jews themselves had not this openess as is self-evident in the Acts (cf. 11,1-18; 15,1-35; 21,17-25, etc.).
63 Cf. O'Toole, Unity, 99-108. In these pages O'Toole tries to review the universality of salvation in Luke-Acts and affirms that "*No one denies that Luke in both his works sees salvation as universal, that is, as directed to both Jews and the Gentiles*" (99). "*...it is beyond dispute that this was a major theological concern of Luke. Yet, most properly, it is subordinated to God's salvific will, since this universality itself was due to that will. Nonetheless so important was this universal dimension of salvation to Luke that he integrated it into his Gospel and the Acts so that it would always, in some sense, be before the eyes of his readers*" (108).
64 Cf. Brown, Churches, 70-73.

Church founded on the stock of Israel, and the impartial "intervention of the Holy Spirit at crucial moments"[65] that touches on both Jews and Gentiles. Like the Gospel of Luke (2,30f), Acts addresses God's salvation to all peoples. In this universal offer of salvation, tensions and conflict must arise and believers in Christ must experience both internal and external divisions[66] which do not exclude even the divinely elected apostolic missionaries[67]. Acts shows a keen awareness of this unresolved problem. Yet salvation is for all peoples because the impartial God has no favourites and his Good News is for a "tolerant, pluralistic world culture"[68].

Acts maintained the connection between gentile Christianity and Judaism; politically, it defended Christianity as a legal religion; and ecclesiastically, it promoted the unity of the various branches and centres of Christianity by tracing their origins to a common Gospel proclaimed to both Jews and Gentiles under the leadership of the Holy Spirit[69].

All these cogent reasons are enough to convince the reader and the evangeliser that the Acts can serve as a paradigm for inculturation in any local Church today.

2.2 Insights on Acts 15 in Particular.

What is said about the whole Acts is valid for Acts 15 traditionally referred to as the Jerusalem Council (**JC**). But Acts 15 seems to have exercised a sort of magnetic influence over many scholars. As E. Haenchen observes,

this chapter has been the subject of passionate debate among scholars. Nearly every one of them has hacked his own way through the jungle of problems, and often it was done in a thoroughly violent fashion[70].

This special attention to Acts 15 is engendered by its position in the whole book, its particular attention to the Jewish/Gentile question, the critical doubts about its sources and historical reliability, its thematic link to the Cornelius episode in chapters 10-11, and its teaching on the resolution of faith-culture conflict between Jewish and Gentile Christians.

---

65 Id., 69; cf. 63.
66 Cf. Ac 6,1; 11,1-3; 15,1-5.
67 Cf. Ac 11,1-3; 13,2-3; 15,36-40.
68 Tannehill, Narrative Unity, 2, 2-3.
69 Culpepper, Paul's Mission, 487.
70 Haenchen, Acts, 455.

2.2.1 Medial Position and Importance of Acts 15.

The almost medial position of Acts 15 in the whole book (chaps. 1-28) and also the mediating role of the Council story in the early Church has given the chapter a special place and attention in the *Acta-Forschung*[71]. Acts 15 is considered to be the watershed, the climax, and also the turning point in the missionary narrative of the Acts[72]. "Up to Chapter 15 all roads lead to Jerusalem" as the spiritual head of the Christendom. "Wherever Christianity is implanted, the town or region concerned is in one way or the other subordinated to Judaea"[73].

But after chapter 15 there is a change of leadership. The apostles mentioned for the last time in 16,4 are now replaced by James and the elders (21,18). Before Acts 15 the Church was under apostolic rule. After it came the period of the rule of the elders. The focus of the apostolic mission also shifted from the Mother Church of Jerusalem to the Church of Antioch and other mission territories like Macedonia, Athens, Corinth, Ephesus up till Rome. From chapter 15 onward the figure of Paul dominates the Church of Acts. All these show that Acts 15 marks a turning point in the whole Acts[74].

Its position might have been "providential" or it might have been an intentional literary design or device of the author to show that after the first missionary enterprise of Paul and Barnabas in Acts 13-14, a new era commenced in the missionary work with its attendant problems.

2.2.2 Jewish/Gentile Relationship.

Having accepted Acts 15 as landmark and a turning point in the history of Jewish/Gentile Christian relationship and in the socio-cultural relationship of all believers in Christ[75], I. H. Marshall notes that

Luke's account of the discussion regarding the relation of the gentiles to the law of Moses forms the centre of Acts both structurally and theologically[76].

---

71 Cf. some special articles on Acts 15: Barrett, Apostles, 14-32; Id., Apostolic Decree, 50-59; Fahy, Council, 222-261; Dahl, People, 319-327; Squillaci, Primo Concilio, 829-834; Boismard, Le "Concile", 433-440.

72 Cf. Haenchen, op. cit., 461-462. Cf. Kee, Good News, 57-58. Wison, Gentiles, 192-293; Pesch, Apg, 85; Bruce, Book of the Acts, 282; Crowe, Acts, 111.

73 Haenchen, op. cit., 461.

74 Id., 461-462.

75 Cf. Barclay, Acts, 112-118; Wilson, Gentiles, 191-195; Weiser, Apg, 386-387.

Scholars generally agree on the importance of the missionary JC theology as a basis for socio-cultural exchange and inter-religious relationship between Jews and Gentile[77].

2.2.3 Sources of Composition and Historicity.

Internally Acts 15 seems to present contradictory accounts about the Jewish/Gentile controversy. *Externally* too, Acts 15 seems to be in conflict with Paul's account in Gal 2,1-10 and his rebuke of Peter over the Gentile question in 2,11-14[78]. This has generated passionate debates about the sources of Acts 15 and its historical worth[79].

Yet the source question will not go away because the convergences between Luke's information and Paul's are too substantial to pass over[80].

The resolution of these apparent contradictions remains the principal but elusive problematique of Acts 15[81]. From the examination of the internal evidence of Acts 15 and 21,25 compared with their parallels in Ga 2,1-14; Rm 14,14-22; 1 Co 8,1-13 and 10,23-30, scholars try to give possible reasons for these contradictions:

Luke must have conflated separate accounts of two different disputes with different solutions. Or he may have used different sources in the composition of the chapter. Or the conflicting accounts and directives may have been due to the narration of the same event by two different persons (Luke and Paul) writing from different perspectives and contexts and with different aims and objectives. Haenchen summarizes what critics are saying about the sources of Acts 15:

Criticism first regard it as a conglomerate of sources. It was a question of sorting out the mixture and discovering from the most reliable source what actually happened. The author came into the picture only as a purveyor of more or less reliable reports. The further research advanced, the more the source-question receded. The author comes into view, and

---

76 Marshall, Acts, 242.
77 Cf. Pasinya, L'Inculturation, 126ff; Pathrapankal, Church, 19ff; Id., Critical and Creative, 97f.
78 Cf. Parker, Once More, Acts and Galatians, 175-182.
79 Cf. Haenchen, Acts, 455-460; Weiser, op. cit., 367-377; Pesch, Apg, 74f; Brown et alii, Der Petrus, 49-51.
80 Dillon, Acts, in: NJBC, 44:80, p. 751.
81 Schneider, Apg, 2, 189f; Weiser, Apg, 367ff; Fitzmyer, Letter to Galatians, in: NJBC, 47:17, p. 783f; Pervo, Profit, 41.

not merely as a transmitter of sources. It becomes clear that he did not write for a history-obsessed twentieth-century generation, but meant his narrative to implant in his own generation the certainty that its Gentile Christianity was in order, authorized by God and by responsible men[82].

2.2.4 Thematic Link with Cornelius Episode.

Acts 15 also marks a turning-point in the "*Vocation of the Gentiles*"[83] already inaugurated in the conversion of Cornelius and his household (cf. 10,1-11,18). The arguments of Acts 15 for the inclusion of the Gentiles in the Church (vv.7-11.13-14) relies heavily on the Cornelius episode[84]. This is why modern scholarship makes a profound nexus between both episodes and regards the Cornelius event as a forerunner of the JC[85]. The conversion of Cornelius and his household is thus "the 'classic' precedent"[86] of Acts 15. And for many of the Fathers of the Church, the Cornelius episode remains the centerpiece of God's call of the Gentiles through Peter[87].

2.2.5 Resolution of Faith-Culture Conflict.

The JC theology is gaining attention as a classic example of the inculturation teachings of the apostolic Church:

According to the most widely accepted opinion, the decree's regulations, which are concerned mainly with food, make sense in the context of Acts as an effort to regulate the practical question posed in Acts 11,3: what must be asked of the new converts so that Jewish Christians can share their meal without legal defilement. They lay out "that which is strictly necessary" (15,28) to make the common life possible. Those for whom the food prohibition are unimportant (Gentile Christians) ought to respect those for whom they are important (Jewish Christians)[88].

---

82 Haenchen, Acts, 457.
83 Cf. Bovon, De Vocatione, 92ff; Id., Tradition, 22-45; Id., Luc, 356-360. See also pages 321-323 for Bovon's collection of authors on the call of the Gentiles.
84 Lukasz, Evangelizzazione, 11; 17; 21; 85 etc.
85 Cf. Wilson, Gentiles, 171-195; Boismard, Le "Concile", 434-440. Haenchen, 458-459.
86 Dillon, op. cit., 44:80, p. 751.
87 Cf. Bovon, op. cit., passim.
88 Dumais, Church of the Acts, 10-11.

In this way the Church is laid open to all peoples and cultures of the world of the Acts and she becomes a home in which any believer can live at ease without losing one's cultural identity, customs and traditions.

2.2.6   Why Acts 15 as a Basic Text for Inculturation?

If the whole theology of the Acts can inspire the whole Church in the task of inculturation, why then focus only on the theology of Acts 15 as an inspiration for inculturation in the Igbo Church? There are some cogent reasons.

The first is for *scientific purpose*. It is true that the whole Acts is dotted with *ta dogmata* on inculturation[89]. The whole book is a narrative of how the Gospel message is gradually but progressively inserted first into the Jewish cultural milieu (chaps. 1-12; 15) and later into the Gentile environment (chaps. 13-14; 16-28). But if one is to study all the 28 chapters of the Acts, the work would be too bulky, unwieldy, imprecise, and out of proportion for a scientific thesis. Hence the study is limited to chapter 15 which provides an exemplar of inculturation theology of the Acts.

Secondly, Acts 15 constitutes a turning point of the whole Acts regarded as an expression of Gentile Christianity[90]. This is supported by the internal structure of the Acts which devotes a large portion of the book after chapter 15 to the story of apostolic mission to the Gentiles[91].

Thirdly, Acts 15 connects the Torah (Lv 17,10f; 18,6ff; Ac 15,22.29) and the OT prophetic call of the Gentiles (Am 9,11f; Ac 15,13f) with the marvels of God for them in the NT apostolic mission through Peter (Ac 10,1ff; 15,7-11), Paul and Barnabas (Ac 13,3ff; 15,12). It also prepares for the future mission *ad Gentes* (Ac 15,36ff) through the apostolic Letter to the Gentile Churches of Antioch, Syria and Cilicia (Ac 15,23f). In this sense its *medial position* (2.2.1) in the whole book plays a *mediating* theologico-missiological role.

Fourthly, although the author of Acts might or might not have taken Acts 15 as the medium or the turning point or the exemplar or the climax of the inculturation texts of the apostolic mission, contemporary research considers it as a basic text for inculturation *(Le text fondamentale sur l'inculturation)*[92]. This is because it tells the story of the resolution of faith-culture conflict between the

---

89   Cf. Amewowo et al., Les Actes des Apotres et les Jeunes Eglises Kinshasa (Zaire) 1990, passim.
90   Cf. Gasque, Historical Value, 81-82.
91   Cf. Ac 15,36-20; 24,11ff; 27-28.
92   Cf. Pasinya, L'inculturation, 126-131.

Jewish and Gentile Christians which can be applied to similar crisis situations in any Local Church.

Fifthly, from a personal reflective reading of the whole of the Acts and a comparison of the biblical texts with inculturation teachings, I derive the insight that Acts 15 has a *special inculturational value*. It highlights the transcultural nature of the christian life (cf. vv. 7-11).

Although in the OT and NT (from Genesis to Apocalypse or Revelation), there are many biblical texts with inculturation value, but Acts 15 surpasses them because it contains the collective authoritative teaching of the apostolic people and special witnesses of Jesus (Ac 1,8). A comparison of key inculturation texts in the OT and NT with Acts 15 can buttress my point.

IN THE OT one reads that by Abraham "all clans on earth will bless themselves" (Gn 12,3). The whole world belongs to God who created heaven and earth[93]. God is the ruler over all the earth, nations, and peoples (Ps 96) and will judge all with justice and truth[94]. Therefore all nations and creatures are bound to praise him[95] and adore him[96] as the Lord of all, so that all flesh will see the glory of God[97].

IN THE NT, the Gospels teach that God "causes his sun to rise on the bad as well as the Good, and sends down rain to fall on the upright and the wicked alike" (Mt 5,45). He so loved the world that he sent his only son Jesus Christ, not to condemn the world, but to save it and all those who believe in him (cf. Jn 3,16-18). This Jesus is the "light of revelation for Gentiles and for (God's) people Israel" (Lk 2,32). Through him "all humanity will see the salvation of God" (3,6). His Good News is for all nations in the name of the triune God till the end of time (cf. Mk 16,15; Mt 28,19) when many shall come from east and west and sit with the patriarchs in the Kingdom (cf. Mt 8,11). This is because God is impartial and fatherly accepts "anybody of any nationality who fears him and does what is right" (Ac 10,35).

For this reason God chose the persecutor Paul to bring his name "before gentiles and kings and before the people of Israel"[98] and through him "opened the door of faith to the gentiles" (14,27) among whom he rooted the Gospel message, beginning from Cyprus through Pisidian Antioch, Lycaonia, Athens, Corinth, Ephesus up to Rome, the centre of the Gentile Kingdom. In these missionary trips, Paul's speeches to Lystrians (Ac 14,14-18) and to Areopagites (17,23-32) exhibit strong inculturation overtones and value.

---

93   Cf. Gn 1,1; Ex 19,5; Dt 5,9-10; 7,9-10.
94   Cf. Pss 24,1; 97,9; 98; 113; 115-15-16; Jl 4.
95   Cf. Pss 19,4; 64; 100; 117; 150.
96   Cf. Is 2,1-5; 45,21; 66,18-23.
97   Cf. Is 40,5; 49,6; 52,10; Jl 3.
98   Cf. Ac 9,15; cf. 13,46ff; 22-23; 24,1ff; 26,2ff.

Also in the Pauline corpus one finds many texts with tremendous inculturation stance[99]. He enunciates the "principle of accommodation" as the best approach to the inculturation of the Good News among every people, person and
culture (1 Co 9,19-23). The seer of the Apocalypse paints glowing pictures
about the integration of the Christian message within "every race, language,
people and nation" redeemed with the blood of Christ the lamb and "made a
line of kings and priests for God to rule the world" (Rv 5,9f)[100]. At the end of
time, all nations and peoples will be judged by God[101]. Then comes a new
heaven and a new earth where God dwells and reigns among the people (Rv
21,1ff).

My contention is that none of the above biblical "*inculturation texts*" surpasses the inculturation text of Acts 15. While the other texts present pertinent
but sporadic teachings on the inculturation of the faith among peoples, the JC
theology is an outcome of a planned meeting and an authoritative teaching of
the leaders of the Church united with the Holy Spirit (Ac 15,28) in order to direct the apostolic people on how to bring the Good News to the Jews and
Gentiles in accord with divine will and purpose (15,7-9). The resulting decision did facilitate the opening of "the door of faith" to other peoples of all
cultures (15,36ff).

Being the first official gathering of the Church to take a decision on faith-
culture issues and to give directives on the rooting of the Good News in the
lives of the Jewish and Gentile peoples, I contend that the proceedings of the
JC and its decree can be taken as a basis for the theory and practice of an inculturated faith in a local Church. By a hermeneutical correlation of the JC
theology to faith-culture conflicts in the Local Churches, one may be able to
resolve the socio-cultural problems and conflicts arising from the proclamation of the Gospel message in our times.

2.2.7   What to do About the Whole Acts.

It is already noted that ever since the *Tendenzkritik* of F. C. Baur and his
Tübingen colleagues up to the time when Acts became Van Unnik's "storm
centre in contemporary scholarship" in the 1970s, the Acts had been subjected
to an intense historical and literary critical studies (see 2.0). Yet the narrative-
inculturation study of the Acts and the use of the Acts as a "handbook" for in-

---

99   Cf. Ga 3,8-9.28; Ep 2,11-22; Rm 1,16; 10.
100 Cf. Cf. Rv 1; 15,1-5; 22,12-21.
101 Cf. Mt 25,31-46; Lk 21,25-28; Rv 20,11-15.

culturation in the modern Church remain part of the *unfinished agenda* of the Acts studies.

In the study of the Acts, the representative works employing the narrative method are, Tyson's "The Death of Jesus in Luke-Acts", Tannehill's commentary on the "Narrative Unity of Luke-Acts", and Pervo's "Profit With Delight". While Tannehill's commentary can be regarded as a unique attempt in the narrative study of the Acts, Pervo's monograph provides the reader with the literary genre of the Acts and the possibility of reading and enjoying the theological work like any other ancient popular narrative.

However what remains is a narrative study of the Acts, not only as a unit with Luke's Gospel, but as a *unique plot* wholly and entirely in its parts. Although the Acts is an *episodic plot*[102], as Tannehill rightly points out, there are sections of the book in the form of a *unified plot*[103]. The study of each section according to its plot-form may lead to a more profitable understanding and application of the theology of the Acts to Christians of each epoch. This accords with Pervo's program of comparing the Acts with ancient popular narratives in order to clarify "the religious and and social values of the milieu in which it emerged"[104].

Furthermore the *inculturation study* of the Acts is more urgent than ever if the Acts is to be meaningful and relevant to the peoples of the 20th century cultures and beyond. In the past, scholars have treated the Jewish/Gentile question very intellectually and academically. While fully aware of the intercultural problems posed by the Acts theology of the inclusion of all peoples into the christian fold[105], scholars have not until recently given much attention to the inculturation value of the Acts, nor did they undertake the study of the whole Acts from the inculturation perspective.

Recent inculturation studies of the Acts by M. Dumais, J Pathrapankal, African Biblicists, Tyson and the colleagues of the SBL's group on Acts are encouraging works on the cultural interpretation of the Acts to be emulated and developed by the Acts-research. These works have given us the blueprint and pattern for a cultural critical study of the Acts and for its use in the resolution of cultural issues facing the Local Churches of our era. But they are only a beginning not the end of such studies, yet a powerful inspiration for all to go

---

102 "In an 'episodic plot' the order of episodes can be changed, the reader can skip an episode without harm; every episode is a unit in itself and does not require the clear and complete knowledge of the former episodes to be understood" (Ska, Our Fathers, 17).

103 "In a unified plot, all the episodes are relevant to the narrative and have a bearing on the outcome of the events recounted. Every episode supposes what precedes and prepares for what follows" (Ska, Our Fathers, ibid.).

104 Pervo, Profit, xii.

105 Cf Haenchen, Acts, 357-350; Bovon, De Vocatione, passim.

further and deeper into the theoretical study and practical application of the inculturation riches and values of the Acts to any local Church.

The inculturation study of the book therefore remains a *compulsory pressing agendum* for the Church today. Scholars may do well to stress the importance of the theology of the Acts for a harmonious intercultural christian relationship between a *Euro-American* acculturated Christian Church and the Local Churches in the non-Euro-American continents. The emphasis should now shift from the mere praise and awesome admiration of the Acts as the "Gospel of the Holy Spirit" to an appreciation of the Acts as a "Story of the Apostolic Church" capable of being a "model of inculturation" or "an inspiration for inculturation" in the Church today.

2.2.8   What to do About Acts 15.

What remains to be done to the whole of the Acts also applies to what is yet to be done to Acts 15. First there is need to study it as a story of "evangelisation, conflict and resolution of conflict" in the apostolic Church. That is, it is advisable to study it as a plot with all its moments, characters, reading positions, points of view, etc. in order to appreciate its entertaining qualities as well as its theological significance in resolving the problem posed by a racist cultural arrogance to any young Church[106]. R. I. Pervo appreciates and highlights this point for current scholars, pastors and readers when he writes that

> Acts 15 is indisputably Luke's most compelling account of a church meeting. Narrative suspense, elegant rhetoric, and correct procedure justify its traditional title[107]. Despite violent contradictions with Galatians 2, this attractive account continues to exert seductive force. Early readers would sense the same attraction and revel in the stateliness of their ancestral assemblies[108].

It is true that some scholars have discussed Acts 15 in all its ramifications and have in various ways prognostically mentioned the inculturation significance of the JC[109], but these studies have concentrated more on the exegetical analysis of the themes of the text and emphasis on the socio-religious contro-

---

106   Cf. Zvarevashe, Racist Missionaries, 117ff.
107   Its traditional title is "apostolic council" awarded to it by M. Dibelius. So Pervo, Profit, footnote, 123, p. 153.
108   The whole indented citation is from Pervo, op. cit., p. 41.
109   Cf. Weiser, Apstelkonzil, 209-210.

versy between the Judaizers and the Gentile Christians[110]. The few studies from the inculturation perspective have not considered a hermeneutical correlation of the JC theology to the particular context of a Local Church[111] which would refuse to embrace "either innocently or uncritically the confessional framework of other peoples"[112] to her disadvantage. This should be the task of an inculturation study of Acts 15.

2.2.9 Acts and the Narrative Method.

As one of two methods selected for the study of Acts 15, there is need to give some details about the narrative method. "Narrative Criticism is the application of rhetorical criticism to stories"[113]. It is the study of a literary or a biblical work as a story. Some of the representatives of this new trend in the Acts studies are C. H. Talbert, A. Walworth, J. B. Tyson, R. C. Tannehill, R. I. Pervo, G. P. V. du Plooy, S. M. Sheeley, and J. Dawsey who differentiates between the older critics and the recent narrative critics:

> What most distinguishes these critics' approaches from older, more familiar ones is the claim that the Bible's historical narratives are imaginative re-enactments of history - thus, in form, more akin to fiction than to theology, biography, or history[114] ... Professors Tyson and Tannehill, and other literary scholars like them, are helping us better discern how these techniques were used in Luke and Acts, thus opening new windows to the characters, the way that the author ascribes intentions to them, the plot, themes, nuances, points of view, uses of irony, and word-plays and associations in the writings[115].

---

110 Cf. Haenchen, Acts, 455ff; Bruce, Acts, 332ff; Phillips, Exploring Acts, 59ff; Arrington, Acts, 149ff; Barrett, Apostles, 14ff; Fahy, Council, 232ff; Crowe, Acts, 111ff; Danielou, La Chiesa, 63ff.

111 Pasinya, L'Inculturation, 126ff; Dumais, Church of the Acts, 9f; Pathrapankal, Church, 19-24.

112 Wimbush, Historical/Cultural, 46.

113 Brown/Schneiders, Hermeneutics, 71:67, p. 1160. Narrative criticism is usually distinguished from narratology which is the stuctural analysis of a story. However in this work, the term narrative criticism shall be understood in terms of the narrative critical method which embraces both narratology and rhetorical criticism (applied narrative criticism). So then narratology, narrative rhetoric and narrative criticism shall be used synonymously and interchangeably, while their meaning shall be determined by their context.

114 Dawsey may not be stating the mind of historical critics by saying that they consider the biblical narratives as immaginative re-enactments of history more akin to fiction than to theology, biography or history.

115 Dawsey, Literary Unity, 48. Cf. Sheeley, Narrative Asides, 102.

While Dawsey tries to point out the difference between the older historical and the more recent literary critics, his point of view may not be wholly acceptable to the older critics. His position is modified or corrected by J. L. Ska who presents "narratology" as "a recent method of literary criticism" which "tries to open a forum for constructive dialogue between exegetes using more classical methods and those who favour this new way of exploring the well-known landscapes of Scripture"[116].

Tyson and Tannehill uphold the "narrative unity of Luke-Acts" and also recommend that the two volumes should be read as one since they are intended to tell a single story and their contents do inform each other. While *Tyson* affirms that the Prologue of the Acts (1,1-3) reveals that the author intended Luke-Acts to be read as a unit, *Tannehill* sees them as an expression of God's controlling purpose or design in salvation history[117] which, in *du Plooy's* view, is developed and realized on a variety of levels in the narrative[118].

One thus sees in the narrative method a dialogal approach to the traditional methods of Acts-research. The apparent lack of this dialogue and improvement of the earlier methods of Acts-research may have led Tannehill to lament the failure of many modern readers and scholars to appreciate the dramatic episodes of the Acts. So he states categorically that

we must study Acts in terms of narrative rhetoric. It is appropriate to speak of narrative rhetoric both because the story is constructed to influence its readers or hearers and because there are particular literary techniques used for this purpose[119].

By insisting that "Luke-Acts is a complex system of influence which may be analyzed in literary terms", Tannehill goes on to explain why he deems the narrative method appropriate for the study of the Acts story:

I make use of narrative criticism in order to understand this narrative's message, a message that cannot be confined to theological statements but encompasses a rich set of attitudes and images that are embedded in the story and offered for our admiration and imitation[120].

This correspond's to R. I. Pervo's program of reading the Acts as a "popular story" and at the same time studying it profitably and delightfully as a serious

---

116 See Ska, Our Fathers, Back Cover.
117 Cf Tyson, Death of Jesus, 4; Tannehill, Narrative Unity (1986) 1,2; Dawsey, Literary Unity, 48-49.
118 Cf. Du Plooy, Design of God, 1 & 5; Author in Luke-Acts,28.
119 Tannehill, Narrative Unity (1990) 2,4.
120 Ibid.

theological treatise[121]. With this approach Pervo aims at letting the "Acts speak for itself". In this sense the Acts story becomes a bearer of theological significance since "narrative development is essential to the consideration of the theology of Acts"[122]. This is plausible because the Acts is basically a *"diegesis"* or narrative (Lk 1,1) about the inspired powers of the apostolic people commissioned by Jesus Christ (Ac 1,5f)[123]. Thus narrative and theology inform each other.

But Pervo is not alone in his methodolgical approach. There is a general consensus among narrative critics on the literary value of Luke-Acts which also

raises some interesting questions about the rhetorical effect of the narrative on its reader, the use of various themes to provide movement within the plot, and the techniques used by the narrators of these two volumes[124].

Advantages of the Narrative Method.

The narrative method recognizes the merits and the demerits of other critical methods. In the spirit of *"methodological pluralism"*, the method incorporates the useful findings of the historical critical and other literary methods in order to understand the first century society and its *historical events* that are also basic to "understanding the Acts as a narrative". To this effect Tannehill says:

I do not understand narrative criticism to be an exclusive method, requiring rejection of all other methods. Methodological pluralism is to be encouraged, for each method will have blind spots that can only be overcome through another approach. I readily draw on past exegesis of Acts. Biblical exegesis has a tradition of detailed textual interpretation that should not be lost as we address literary questions[125].

Narrative criticism is therefore not exclusivistic but accomodative and incorporative of other critical methods which in turn should mutually correct, supplement and complement one another. This approach to Acts thus represents a serious effort at a synchronic study that is frequently in "dialogue with

---

121 Cf. Pervo, Profit, xi-xii. Pervo says that he drew his inspiration from **Horace**, *Ars Poetica* 343-344: "The one who combines profit with delight, equally pleasing and admonishing the reader, captures all the plaudits". In **Latin**: *Omne tulii punctum qui miscuit utile dulci, Lectorem delectando pariterque monendo.* Similar inspiration guides me in my attempt at the narrative-inculturation study of Acts 15.
122 Gaventa, Toward a Theology, 157.
123 Cf Wall, Acts, 22.
124 Sheeley, Narrative Asides, 102.
125 Narrative Unity (1990) 2,4.

past scholarship" - a synchronic approach with a sufficient "dosage" of diachronic insights. Nevertheless the narrative method has the additional advantage of helping the researcher relate one's findings to the actual human situation, values and beliefs.

The vital issue in the study of Acts is not whether it is historically accurate but whether
it promotes values worthy of respect and presents models worthy of imitation. Since Acts is
a narrative, these issues cannot be adequately discussed without the knowledge of the ways
in which narrative promotes values and beliefs[126].

In my opinion one of the best ways to uncover how narrative promotes values and beliefs is by the application of the narrative and inculturation methods
to the study of that narrative. This is because culture embraces the promotion
of human values and beliefs worthy of respect and emulation, and the inculturation process precisely aims at the integration of the cultural values into the
Good News.

2.2.10 Acts and the Inculturation Method.

The cultural critical or inculturation method is the second method selected for
our study. It is a recent biblical/theological method with different perspectives
(cf. 1.4.1). Here it is a particular way of studying the biblical word or message
by situating it within a people's historical cultural context. The method came
in vogue after the introduction of the term "inculturation" into the biblical and
theological sciences. It begins with an analysis of the situation or the socio-
cultural context of a people to which a particular biblical message is to be
applied[127]. Scholars of this method are convinced that

theologizing is a matter of dynamic-equivalence transculturation and of witness to
Christianity in terms of culture. All theologizing is culture-bound interpretation and communication of God's revelation. Good theologizing is Spirit-led, even though culture-
bound[128].

The method arose from the growing awareness that in the religious sphere
(as also in other spheres of life) all peoples in their various socio-cultural mi-
lieux need self-knowledge, self-assessment, self-remedy and self-healing[129].

---

126 Id., 3-4.
127 Cf. Sarpong, Evangelisation, 4-7.
128 Kraft, Christianity, 291. This citation is also the sub-title of the book.
129 Cf. Clement et al., Cross-Cultural Christianity, 1-12; Hesselgrave, Communicating
     Christ, 199f; Kraft, op. cit., 75f; 277f.

This is so because each cultural group has its own history, experience and its own socio-religious context[130]. It follows then that not all culture-bound religious prescriptions for salvation should be at all times and in every place unconditionally and absolutely binding on each and every people. Rather the application of such prescriptions should make allowance for cultural practices that are not at variance but consonant with authentic faith and practice. This is what the inculturation method seeks to achieve.

By cultural criticism of a religious text therefore, I mean an affirmation of an indigenous hermeneutic that would help any people with a specific culture understand themselves as a people with a religious heritage and with a future in which that heritage is to be expressed. It is a hermeneutic that would involve a cross-cultural analysis of the religious text as of prime importance and also take into account the historical critical interpretation of such a text with its distancing, dissembling and relativizing effects[131].

In the biblical context, V. L. Wimbush stresses that

cross-cultural analysis is necessary in order to interprete the symbols and referents of biblical cultures and contemporary dominant cultures, so as to determine which symbols and referents from any culture are relevant and affirming[132].

Biblical cultural criticism seeks to rid God's word of any form of "cultural and linguistic imperialism" so that this word may be read and heard in languages other than Hebrew, Greek or Latin or in any of the modern, imperialist, colonial languages (English, French, Spanish, German, Portuguese)[133]. Thus every reading and interpretation of a biblical text "must always be recognized as culture-specific"[134].

To the formerly colonised and oppressed Africans in particular, the cultural method counsels that

the Bible should be the focus of the challenge that Afro-Christian Churches must begin to address in order to embrace and define Christian traditions anew for affirmation and liberation. For without an increased measure of hermeneutical control over the Bible, it will prove impossible for Afro-Christian Churches to articulate self-understanding, maintain integrity as separate communities, and determine their mission in the world[135].

---

130 Cf. Hesselgrave, op. cit., 90f; 121ff.
131 Wimbush, Historical/Cultural Criticism, 50-51.
132 Id., 43.
133 Cf. Lan, Discovering the Bible, 25.
134 Wimbush, op. cit., 44.
135 Id., 47-48.

Since it is culture-specific, the inculturation method starts with the analysis of the human situation and context in which the biblical word is being preached or heard or received. Then it relates this situation to the context of the biblical message in order to draw appropriate lessons for the situation or context of the recipient or audience. The method proceeds from anthropological questions to the Gospel message. This means that the Christian teaching is learnt through a people's language and culture.

"There is true inculturation only when the anthropological (cultural forms and expressions, patterns of thought and social relationship) precedes the theological (faith, mystery of the Church, grace), and not the other way round"[136]. "The anthopological and the cultural become the way through which the theological is approached, perceived, appropriated, integrated and lived"[137].

In other words, the situation and problems of the believing community are the point of departure for the cultural critical study and application of the biblical word to the life of the people[138]. Seen in this light, the inculturation method involves as alredy noted in chapter one the context of the audience or recipient of the divine message, the context of the preacher of the message and the context of the divine message. These three contexts or poles of cultural relationship between the divine word, pastoral agent and the audience are a *sine qua non* for the inculturation of the Gospel in every stratum of the human community[139].

Applied to the Acts, the inculturation method, unlike the other methods, has the advantage of combining theory with practice. Two examples of the use of this method can highlight its validity and importance for contemporary Acts studies. The one is promoted by M. Dumais and J. Pathrapankal, the other by the Congress of African Biblical Theologians (2.1.10).

Dumais' approach is a combination of the inculturation method with the historical exegetical method, that is, a historical/cultural approach to the study of the Acts in the style of Wimbush's proposal for a historical/cultural approach to biblical texts[140]. It is a diachronic inculturation method of Acts-research whose end-result is expected to be an appreciable cultural interpretation of the whole Acts that reflects the historical situation of the apostolic people with a hermeneutical relevance to the people of our own era. Using the same historical/cultural method, the members of the Congress of African Bib-

---

136 Wilfred, Inculturation, 186.
137 Id., 194.
138 Arrupe, Message, in : Crollius, Inculturation, 1, xi
139 Cf. Schineller, Handbook, 62-72; Hesselgrave, Communicating Christ, 72-78.
140 Cf. Wimbush, Historical/Cultural Criticism, 43-55.

licists in their Ibadan (Nigeria) Seminar in 1984 made a serious contribution to the inculturation study of the Acts[141] (2.1.10).

Advantages of the Inculturation Method.

When rightly employed, the cultural critical method will no doubt facilitate a "dynamic biblical theologizing in crosscultural perspective"[142]. The method does not dwell so much on the historical reliability of a biblical text. Rather it takes the texts as it sees it, examines its message in its socio-religious context, allows the text to speak for itself and applies its message to a particular audience.

In this sense the inculturation method involves a certain measure of the narrative method which considers a narrative text as a story about some historical event that can be used to foster and promote values and beliefs worthy of emulation by the recipients or audience of the text. Hence the cultural critical method may be regarded as the hermeneutical centre of the historical and literary methods.

The inculturation method is also related to the historical critical method by its emphasis on human cultures, and to the narrative method by its emphasis on the contexts of the story, its narrator or preacher or pastoral agent, and its hearers or audience. This relationship to both the historical and contextual methods gives the inculturation method a growing popularity especially in the comparative study of the life of the apostolic Church of the Acts with the life of the young Churches of Africa, Asia and Afro-America[143].

2.3 Delimitation of Narrative Units of Ac 15,1-35.

One of first tasks of a literary analysis is the delimitation of the narrative units which are sometimes called macro- and micro-units (longer narratives and their subdivisions)... In determining the main units of a narrative, the chief criteria are dramatic criteria: change of place, change of time, change of characters (characters entering or leaving the "stage"), or

---

141 Bishops, Priests, Religious and Lay people qualified in "re biblica" are members of this Congress. I am also happy to be identified with this body of biblical inculturationists.
142 Cf. Kraft, Christianity, passim.
143 Cf. Waliggo, Acts of the Apostles, 26ff; Arowele, Mission and Evangelisation, 235f; Balembo, L'Autonomie des Jeunes Eglises, 91ff.

change of action.... Stylistic criteria are also very useful (repetitions, inclusions, shift in vocabulary....)[144].

Using these criteria, Ac 15,1-35 can be divided into six major units[145]. These units can be studied as "scenes" in the narrative[146] comparable to the "*scenic study*" of the Cornelius episode by J. Crowe and R. Dillon[147].

2.3.1   Acts 15 as a Story and a Plot.

The story[148] of Acts 15 comparable to ancient biblical and non-biblical narratives[149] focuses more on the deeds or actions of the characters in order to communicate a message to the audience. As J. Crowe rightly observes,

> Acts is a "story", a connected narrative of events involving movement, conflict, change. It includes the lesser "stories" of so many individuals or groups; Luke connects them into a pattern which constitutes the larger story. This offers him the possibility of using material of many kinds... It is well to attend to the "story" character of Acts to avoid common misunderstandings. Luke has an excellent claim to the title of historian, but he is primarily engaged in telling a "story". It is through the literary medium of the story that he communicates[150].

Its plot[151] or the "ordered arrangement of incidents"[152] is a plot of action or resolution because the tense and charged atmosphere at the beginning of the

---

144   Ska, Op. cit., 1. Cf. also Mlakuzhyil, Structure, 87-136; Bar-Efrat, Narrative Art, 96-111.
145   Cf. Barclay, Acts, 112-119; Barrett, Apostles, 16-25; Tannehill, 183-193; Dillon, Acts, 44:81-85, pp. 751-752; Marshall, Acts, 247-256. Weiser, Apg., 365-366; Id., "Apostelkonzil", 199-209; Bruce, Book, 285-300. The best division of these literary units is by A. Weiser and F. F. Bruce.
146   I must point out that other methods are possible as already shown in the survey of Acts-research in chapter two. But in the spirit of the conciliar teaching I have, as a student of the Bible and Theology, selected the narrative/inculturation method in order to present the divine word to the contemporary peoples.
147   Cf. Crowe, Acts, 71-82; Dillon, Acts, 44:59-65, pp.745-747.
148   "Story" here means an abstract reconstruction in which the elements of a concrete narrative or discourse are orderly and logically placed or replaced chronologically while also supplying what is missing.
149   Cf. Edwards, Acts of the Apostles, 363f. 376f; Sterling, Luke-Acts, 337-342; Dawsey, Characteristics, 324f; Balch, Genre and a Political Theme, 360f.
150   Crowe, Acts, xi.
151   The Italian scholar G. Ravasi following the thoughts of E. Haenchen gives a fair summary of how to read and study the Acts as a story and a plot: "Nell'articolo "Apostelgeschichte" della "die Religion in Geschichte und Gegenwart" l'esegeta tede-

JC (vv.5-6) changes for the better at its end (vv.30-35). The events are ordered, chronological and logical in the sense of temporal succession of events following the basic principle of "*post hoc, propter hoc*". One event in the pericope logically leads to the other until some solution (vv.22-29) is given to the initial problem (vv.1-5), and the situation is transformed as in a plot of resolution (vv.30-35).

It is a "unified plot" because each episode or unit of the story leads to the other and supposes what precedes it while it prepares for what follows it. That is, each unit is relevant to the narrative[153] and has a bearing on the outcome of the whole story[154]. The subsequent analysis of the text shall elaborate on these points.

2.3.2 Formal Structure or Theme of Ac 15,1-35.

Since conflict and ignorance give rise to a plot[155], the conflict created by the ignorance of the over-zealous Judaizers about what is necessary for salvation

---

sco Ernst Haenchen definiva gli Atti degli apostoli piu stories che history a causa del robusto intervento redazionale dell'estensore... L'opera, infatti, piu che su di un'esposizione narrata degli eventi e basata su un episodio emblematico o su una missione apostolica, il tutto collegato frequentemente da sommari di coordinamento. Lo spazio "drammatico" interno ai singoli quadri e distribuito sulla tensione del crescendo, accompagnato da un sapiente dossaggio di "elementi ritardanti" che accrescono l'intensita e la suspense del risultato narrativo finale" (Studi, 7-8).

152 "The ordered arrangement of the incidents is what I mean by plot" (Aristotle, Poetics, 6). To this modern scholars add, "Plot can be defined as the dynamic, sequential element in narrative literature" (ScholesKellog, Nature, 207). Cf. Egan, "What is Plot", 455-473. Dipple, Plot; Bar-Efrat, Narrative Art, 47-92.

153 Technically "Narrative" refers to a specific literary genre whose methodology we have already described. But ordinarily it is synonymous with "story". Context will determine the meaning of its usage.

154 Cf. Ska, Our Fathers, 17-19.

155 A complete scheme of the structure of a narrative text as presented by Chatman consists of seven elements: Real author, Implied author; Narrator, Narration, and narratee; Real reader and Implied reader. In Biblical narratives the distinctions are mainly between real and implied author and between real and implied reader. The implied author (discernible in the value-systems, interests, norms, world-view and creative power in a narration), is a projection of the real author. In the same way, the implied reader is less a person than a role performed by every individual reader with his/her value judgments, feelings and world-views (cf. Chatman, Story, 151; Ska, Fathers, 40-43).

gives rise to the plot with the formal structure or theme[156] of conflict/resolution; problem/solution; difficulty/difficulty removed. This is so because it resolves, at least temporarily, the socio-religious conflict between the Judaizers and the Gentile Christians. This is also obvious if one compares the contentious beginning of the narrative (vv.1-5) with its happy conclusion (vv.30-35). The quarrels and conflicts in vv. 1-5 disappear completely in vv.30-35.

2.3.3 Moments of the Plot of Ac 15,1-35.

The various stages of a plot constitute its different moments. These moments form the backbone of the narrative and articulate the main stages of an action although they may not correspond exactly to the principal units of a properly delimited text of a narrative. Aristotle gives us a three-part division of a plot or story (and of drama): beginning, middle, and end, or in other words, complication, climax, and unravelling.

In line with the Aristotelian division, G. Freytag's theory of a typical plot states that it begins with an action that continues to rise until it reaches a climax and then comes to an end with a falling action[157]. Now let us apply these moments to the analysis of the Acts 15,1-35.

2.3.4 Exposition (Vv.1-2b.3-4).

The exposition acts as the introduction (*Einleitung*)[158] to the whole story and often outlines for the reader a laconic, generic and abstract background information about the who, the where, and the when of the narrative. It thus pro-

---

156 "Theme" may somtimes be another term for the formal structure of a story and it is discovered by comparing the initial part of the narration with its final stage. The formal structure, which different from the concrete narration, is an initial, abstract way of classifying a text in a pair of words that stand in simple opposition.

157 Cf. Freytag, Technique of Drama (1908), passim; Sternberg, Expositional Modes, 5-8; Ska, Our Fathers, 20f.

158 Note the narative terms used and their equivalents in German language: Exposition (Einleitung); inciting moment (das erregende Moment); complication (Steigerung); climax (Hohepunkt); turning point (das tragische Moment); falling action or resolution (Auflosung; also Fall or Umkehr); last delay (das Moment der letzten Spannung); dénouement or conclusion (Katastrophe). In the context of a Greek tragedy "katastrophe" signifies the final outcome of an event at which tension and suspense come to an end. (Cf. Ska, op. cit.,109-110; Best, Handbuch, 120).

vides basic information about the main characters of the story, their relationships and the setting of the narrative which are necessary for a better grasp of the story. Hence exposition is fittingly defined as

> the presentation of indispensable pieces of information about the state of affairs that precedes the beginning of action itself... Logically the exposition is the first moment of a narration, but concretely the action can begin in **media res**... and the exposition can come afterwards[159].

In Acts 15 the exposition follows the logical order because the description of the state of affairs in Antioch is already begun in 14,27 where Paul and Barnabas report their missionary success which is immediately followed by 15,1 where the Judaizers initiate their troublesome demands from the Gentile Christians. The exposition is continued in 2b-4 which tells of the journey of the Gentile delegates from Antioch to Jerualem and their initial welcome by the Jerusalem community.

Thus in three and half verses, the exposition in a way summarises the story of Acts 15, giving the reader the setting of the narrative, introducing the main *dramatis personae* in the Churches of Antioch and Jerusalem and the relationship between them. These are necessary informations about the situation that incites the action of the plot.

2.3.5   Inciting Moment (Vv.1-2a.5).

The inciting moment is the time of the first spur or awakening of action. It is clarified by the German word "*erregend*" - the exciting or arousing or provoking or "infuriating" moment. In a plot of action/resolution, it is

> the moment in which the conflict or the problem appears for the first time and arouses the interest of the reader. Often it is the "*what*" of the exposition of the story. In many cases, it is difficult to distinguish it from the exposition or the beginning of complication[160].

15,1-2a tells us for the first time of the great conflict between the Antiochian Church and the Judaizers who arrived from Jerusalem. As a reader, one's interest is then aroused and one becomes very expectant of what will happen. 15,5 recharges the interest by the presentation of the confict in terms of a double demand by the Christians of the "sect of the Pharisees".

---

159 Ska, op. cit., 21.
160 Id., 25.

The incitement and excitement take place in both centres of Christianity. There is dramatic tension with suspense and as the reader expects what will happen, his attention is oriented towards the future. As is sometimes possible, the inciting moment (vv. 1-2a.5) here overlaps and intertwines with the exposition (vv. 1.2b-4) and this is why one may not easily identify or differentiate them in this context.

2.3.6 Complication (Vv.2b.6-7a).

The German words "*Steigerung*" (intensification, heightening, raising) and "*Entwicklung*" (development) may well explain the concept of complication in the narrative context. It is the gradual raising or intensification of an action, a "*crescendo*" movement of an action to a height. In complication, conflict and tension build up, yet various steps are taken to resolve them, or transform the situation by trying as far as possible to come near to the truth. At the same time the narrative unfolds and suspense is created while the reader's appetite is whetted for what will next happen[161].

15,2b tells of the great dispute and arguments between the Antiochian Church and the legalistic Judaizers who ignited the conflict. The contensions are part of the attempts to resolve the Gentile question. When all the arguments failed to resolve the problem, the Antiochian Church arranged for another "peace-talk" in Jerusalem where the tension continued to build up and intensify because the Judaizers increased their demands from the Gentiles. V.6 tells of the efforts made by the apostles and elders to settle the matter. V.7a summarises the great deal of dispute that preceded Peter's "pastoral" intervention and directives. Thus vv.6-7a act as a type of transition to Peter's speech.

2.3.7 Peter's Speech (Vv.7b-11).

Peter's speech is the *first real scene* of the story because one sees in it a change of rhythm[162]. His intervention changes the tempo or movement of the narrative which, up to this moment, has centred on the heated arguments between

---

161 Id., 25-27.
162 "A rhythm is a regular movement or beat"; it is "a strong pattrern of sound or movement that is used in music, poetry, or dancing"; "if a movement is rhythmic or rhythmical, it is repeated at regular intervals, forming a regular pattern or beat" (Pons Collins Dictionary, p. 1246). In a narrative scene a change of rhythm is the change of time-ratio of a summary concluding the scene due to the addition of a new element required to continue the action. (cf. Ska, Our Fathers, 33).

the opposing Jewish and Gentile parties. As Peter stands up to speak, the narrator[163] abdicates his role to Peter. And the speech, though brief, is unique and concrete, for it makes references to the past events which will never recur as such, but are useful for the solution of the present conflict. Being the first real attempt to resolve the problem, and as a preparatory scene, Peter's speech heightens the narrative tension and equally prepares the way for the climax of the JC story.

2.3.8 Report of God's Wonders Among Gentiles (V.12).

The *second real scene* astonishingly consisits of v.12 where the silenced assembly (*pan to plethos*)[164] of the Church, apostles and elders (vv.2.4-7) listen attentively to Paul and Barnabas as the narrator recounts their God-inspired missionary success. The events which are here narrated in one sentence and in so short a time embrace the initial evangelical tasks of the two missionaries in 13,4-14,28. Such a period of "real" time is known as the time of the narrative, or the "narrative time" or the "narrated time" (*erzählte Zeit*), while the "material time" devoted to the summary of the events in one verse is called the "narration time" (*Erzählzeit*)[165].

Normally narrative time is longer than narration time, and their ratio helps the reader assess the narrator's necessary choices and the effects he intends to produce[166]. V.12 is part of the attempt to resolve the conflict. It is then a second preparatory scene that eventually prepares for the climax, the decisive intervention of James, the leader of the Jerusalem Church.

---

163 The narrator is a function, a role or a voice within or outside the story. He is like a speaker's voice in a radio or like someone who reads a text aloud to the hearing of an audience, and can tell his own story or the story of somebody else in a narrative (cf. Chatman, Story, 147-151; Genette, English, 212-262.

164 In the NT the expression *"pan (hapan) to plethos"* is peculiar to Lukan works and so it can be regarded as Luke's manner of generalisation. Cf Lk 1,10; 8,37; 19,37; 23,1; Ac 6,5; 21,22; 25,24; Weiser, Apostelkonzil, 196.

165 Genette Figures, III, 77 = Narrative Discourse, 33-34; Ska, Our Fathers, 7-8.

166 "Time" is very basic to narratives for two reasons: (a) a narrative recounts events that took place in time; (b) the act of narration presupposes a certain time and "an arrangement of events in a certain temporal order" (Ska, id., 7).

2.3.9 Speech of James as Climax (Vv.13-21).

The speech of James is the third real scene of the plot and forms both the climax (*Höhepunkt*) and the turning-point (*das tragische Moment*) of the whole story. The "climax" is not easy to define but in Greek tragedy it is the apex of the fortunes of the hero. In a narrative however,

> it can be the moment of highest tension, the appearance of a decisive element or character, the final stage of a narrative progression[167].

The turning-point initiates the falling action and introduces an element that will be decisive in bringing the movement of the story to its conclusion. This is why the turning-point can sometimes coincide with the final resolution of a plot, thus blurring their differentiation in a story.

As the climax of the episode, the intervention of James is the apex of the whole disputes, debates and speeches on the Gentile question (vv.13f). The opposing parties have put forward their views for and against the unconditional admission of the Gentiles into the Church. But the problem remains unresolved. Tension continues to mount and reaches its climax in the decision of James in favour of the Gentile cause (v.19). All listen attentively to him and accept his final verdict to allow Gentiles into the Church with or without the observance of Jewish Law and practices (v.22).

The climax is immediately followed by the turning-point. The decision of James includes a compromise formula that will at least facilitate christian relationship between the Judaizers and the non-Jews. The Gentiles are to refrain from certain dietary and social practices not acceptable to the Jews and his proposal wins a general acceptance (v.20). With this comes a hopeful expectation for the resolution of the problem.

2.3.10 Resolution (Vv.22-29).

This is the fourth real scene of the plot. Resolution (German: *Auflösung*) is an important stage of a plot. In Greek tragedy the resolution is called "*peripeteia*" (falling upside down). It refers to a sudden change of action or reversal of state of affairs to its exact opposite if it occurs in a plot of action (resolution). But it is called "*anagnorisis*" (recognition) if it occurs in plot of knowledge (discovery or revelation)[168]. It is the end of the suspense of a dramatic action (*das Moment der letzten Spannung*). The resolution brings about an unex-

---

167 Ska, Our Fathers, 27.
168 Cf. Chatman, Story, 85; Sternberg, Poetics, 172; 308.

pected dramatic turn of events. It is the moment most awaited for by the reader of a plot. Hence it is of utmost importance to pinpoint this moment, since it provokes a downward plunge of the dramatic tension which may even completely ease off before the introduction of the final scene.

In 15,22-29, the resolution is a reverse action. There is a sudden change of attitude by the characters in the story. The state of unhappiness and dispute that marked the beginning of the JC suddenly gives way to a state of agreement, and the members of the assembly suddenly pass from the initial state of disunity, rancour and bitterness to a state of brotherly understanding, unity and happiness.

In the concrete, the resolution is embodied in the "Letter to the Gentile Christians" which frees them from the yoke of Jewish Law, but obliges them to refrain from idolatrous and immoral practices as the "basic Law" for social interaction with Jewish Christians. Thus the Letter resolves the serious conflict between the two "christian races", and sets the stage for the final outcome of the narrative.

2.3.11 Dénouement (Vv.30-35).

The French word "*dénoument*" means the untying or undoing of a knot or a plot. In Greek tragedy *dénoument* signifies the moment when the plot is untied or "unknotted" and suspense and tension completely disappear, hence the alternative use of the technical term "catastrophe" to describe this moment of the plot. M. H. Abrams defines dénoument as

"the precipitating final scene" during which "the action or intrigue ends in success or failure for the protagonist, the mystery is solved, or the misunderstanding cleared away"[169].

Dénoument is the conclusion of a narrative, subsequent to the resolution of the plot. It contains the result of the resolution of the plot. It is the epilogue of the story, the final state of affairs, the final scene of the action.

15,30-35 is the final scene of the story of the conflict between Jewish and Gentile Christians. The reader experiences a total disappearance of tension. After reading the Letter to the Gentile Christians, there is great joy and relaxation among them. The delegates have successfully presented and defended their cause. Misunderstanding and conflict are set aside and there is calm, peace and happiness at last.

---

169 Abrams, Glossary, 141.

CONCLUSION.

The division into scenes makes the story in Acts 15,1-35 more vivid by presenting the whole episode like a plot with several scenes. Using this approach the characters can be better understood and the event described therein may become more real while the words, actions and decisions of each character may become more true to life. This is an advantage of the narrative critical method over the other methods.

But by this narrative analysis, I am in no way intimating that Luke the author intentionally employed the Aristotelian plot-model in composing the Acts. He might have employed it (as was the case in ancient historiography) but I am not very certain about it. I have only tried to demonstrate that the story of Acts 15 can be considered as falling within the category of a unified plot of resolution and can also be read and enjoyed as a story by applying the Aristotelian plot-model to it without in any way diminishing its edificatory theological significance as Pervo has demonstrated in his discussion of ancient historical novels[170].

Next is the exegetical study of each of the narative units or scenes with the narrative-inculturation method. Following the narrative method, a suitable title shall be given to each unit which constitutes a chapter of the work.

---

170 Cf. Pervo, Profit With Delight, 115-135.

Part Two.

Exegetical Study of Acts 15,1-35.

Preamble.

This exegetical section consists of chapters three to eight. The preamble to an exegetical study of a text requires a presentation of its delimitation, historical context, structure and form. Such a procedure helps to focus on the text at hand and to back up and corroborate the narrative method. It helps to indicate that the method takes into account the fruitful results of the previous approaches to the Acts-research.

1. Delimitation of Ac 15,1-35.

Ac 15,1-35 is situated immediately after the successful conclusion of the first missionary journey of Paul and Barnabas (13,4-14,28) and before the beginning of the second enterprise during which Paul and Barnabas disagreed and separated from each other (15,36-41). So the text is situated within the context of the official ecclesial evangelization and mission to the Gentile World with a mixture of Jewish population[1]. Within this context of missionary evangelisation it narrates the frequent conflicts between the evangelized Jewish and Gentile peoples and also between the evangelizers themselves[2].

2. Historical Context of Ac 15,1-35.

On their arrival from their first mission to the Gentiles, Paul and Barnabas assembled the Church of Syrian Antioch, told them about the wonderful signs and deeds by which God "had opened the door of faith to the gentiles" (*hoti enoixen tois ethnesin thuran pisteos* 14,27). As they spent their missionary break in Antioch, some Judaizers came from Jerusalem and stirred up tumult among the Gentile converts by insisting that they must be circumcised and observe the Mosaic Law as a necessary condition for salvation. The ensuing

---

1   Cf. Ac 13,13-43; 14,1-7.19-20.
2   Cf. Ac 13,6f.34f; 14,4f.19f.

controversies resulted in the assembly at Jerusalem of the representatives of the Jewish and Gentile Christians to settle the socio-religious dispute.

3. Textual Structure and Form of Ac 15,1-35.

Textual critics have structured this traditionally accepted "central text"[3] of the whole Acts as follows:

Vv. 1-5, the report of the dissension in Antioch and Jerusalem which is the introduction or the background or the prologue to the convocation of the JC.
Vv.6-29 are the main account of the four part Council proceedings:
Vv.6-7a.7b-11, convocation and Peter's speech.
V.12, a reported account of the Gentile mission of Paul and Barnabas.
Vv.13-21, speech of James favouring a Law-free Gentile Church.
Vv.22-29, the Letter to the Gentiles.
Vv. 30-35, arrival of the bearers of the Letter and delegates at Antioch; epilogue and a happy conclusion of the episode[4].

This structure corresponds to the already delimited six narrative units of the text (cf. 2.3) with a prologue and an epilogue and whose plot-moments are outlined in terms of conflict/resolution of conflict. Therefore the "structure and cohesion of the Lucan composition"[5] exhibits a formally well-closed and balanced unit of work in which the "conflict prologue" and the "happy epilogue" rams in the proceedings, thus establishing the formal structure of conflict/resolution of conflict. This inner textual cohesion is further attested to by the frequent mention or repetition of the important motifs in the story.

Eleven of such motifs are spread out throughout the narrative[6]. In the order of their occurrence they are: Some men (*tines*) enforcing circumcision on the Gentiles (vv.1.5.24); the big conflict described as dissension and controversy

---

3   Even literally and coincidentally too, in the Nestle-Aland's "Novum Testamentum Graece" (1983/85), Acts is found midway (pp. 364-367) in the 320-408 page presentation of the greek text of the whole chapters 1-28. In other words, it is preceded by 44 of its 88 pages in the Nestle-Aland version. (Cf. Haenchen, Acts, 461, for a similar remark with regard to Nestle' 1963 edition of the greek text).

4   Cf. Weiser, Apg., 365-366; Id., "Apostelkonzil", 186-188; Monsengwo, L'inculturation, 126; Dillon, Acts, 44:80-85, pp. 751-752.

5   Haenchen, Acts, 461.

6   In a narrative, the narrator is the one who conveys linguistic message to an audience or addressee. The message is the narration, while the addressee is the narratee. "A narrative is a linguistic message conveyed by a narrator to an audience (addressee). The sender is the narrator, the message the narration and the addressee is called the narratee" (Ska, Our Fathers, 40; cf. Chatman, Story, 151).

(*stasis kai zetesis*) and as the upsetting (*tarasso*) of the mind of the people (vv.2.7.24); the Jerusalem authorities referred to as *apostoloi* and *presbyteroi* (vv.2.4.6.22.23); the disturbed Christians called *ethne* or Gentiles (vv.3.7.12.14.17.19.23); the report of the divinely inspired Gentile mission (vv.3.4.12); the participation of the *ekklesia* of both Antioch and Jerusalem in the resolution of the conflict (vv.3.4.22); the mention of Moses and his customs (*ethei*, vv.1.5.21); God's pre-election of the Gentiles through Peter (vv.7.14); the pleading or decision not to lay unnecessary yoke (*zugon*) on the Gentiles (vv.10.19.28); the Jacobian "clause" (vv.20.29); the mission and encouragement by Judas and Silas (vv.22.27.30.31.32.33)[7].

A closer look at these motifs shows that *ethne* occurs 7 times; the mission of Judas and Silas 6 times; the mention of Jerusalem authorities 5 times. The pre-election of the Gentiles and the Jacobian clause occur twice each, while the rest occur thrice each. Since the JC lays emphasis on the motifs of more frequent occurrence, the Gentile or *ethne* question takes precedence over all other motifs.

---

7   Cf. Weiser, Apostelkonzil, 187-188.

3. Chapter Three.

No Salvation Without Mosaic Law and Customs (15,1-5).

3.0 Greek Text of Ac 15,1-5.

1. Kai tines katelthontes apo tes Ioudaias edidaskon tous adelphous : "Ean me peritmethete to ethei to Moüseos, ou dunasthe sothenai".
2. Genomenes de staseos kai zeteseos ouk oliges to Paulo kai to Barnaba pros autous, etaxan anabainein Paulon kai Barnaban kai tinas allous ex auton pros tous apostolous eis Ierousalem peri tou zetematos toutou.
3. Hoi men oun propemphthentes hupo tes ekklesias dierchonto ten te Phoiniken kai Samareian ekdiegoumenoi ten epistrophen ton ethnen kai epoioun charian megalen pasin tois adelphois.
4. Paragenomenoi de eis Ierousalem paredechthesan apo tes ekklesias kai ton apostolon kai ton presbyteron, anengeilan te hosa ho Theos epoiesen met' auton.
5. Exanestesan de tines ton apo tes haireseos ton Pharisaion pepisteukotes legontes : "Dei peritemnein autous parangelllein te terein ton nomon Moüseos".

3.1 Narrative and Stylistic Features of Vv.1-5.

This introductory unit or prologue contains the exposition and the inciting moment of the plot. Here refer to (2.3.6 and 2.3.7). In these five verses narrating events which might have lasted for many days or several weeks (judging from the time of the arrival of the Judaizers at Antioch up to the arrival of the disputing parties at Jerusalem), the story presents the reader with its exposition and inciting moment while at the same time revealing the identitiy of the Judaizers (v.1.5), of the many personages involved in the dispute (vv.2.3.4), and the initial effort by the Antiochian Church to settle it at least temporarily (v.2).

V.1 is introduced by the greek quotation particle "*hoti*" while v.5 is introduced by the usual *verbum declarandi*: "*legontes*" (saying). Here the narrator[8]

---

8   "The narrator is the 'mediator' between the world of the narrative and the world of the audience. He presents or summarizes the events, gives the pace of the narration, introduces the characters and decides to let them speak for themeselves or not" (**Ska, Our Fathers**, 2). Please, note that narrator and plot are the main elements of a narrative. Furthermore the narrator is not to be confused with the author or writer of the story. The "Narrator" is a function or a role or a voice and "is always present in the narrative as part of of its structure" even after the demise of the author (here: Luke) "because he is the "voice" that tells the story" (Ska, Id., 44; cf. Genette, Discourse, 247-252).

finds it necessary to cite verbatim and in a summary form the teaching of the circumcision party which is the cause of the tumult (*stasis kai zetesis*) in the early Church. Vv.2-4 are told in a free indirect style while vv.1.5 are in the free direct style.

The "omniscient" narrator's voice sounds through all the five verses. As the narrator with the privilege of "omnipresence"[9] which one can liken to that of God, he is ever present in Antioch, Phoenicia, Samaria and Jerusalem, reporting the words, feelings and emotions of each character in this unit. He has the "inside views" of every happening and speaks authoritatively and boldly about the conflict and about all involved in it[10]. The narrator can be described as the "Holy Spirit of the narrative" because he is a God-like artist, "invisible and omnipotent, so that one can feel him everywhere, but one cannot see him"[11]. The narrator can tell the story from within (intradiegetic) or from without (extradiegetic) but he remains the authoritative and invisible teller of the story[12]. In Luke-Acts the narrator appears explicitly in the two different prologues (cf. Lk 1,1-4; Ac 1,1-5).

Stylistically the first unit of the text (vv.1-5) which poses the state of the question, is a chiastic literary unit and forms a concentric structure centred around the joy-arousing conversion of the Gentiles which is a favourite theme of the Acts[13]. The renewed controversy over circumcision with additional demand for the observance of the Mosaic Law in v.5 indicates a progression of the initial controversy of v.1 in which circumcision alone is demanded. Here is an outline of the concentric pentacolon structure[14] of vv.1-5:

---

9 "The classical narrator of ancient and traditional narratives is omniscient. He is almost like God: he knows everything and speaks with unabashed authority" (Ska, op. cit.., 44.). This is also true of lthe biblical narrator who, for most of the time, remains invisible and undramatized

10 Cf. Ska, Id., 44-45.

11 Id., 46. This is part of Ska's citation of G. Flaubert's "classical theory about the narrator" in his Letter to Leroyer de Chantapie in 18.03.1857.

12 In the Gospel narratives, the Evangelists tell the story of Jesus from outside. So also is the story of the Acts. Within the narration itself one can tell the story of oneself, as Peter does in his speech (cf.vv.7-21 of our text). This point is deferred to the treatment of the petrine speech.

13 Cf. 8,8; 11,23; 13,48.51.

14 Cf. Monsengwo, L'inculturation, 127. For more on chiastic pentacolon structure confer: Watson, Chiastic Patterns, 130.

V.1 Circumcision following Mosaic Customs (Antioch)	A.
V.2 Reference to Apostles and Elders (Jerusalem).	B.
V.3 News of Gentile Conversions (Phoenicia/Samaria)	C.
V.4 Reception by Apostles and Elders (Jerusalem)	B[1].
V.5 Circumcision *plus* Mosaic Law (Jerusalem)	A[1].

Chiasmus "systematically serves to concentrate the reader's or hearer's interest on the central expression"[15]. Employing this chiasmus for the analysis and interpretation of this pericope one can easily observe that at the heart or center of this literary unit is the joyful news about the conversion of Gentiles (C). It is encircled at the periphery by the Judaizers' double demand for circumcision and the additional demand for the observance of the whole Jewish Law (A/A[1]). This structural position perharps indicates that the narrator probably places these demands at the "periphery" of the happy conversions of the Gentiles. The Jerusalem Apostles and Elders (B/B[1]) are positioned at each stage of disputes and disagreements as mediators in the conflict between the Gentile converts (C) and the Judaizers (A/A[1]). They are placed here like overseers or custodians of the converted Gentiles.

Another noteworthy fact is the prominence of Jerusalem (= Judaea v.1) in this pericope. Other cities are mentioned once, but Jerusalem thrice, thus stressing its importance as the prime "headquarters" of the early Christian Church. The two-way directional journeys are completed by each group in the dispute: the Judaizers set out from Jerusalem to Antioch and returned from Antioch to Jerusalem to insist on their demands. In a similar way the Antiochian delegation sets out from Antioch to Jerusalem (15,3-4) and shall later travel back from Jerusalem to Antioch (15,30).

Now back to vv.1-5. In narratives, as in literatures, a chiasm has an important role to play in the dramatic action as shaped by the narrator. Thus this

---

15 Welch, Chiasmus, 7. Welch defines chiasmus as inverted parallelism (p.9). And Yelland's *Handbook of Literary Terms* defines it as a type of antithesis in a "passage in which the second part is inverted and balanced against the first" (p.32). Welch goes on to point out that this simple inversion or repetition pattern "can draw unusual attention to the central terms, which are repeated in close proximity to each other..... An emphatic focus on the center can be employed by a skilful composer to elevate the importance of a central concept or to dramatize a radical shift of events at the turning point. Meanwhile, the remainder of the system can be used with equal effectiveness as a framework through which the author may compare, contrast, juxtapose, complement, or complete each of the flanking elements in the chiastic system. In addition, a marked degree of intensification can be introduced throughout the system both by building to a climax at the centre as well as by strengthening each element individually upon its chiastic repetition" (p.10).

stylistic structure can also help towards the exegetical study of this literary unit which in turn has three sub-divisions or sub-units: the scene at Antioch; the scene in Phoenicia and Samaria; the scene at Jerusalem. Note that in terms of the movements, journeys and events, Jerusalem stays at the centre and is in the thick of things. It is the central city of activity and the reference point for the mission to Jews and Gentiles alike.

From this perspective, the overall structure of Ac 15,1-35 assumes the chiastic tricolon pattern: Antioch -A, *Jerusalem* -B, and Antioch -A[1]. A diagramatic presentation of the chiastic structure leads into the exegesis of the scene at Antioch.

In Antioch + journey to Jerusalem (15,1-4)	A
In Jerusalem (15,5-29)	B
From Jerusalem + journey to Antioch (15,30-35)	A[1]

3.2 Circumcision According to Mosaic Custom is Necessary for salvation (Ac 15,1-5).

3.2.1 Some People Came from Judaea (V.1a).

Who are these people coming from Juadea? The narrator does not at the onset say who they are or tell of their place of origin. He denies the reader the knowledge of their specific identity, thereby arousing curiousity, questionings and cognitive interest about them. The reader wants to know who the "some" are, from where they have come to Antioch, why they have come, and who has sent them. What is happening? What will happen? Who is/are responsible? Such are the curious questions. Thus the narrative begins with "a character elevating position"[16] whereby the characters at Antioch know more at this stage than the reader(s). In this unclarified state of affairs, only one thing is clear: the presence of these men in Antioch is not for the peace and happiness of the Christian community.

After a "narration time" of four verses the identity of the *tines* (some) comes to light: they are "certain members of the Pharisees party who had be-

---

16 Narrative critics speak of three basic reading positions: character-elevating (character knows more than the reader); reader-elevating (reader knows more than the character); evenhanded (both reader and character are at the same level of knowledge). (Cf. Sternberg, Poetics, 163-172).

come believers *(tines apo tes haireseos ton Pharisaion pepisteukotes*, v.5)"[17].
In the story about Peter's reception of Cornelius and his household into the
Christian Church and the dispute which resulted from that event, they are described as "those of the circumcision" *(hoi ek peritomes*, 10,45; 11,2). In
21,20, James refers to such a group of believers as the zealous upholders of
the Law *(zelotai tou nomou hyparchousin)*. But in a parallel passage in *Galatians*[18], Paul refers to them as false brothers *(pseudadelphous*, Ga 2,4), as
certain people from James *(tinas apo Iakobou* 2,12) and as trouble-makers
(tarassontes, 1,7) who are seeking to pervert Christ's Gospel.

In theological language, the "*tines*" from Jerusalem are variously referred to
as Circumcision Party, Pharisee Christians, Judaizing Christians, Jewish-Law
Christians Judaizers (from the verb, *ioudaizein* = to live according to Jewish
religious regulations), etc[19]. Through their spokesman Tertullus, the Judaizers
describe Paul as "a pest" *(loimon)* who "stirs up trouble *(kinounta staseis)*
among Jews the world over and is a ringleader *(protostates)* of the Nazarene
sect *(haireseos)*" [Ac 24,5].

Thus from the text and its parallels the narrator clearly tells the reader that
Paul and the Judaizers are engaged in a bitter conflict, each side accusing the
other of being guilty of similar offenses of sectarianism and insurrection. In
his Letters Paul confirms this frequent conflict with the legalists and sectarian-
ists in the christian fold[20].

3.2.2   Teaching the Brothers (V.1a).

The Jewish-Law Christians from Judea assume the role of teachers at Antioch.
They were teaching *(edidaskon)* the brothers *(tous adelphous*, accusative plural of *hoi adelphoi)*. Again this is character-elevating position, for the reader is

---

17   In the Western text this v.5 is already added in v.1 which reads: "Some men of the
      party of the Pharisees, who were believers...".

18   Despite the fact that the correlation of this Galatian incident with Acts 15,1-35 is "one
      of the most difficult exegetical problems of the NT, however, one cannot escape the
      impression that Gal 2 refers to the same event as that in Ac 15 (at least vv 1-12) - all
      other attempts to identify it otherwise notwithstanding. Yet many problems remain"
      (Fitzmyer, Galatians, 47:17, p.783). And C. K. Barrett affirms that the many difficul-
      ties involved in taking Gal. 2 and Acts 15 to be roughly parallel are far less than the
      difficulties invloved in taking them as two separate incidents (cf. Apostles, 15-16).

19   Cf. Cassidy, Society, 71. Following Cassidy, these appelations shall be used in-
      terchangeably in this work to stand for the "tines" at Antioch and Jerusalem (vv.1.5).

20   Cf. Ga 2,1-14; 3,6-29; Rm 2,12-29; 4,9-12; 7,1-6; 2 Co 11.

not given the specific identity of these brothers, but it is known to the narrator and the characters. Who then are the "*adelphoi*"?

In Acts 15 *adelphos* occurs eight times (6 in vv.1-35). In v.1 it refers to the Christians of Antioch. In v.13 the representatives of the Jerusalem and Antiochian Churches are "*andres adelphoi*". In v.23 the Apostles and Elders are the *adelphoi* writing to the *adelphoi* in Antioch, Syria and Cilicia. So the Jewish and Gentile Christians regard themselves as *adelphoi* (v.23.31). And all Christians in every city are brothers whom Paul and Barnabas would like to visit (v.36). The Antiochian brethren commend Paul and Silas to the grace of God, as they set out on the next phase of their evangelisation of the Gentiles (v.40).

Adelphoi is thus a common term for the men and women disciples of, or believers in, Jesus Christ. In Ac 1,16 Peter calls the one hundred and twenty initial followers of Jesus *andres adelphoi* (cf.v.15). The same word stands for the crowd of Jews and God-fearers in his Pentecost address (2,29) and the repentant crowd equally addresses the Apostles as *andres adelphoi* (2,37). The *adelphoi* provide safe conduct and journey for the converted but endangered Saul (9,30).

Six *adelphoi* accompany Peter from Joppa to Cornelius in Caesarea (10,23; 11,12). And Peter's miraculous escape from prison is to be reported to "James and the brethren" (12,17). At Iconium the unbelieving Jews stir up the Gentiles against the brethren (14,2). Christians at Lystra and Iconium are called brethren (16,2). So also are those in Thessalonica (17,6.10), Boerea (17,14), Corinth (18,18), Ephesus (18,27), Ptolemais (21,7), Puteoli (28,14) and in Rome (28,15).

But *adelphoi* is not reserved to the christian community alone. Acts uses it to designate Jewish communities within the Roman Empire of that era. Hence Stephen addresses the Chief Priests and the audience at his trial as *andres adelphoi* (7,2). The synagogue worshippers at Pisidian Antioch are *andres adelphoi* who are children of Abraham and God-fearers to whom are promised the Messiah (13,15.26.28). The Jews of Damascus (22,5) and Jewish visitors to Rome are *adelphoi* (28,21).

To refer to the covenant community members as "brothers" was not a christian innovation. Acts shows that this was a general and widely-used way of designating those in the Jewish community from Jerusalem to Rome... Thus brotherhood, with all of its male chauvinist connotations, was seen as the appropriate way to designate the covenant people of God as the author of Acts portrays Judaism in this period[21].

The evidence of the Acts therefore shows that *adelphoi* is a term for all Christians of the early Church and for the Jewish community. "Brotherhood" is for the Jews symbolic of their familial covenant relationship as the chosen people of God. For the Christians it depicts their "brotherhood" and fellowship as the family of Jesus Christ. This accords with the usage of the term in biblical tradition[22]. Within and outside the Acts, *adelphoi* reflects the socio-religious situation of the first century.

In the context of Acts 15,1-35 *adelphoi* refers to both Jewish and Gentile Christians. This is supported by the evidence of Ac 11,19-26 which tell of the foundation of the Church of mixed races of Jews and Gentiles to whom the title "Christians" (*christianous*, v.26) is given and by the report of the mixed-race prophets and teachers of the *ekklesia* of Antioch from whom the Holy Spirit selected Saul and Barnabas for their work[23].

The unfortunate problem in Acts 15,1 is that some of the Jewish *adelphoi* do not want the Gentile brethren to enjoy unconditionally the fellowship of brotherhood arising from their common belief in Christ (cf. Ga 2,4-6). They must observe Mosaic ceremonials if they want to enjoy this fellowship with Jewish believers in Christ.

3.2.3   Unless Circumcised According to Mosaic Custom.

The Judaizers teach that "Unless you are circumcised (*ean me peritmethete*) according to the custom of Moses (*to ethei to Moüseos*) you cannot be saved (*ou dunasthe sothenai*)". The protasis of this conditional sentence introduced by "unless" (*ean*) is the question of circumcision and Mosaic practice while the apodosis deals with the key issue of salvation. Let us begin with the protasis.

---

22   The NJB summarises the biblical usage and meaning of "brother" thus: "Besides its strict sense the word 'brother' has often in the Bible wider senses, a relation more or less distant, Gn 9:25; 13,8, a compatriot, Gn 16:12; Ex 2:11; Dt 2:4; 15:2; Ps 22:22. From there it passes to a deeper relationship by communion in the covenant. In the NT it very frequently denotes Christians, disciples of Christ, 6:3; 9:30: 11:1; 12:17; Matt 28:10; Jn 20:17; Rm 1:13, who like him do the will of the Father, Mt 12:50 and par., children of the Father of whom he is the First-born, Mt 25,40; Rm 8,29; Heb 2:11,17, between whom brotherly love reigns, Rm 12:10; I Th 4,9; 1 P 1:22: 1 Jn 3:14" (p. 1799).

23   Cf. 13,1-3; cf. 14,24-28.

3.2.3.1 Unless You are Circumcised (V.1b).

The form "*peritmethete*" (aorist, subjunctive, passive, second person, plural) of the verb "*peritemno*" is the LXX translation of the MT Hebrew verb "*mul*", to circumcise[24]. The Latin Vulgate translates *peritemno/mul* with "*circumcidere*", literally, to cut around. In the NT the forms of *peritemno* are used 17 times while the noun-forms occur 35 times[25]. In the bibical sense, the corresponding noun *milah/mulah* or *peritome* or *circumcisio*, signifies the act of circumcision, which is a distinct mark of a Jew or a Judaizer and a symbol of membership in the Jewish Christian community[26].

From the divine command and its execution (Gn 17,1-14.23f), it is clear that circumcision which is the cutting of the loose foreskins'of a male's penis[27], is binding only on male Jews. In the biblico-Jewish context, circumcision serves as an initiatory rite to the life of the clan and to marriage[28]. So it celebrates a man's attainment of maturity. It is above all a sign of fidelity to God's covenant with Abraham[29]. An uncircumcised man is as unclean as the fruit of a young tree not yet consecrated to God (cf. Lv 19,23).

By the same analogy of uncleanliness, no uncircumcised male whether slave or alien, is allowed to keep or eat of the Passover ritual. So then, even if circumcision was/is not a practice peculiar to the Jews, yet it remains for the people an obligatory and a very important, covenantal and eighth day socio-

---

24 Let us take an example of the translations from Gn 17,10-11: MT text: Himmon lakhem kol zakar. Unemaltem 'eth besar 'orlathkhem. LXX text: Peritmethestai humon pan arsenikon kai peritmethesesthe ten sarka tes akrobustias humon. Latin Vulg. text: Circumcidetur ex vobis omne masculinum, et circumcidetis carnem praeputii vestri. In the MT text, "mul" occurs 26 times while milah/mulah occurs 4 times.

25 Cf. Moulton-Geden, Concordance, 799-800; Aland, Konkordanz, 1120-1121; Morgenthaler, Statistik, 132. Note that most of the occurrences of "peritome" are in Romans (14 times) and Galatians (7 times) where Paul engages himself over the question of circumcision.

26 Cf. Betz, Peritome, in: EWNT (1983 & ²1992), 186-188. In contrast to the Judaizers whom he ridicules as "katatome" or self-mutilators Paul refers to himself and the Christians as "he peritome" (the true people of circumcision) because they worship by the spirit of God and make Jesus Christ their boast, without relying on physical qualifications (cf. Phil 3,2-3).

27 Some peoples and cultures also practice "female circumcision" or clitoridectomy as part of their initiation rites. The Igbo circumcise both male and female few days after birth. Cf. Mbiti, Introduction, 91-95; Id., African Religions, 122-126; Parrinder, Religion, 102-104.

28 Cf. Gn 34,14-24; Ex 4,24-26; 12,43-48; Lv.12,3; 19,23.

29 Cf. Gn 17,10-14.23-27.

religious ritual dating back to the patriarchal times and passed on from generation to generation[30].

In the exilic times circumcision was the distinctive mark of an Israelite or a Jew deprived of his national identity and temple rituals. In the post-exilic period it assumed a greater religious significance. The Maccabean era demonstrated how the Jews of that epoch valued and clung steadfast to the practice of circumcision, despite terrible persecutions and death in the hands of King Antioochus IV Epiphanes[1].

Following the patriarchial practice and the pentateuchal prescription (Lv 12,3), circumcision then took the form of an obligatory infancy ritual for males. At the beginning of the NT period, it was already combined with the naming ceremony of the male child eight days after birth. Thus John the Baptist and Jesus the Messiah were circumcised and named on the eighth day (cf.Lk 1,59-63; 2,21). And during the ministry of Jesus Christ the practice of circumcision had attained such a religious prominence that its performance on the Sabbath Day was considered right and lawful as is evident from the Lord's dispute with some Jews.

> Moses ordered you to practice circumcision - not that it began with him, it goes back to the patriarchs - and you circumcise on the Sabbath. Now if someone can be circumcised on the Sabbath so that the Law of Moses is not broken, why are you angry with me for making someone completely healthy on a Sabbath? (Jn 7,22-23).

In Ac 7,8 Luke continued the story of the patriarchal "covenant of circumcision" on the eighth day and later reported the protest by the circumcised Jewish Christians (*hoi ek peritomes*) against Peter's commensality with uncircumcised people (*andras akrobustian echontes*, 11,3)[32].

---

30   Cf. Gn 17,12; 21,4; Lv 12,3.

31   "Women who had their children circumcised were put to death according to the edict (of King Antiochus) with their babies hung round their necks, and the members of their household and those who had performed the circumcision were executed with them" (1M 1,60-61; cf. 2M 6,10, from NJB).

32   "These men having foreskin (akrobustia)" are Cornelius and his household whom Peter under divine guidance baptised and received into the Church without their performance of the rite of circumcision. Note that the hebrew verb for "to be uncircumcised" is *'arel* and the noun is *'orlah*. In the OT the Isralelites scornfully called the Phillistines "uncircumcised" (*'arelim*, Jg 14,3; 15,18; 1 Sm 14,6; 31,4, etc.). Acts shows that "akrobustia" is a pejorative term hurled by Israelites or Jews on the non-circumcised Christians or Gentiles (11,2) who in turn ridicule the Jews by calling them "those of circumcision" (*hoi ek peritome*, 10,45; 11,2. Cf. Gal 2,7-10). The Letter to the Ephesians brings out this bilateral disparagement clearly: *"Do not forget, then, that there was a time when you who were gentiles by physical descent, termed*

Fidelity to this covenant and deference to the Jews of Lystra led Paul to circumcise his future missionary companion Timothy, a half-Jew through his mother (Ac 16,1-3). And although Paul strongly opposed those who would force circumcision upon non-Jewish Christians, he himself was proud of his own circumcision on the eight day (Phil 3,5) and regarded it as a "sign and guarantee" of the faith received by Abraham before his circumcision (Rom 4,11). In this way Abraham became the ancestral representative of all circumcised and uncircumcised believers in Christ (v.12). To this effect Bruce comments:

> There were indeed some Jews in those days who thought that the outward rite of circumcision might be omitted, if only its spiritual significance was realized; but these formed a negligible minority. The vast majority, including such a hellenized Jew as Philo of Alexandria, insisted on circumcision as indispensable for all males in the commonwealth of Israel, whether they entered it by birth or by proselytization. This was probably the attitude of the rank and file in the Jerusalem church - "zealous for the law...." (21,20)[33].

In any case the Torah and the Prophets place the circumcision of heart and ears (spiritual circumcision) above mere physical circumcision[34]. That is, a right spiritual condition is worth more than, and preferable to, a mere correctness of ritual and forms. In the post biblical era and in rabbinical tradition, circumcision remained a common practice to be performed even if the eighth day after birth fell on a Sabbath or on the Holy Day of Atonement (*yom kippur*). And astonishingly this custom continues today among the Jews.

> In modern-day Judaism circumcision is still practised by both Orthodox and Reformed elements. The male infants are circumcised on the 8th day after birth, even if it is a Sabbath or Day of Atonement. Among the Orthodox, the rite is carried out by a functionary called a mohel (circumciser). The Reform Jews allow the rite to be performed by a physician; contrary to the practice of the Orthodox, they do not require it for adult proselytes[35].

This brief overview of the origin, history and practice of circumcision among the Jews from Abraham to our era gives an insight into its religious significance and importance for the people: It is for them a sign of the covenantal relationship between Yahweh and Israel and is a supreme religious act that supersedes the religious ordinance of the Sabbath rest. This may certainly provide a clue to anyone who may be wondering why such a mere physical

---

the uncircumcised by those who speak of themselves as the circumcised by reason of physical operation" (Eph 2,11). Cf. also, Marcus, Circumcision, 73-81.

33   Bruce, Book of the Acts, 286-287. See also his foot note (no.23, p. 287) on Philo's position on circumcision in his "Migration of Abraham", 89-94.

34   Cf. for example, Lv 26,41; Jr 4,4: 6,10; Ac 7,51.

35   Polan, Circumcision, 879.

operation was insisted upon by the orthodox Judaizers as a necessary condition for the salvation of non-circumcised Christians (Ac 15,1.5).

3.2.3.2 Circumcision According to Mosaic Custom.

What is Mosaic custom (*ethos Moüseos*)? And how does one understand it in Luke-Acts? To know what it is let us first of all consider the NT use of the term "*ethos*". It is mainly a *Lukan terminology*, occurring ten times (out of the twelve times in the NT) in Luke-Acts[36]. It is used three times in Luke to refer to the priestly custom of casting lots for the ministry in the Lord's sanctuary (1,9), to the Jewish religious custom binding every twelve-year old to go to Jerusalem for the Passover feast (2,42), and to Jesus' practice of going to the Mount of Olives (22,39).

In Acts *ethos* refers to Roman custom or habit (25,16), to Jewish customs or practices (16,21; 26,3), to Jewish ancestral customs (28,17), and to the customs handed by Moses[37] to the people (6,14; 21,21). Culturally, *ethos Moüseos* and *nomos Moüseos* designate a norm of life for the Jewish people, a norm that distinguishes them from other peoples or religious groups[38]. In the Lukan sense *ethos* substantially carries the same signification as a community's normative, habitual usage (*nomos*) or as part of a people's way of life.

Therefore in the NT "the custom of Moses" can be understood in two ways: firstly as the normative way of life regulated and impressed on the people of Israel (Jews) by their powerful leader Moses; secondly as the normative, habitual usage of that which is handed down from Moses to the people of Israel. In this latter sense *ethos* is synonymous with tradition. In this context circumcision and the observance of the Torah are the essential components of the "Mosaic custom".

Two NT texts summarise the biblical teaching on *circumcision according to the Law of Moses*. In his dispute with the Jews, Jesus said that Moses ordered them to practice circumcision although the practice begun with the Patriarchs (Jn 7,22). And in his contention before the Sanhedrin Stephen mentioned the

---

36 The other two occurrences in the NT are in Jn 19,40 which reports the burial of Jesus according to the Jewish custom (εθος τοισ Ιουδαιοισ). The second is in Heb 10,25 which urges christians not to absent themselves from their assemblies as some are accustomed to do (καθος ετησσ τισιν). For more details confer, Weiser, Critica della Legge, 144-146.

37 Luke is fond of telling about the performance of Jewish religious custom according to the law of Moses (cf. Lk 1,59; 2,21-24.39; 41-43) or about the suffering of Jesus according to the Law of Moses and the scriptures (Lk 24,27.44).

38 Cf. Weiser, Critica, op. cit., 146.

patriarchal covenant and practice of circumcision on the eighth day after birth (Acts 7,8).

Since circumcision was originally a covenantal patriarchal rite, why then did the Judaizers insist on its practice according to Mosaic custom (*to ethei to Moüseos*)? Dillon's suggestion is that "this means, of course, that circumcision was prescribed by the Pentateuch which came from Moses"[39].

After the divine command and the execution of circumcision in Gen 17,23-27 and 21,4, one later reads of the Mosaic or pentateuchal positive legislation on circumcision in Ex 12,43f and Lev 12,3. It is urgent to cite the two texts here:

In Ex 12,43.48-49, "Yahweh said to Moses and Aaron, 'This is the ritual for the Passover: no alien may eat it, but any slave bought for money may eat it, once you have circumcised him... Should a stranger residing with you wish to keep the Passover in honour of Yahweh, all the males of his household must be circumcised: he will then be allowed to keep it and will count as a citizen of the country. But no uncircumcised person may eat it. The same law will apply to the citizen and the stranger resident among you'". Lev 12,3 reads: "On the eighth day the child's foreskin must be circumcised".

So then, although circumcision is a patriarchal tradition and custom, it is performed according to the stipulations of the "Books of Moses" or the Torah. Its religious performance by male Jews prepares them for the Lord's Passover meal and acts as a guarantee of righteousness and salvation. Therefore,

to countenance any relaxation in the terms of the covenant with Abraham, sealed in the flesh by circumcision, would be to forfeit all claim to remnant righteousness, all claim to salvation on the last day[40].

For this reason, strict religious Jews insist on the observance of the whole of the Mosaic *ethos* or *nomos* as a necessary condition for salvation for themselves and for all those associated with the Jewish religious tradition. This is why the Judaizers teach that Gentile Christians now members of an originally Jewish Christianity must be circumcised and obliged to keep the custom of Moses in order to be saved.

3.2.3.3 You Cannot Be Saved? (V.1c).

The Judaizers were quite categorical over the question of circumcision without which the male Jews cannot be saved. *Sothenai* is the aorist, infinitive, passive of *sozo* which has a wide range of meanings about physical health, security

---

39   Dillon, Acts, 44:81, p. 751.
40   Bruce, Book, 287.

and spiritual salvation, namely: to rescue, to deliver, to keep safe, to preserve, to cure, to make well, to save. Its corresponding noun, *soteria* or *soterion* means preservation, release, saving power, deliverance, salvation[41]. Hence soteria signifies the deliverance or rescue from any kind of evil whether physical, moral or spiritual. *Sozo* in the NT usage[42]

> normally connotes deliverance from dangers to christian destiny and (positively) the fostering of those conditions that ensure its attainment. Elsewhere in Rom (5:9-10; 8,24; 10:9,13; 11:11,26; 13:11) it refers to a future eschatological reality conceptually distinct from justification or reconciliation"[43].

Peter's address to the Sanhedrin after the healing of a cripple clearly brings out the salutary meanings of *sozo*.

> 8. Rulers of the people, and elders! 9. If you are questioning us today about an act of kindness to a cripple and asking us how he was healed (*sesotai*), 10. you must know, all of you, and the whole people of Israel, that it is by the name of Jesus Christ the Nazarene, whom you crucified, and God raised from the dead, by this name and by no other that he stands before you cured... 12. Only in him is there salvation (*he soteria*) for of all the names in the world given to men, this is the only one by which we can be saved (*sothenai*) (Ac 4,8-10.12).

In v.9 *Sesotai* refers to bodily or physical healing while *soteria* and *sothenai* in v.12 refer to spiritual deliverance or redemption. This salvation comes through faith in the name of Jesus the Saviour (*soter*) or through his grace. Salvation then does not depend on any human effort or custom or tradition, but is purely and solely God's gratuitous gift which demands faith in Jesus Christ from the potential recipient.

Since salvation comes from God alone, one can then imagine the great danger posed by the teaching or "new Gospel" of the Judaizers who at Antioch made circumcision the only condition for salvation! By their categorical im-

---

41   Hence the term "soteriology" for the theology of salvation. In the LXX *sozo* is often used to translate the MT hebrew verb, *ysr*, and sometimes *plt* and *mlt* (cf. Jl 3,5). Its noun Yeshuah (in Greek, Iesous) means help, deliverance, rescue, salvation. (For more on this confer, Foester, *sozo* in TWNT, vol. 7, 966-970; Fohrer, id., 970-981).

42   For the NT usage and meaning of *sozo* confer,. Ac 2,21.40.47; 4,9.12; 11,14; 14,9; 15,1.11; 16,30-31; 27,20.31. And for the Gospels confer for example, Lk 7,50; 8,48; Mt 9,22; Mk 5,34; 10,52; Jn 3,17; 5,34; 10,9; 11,12; 12,27.47. And for "Paul's Christocentric Soteriology" confer, Fitzmyer, Pauline Theology, NJBC 82:24-80, pp. 1388-1402, especially 82:71 on "Salvation", p. 1398. See also Moulton-Geden, Concordance, 928-929.

43   Fitzmyer, Romans, 51:20, p. 834.

perative for salvation the Jewish-law Christians laid the axe at the very root of the teaching and salutary work of Christ and the apostolic people. The implication is that even those who are circumcised, but not according to the Mosaic prescriptions, have no hope of salvation. What happens also to the female Christians who were not bound by Mosaic law of circumcision? By what then shall they be saved? So by their circumcision teaching, the Judaizers were really setting a dangerous precedent in the evangelical mission of the Church. The subsequent prolonged dispute and strife were the logical outcome of their false evangelism.

3.3 Lengthy Dispute and High-Powered Delegation (V.2).

3.3.1 Narrative Features of V.2.

It is already noted that v.2a pertains to the inciting moment while v.2b belongs to the exposition of the story (cf. chapter two). In a narration time of one verse, the narrator finishes the exposition of the origin, cause and course of the conflict at Antioch (v.1). The tale lasts for a narrative time of few seconds. Then in v.2 he shows that the conflict lasted for a long time by the phrase, *"genomenes de staseos kai zeteseos"* (2a). But it is not enough to spend time arguing and disputing on the question of the circumcision of the Gentile Christians. Some positive step should be taken to resolve the conflict. So the narrator exposes in v.2b the initial step being taken to come to a solution: "they appointed (*etaxan*)[44] Paul and Barnabas[45] and some others to go up to the apostles and elders in Jerusalem about this question" (v.2b).

---

44   The subject of the verb, "etaxan" is not expressed but implied in it. "They" may refer to the Church of Antioch or its leaders (cf. Bruce, Acts, footnote no. 20, p. 286 for similar opinion).

45   The order of mentioning the two missionary companions has been already changed. Initially the narrator mentions Barnabas before the newly converted "Saul of Tarsus" (cf. Ac 11,25.30; 12,25; 13,1-2.7). Even the Holy Spirit names Barnabas before Saul (13,2). But at Paphos during the contest with the Magician Barjesus (Elymas) over the belief of the Proconsul Sergius Paulus, Saul's name is suddenly changed to "Paul" (13,9). Perharps in accordance with the custom of the Graeco-Roman World, the narrator gives Saul his Roman name for the first time as he launches into his divine mission in this area. From now on the name "Saul" ceases to be used; the new Paul comes into prominence and takes precedence over Barnabas, as the leader of the gentile missionary leader par excellence (cf. 13,13.43.46.50.; 14,3.20; and here, **15,2** where both are mentioned twice and Paul comes first in each case). An exception is in 14,14 where Barnabas is named before Paul probably because the Lycaonians (Lystrans)

The omniscient narrator who knows all that is happening does not tell the reader "who" it was that appointed the delegates. He is only "showing" and not "telling"[46] what is actually taking place. The reader only guesses or assumes that the decision to send a delegation to Jerusalem is made by the Antiochian Church.

By the mention of Jerusalem early in this verse, the narrator is gradually shifting the scene from Antioch, the citadel of Gentile Christianity to Jerusalem, the headquarters of Jewish Christianity. Of course there is a narrative interval of time and space before the Jerusalem scene is shown to the audience.

3.3.2   Prolonged Dissension and Contention (V.2a).

15,2a speaks of the considerable dispute (*stasis*) and contention (*zetesis*) that erupted from the teaching of the Jewish-law Christians. This is clearly explained by the use of the characteristically Lukan litotes "*ouk oligos*" to qualify the long drawn out conflict[47].

Stasis means dispute, argument, discord, riot, revolt, rebellion[48]. It is a typically Lukan word, occurring only twice outside Luke-Acts[49]. In the Gospels it describes the revolt and riot in which the criminal Barsabbas and some others committed murder (Mk 15,7; Lk 23,19.25). The riot of the Ephesian silversmiths is *stasis* (Acts 19,40). The same is true of the discord between the Pharisees and the Sadducees of the Sanhedrin (23,7.10). Tertullus accuses Paul of stirring up *stasis* among the Jews (24,5).

---

thought that the "dignifying-looking" Barnabas was the chief god "Zeus", while the oratorical Paul was Hermes, the messenger of the gods.

46   "Telling" is the direct address of the reader by the narrator. It is not to be identified with description or normal narration of a story. The "telling" sections of a story are more of intrusions by the narrator whose intruding presence can be easily felt by the reader. "Showing" is not to be confused with a "dialogue". It is more of a "scenic" or "dramatic" presentation of a story. In the Bible most of the narration is scenic or showing mode (cf. Chatman, Story, 196-262; Booth, Rhetoric, 2; Ska, Our Fathers, 53).

47   A litotes is a figure of speech which expresses an idea by denying the contrary (cf. Acts 1,5; 12,18; Zerwick, Analysis, 350).

48   Newman, Dictionary, 166.

49   Cf. Lk 23,19.25; Ac 15,2; 19,40; 23,7.10; 24,5. In Mk 15,7 (= Lk 23,19.25) it means revolt or uprising: "Now a man called Barsabbas was then in prison with the rebels who had committed murder during the uprising (en te stasei). And in Heb 9,8 it means standing, existence (eti tes protes skenes echouses stasin = as long as the old tent stands.

Zetesis means discussion, debate; controversy, controversial issue; investigation, speculation[50]. In the Acts (15,2.7; 25,20) it occurs three out of the seven times in the NT. In Jn 3,25 "a discussion (*zetesis*) arose between some of John's disciples and a Jew about purification". The three Pastoral Letters advises the pastor against debates and controversies (*peri zeteseis kai logomachias*, 1 Tim 6,4), and admonishes him to desist from foolish and ignorant speculations (*zeteseis*, 2 Tim 2,23; cf. Tit 3,9).

The meanings and nuances of *stasis* and *zetesis* qualified by the Lukan litotes "*ouk oligos*" depicts very well the intensity and the extent of the dissension, contention and quarrel that took place in the Antiochian "religious riot" between the "circumcision fanatics" and the Gentile Christians (Ac 15,2). Such a chaotic atmosphere deserves an immediate pastoral attention and an authoritative ecclesial solution and hence the reasonableness of the delegation to the Jerusalem.

From this negative picture of the scene at Antioch the narrator goes on to paint a positive picture of the Antiochian dispute. The dispute is a type of "*felix culpa*" that will yield later positive fruits for the Gentile Christians. While describing the existing tensions, the narrator inserts some element of humour into the dispute so that the reader has some profitable delight as he reads through the unravelling of events[51]. The chaotic scene is a very short story with great theological result: the appointment of a Gentile delegation to settle faith-culture conflict with the Jewish Christians.

3.3.3 A High-Powered Delegation (V.2b).

This verse is part of the complication of the plot (2.3.8). The Antiochian Christians are unable to resolve the long heated dispute with the circumcision party. So they arrange to send a delegation led by Paul and Barnabas to go to Jerusalem and settle the problem (*zetema*) with the *apostoloi* and the *presbyteroi*. *Zetema* means controversial question, point of disagreement, matter under debate. It is a Lukan loan word and occurs only five times in the Acts[52]. In each case it refers to matters of argument, debate, dispute or controversy. Here

---

50 Newman, op. cit., 79.
51 For detailed descriptions of similar "burlesque and rowdy episodes" and humorous scenes with theological import, cf. Pervo, Profit, 61-66. The texts which he discusses are: Ac 5,17-25; 12,5-17; 14,8-18; 16,16-18; 19,14-16; 19,21-20,1; 20,7-12; 23,6-10; 28,1-7.
52 Cf. 15,2; 18,15; 23,29; 25,19; 26,3.

the apostles and the elders[53] have to say the final word over the disagreement and conflict in the Church of Antioch. Who are these *apostoloi* and *presbyteroi*?

3.3.4 The Apostles.

In secular Greek "*apostolos*" is from the verb "*apostellein*", to send. "It refers to a fleet or an army sent on an expedition; the command of an expedition; a colonist sent to settle; a bill or an invoice"[54]. But this etymology does not help much in understanding its NT usage. The basis for the NT concept may be sought first in Ex 3,10 where God said to Moses: "So now I am sending you (*we'eshlahaka*) to Pharaoh, for you to bring my people the Israelites out of Egypt".

A second basis can be found in Is 61,1: "The spirit of the Lord Yahweh is on me... He has sent me (*shelahani = apestalken me*) to bring the good news to the afflicted". At the commencement of his ministry Jesus applied the Isaian passage to himself and his mission from the Father (cf. Lk 4,18). Also in 1 Kg 14,6, the MT Hebrew passive participle "*shaluah*" (root = *slh*) is translated by the LXX as "*apostolos*" in a text which refers to Prophet Ahijah as the one sent by God with a tragic message for King Jeroboam. Thus those sent on a similar message are known as the "*sheluhim*".

In the talmudic circles the disciples of the Rabbis are often called their *sheluhim* or apostles. R. E. Brown thinks that

a plausible thesis is that from the OT usage involving "*slh*" in a religious sense came both the rabbinic institution of *sheluhim* and the NT apostolate as parallel, independent developments[55].

From this biblical usage and development of the term, one can without doubt consider the NT apostle as the prophetic or evangelistic messenger of Christ[56]. In the NT *Apostolos* occurs 80 times[57]. Jesus choses from the circle

---

53 Note that in the relief mission of Ac 11,30 only the elders are mentioned, and later in 21,18 the apostles also omitted. Only James and the elders are present to hear Paul's "detailed account of all that God had done among the Gentiles through his ministry".

54 Brown, Aspects: The Twelve, 81:149, p. 1380.

55 Id., 81:152, p. 1380.

56 But the term "apostle" has also a wider application: it applies to those who had not see the risen Jesus but joined themselves to the mission of his eyewitnesses; it applies to those who go on a false mission or counterfeit apostles and prophets (2 Cor 11,13; Rv 2,2.20).

of his disciples (*mathetai*) twelve men whom he called *apostoloi* (Lk 6,13-16)[58]. Later during his public ministry he sends them out on a mission of evangelisation and exorcism[59]. And after the ascension[60] Matthias is chosen by the pre-Pentecost witnesses of Jesus to replace Judas Iscariot (Ac 1,15-26). Upon this first community of Jesus came the Holy Spirit giving them courage and boldness to proclaim the marvels of the Lord to people "from every nation under heaven" (Ac 2).

In the Acts the apostles strictly speaking are the Twelve whom Jesus "had chosen through the Holy Spirit" and instructed on their mission (Ac 1,2). In his pre-Pentecost speech Peter lays out what is now considered as the "*Magna Charta of the Apostolate of the Twelve*"[61] : A member of the apostolic band must be one of the men who had been with them throughout the earthly life of Jesus - from the baptism of John up to his Ascension. His duty will be to serve with them as a witness to the resurrection (Ac 1,21-22).

In the Lukan concept, "apostle" is identified with the "Twelve"[62] and apostleship is service with the all-important function of witnessing to Jesus unto the ends of the earth. Hence the Acts presents the Twelve in particular as primarily servants and preachers of the divine word (Ac 2,14-26), and they make it quite clear that it is not right for them to neglect the word of God in order to share out food to the christian community (Ac 6,2). Their task comprises teaching preaching, fostering community fellowship, breaking of bread and devotion to prayer services (2,42; 4,2)[63].

Preaching is the basic concern of every apostle within and outside the circle of the Twelve and also of the "apostles" Paul and Barnabas (cf. Ac 14,14) who

---

57   It is spread out as follows: 1 in Mt, 1 in Jn, 2 in Mk, 34 in Luke-Acts, 34 in Pauline corpus, 5 in the Pastoral Letters, and 8 in the rest of the NT books (cf. Buhner, Apostolos, in: EWNT, vol, 1, 344).

58   Cf. Mt 10,2-4; Lk 6,12-16; Ac 1,13. Mk 3,16-19 makes a list of the appointed twelve who were to be the "companions" of Jesus and were "to be sent out to proclaim the message with power to drive out devils". Note that in Lk-Ac the verb "apostellein" occurs 25 times in Luke and 24 times in the Acts. The noun "apostolos" occurs 6 times in Luke and 28 times in the Acts. (Cf. Morgenthaler, Statistik, 77). Thus apostleship is a major theme of the Acts.

59   Lk 9,1-6; Mt 10,1.4-16; Mk 6,7-13.

60   After his resurrection Jesue orders the remaining eleven to go and proclaim the Gospel to all creatures and make all peoples his disciples while at the same time assuring them of his abiding presence and protection from every evil. This time the Twelve are not called *apostoloi* but *mathetai* (Mt 28,16-20; Jn 20,19-21). In the absence of Thomas they receive the Holy Spirit and power to forgive sins (Jn 20,22-23).

61   Cf. Weiser, Apg, 1, 71.

62   Cf. Roloff, Kirche, 212-214.

63   Cf. Id., 214-220.

were not members of the "Twelve" but were chosen by the Holy Spirit for their Gentile mission (cf. Ac 13,1-3). The Apostles assiduously carried out their task of preaching and teaching despite oppositions and persecutions from the rank and file of the people[64].

In the Gospels apostleship is restricted to the circle of the Twelve chosen by Jesus. In this sense Paul is not an apostle. The same is true of the early chapters of the Acts before the conversion of Saul (Paul). They are the leaders of the Jerusalem community of believers and devoted to preaching the Gospel message[65].

In his Letters, Paul applies to himself the title of "Apostle" of Jesus[66] in order to stress his calling and authorization by the risen Lord to minister to the Gentiles. He extends this title to his missionary comrades like Andronicus and Junias (Rm 16,7) or to a larger group than the twelve (1 Co 15,7)[67]. In this sense the missionaries are called apostles.

However the NT gives a special place of honour to the Twelve as eyewitnesses of Jesus and members of the apostolate commissioned before and after his resurrection. They are the first important group to enjoy the presence of the risen Lord (1 Co 15,5). Except for the sad case of Judas Iscariot who fell away from his ministry and was replaced by Matthias (1,15-26), the Twelve are not replaceable. Their membership is permanent and this may account for the non-replacement of James, the son of Zebedee after his martyrdom (Ac 12,2).

Their permanency may be probably due to the fact that the Twelve symbolically represent the "new Israel" who at the end of time shall play the role of judges seated on the twelve thrones of judgement[68]. In Ep 2,20 the Apostles and the Prophets constitute the foundations of the household of God whose corner-stone is Christ himself. Rv 21,14 depicts the twelve as the foundation stones of the city of God.

---

64 Ac 4,1f; 5,17f; 11,1f; 13,7.17f.44f; 14,2f.4f; 17,1f.10f; etc. Paul bears glowing witness to the apostolic zeal in preaching in the following words: "I was given grace to be a minister of Christ Jesus to the gentiles, dedicated to offer them the gospel of God... From Jerusalem and all round, even as far as Illyricum, I have fully carried out the preaching of the gospel of Christ ...." (Rom 15,16-21; cf. Rm 1,9.15; 2 Co 3,12; Tm 4,5, etc.).

65 Ac 4,35.37; 5,2; 6,6.

66 Cf. Rm 1,1; Ga 1,15, 2,8; 2 Co 5,19; 1 Th 2,4-9.

67 In the NT Apostles other than the Twelve include James the "brother" of the Lord (Ga 1,19), Paul (Rm 1,1-2; 1 Co 1,1; Ga 1,1 etc.), Barnabas (Ac 14,14; I Co 9,6 etc.), Andronicus and Junias (Rm 16,7), and many others whose not mentioned by name (cf. 1 Co 4,9; 1 Th 2,6; Buhner, Apostolos, in: EWNT, vol. 1, 348-350).

68 Cf. Lk 23,30; Mt 19,28.

Biblical evidence thus confirms the pride of place enjoyed by the Jerusalem apostles as chief representatives of the Church through their special election as messengers of the Good News of Christ. They are better placed to understand and handle the problem arising from the mission of those who are not authorized as they are. Such was their role before the group of elders came into prominence and became co-policy makers for the young Church[69]. And this is precisely their role in Acts 15. This must have accounted for the decision of the Antiochian Church to send delegates to the apostles and the elders to settle the culture-faith conflict in their community[70]. Now who are the elders?

3.3.5   The Elders (Presbyteroi).

The term *presbyteros* is the LXX translation of the MT hebrew "*zaqen*" (elder, old man). It occurs 18 times in the Acts out of the 65 times in the NT[71], and refers to both Jewish and Christian Leaders with specific functions among the people. In the OT elders (*zeqanim*) were selected to act as judges or arbitrators and could be just or corrupt men (cf. Dn 13,5-63). In the Greek period, between 300 and 200 BC, the council of elders or gerousia served as a ruling board with the High Priests. As lay members of the Sanhedrin the elders were selected from wealthy families and were the allies of the high-priestly families[72].

In the Acts *presbyteroi* (old men) occurs first in 2,17: "And your old men shall dream dreams"[73], which is part of Peter's citation of Prophet Joel in order to buttress his teaching on the outpouring of the Holy Spirit on the Pentecost. But in the Christian context elders are mentioned first in Acts 11,30 where they receive from the deputies of the Antiochian Church, Barnabas and Saul, the relief for the famine stricken Church of Judaea/Jerusalem. In 14,23 Paul and Barnabas appoint *presbyteroi* for the Churches founded by them[74].

Here in Ac 15 the presbyters are mentioned five times as co-policy makers with the apostles (vv.2.4.6.22.23) and their decisions are later passed on by Paul to the Gentile Churches (16,4). At Miletus Paul gives his farewell address

---

69   Cf. Kee, Good News, 70-77.
70   Note that the narrator does not tell us the number of the Apostles and Elders who participated in the deliberations to resolve the dispute. Suffice it to say that all who were in Jerusalem took part in the proceedings.
71   Cf. Morgenthaler, Statistik, 135.
72   Cf. Mt 21,23; 26,3.47; 27,1.3.12.20; 28,12; Lk 22,66; Ac 4,5; 23,14.
73   "Hoi presbyteroi humon enupniois enupniasthesontai" (Jl 3,1). In Hebrew: "ziqnekhem halomoth yahalomun".
74   Cf. 2 Jn 1; 3 Jn 1.

to the elders of Ephesus, exhorting them to vigilance, selflessness and charity (20,17-35). In the Church of Ephesus they are also the *episkopoi* (overseers) to whom the Holy Spirit has entrusted the guardianship and pastoral care of the Church of God established with the blood of his son Jesus (v.28)[75].

In the time of Jesus the elders were such a powerful institution that their tradition was strictly adhered to and respected by a religious Jew as the Gospel stories attest[76]. As civil leaders (Mk 11,27; 15,1) they could plead to Jesus on behalf of their centurion benefactor (Lk 7,3-5). But they were grouped with the Scribes and Pharisees as the "triplets" who plotted the death of Jesus[77].

In the Pastoral Letters the appointment and establishment of presbyters in every city is encouraged so that the apostolic mission may be continued as the apostles and the early witnesses gradually depart from the missionary scene[78]. The Letter of James positively describes the pastoral role of the earthly *presbyteroi* in healing the sick Christian:

> Any one of you who is ill should send for the elders of the church and they must anoint the sick person with oil in the name of the Lord and pray over him. The prayer of faith will save the sick person and the Lord will raise him up again; and if he has committed any sins, he will be forgiven (5,13-15).

In Hb 11,2 the *presbyteroi* are the saintly ancestors from Abel to the Judges and Prophets whose examplary faith is to be emulated by later generations of Christians (cf. 11,3-40). These may be compared to the 24 *presbyteroi* of the book of Revelation who are represented as heavenly creatures clothed in white garments, and together with the innumerable Martyrs from all peoples (Rv 7,9-17) they perform cultic function before the throne of God[79].

So then, many texts in the NT recognize the high status of the *presbyteroi* as pastors, cooperators and co-policy makers with the apostles. Their frequent mention in Ac 15 emphasizes the importance of their cooperative "episcopal role" (cf. Ac 20,1f.28) in resolving the pastoral problems posed to the early Church of Antioch.

---

75   Cf. Campbell, Elders, 515f; 520f; 525f.
76   Mt 15,1-9; Mk 7,3-13.
77   Cf. Mk 8,31; 11,27; 14,43.53; Lk 9,22; 20,1.
78   Cf. Tt 1,5-9; 1 Tm 3,1-7; 5,17-19.
79   Cf. 4,10; 5,6.8.11.14; 11,16; 19,4. Cf. Rhode, Presbyteros, in: EWNT, 3 (1983), 356-359 for more details on this theme.

3.4 Delegates Seen off by the Ekklesia (V.3).

3.4.1 Narrative Features of V.3.

This verse of "two parts", 3a and 3b, is also part of the exposition which provides the reader with pieces of information about some of the main characters of the story and the state of affairs after the uproar described in vv.1-2a. The Judaizers seem to have left the stage, and the decision to send delegates to Jerusalem is being carried out in 3a. But the omniscient narrator does not tell the reader the criteria for the selection of each delegate. The events are simply bypassed in a narration time of one verse. Only the reader can perhaps make up for this "ellipsis"[80] and supply what is missing through his active participation in the scene.

In this character-elevating exposition, the characters know the criteria and the processes of the selection while the reader is only told the outcome. Moreover the narrator denies the reader the names of all but two delegates, Paul and Barnabas. The Church of Antioch bids the delegation farewell as they go to confer with the apostles and elders in Jerusalem. That they are so sent off indicates that they are truly acting in the name of the Antiochian Community[81].

V.3b describes their *journey* by way of Phoenicia and Samaria. The whole travel-story told within a narration time of few words is narrated from the character-elevating position because the delegates involved in the journey know more of the happenings than the reader who is not given the details of the events that have taken place in the cities visited by them. But the omniscient narrator is ever present at every stage of the journey, informing the reader about the conversion of the Gentiles and the joy which it arouses among the ecclesial communities that heard such news.

This journey is not only an important element in this verse or episode but in the whole of the Acts-narrative[82]. The author uses it to create a unity between the different episodes and scenes of the story. This is true of the journey from Antioch to Jerusalem and back to Antioch which is like a thread linking the different scenes and highlighting the unity of the plot. Not only does one event lead to the other in Ac 15 but the departure/arrival adds to the concentric structure and wholeness of the story. "Journey" is thus an important connect-

---

80   An ellipsis occurs when the events of a story are simply bypassed in the discourse or concrete narrative presented to the reader (cf. SKa, Our Fathers, 13).

81   A similar escort and bidding of farewell is carried out by the elders of the Church of Ephesus (20,38) and the disciples at Syria (21,5).

82   Cf. 8; 9; 10-11; 12,12-17; 13-28: The Good News is spread by itinerant preachers.

ing thread or element of this plot (as it is in some other biblical plots)[83]. At the end of their mission in Jerusalem the delegates will again be sent off to report its result to the *ekklesia* of Antioch (15,30).

What is very striking in this verse is the title of *"ekklesia"* (church, congregation, gathering, assembly) for the Christian communities of Antioch and Jerusalem, a sign that both enjoy similar (if not equal status). In chapter one (see 1.7) I tried to explain the meaning and nuances of *ekklesia* but its usage in the Acts is a point of interest for our study.

3.4.2 Ekklesia in Acts.

In Acts *ekklesia* occurs 23 times[84]. It does not refer to christian community alone since it is applied to the gathering of the tribes of Israel on Mount Sinai (7,8) and to the civic assembly of the rioting silversmiths in Ephesus (19,32.39.40). Nevertheless it is one of the terms to describe the new Christian community[85]. It occurs for the first time in Ac 5,11 which reports that after the fraud and the punitive sudden death of Ananias and Sapphira, "a great fear came upon the whole Church (*holen ten ekklesian*) and on all who heard it". This *ekklesia* of Jerusalem (8,1) is forced by persecution to spread throughout Judaea, Galilee and Samaria and enjoys peace only after the conversion of the chief persecutor Saul (9,13). Later on some members of the *ekklesia* of Jerusalem are persecuted or killed by King Herod Agrippa 1 (12,1)[86].

Ekklesia thus stands for local congregations or assemblies in Jerusalem[87], in Antioch[88] and in Ephesus (20,17) where, as already noted, the *ekklesia* had presbyters who as overseers were charged with the vigilant shepherding of the christians (20,17.28). It is also to be recalled that the *ekklesia* of Antioch was

---

83   Compare the plot of this apostolic journey to and fro between Antioch and Jerusalem (15,1-35) with the plot of the evangelizing journey of Jesus to and fro between Cana and Jerusalem at the beginning of his ministry (Jn 2,1-4,54). Compare this also with the plot of the Jacob story and his journey to and fro between Canaan and Haran in Paddan-Aram (Gen 28,1-33,20).

84   Cf. Morgenthaler, Statistik, 93. Ekklesia is also found once each in James and Peter, 2 times in Hebrews, 3 in Johannine letters, 3 in Matthew, 20 in Revelation and 62 in Pauline corpus.

85   Other terms to describe the new christian community include believers (pisteuontes, 5,14 etc.), brethren (adelphoi), saints (hagioi, 9,13; 26,10) and disciples (mathetai, 9,1 etc.). See also Kee, Good News, 81-86.

86   Cf. NJB, footnote "12 a", p. 1819.

87   Cf. Ac 11,22.26; 12,5; 15,4.22.

88   Cf. Ac 13,1; 14,27; 15,3.

founded, not by the apostles, but by those unnamed Jewish and Hellenist believers who fled from persecution and death (11,19-20). The Church of Jerusalem exercised apostolic authority over them by sending Barnabas and Saul to confirm them in their new faith. They were so outstanding in their emulation of Christ that they received the title *"christianoi"* (11,26) which has now become the proud title/name for every believer in Christ. The Antiochian *ekklesia* had its prophets and teachers[89] and had authority to appoint apostolic delegates to represent their interests in the *ekklesia* of Jerusalem (15,3-4).

What is very special and pecular about the *ekklesia* of Antioch is its interracial and international structure. From the time of its foundation by fleeing Hellenists, it was a mixture of the two major races of Jews and Gentiles who received the faith preached to them without cultural preconditions[90]. Cultural pluralism and exchange was basically the bulwark of the Antiochian *ekklesia*. It is this interculturated Church that sent off their high-powered delegation to Jerusalem to settle the cultural problem incited by the circumcision party.

3.4.3 Journey to Jerusalem via Phoenicia and Samaria (V.3b).

From both literary and theological points of view, the route taken by the delegates calls for the attention of the reader. In this journey from Antioch via Phoenicia and Samaria the author[91] seems to adopt the literary device of recasting past events by retracing the missionary route of the fleeing Christians first scattered throughout the districts of Judaea and Samaria (8,1). Philip one of the "seven" (6,3f) evangelizes Samaria and Azotus (8,2-40) and by the time of the lull in persecution the Church is already established in Judaea, Galilee and Samaria (9,31) to which the chief apostle Peter pays pastoral visitations

---

89 Cf. Ac 11,27; 13,1; 15,32.
90 Cf. Note tha from 11,19 one can infer that the first group of evangelizers in Antioch practised christian apartheid by proclaiming the message only to Jews. But the arrival of the second group of missionaries (11,20) immediately rectified this cultural segregation.
91 In the narrative context, the "author" here is the "implied" author who is the projection of the "real" author in the work. The implied author corresponds to the implied reader, but it is not easy to perceive the difference between the real author and implied author. Perharps an example from a pauline letter may help us. In Corinth Paul's opponents and detractors ridiculed the "real" author Paul for being "lowly in their presence" (tapeinos en humin) while the "implied" author - the projection of the real Paul - "is full of boldness at a distance from them" (apon de tharro eis humas) as he himself testifies in his "apologia" (2 Co 10,1-11).

(9,32-43). Ac 11,19 resumes the dispersion story of 8,1 and tells the reader about the founding of the Church in Phoenicia, Cyprus and Antioch.

Just as persecutions by orthodox Jews led to the flight of the believers from Jerusalem to Samaria, Phoenicia and Antioch, so now a new sort of persecution by the Christian Judaizers elicits a journey of a delegation of some believers from Antioch to Jerusalem by way of Phoenicia, Samaria and back again to Jerusalem[92]. The delegates are thus presented as a people returning to their cultural roots, to their "motherland" from which the faith and the *ekklesia* spread to the other regions outside Palestine, with Antioch as the official headquarters of the Gentile *ekklesia*.

Theologically the journey from Antioch to Jerusalem throws some light on the partial fulfilment of the divine purpose in the Acts as programmed in 1,8. It shows that the disciples of Jesus have witnessed to him not only in Jerusalem, Judaea and Samaria, but also outside Palestine and are gradually moving outwards unto "the ends of the earth". Meanwhile the Good News has gone out from Antioch up to Derbe and back to Antioch (13-14) and this is the theme of the Antiochian delegates as they journeyed to Jerusalem.

3.4.4 News of Conversion of the Gentiles (V.3b).

The delegation led by Paul and Barnabas "went through Phoenicia and Samaria, relating in detail the conversion (*epistrophe*) of the Gentiles (*ton ethnon*)". *Epistrophe* is a Lukan loan word, occuring only in this verse throughout the whole of the NT[93]. On the contrary, its corresponding verb *epistrephein* occurs 36 times in the NT. It has both transitive and intransitive usages and means "to turn back, to return, to turn around". It occurs 11 times in the Acts and it is used 10 times to describe the act of turning to the Lord or conversion to the christian faith by both Jews and Gentiles[94].

Ta ethne is the LXX translation of the Hebrew word *goyim* (plural of *goy* = *to ethnos*, nation or people). Used in opposition to the term "Jew", *ta ethne* means non-Jews, Gentiles, pagans, heathens, unbelievers, or nations (*goyim*). Occurring 43 times in the Acts alone, it is a frequent and an important biblical theme. It is one of the key concepts in the biblical inculturation of the faith

---

92 Note also that Paul's last journey to Jerusalem is by way of Phoenicia (Ac 21,2).

93 Cf. Morgenthaler, Statistik, 100. There are many such loan words in Luke-Acts which may be an indication of Luke's compositional ability as the prologues of Luke-Acts shows the reader.

94 Cf. Ac 3,19; 9,35; 11,21; 14,15; 15,19.36; 16,18; 26,18.20; 28,27. Once it describes Peter's turning to the dead body of Tabitha to raise her up from the dead (9,40) [cf. Moulton-Geden, Concordance, 372; Morgenthaler, op. cit., 100].

among Jews and Gentiles. In the Acts *ta ethne* refers to the Gentiles[95] but here the discourse focuses on its usage and import in 15,3b.

As they travel to Jerusalem, Paul and Barnabas report the conversion of the Gentiles to the Churches. Prior to this mission *ad Gentes* God had already effected the conversion of the Roman soldier, Cornelius and his household, through the agency of Peter (Ac 10,1-48). Peter later had to defend this Gentile ministry before the remonstrating members of the circumcision party (11,1-18). The Gentiles of 15,3b are the non-Jews converted in the first missionary journey by Paul and Barnabas at Cyprus (Salamis and Paphos), Antioch in Pisidia, Perga in Pamphilia, Attalia, Iconium, Lycaonia (Lystra and Derbe) [13,3-14,26].

Of special mention is the conversion of the Roman official Sergius Paulus after seeing Paul's miraculous power that could strike Elymas the magician blind. In these two chapters *ta ethne* occurs 8 times, three of which refer to the nations of the earth (Ac 13,19.47; 14,16). 13,47 is a citation of Is 49,6 which is here used as a support for Paul's Gentile mission: "I have made you a light to the nations, so that my salvation may reach the remotest parts of the earth".

At Pisidian Antioch Paul and Barnabas turn to the Gentiles (*eis ta ethne*) because the Jews have rejected their message and by implication the eternal life offered by the message (13,46). And *ta ethne* rejoice at hearing that the two missionaries are God's light to them and that the message of salvation is for them (13,48). In Iconium the unbelieving Jews poison the minds of the Gentiles (*ton ethnon*) against the brothers (14,2) and eventually both Gentiles and Jews plan to attack and stone the missionaries (v.5). But they are undaunted by persecutions. At the end of their first mission they could report with satisfaction to the Antiochian community that God has "opened the door of faith to the Gentiles (*tois ethnesin*, v.27).

It is particularly this news of the conversion of the Gentiles in the Gentile culture areas of the first missionary journey that is being announced to the christian communities of Phoenicia and Samaria in 15,3b as the Antiochian delegates travel to Jerusalem to settle the question of circumcision for the Gentile males (v.1).

That the Phoenician and Samarian Christians receive the news of the conversion of the Gentiles with great joy (*charan megalen*) may be a pointer to the fact that the Judaizers do not enjoy a popular support even in the Jewish (Palestinian) culture area, for here no mention is made of male circumcision as necessary for salvation for the Gentile converts. Rather the friendly reception of the missionaries can be regarded as a sign of the approval of the manner

---

95   Cf. Jervell, Luke, 56.

and art of their law-free Gentile mission. It may also be a subtle neutralization of the legalistic, Christian Party of the circumcision.

Finally the mission to the Gentiles is a confirmation of the progressive movement of the apostolic message from Jerusalem towards the ends of the earth[96]. From the narrator's perspective, this mission is the will of God and it is consequent on the rejection of Jesus and his messengers by the people of Israel[97].

3.5 Arrival and Reception in Jerusalem (V.4).

3.5.1 Narrative Features of V.4.

V.4 continues the exposition of the story. The delegates of the *ekklesia* of Antioch have at last reached Jerusalem and are warmly received by the whole *ekklesia* of the mother Church. The locus of the scene has shifted from Phoenicia/Samaria (v.3) to Jerusalem (v.4). But the travelling personages are the same delegates mentioned in vv.2b-3. V.4 is linked to v.2b by the mention of the apostles and the elders as the men of authority in Jerusalem.

The narrator does not give the reader the details and means of the travel. What took place within a narrative time of many days is told in a narration time of one verse. As part of the exposition of the plot, v.4 continues to furnish the reader only with a laconic, generic information about the journey and its happy ending - the friendly disposition of the Jerusalem Church and leadership towards the Church of Antioch and her representatives.

The narrator does not also disclose the actual time, duration or particular place of the reception. The reader does not know if it took place in the Temple or synagogue or in the house of one of the leaders as was the custom of the early Christians[98]. The details of the events are known only to the omniscient narrator and to the characters involved in them.

V.4 therefore gives a character-elevating report and is closely related to that of v.3 by its repetition (in another form) of the news about the conversion of the Gentiles through the tales[99] of Paul and Barnabas to the Jerusalem community. The lack of details or the information gaps may be the narrator's de-

---

96   Cf. Ac 1,8; Lk 24,24.25; Haenchen, Acts, 443-444; Weiser, Apostelkonzil, 200.
97   Cf. Tannehill, Rejection, 83-101; Wilson, Gentiles, 219-238. Note that not all the Jews or the people of Israel reject the Gospel message. There is always a faithful remnant among them (cf. Rm 9-11).
98   Cf. Ac 2,45; 3,1ff; 9,1-2.
99   These stories are already told in 14,27 and will be summarily repeated in 15,12.

vice of increasing suspense and the reader's curiousity in an effort to retain his/her interest.

3.5.2   Import of the Reception (V.4).

The reception in Jerusalem is significant. It seems to confirm the joy of the Chrisitian communities of Phoenicia and Samaria and imports the continued joy and satisfaction of the majority of the Jewish Christians with the Gentile Christians. One can assume that the narrator is doing all he can to "show" the reader that despite the conflicts and complications of vv.1-2 everything seems to be working out in favour of the Antiochian delegates opposed to the Jewish-law Christians. Haenchen summarises the import of the Jerusalem reception thus:

> The solemnity with which the delegates were sent off is marched by a similar reception: the delegation is received in a gathering of the whole congregation in which the governing body appear in person, and is immediately allowed to present its report... Luke does not mechanically repeat the whole expression from 14,27; but as verses 3 and 5 show, what is meant is not only the miracles but also the great success of the mission, the conversion of numerous Gentiles[100].

These miracles and conversions are purely the gratuitous work of God that plays down any dependency of the *missio ad Gentes* on any human decision or effort like that advocated by those of the Circumcision Party in v.1 and later in v.5.

3.6   Some Christian Pharisees Insist on Circumcision and Mosaic Law for Gentile Christians (V.5).

3.6.1   Stylistic and Narrative Features of V.5.

With v.5 is completed the chiasmus of vv.1-5 (A, B, C, B^1, A^1 demonstrated above). The verse is an indication of a shift of scene and also a change of time, character and action. After the missionary report of Paul and Barnabas, some of the Christians from the *hairesis* of the Pharisees rise up to renew their demand for the circumcision of the male Gentile Christians and the observance of Mosaic law. Thus v.5 is thematically connected to vv.1-2a as the inciting

---

100 Acts, 444. Cf. Loisy, Actes, 570.

moment of the plot for it is the demand of some of the *hairesis* that triggered off the conflict which requires resolution.

V.5 intensifies the incitement by pinpointing the characters responsible for the controversy. Here the omniscient narrator is plain and straightforward and shares his knowledge with the reader of the story. The reader thereby stands at an even-handed reading position with the characters of the story since he now knows as much as the characters about the trouble-shooters. The *tines* belong to the party of Pharisees converted to the christian faith.

3.6.2 Some of the Sect of the Pharisees (V.5a).

Who are really this *tines* of the *hairesis* of the *Pharisaios*?[101] As already indicated, they may be identical with the *tines* of v.1 and are possibly identifiable with those of the cicumcision who were companions of Peter at the conversion of Cornelius (Ac 10,45; 11,2) or with the myriads of the Jewish Christians zealous for the Law (20,20 or with those Jews who always persecuted Paul in his ministry and swore never to eat or drink till he was dead[102] or with those people sent by James to Antioch (Ga 2,12) or still with the trouble-makers in the Churches of Galatia (1,7).

Hairesis means division, faction, religious party, and false party or teaching[103] and the Acts applies it across the spectrum of Judaism to Sadducees (5,17) and Pharisees (26,5). Even Christians are referred to as a *hairesis* which "encounters opposition everywhere" (24,5.14; 28,22). Technically speaking, *hairesis* means a "school of thought". Hence the term "heresy" is used to describe false religious teachings, beliefs or schools of thought. So then the *hairesis* of the Pharisees means the sect, party, or school of thought of the Pharisees.

Pharisaios, derived from the Aramaic word "*perisaye*" (Hebrew, *perushim*) means separatists, deviants, heretics. The Pharisaic sect then was a party of "Separated Ones", a scornful epithet hurled on them by their opponents probably "because of their professed strict avoidance of Gentiles, of unclean persons, of sinners, and of Jews less observant of the Torah"[104]. Josephus de-

---

101 A lot has been written on the Pharisees and their beliefs, functions, and practices and influence in Judaism. So I shall only be concerned with what is pertinent to the context of our work. For more on the Pharisees confer, for example: Muller, Pharisaer, 1002-1003; Rivkin, Pharisees, 269-272; Box, Pharisees, 831-836; Benhayim, Jews, 25-29; Cassidy, Society, 7, 16, 71.

102 Cf. 21,27-28; 22,22-24.30; 23,12-15; 24,1-8; etc.

103 Newman, Dictionary, 5.

104 Wright/Murphy/Fitzmyer, History, in: NJBC, 75:146, p.1243.

scribed them as one of the Schools of thought that flourished in Israel from the Hasmonean times to the destruction of the second temple (ca 150 BC-70 AD)[105] and well into the second century. They were perhaps closely associated with the *asidaioi* (Hebrew, *hasidim*) or "Pious Ones" who at first supported the Maccabean revolt but later distanced themselves from Maccabeanism when it became too politicized and secularized.

Rooted in the lay scribes (*grammateis*, Mt 5,20) or teachers of the law (*nomodidaskaloi*, Lk 5,17) who emerged in the post exilic hellenistic era, the Pharisees were mainly a party of lay people who accepted the normative character of both the written Law from Moses (*Torah she-biktav*) and the oral Law (*Torah she-be 'al-peh*) handed down from the forefathers (*avoth*) but not recorded in the Mosaic Law.

This oral Law comprised scribal interpretations and elaborations designed to be a protection for the Law or as "a fence around the Law" and were later codified in the Mishnah as an inseparable part of the Sinai Covenant (cf. Ex 19-24).

From the national-religious standpoint, the most significant stream of Jewish life reflected in the New Testament was that of the Pharisees. They were the true fathers of traditional Orthodox Judaism as it was destined to crystallize and dominate Jewish life after the destruction of the Second Temple in A.D.70[106].

The Pharisaic strict interpretation of the Torah separated them from the people of the land (*'am ha-aretz*) whom the Pharisees described as the rabble without the knowledge of the law (cf. Jn 7,49). The Law was a guarantee of the piety of every Pharisee. Hence they meticulously kept the Sabbath rules, ritual purity regulations, the rules of fasting and the paying of tithes[107]. Nevertheless they could adjust themselves to new situations and contigencies by their oral re-interpretations of the Law.

Their principal religious convictions include belief in the interplay of fate and free will under divine providence, in the advent of the Messiah, in the Angels, immortality of the soul and general resurrection of the body on the Last Day[108]. As a religous party, the Pharisees promoted religious fervour in Judaism and exercised much influence on the lives of the people. So great was

---

105 Cf. Jewish War, 2.162-163; Jewish Antiquities, 13.171-173. The other two haireseis are the Sadducees and the Essenes. Cf. Benhayim, Jews, 25.
106 Benhayim, Ibid.
107 Cf. Mt 12,2; 15,1-9; Mk 2,16; 7,1-7; 12,13; Lk 6,6; 18,12; Jn 7,45-52; 11,45-54, etc.
108 Cf. Ac 23,8; Mt 22,41-46; Mk 12,35-37; Lk 20,41-44; Benhayim, Jews, 27.

their influence that Josephus reported that "all prayers and sacred rites of divine worship were performed in accord with their exposition"[109].

These facts are complemented by Paul's presentation of himself as an orthodox, circumcised Israelite or Hebrew and a fervent Pharisee, zealous and faultless in upholding the Law[110]. Fitzmyer's comment gives a summary portrait of the sect:

> the fundamental religious outlook of the Pharisees enable them to make a permanent mark on Judaism... After the destruction of the temple of Jerusalem, when the temple cult was no longer possible, Pharisees rallied the Jews. Their tradition developed into rabbinic Judaism and persists to some extent in orthodox Judaism of today[111].

In Luke-Acts *Pharisaios* occurs 27 times in Luke and 8 in Acts. In Luke the Pharisees are five times presented as working in union with the Scribes (6 times if the *nomodidaskaloi* of 5,17 also stands for *grammateis*). But they act alone for 21 times which may indicate that they have a very influential role in the Lukan *ekklesia*. The group is twice referred to as *"hairesis"* (15,5; 26,5). Except for Mt 12,38 where *"tines"* of the Scribes and Pharisees seek a sign from Jesus, the use of the adjective *"tis"* to qualify the sect is particularly Lukan[112].

This creates the impression that not *all* but only *some* of the Pharisees of the Lukan community are actually hostile to the Jesus circle. Just as not all Jews of the Acts are hostile to the apostolic Christianity, so also not all the members of the pharisaic sect of the Acts are hostile to the "Christian sect" (even if the narrator does not explicitly say that). Salmon confirms this point by noting that

> In Acts 13:42-43, "many Jews and devout converts to Judaism " urge Paul and Barnabas to continue their preaching. In 14:1-2 Jews are included among those who believed, and it is specifically "unbelieving Jews" who stir up the non-Jews. Some are persuaded in Thessalonica (17:4), and in Boerea noble Jews receive the word with eagerness, and many believed (17:11-12). Paul persuades Jews at Corinth (18:4), and Jews at Ephesus urge him to stay (18,20). At the end of the narrative Paul convinces some in Rome, and there is disagreement among them (28:24-25)[113].

---

109 Antiquities, 13.298.
110 Cf. Phil 3,5-6; Acts 23,6; Rom 9,2-4.
111 Wright/Murphy/Fitzmyer, History, 75:147, p.1243.
112 Cf. Lk 6,2; 13,31; 19,39; Ac 5,34; 15,1.5; 23,9.
113 Salmon, Insider, 81.

Acts therefore distinguishes between the believing and non-believing Jews, between the believing and non-believing Pharisees, and between the hostile and friendly Pharisees.

In Luke, the Pharisees criticize Jesus and his disciples for eating with tax collectors and sinners (Lk 5,29-32; 15,1-2). Jesus in turn remonstrates with his Pharisee friend Simon for his spiteful attitude to the sinful womman (7,36-50), rebukes the Pharisses for their objection to his healing on the Sabbath (14,1-6), and upbraids them for placing external rituals and practices above justice and the love of God (11,37-54)[114].

As a self-righteous and an avaricious group, the Pharisees are unable to accomodate themselves to the teachings of Jesus on the right use of money (Lk 16,9-15), on almsgiving (12,33f), on love and mercy for one's neighbour (18,1-14) and on attitude to Samaritans (17,11-19). Every good disciple of Jesus must therefore beware of their "leaven" of narrow-mindedness and hypocrisy (12,19).

In the Acts the Pharisees are four times presented as acting in concert with the Sadducees in the Sanhedrin[115]. The Pharisee Gamaliel, the highly respected teacher of the law (5,34) and Paul's educator (22,3), successfully counselled the Sanhedrin to tolerate the christian movement (5,38-41). Paul himself is a stunch Pharisee who claims that he is brought to judgment because of his hope in the resurrection of the dead (23,6; 26,5), and is defended by the Pharisee members of the Sanhedrin[116]. Therefore the Pharisees of the Acts community generally seem to be more tolerant of the apostolic community than the Pharisees of the Gospels[117].

The Acts community in turn is very faithful to Jewish Law and practices and share the same messianic hope and eschatological beliefs with the *hairesis* of the Pharisees. But they differ very much on the question of circumcision and the observance of the Jewish Law for the Gentile Christians. While the converted Pharisees want all the Jewish norms to be imposed on the Gentile converts, the mainstream of the Church of Acts is advocating a Gentile christian community free from the observance of Jewish Law and custom.

The observation of the Jewish scholar, Menahem Benhayim, on the relationship between the Pharisees and the apostolic community provides us with a noteworthy summary of the points of contact and the tensions existing between the young Christian movement and Christian pharisaism.

---

114 Cf. Kingsbury, Pharisees, 1500-1503.
115 5,34; 23,6.7.8.
116 The Sadducees who are opposed to pharisaic beliefs are naturally the enemies of the Apostles preaching the resurrection of Jesus (Ac 4,1f; 5,17f; 23,6f).
117 Cf. Kingsbury, Pharisees, 1503-1512.

There was, therefore, a considerable area of common ground which could permit "certain of the sect of the Pharisees which believed" in Jesus the Messiah to be active in the 1st Century Christian movement (Acts 15:5). Doubtless these Pharisees were part of that large group "among the Jews which believed and are all zealous for the Law" to whom the apostle and the Jerusalem elders referred when they spoke to Paul during his last visit to Jerusalem (Acts 21,20). As the Christian movement gained momentum, it became more clear in its differences with the mainstream of the Pharisees despite important points of contact. The fact that an "*am ha'aretz*", an unlearned commoner like Simon Peter the fisherman, was a force in the Messianic movement no less than a scholar and Pharisee like the Rabbi Saul of Tarsus, the apostle Paul, is of greatest significance[118].

But if the Pharisees of the Acts are depicted as being more friendly to the apostles and more tolerant of the Christian movement than the Pharisees of the Gospels, what then do the Gospels say of the *pharisaioi*?

The Gospels generally paint a bad image of the Pharisees and discredit their religious practices. They are frequently presented as the opponents of Jesus and his disciples. In their opposition they act either in league with the scribes or teachers of the Law, or with the Sadducees and Chief Priests, or with Herodians[119]. Jesus in turn strongly criticizes them for their hypocrisy, narrow, religious views and corrupt practices with a sarcastic, prophetic vehemence as summarised in Lk 11,37-54 and Mt 23,1-32. The citation of some verses can elucidate our point here:

You Pharisees! You clean the outside of cup and plate, while inside yourselves you are filled with extortion and wickedness. Fools! Did not he who made the outside make the inside?... Alas for you Pharisees, because you pay your tithe of mint and rue and all sorts of garden herbs and neglect justice and the love of God! (Lk 11,39.42).

Alas for you, scribes and Pharisees, you hypocrites! You pay your tithe of mint and dill and cummin and have neglected the weightier matters of the Law- justice, mercy, good faith! These you should have practised, those not neglected. You blind guides, straining out gnats and swallowing camels (Mt 23,23).

Jesus also warns his disciples to beware of the pharisaic hypocrisy (cf. Lk 12,1; Mt 16,6f). Nevertheless the Gospels tell about the truly pious Pharisees friendly to Jesus. These include his hosts at two meals (Lk 7,36f; 14,1f), Nichodemus[120], and his secret disciple, Joseph of Arimathea who, along with Nichodemus, buried him[121]. There is no doubt that Jesus shared with the Pharisees common doctrines of messianic hope, personal immortality and res-

---

118 Benhayim, Jews, 28-29.
119 Cf. Kingsbury, op. cit., 1502f.
120 Cf. Jn 3,1-21; 7,50-52; 19,39.
121 Cf. Jn 19,38-42; Mk 15,42-46; etc.

urrection of the dead (Lk 20,27-40)[122]. Like them he was faithful to Jewish law, rites and festivals[123]. But he disagreed with their rigid legalism and sanctimonious attitudes.

Initially it seems that only the *tines* (some) of the Pharisees of the Acts are insistent on the question of obedience to the Mosaic *ethos* by the Gentile converts (Ac 15,1.5), but later the reader learns that thousands of Jewish believers zealous for the Law (*myriades... en tois Ioudaiois ton pepisteukoton... zelotai tou nomou*, 21,20f) join in the uncompromising demand for the observance of the Jewish Law and practices by the Gentile Christians. As members of a very strict Jewish religious sect (*akribestaten hairesin*, 26,5) converted to Christianity, the Pharisees want all the Gentile Christians to follow their strict way of life[124].

3.6.3 Christian Pharisees Demand Obedience to Jewish Torah as Necessary for Gentile Converts (V.5b).

The first demand of the Pharisee believers in this verse is circumcision: *dei peritemnein autous* - it is necessary to circumcise them (Gentiles), and the second is the observance of the Law of Moses: *autous parangellein te terein ton nomon Moüseos*. Circumcision is already treated in v.1. Let us briefly consider the question of the *nomos Moüseos*.

3.6.4 The Nomos of Moses.

Nomos (hebrew, *Torah*) is a major NT theme[125]. It occurs 31 times in the Gospels (9 in Luke) 17 times in the Acts, 119 times in the Pauline corpuss, 14 times in the Letter to the Hebrews, and 10 times in the Letter of James. Its nuances of meaning include law, principle, rule, norm. Its synonyms are divine

---

122 Cf. Mt 22,23-33; Mk 12,18-27; Jn 7,31-52; 11,21-44, etc.
123 Mt 5,17-19, Lk 2,21-50; Jn 2,13-25; 7,1-30, etc.
124 Here the presentation of the attitude of the Pharisees points to a period of tension between Judaism and Christianity especially after 70 A.D.
125 The total NT occurrences are 191. Cf. Moulton-Geden, Concordance, 667-669; Morgenthaler, Statistik, 123. Nomos or Torah is the most basic theme of the Bible. It is in fact a synonym for the whole of OT. Since it is a concept that runs through the whole sacred sciptures, it will be too unwieldy to present it in detail here. It is enough to say only what is relevant to our work and context. For more details confer, Kertelge, **La Legge**. The whole book is a collection of scholarly articles on "The Law In The NT".

precepts, commandment, instructions, judgements, and finally the word of God (cf. Ps 119,1-176).

In the Acts Stephen is accused of speaking against the Temple and the Law (Ac 6,13). In his subsequent address to the Sanhedrin he rebukes the members for failing to keep the Law given them through the Angels (7,53). Paul who consented to the stoning of Stephen is attacked and taken to the court of Gallio at Corinth for teaching the people to worship God contrary to the Law (18,13.15). And in Jerusalem he (like Stephen) is accused and attacked by thousands of stunch upholders of the Law for preaching against the Law and the Temple (21,20-28). In his defenses Paul emphasizes his unalloyed loyalty and fidelity to the Law (24,14; 25,8). And in Rome he argues from the Law and the Prophets in order to persuade the Roman Jews to accept the christian faith (28,23).

The Acts story also presents the unconverted Saul as being even more fanatical about the Law than his Jewish Law Christian opponents or counterparts. He was then Saul the persecutor who was "breathing out threats to slaughter the Lord's disciples"[126]. He was Saul the Pharisee, (23,6; 26,4-8) who outstripped his Jewish colleagues in keeping the ancestral law and traditions (cf. Ac 22,3f; Ga 1,13-24)[127].

From the internal evidence of Luke-Acts, what then is the Lukan attitude to the Law?. Jacob Jervell[128] demonstrates that besides Lukes's peculiar terminology for the Law[129], he has a basically conservative attitude to the Law.

In the Gospel, Luke presents Jesus as being completely faithful to the Mosaic Law (Lk 2,22-24) which is also called the Law of the Lord (*nomos kyriou*, 2,23-25.39). His mother observes the Law of purification (Lk 1,22) as found

---

126 Ac 8,1.3; 9,1f; cf. 22,1-9; 26,9-16.

127 In the Pauline Letters and theology *nomos* is a recurring theme with different connotations. It means law in general (Ga 5,23; Rm 5,13), but figuratively, it is a principle (Rm 3,27; 7,21), sin (Rm 7,23.25), sin and death (Rm 8,2) or human nature (Rm 2,14). *Nomos* also refers to faith (Rm 3,27), to Christ (Gal 6,2), to the Spirit (Rm 8,2). It stands for the OT books: either the Prophets (1 Co 14,21), the Psalms (Rm 3,19), or especially the Torah (Gal 3,10; 1 Co 9,9). But Paul uses *nomos* about 97 times to refer to the Law of Moses, an indicator for the importance and intricacy of this theme in his theology, ministry and life. Its discussion, however, is restricted to Rm, 1-2 Co, Ga, Phil (referred to in Ep 2,15) where Paul engages himself with the Judaizing problem of the ηαιρεσισ of the Pharisees (cf. Fitzmyer, Theology, in NJBC, 82:89-100, p. 1403-1406; Bultmann, Theology, 1, 259f).

128 Cf. Jervell, Luke, 133-151.

129 Luke's peculiar terms for the Law are: nomos kyriou, nomos (Lk 2,23), Mouseos (Lk 2,22; Ac 13,38, etc), tou patreoou nomou (Ac 22,3), and living words, *logia zonta* (Ac 7,38). They are borrowed from the LXX and from other Hellenstic Jewish sources like Josephus and Philo (cf. Jervell, Luke, 136-137; see also his footnote nos. 12-18).

in Lv 12,2-8. He is consecrated as the firstborn male (Lk 1,23-24) as found in Ex 13,1-2. His presentation in the Temple is similar to that of Samuel in 1 Sm 1,22-24 and is a fulfilment of the prophecy of Mal 3, 1-2. At the age of twelve he goes to Jerusalem to celebrate the Torah feast of the Passover[130].

Luke further demonstrates the fidelity of Jesus to the Law by pointing that he is the one about whom Moses wrote in the Law and the Prophets. He has come to fulfil what is written in the Law, the Prophets and the Psalms (Lk 24,44). He requires his followers to give similar respect to the Law (Lk 16,17)[131]. The Acts presents the apostles, elders and Jewish Christians as being faithful to the Law and as religiously "observant Jews"[132], but it is against the imposition of Jewish Law and practices on the Gentiles or non-Jews (15,10).

In the OT usage, *nomos* represents the first five books of the Bible (the Pentateuch) which is the Law of Moses, the Torah par excellence. When paired with the prophets (*ho nomos kai hoi prophetai*), it means the "Old Testament". Finally it refers to the entire Jewish sacred tradition[133]. The whole of Ps 119 is devoted to the praise of the divine *nomos*[134] and shows explicitly the great respect and love which the average Jew rendered to the Law. The Law is the delight of the orthodox Jew who would love to keep it without fail (v.44). Some verses of the Psalm are more incisive than others:

V. 1 How blessed are those whose way is blameless, who walk in the Law of Yahweh!

V. 34 Give me understanding and I will observe your Law, and keep it wholeheartedly.

V. 72 The Law you have uttered is more precious to me than all the wealth in the world.

V. 92 Had your Law not been my delight, I would have perished in my misery.

V. 97 How I love your law! I ponder it all day long.

V. 165 Great peace for those who love your law; no stumbling blocks for them!

---

130 Cf. Lk 2,42f; Ex 23,14-17; Dt 16,16.
131 Cf also Mt 5,17; Jn 2,13,25; 5,1f; 7,2-14, etc. Jesus is often engaged in debate with the scribes and Pharisees over the true meaning and demands of the Law (Mt 12,5; 23,23, etc) which, in Jesus' teaching, is summarised in the two commandments of the love of God and neighbour (22,36) The weightier matters of the Law are justice, mercy and good faith (Mt 23,23). The Law was given through Moses, but grace and truth came through Jesus Christ (Jn 1,17). Despite all his fidelity to the Law, the Jews demand that Jesus must die according to the Law for breaking the Law by claiming to be God's Son (Jn 19,7).
132 Cf. Salmon, Insider, 79. Cf. Ac 2,46-47; 3,1f; 13,14f; 21,23-26.
133 Cf. Newman, Dictionary, 121.
134 In the LXX and the Vulgate it is Ps 118. Cf. Mussner, La Vita, 25-26.

From this biblical evidence it is therefore not surprising that the Pharisaic Party would strive to make the observance of the Torah a universal condition for the salvation of anyone who professes the same faith with them. Hence the position of the Circumcision Party at Antioch (Ac 15,1) is here resumed by the believers of the Pharisaic Party (v.5) who insist on the necessity of circumcision for the male Gentile converts.

As already pointed out, the two groups of the circumcision movement (Ac 15,1.5) are most probably of the same party. The first group said to the Gentile converts at Antioch, "unless you are circumcised according to the custom of Moses you cannot be saved" (v.1). And the second group insists before the Antiochian delegation and the Jerusalem Church that "it is necessary to circumcise them and enjoin them to keep the Law of Moses" (v.5)[135]. The "necessity of circumcision" here is with reference to what is necessary for salvation.

3.7 Absurdity of Law and Circumcision for Salvation.

So if a Gentile, for example, is to ask an apostolic preacher as the rich aristocrat asked Jesus, "Good Master, what shall I do to inherit eternal life?" (Lk 18,18), or like the Philippian gaoler to Paul and Silas, "Sirs, what must I do to be saved?" (Ac 16,30), the response would run thus: "Believe on the Lord Jesus Christ, be circumcised, observe the rest of the law of Moses, and you will be saved"[136].

Therefore the Gentile converts have no other option. For their salvation, it is necessary to circumcise them and command (parangellein) them to keep (terein) the Law of Moses. They cannot but observe the mosaic nomos and ethos if they really want to be saved. That is the force of the "autous parangellein te terein ton nomon Moüseos" (v.5).

But since circumcision according to Jewish or Mosaic Law would affect only male Jews and Gentiles, what then happens to the female Jews and Gentiles who are not bound by the law of circumcision? Will they be saved or not? And what is the condition for their own salvation? If they can be saved without circumcision, will that not imply the application of a double standard to the christian message of salvation?

---

135 Note that in contrast to the Western text which identifies the representatives of legalistic piety in verses 1 and 5, "Luke does not make the same men press for cicumcision in Antioch and Jerusalem: only a small group in Jerusalem think - understandably, given their background - in strict legal terms" (Haenchen, Acts, 444).

136 Barrett, Apostles, 16.

Perhaps the loophole in the circumcision demand of v.1 which does not include women (v.1) may have been responsible for the inclusion of the Law of Moses in v.5 in order to include all the Gentile converts in the Mosaic dispensation. But by insisting that the christian preaching must contain reference to circumcision and Mosaic prescriptions[137], is the pharisaic sect not restricting the gift of salvation to Jewish way of life and thereby making a caricature of the christian message? Such a mentality is certainly a narrow view of the way to salvation and makes the reception of the novelty of the Good News of Jesus very difficult for the Gentiles.

For infants, circumcision is painful enough. For adults, it is all the more painful and debilitating (cf. Gen 34,14-25). To demand it from adult Gentiles who have already renounced a large part of their natural way of life in order to take up their cross daily and follow Jesus (Lk 9,23f; 14,25f) is to increase the weight and burden of that cross for the willing disciples who may find it unbearable in their new christian faith. But in the view of the pharisaic sect, salvation which is of the Jews must be obtained by becoming a Jew. And so outside the Jews there is no salvation (*Extra Judaeos nulla salus*). Thus the door of faith which God in his love and mercy had already opened to the Gentiles (Ac 14,27) is now being slammed against them by *the Pharisee Christians*.

Paul was clearly aware of the dangers posed to the Gentile Church by this heretical Gospel and he did not spare time and energy in refuting it in order to direct his converts unto the right way of salvation, a way free from the demands of Jewish Law and practices, a way of faith and good life in Jesus Christ. Part of Paul's non-recorded dispute and debate with Judaizers may probably run thus:

Faith is what counts, since, as we see it, a person is justified by faith and not by doing what the Law tells him to do. Do you think that God is the God only of the Jews, and not of gentiles too? Most certainly of gentiles too, since there is only one God; he will justify the circumcised by their faith, and he will justify the uncircumcised through their faith[138].

So then salvation comes, not through Jewish legal and cultural practices, but through faith in God and his son Jesus Christ. If the pharisaic sect with its understandable but misconceived rigourism does not accept this fact, then the controversy over faith and cultural practices will continue to rage on - *ad infinitum*.

---

137 Cf. Barrett, ibid.
138 Rm 3,28-31. Cf. Ga 1,6-3,29.

3.8 Theological Overview of Ac 15,1-5.

What is the narrator telling or showing the reader in these first five verses? There is faith and culture conflict. The influx of the Gentiles into the Church has caused a dilemma over their admission and integration in a Church that was originally an exclusive Jewish movement. The five verses indicate that the problem is twofold: Should a male Gentile convert be obliged to circumcision and to the observance of the whole Mosaic ordinances? That is, must the Gentile first become a Jew before becoming a Christian? Or can he be simply received into the Church with all his *"Gentile-ness"*? Since an orthodox or strict Jew cannot legally have any social intercourse with a Gentile, how far can Jewish Christians associate with those Gentile Christians without violating the prescriptions of the Mosaic Jewish Law?[139] These questions are framed in another way by Menahem Benhayim:

> Could the Gentile believer remain a gentile nationally and personally while entering spiritually into one of the streams of Judaism rooted in a Jewish national faith? Or was he obliged, like Ruth the Moabitess, to forsake not only the gods and religion of his forefathers, but his ethnic identity as well? For the male believer, physical circumcision was the crucial sign and seal of such a commitment?[140]

This is not only a religious question but a socio-cultural problem confronting both Jewish and Gentile Christians of the early Church. This problem which had caused much uproar, dispute and dissension in Antioch and Jerusalem must not be taken lightly if the "young Church" were to avoid an impending schism. Therefore the apostles, elders and the whole Church must have to do all they could to resolve the problems posed by the hardline Jewish converts. This seems to be what the narrator is telling or "showing" the reader in this "prologue". As the introduction to the JC,

> it leads with conscious aim to the great conflict, men of Antioch *versus* Pharisees. What will happen now that they are confronted? It is time for the Apostles and elders to move into action[141].

---

139 Cf. Barclay, Acts, 112.
140 Benhayim, Jews, 52.
141 Haenchen, Acts, 458.

4. Chapter Four.

Formal Assembly and Peter's Speech: Salvation for Jews And Gentiles Alike (15,6-11).

4.0 Greek Text of Ac 15,6-11.

6. Synechthesan te hoi apostoloi kai hoi presbyteroi idein peri tou logou toutou.

7. Polles de zeteseos genomenes anastas Petros eipen pros autous: andres adelphoi, hymeis epistasthe hoti aph' hemeron archaion en hymin exelexato ho Theos dia tou stomatos mou akousai ta ethne ton logon tou euangeliou kai pisteusai.

8. kai ho kardiognostes Theos emarturesen autois dous to pneuma to hagion kathos kai hymin

9. kai outhen diekrinen metaxu hemon te kai auton te pistei katharisas tas kardias auton.

10. nun oun ti peirazete ton Theon epitheinai zugon epi ton trachelon ton matheton hon oute hoi pateres hemon oute hymeis ischusamen bastasai?

11. alla dia tes karitos tou kyriou Iesou pisteuomen sothenai kath' hon tropon kakeinon.

4.1 Stylistic and Narrative Features of Vv.6-11.

This is also part of the complication of the plot (2.3.8). A suitable introduction to the stylistic and narrative features of this first real scene of the plot (2.3.9) is the dramatic and picturesque presentation by Haenchen and Pervo:

> Christian Pharisees politely demand obedience to the Torah (v.5). The audience receives this proposal as if it were a brand-new motion. Orderly debate, managed by the leaders, ensues until, "when excitement and conflict have reached their peak, Peter intervenes and with one stroke clarifies the situation"[1]. Reminding them of the evidently overlooked case of Cornelius and dismissing the Torah as impossible of observance, Peter closes with a touch of "Paulinism"[2].

As the first real scene of the episode, Peter's speech or intervention changes the rhythm or tempo of the narrative. There is change of time (*polles de zeteseos genomenes*), action (from sitting to standing, *anastas*), character (from a contentious assembly to one listening to Peter). The place of the assembly is not mentioned, but it can be presumed that it may differ from the place of the

---

1   This citation in inverted commas is from Haenchen, Acts, 445. See Pervo's footnote no. 120, in: Profit, 152.

2   Pervo, op. cit., 41.

reception of the Antiochian delegates (v.4) - a place roomy enough for the crowd present at the Council.

Polles de zeteseos "indicates the situation prevailing when Peter rose to speak: speech and counter-speech alternate in the assembly"[3]. Thus vv.6-7a act as the transitional event to the eighth[4] and last recorded speech of Peter in the Acts. It is remarkable that after this speech which states the apostolic Church's policy on the admission of the Gentiles into the Church without the prerequisites of Jewish Law, Peter vanishes from the scene of the Acts.

But why then does one consider this as the first real scene of this episode? Are the foregoing events not real? In the first six-and-half verses (1-7a) before the beginning of the speech in 7b, the narrator continues to provide the reader with pieces of short informations about the conflicts in Antioch, the decision to resolve the conflict in Jerusalem, the journey of the Antiochian delegates, their arrival and reception by the whole Jerusalem Church and the continuation of excitment and conflict in Jerusalem despite the warm reception accorded to them (vv.1-5). For this reason the Jerusalem Leaders convoke a formal assembly (*synechthesan*) to look into the matter (v.6). After much dispute (v.7a) reminiscient of the earlier dispute in Antioch (v.2), Peter rises up to speak, as it is his custom at strategic moments of the apostolic mission[5].

The movement from Antioch to Jerusalem (vv.1-5), the gathering of the assembly and the subsequent dispute (vv.6-7a) form the background and therefore the *transitional event* to Peter's speech which, like in a drama, pictures the whole assembly as listening attentively to the voice and argument of an actor, (here the Chief Apostle Peter) speaking at a critical and tense moment of the life of the young Church.

Unlike the foregoing schematic reports of vv. 1-7a, the speech of vv.7b-11 is like an action being dramatised on a stage, brief and compact with unique concrete details and references to the foregoing Cornelius event that will never recur[6]. Just as the transition from Jewish to Gentile mission began with Peter (Ac 10,1-11,18), so now the transition from the chaotic to orderly scene on the question of Jewish/Gentile relationship begins with Peter (15,7b-11). It is the outset of the action of JC, a shift from noisy debates to serious a attempt at a proposal for the resolution of the dispute raging from Antioch to Jerusalem. These are the reasons for considering it as the *first real scene* of the plot.

---

3 Haenchen, Acts, 445.
4 The other seven speeches are found in: 1,16-22; 2,14-36; 3,12-26; 4,8-12; 5,29b-32; 10,34-43; 11,5-17).
5 Cf. Ac 1,15; 2,14; 10,34; 11,4.
6 In a plot these are the characteristics of a "real scene" (cf. Ska, Our Fathers, 22).

The scene itself is an appeal to a divine precedent in missionary evangelization. In narrative language, it is called a "flashback" or "analepsis, the telling of events after the moment in which, chronogically, they took place"[7]. Within a relatively short temporal distance the Cornelius event now belongs to the "classical" past[8]. The event which took place within a narrative time of many days, - from the vision of Cornelius in Caesarea (Ac 10,1f) through Peter's arrival at Caesarea (10,24f) up to his return to, and defense before the circumcision party in Jerusalem (11,1-18), is now perused within a narration time of three verses (15,7b-9).

The place of the event is at Caesarea but it is retold twice in Jerusalem (first 11,1-18 and now here). This repetition or "frequency" of narration is part of the techniques of a discourse or narrative whereby a singular event is told more than once in order to stress the importance attached to that event by the author or narrator[9].

The reading position of this scene is "evenhanded" for the reader knows as much as the characters about the Cornelius episode which Peter is referring to. However, it may be reader-elevating for those characters (e.g. the Gentile delegates) who might not have known anything about the Cornelius story before the meeting of the plenary assembly.

Peter's appeal to the divine initiative will later be capitalised upon by James in his own speech (15,14) thereby "showing the structural parallelism and complementarity of the two speeches"[10]. Peter's speech itself is a combination of theology and rhetoric. The rhetorical question of v.10: "Why do you put God to test now...", is pressed by the theocentric recital of the three preceding verses[11].

The stylistic and narrative features thus presented, let us now go into the exegesis of Peter's theocentric speech after the long debate among the councillors.

4.2 A Church in Council and in Conflict (Vv.6-7a).

"Apostles in Council and in Conflict" is C. K. Barrett's title for the whole of Ac 15,1-35, but such a title is better suited to the preliminary or complicatory stage of the Council (vv.6-7a) where the narrator tells the reader with the

---

7 Ska, Id., 8; cf. 23.
8 Cf. Dillon, Acts, 44:82, p. 751; Dibelius, Studies, 94-95.
9 Cf. Ska, Our Fathers, 14. In the same way the conversion of Sauλ (Paul) is told thrice in 9,1-19; 22,4-16; 26,9-18.
10 Dillon, 44:82, p.751. Cf. Dupont, Un Peuple, 323.
11 Dillon, ibid.

phrase "*polles de zeteseos genomenes*" that there is really a big controversy. Soon after Peter has begun to speak in v.7b, the conflict described in v.7a seems to be disappearing because of the gradual ebbing of the complication as Peter addresses the disputing *andres adelphoi* who now listen to him attentively.

Strangely enough, only the apostles and the elders are mentioned in the gathering of v.6 while the *ekklesia* of v.4 is seriously omitted here. But one may infer from the much dispute of v.7a that all parties to the conflict are present at the assembly. This inference can be supported by the report of the aftermath of the speech in v.12a which says that the whole crowd is silent (*esigesen de pan to plethos*). But what has silenced this unknown number of Jewish and Gentile Christians? It is Peter's convincing God-centred speech.

4.3 Through Peter God Spoke to Gentiles (V.7b).

With a *captatio benevolentiae* "*andres adelphoi*", Peter the leader of the apostles, stands up among the assembly and introduces himself as the initiator of the gentile mission. God has chosen (*exelexato*) him for this purpose. *Eklegesthai* means to choose, select. In the LXX it is used to describe the divine selection of one of the sons of Jesse to be King (I Sm 16,8-10), and consequently in the divine choice of David (1 Kg 8,1). Of the 22 times it occurs in the NT *eklegesthai* is found 11 times in Luke-Acts[12].

The Apostles are chosen (*exelexato*) by Jesus (Lk 6,13: Ac 1,2) as God chose David. In the same way God chose (*exelexato*) the Gentiles through Peter. So then there is no need for dispute and dissension over the admission and integration of the Gentiles into the christian fold for the matter had been settled "from the days of old" (*aph' hemeron archaion*) through Peter. *Aph' hemeron archaion* is reminiscient of a divine, predetermined intervention in salvation history[13]. Peter is obviously referring to his divinely approved mission to the Roman centurion Cornelius and his friends stationed at Caesarea[14] as narrated in Ac 10 and recapitulated in Ac 11.

Cornelius was a devout soldier (*eusebes*), a Godfearer (*phoboumenes ton Theon*), a charitable man (*poion eleemosynas*), and a very prayerful man (*deomenos tou Theou dia pantos*) whom an Angel of God mandated in a vi-

---

12 *Eklegesthai* is used 10 times in the Gospels, 7 times in the Acts, 4 times in Paul and once in Hebrews. The adjective "eklektos" (chosen, elect) also occurs 22 times (Morgenthaler, Statistik, 93. Unless otherwise stated the statistic of words in the NT are made from the relevant pages of this book).

13 Is 37,26; Lm 1,7; 2,17. Also cf. Weiser, Apostelkonzil, 202.

14 Cf. Nolland, Fresh Look, 108.

sion to send for Simon Peter who was then lodging at the house of Simon the tanner in Joppa. Cornelius obeyed and sent one of his devout orderlies and two servants to Caesarea (10,1-8). As the three were nearing Joppa, Peter who was praying at the housetop, had a vision of clean and unclean beasts[15] in which he learnt not to call common (*koinon*) and unclean (*akatharton*) what God himself had cleansed (*ekatharisen*, vv.9-16).

Peter was bewildered by his vision and as he pondered over its meaning, the three messengers from Cornelius arrived. Inspired by the Spirit, he welcomed the men who told him of the centurion's angelic vision which required him to send for Peter (vv. 17-23). Arriving at Caesarea with some *adelphoi* from Joppa, Peter spoke of the lesson of his visionary experience to the group at the house of Cornelius:

> You know it is forbidden for Jews to mix with people from another race and visit them; but God has made it clear to me that I must not call anyone profane or unclean. That is why I made no objection to coming when I was sent for; but I should like to know exactly why you sent for me (vv.28-29).

Cornelius then narrated his own visionary experience and declared their readiness "to hear all the instructions" which God had given to Peter (vv.30-33). Peter's first theo-christocentric homily to a gentile audience began with his conscious affirmation of divine impartiality:

> In truth I have come to understand that God has no favourites; but that in every nation he who fears him and acts righteously is acceptable to him (v.34)[16].

Then Peter went on to tell them about the Good News of peace which God sent to the people of Israel through Jesus, the Lord of all, and to remind them about the whole Jesus event. God anointed and equipped Jesus his Son with the Holy Spirit and with power. With this divine power Jesus went about doing good and exercised the ministry of healing.

Despite his goodness the people crucified him, but God did raise him to life on the third day. Peter and other preachers are witnesses to this living presence of the crucified and risen Jesus whom God has appointed the judge of all the living and the dead. The Prophets have also borne witness that all who believe in Jesus (*panta ton pisteuonta eis auton*) will obtain forgiveness of their sins through his name (vv.35-43).

15　For more on clean and unclean animals and on the theology of unclean food, confer: Derret, Clean, 205-221; Wenham, Theology, 6-15.

16　Note that because of its inculturation importance this verse may be cited as often as it is needed in this work.

In the course of his homily the Holy Spirit fell upon the gentile Cornelius and his friends (*ta ethne*) and in ecstacy they began to speak in tongues and to praise God (*lalounton glossais kai megalunonton*) as the apostles and the disciples did on the Pentecost day (2,11). This phenomenon amazed the Jewish Christian companions of Peter. It was an approving sign that God had given his Spirit to the Gentile converts in the same way as he gave him to the Jewish converts.

Baptizing them there and then was the logical conclusion of this divinely inspired *missio ad Gentes*. After their baptism the new converts requested Peter to stay with them for some days (vv.44-48). In this way the Gentiles gained entry into the Church without any pre-condition of circumcision or the observance of the Mosaic Law.

Meanwhile the news of the conversion and free admittance of the Gentiles reached the *apostoloi* and the *adelphoi* of Judaea even before the return of Peter and his companions from Caesarea to Jerusalem. Upon his arrival the Circumcision Party Christians took him to task and criticized him for associating with the uncircumcised and for his commensality with them. Peter had no option but to defend himself by summarily retelling the Cornelius episode as found in Ac 10. He had six brethren who could equally testify to his conduct and mission among the Gentiles. At the end his story convinced the protesting Judaizers who glorified God for granting life-giving repentance to the Gentiles (11,18).

In contrast to the demands of the Judaizers in 15,1.5 the Cornelius event shows that God has approved the salvation of the Gentiles without male circumcision and the observance of Mosaic Law. Jews and Gentiles are now God's *eklektoi*. This is Peter's emphasis in the first three verses of his speech.

4.4 By Holy Spirit God Approves of Gentiles (V.8)

In this verse there are three key themes: God the knower of hearts (*ho kardiognostes Theos*); bore witness (*emarturesen*); the Holy Spirit (*to pneuma to hagion*). Peter stresses that the granting of the Holy Spirit to the Gentiles is a sign of the omniscient God's approval of their reception into the Christian Church. God performed the wonder of the gentile mission, the God who does not judge by outward appearances (*prosopolemptes*, 10,34) but knows and reads the heart of every person. Nothing is, or can be, hidden from him.

God's title as *kardiognostes* occurs only twice in the NT and are found in the Acts alone. The first is Ac 1,24 in the prayer of the pre-Pentecost *adelphoi* for the election of the candidate to replace Judas Iscariot:

You Lord, knower of the hearts (*kardiognosta*) of everyone; do show us which of these two you have chosen to take the place of this ministry and of apostleship from which Judas fell away and went to his own place.

God, as the knower of every heart is the supreme witness to the activities of every individual. This point can be highlighted by a citation of some verses of Psalm 139 which is devoted to the praise of God's omniscience:

Yahweh, you examine me and know me, you know when I sit, when I rise, you understand my thoughts from afar. You watch when I walk or lie down, you know every detail of my conduct (vv.1-3)... Where shall I go to escape from your spirit? Where shall I free from your presence? If I scale the heavens, you are there, if I lie flat in Sheol, there you are (vv. 7-8). You knew me through and through, my being held no secrets from you, when I was formed in secret, textured in the depths of the earth (v.15).

God knows and scrutinizes everyone through his Holy Spirit who also explores the depths of every being and reveals them to human beings as Paul glowingly notes in I Co 2:

God has given revelation through the Spirit, for the Spirit explores the depths of everything, even the depths of God. After all, is there anyone who knows the qualities of anyone except his own spirit, within him; and in the same way, nobody knows the qualities of God except the Spirit of God. Now, the Spirit we have received is not the spirit of the world but God's own Spirit, so that we may understand the lavish gifts God has given us (1 Co 2,10-12).

Through the same Spirit this all-knowing God has borne witness (*emarturesen*) to the reception of the Gentiles into the Church. The verb *marturein* occurs 76 times in the NT and is distributed as follows: 35 times in the Gospels, 11 in the Acts, 8 in Pauline Writings, 10 in Johannine Letters, 8 in Hebrews, and 4 in Revelation. It is found 12 times in Luke-Acts[17]. *Marturein* denotes the activity of a witness (*martus*, martyr)[18]. It means to bear witness, to testify, to be witness; to attest, to affirm, confirm; to speak well of, to approve of, to give a good report about the good conduct or nature of someone. In the *passive voice* it means to be well spoken of, to receive approval[19].

---

17 In the Gospels it occurs once each in MT and Lk, none in Mk, but 33 times in Jn. The noun marturia occurs 14 times. So then the act of witnessing is a preponderantly Johannine theme.

18 From "martus" is derived the English word "martyr", that is, one who suffers or is killed because of his witnessing to Jesus and thereby strengthens others to do likewise.

19 Cf. Newman, Dictionary, 111.

The act of a witness is a testimony, a witness, an evidence, a proof (*marturia*; *marturion*). In 1 Tm 3,7 *marturia* means reputation while in Lk 21,13, it is an opportunity to testify. It also means an emphatic declaration based on one's first hand knowledge or information about a person, an act, or an experience. In the evangelistic sense, it means bearing testimony to the Christ event through proclamations, mighty works and emphatic attestations in order to win converts to Christ or to make disciples for him[20].

This apostolic witness is a favourite theme of Luke-Acts where the verb *marturein* occurs 12 times as already pointed out[21]. It is used 4 times in the passive voice (*marturoumai*) and 8 times in the active (*martureo*) with datives of advantage to the recipient of the witness.

Passively the seven men selected for the service of the christian community are attested men (*marturoumenos hepta*, 6,3). In the same way Cornelius (10,22), Timothy (16,2), Ananias (22,12) are highly regarded men.

In the *active sense* the people in the Synagogue bear witness to Jesus who wins the approval of all (*pantes emarturoun auto*) who are astonished by the gracious words that come from his lips (Lk 4,22). All the prophets (Ac 10,43) and Paul (23,11) bear witness to Jesus. God himself bears witness to David (13,22) and to the Gentiles (15,8) and the Lord bears witness to the words of his grace by allowing signs and wonders to be performed by Paul and Barnabas(14,3). The High Priests attest to Paul's zeal as a Judaist (22,5) while the Jews can testify to his life as a Pharisee (26,5)

Witnessing is precisely the mission of the Apostles who, at the beginning of the Acts story, are commissioned by the ascending Jesus to be his witnesses from Jerusalem unto the ends of the earth (1,8: *esesthe mou martures*). In Luke the apostles are going to be the *martures* of his suffering, death and resurrection and shall preach to all nations repentance for the forgiveness of sins (Lk 24,47-48).

But there can be a false witness who falsifies a true evidence with some evil intent to shield oneself from an embarrassment or to discredit the other. Such were the false witnesses (*marturas pseudes*) who accused Stephen of blasphemy against the holy place and the Law (Ac 6,13) and later joined hands in executing him by stoning (Ac 7,58). Before Stephen, Jesus had suffered similar false charges during his trial before the Sanhedrin (Mk 14,55-58). In Mt 23,31 Jesus says that the words and deeds of the scribes and Pharisees are witnessing against them (*martureite heautois*).

---

20 Cf. Strathmann, Martus, in: TWNT, vol. 4, 477f.
21 The common noun "marturia" occurs once, and "marturion" twice. The proper noun "martus" is used 3 times in Luke-Acts out of its 35 occurrences in the NT (cf. Morgenthaler, 118.).

In *John's Gospel* witness is borne either by God the Father (Jn 5,37; 8,18b), or by Jesus[22] or the Spirit (15,26) or John the Baptist[23] or John's disciples (3,28), or the apostles (15,27). Any person can also bear witness to an event by pointing it out as true or rejecting it as false[24]. The Samaritan woman's witnessing to Jesus as the Messiah brought many Samaritans to believe in him (4,39). The witness is borne in word and deed (Jn 5,36) by a reliable *martus* who attests to the truth or falsity of an event. He gives evidence that something exists or has happened.

For John the whole OT Scritpures bear witness to Jesus (Jn 5,39). God approves the work of Jesus through his signs and wonders (8,18b). These works in turn bear witness to Jesus as God's Son (10,25; 14,10-11). Jesus also bears witness to the Father through his own words and works. At his trial before Pilate, he boldly declares that the purpose of his coming into the world is to bear witness to the truth and all who are on the side of truth listen to his voice (18,37).

John the Baptist attests to the coming of Christ as the one greater than himself (Jn 1,19-34). John's disciples also bear witness to his word and works. Along with the Paraclete Spirit of truth, the Apostles who have been with Jesus from the beginning will also witness to him (15,27).

As the apostles testified to the world of the veracity of Christ event, so did God bear witness to the propriety of the reception of the Gentiles into the Church. God's approval of the manner of life of the Gentiles is made through the Holy Spirit (*to pneuma to hagion*).

In the NT *to Pneuma to Hagion* is at the heart of the mission of Jesus right from his conception until his ascension. The Spirit is also the prime mover of the apostolic mission as is clear from the frequency of references to him in the NT. *Pneuma* occurs 379 times while spirit-moved (*pneumatikos*) activities are found 26 times as adjective and twice as adverb. In Luke-Acts *pneuma* is used 106 times[25]. It is the LXX translation of the MT Hebrew *ruach* (Latin Vulgate: *spiritus*, hence the English, *spirit*). *Pneuma* is used in varied ways and has many nuances of meaning[26] but when qualified by *to hagion* it refers to the Holy Spirit (*ruach qadosh*).

---

22   Cf. Jn 3,11.32; 7,7; 8,14.18a.

23   Cf. 1,7-8.15.32.34; 3,26.

24   2,25; 3,11; 18,23; 19,35.

25   Out of the 379 times pneuma is found 19 times in Mt, 23 in Mk, 36 in Lk, 24 in Jn, 146 in Pauline Letters, 12 times in Hb, 12 in John's Letters, 9 in Pt, 2 each in Jm and Jd, and 24 in Rev. Pneumatikos is 25 times in Paul, 2 times in Peter, and once in Rev (cf. Morgenthaler, Statistik, 133).

26   The various meanings of "pneuma" in the NT are: Spirit (of God); spirit of prophecy, spirit, spirit being or power; ghost, apparition; breath, wind; power of evil spirits; in-

Other synonyms for the Holy Spirit are the spirit of God; the spirit from God; the spirit of the Lord; the spirit of Jesus; the spirit of Christ[27]. In order to understand the role of the Spirit in the Acts, it is proper to have a bird's eye view of his place in biblical and extra-biblical traditions[28].

In the first servant song of Is 42 which is traditionally applied to Jesus Christ, the Prophet indicates that the choice of this servant is accompanied by the outpouring of the Spirit on him as on the OT charismatic leaders[29]. Is 61,1 lets us understand that the prophetic mission is carried out through the anointing by the spirit of the Lord God[30]. In Ezekiel (36,25-27) God promises to cleanse his people, put a new spirit in them and impart his Spirit to them so that they may keep his laws and respect his will.

In Joel (3,12-2) the sign of the new age and the day of the Lord is the outpouring of the Spirit on all humanity[31] so that all sons and daughters may prophesy, see visions and give oracles (cf. Ac 2,17-21). The Qumran *Rule of the Community* points out that the spectacular manifestation of the Spirit ushers in a new age in which

> God will purify by his truth all the deeds of man, and will cleanse for himself some of mankind, so as to destroy every evil spirit from the midst of his flesh and cleanse him by the holy spirit from all his wicked deeds. He will sprinkle the spirit of truth upon him like water of purification from every false abomination[32].

While in the NT the two passages from Isaiah are applied to the mission of Jesus, the pericope from Joel is applied to the mission of the first disciples of Jesus and their associates, and possibly to all those connected in any way with the apostolic mission.

John the Baptist, the precusor of Jesus, is filled with the Holy Spirit right from the womb of his mother who is also filled with the same Spirit (Lk 1,15.41). Zachary his father prophesies under the influence of the Holy Spirit

---

   ner life, self, disposition, state of mind, (cf. Newman, Dictionary, 143). Here we are only concerned with "Pneuma" as the Holy Spirit.

27   Cf. Moulton-Geden, Concordance, 819.

28   Pneuma is a very extensive NT theme, but we shall limit ourselves to the role of the Holy Spirit in the NT and particularly in the Acts. For pertinent articles on "to pneuma to hagion" confer, Bruce, Holy Spirit, 166-183; Wong, Holy Spirit, 57-95; Kee, Good News, 28-41.

29   "Nathatti ruchi 'alaw", v.1; "Theso to pneuma mou ep auton", Mt 12,18.

30   "Ruach adonai Yhwh 'alay; pneuma kuriou ep eme", Lk 4.18.

31   "'Eshpok 'eth-ruchi 'al kol-basar,...'eshpok 'eth-ruchi: ekcheo apo tou pneumatos mou epi pasan sarka... ka ge epi tous doulous mou ... ekcheo apo tou pneumatos mou" (Ac 2,17.18).

32   1 QS (Serek ha-Yahad) lv. 20f.

(v.67f). The pious Simeon enjoys the indwelling and guidance of the Spirit (2,25-27). John the Baptist witnesses that Jesus, upon whom the Holy Spirit will descend and rest like a dove (Mk 1,10; Jn 1,32-33), is the one who will baptise the people with the Spirit, fire and water[33].

The Gospels teach that from his conception to ascension Jesus is united with the Holy Spirit as he is with God the Father. At his conception the Holy Spirit, as the power of the Most High, comes upon, and overshadows, his mother Mary (Lk 1,35). And as he is praying after his own baptism the Holy descends on him in a bodily form, like a dove (3,22). The Spirit is with him during his temptation in the desert (Mk 1,12; Lk 4,1) and at the beginning of his Galilean ministry (4,14). In the synagogue at Nazareth Jesus applied to himself the text of Is 61,1-2 which witnesses to the Lord's Spirit reposing on him so that he may proclaim the Good News to all who are socially disadvantaged (Lk 4,18-21). The Holy Spirit accompanies him throughout his ministry and fills him with joy that prompts him to bless God the Father (10,21) who readily gives the Spirit to those who ask him (11,13; Jn 3,34). This ubiquitous Spirit (Jn 3,8) is God himself (4,24). He is the one whom Jesus himself is to send to us from the Father and will bear witness to Jesus (15,26).

Therefore anyone who blasphemes against this Spirit will never be forgiven either in this world or the next (Mt 12,32; Mk 3,29). He is the Paraclete and the Spirit of Truth (Jn 14,16-17; 16,7) who will lead us to complete truth (14,26; 16,13) and must be worshipped in spirit and truth (4,23). On the day of his resurrection Jesus breathes the Holy Spirit on his disciples (Jn 20,22), but they are to wait in Jerusalem until they are clothed with this promise of the Father, this power from on high (Lk 24,49), before they launch out to evangelize all peoples and baptise them in the name of the Father, the Son and the Holy Spirit (Mt 28,18-19. It is thus clear that the ministry of Jesus is carried out in the unity of the Father and the Holy Spirit.

In the Acts the presence of the Holy Spirit is so real and tangible that the book itself has been called the "*Acts of the Holy Spirit*"[34]. From the first to the last chapter of the Acts the Spirit is very powerful and operative. He is referred to many more times in the Acts than in the four Gospels together[35]. But here the study of his role shall be limited to the chapters that precede the Jerusalem Council.

---

33 Cf. Mk 1,8; Lk 3,16; Jn 3,5.
34 Cf. Bruce, Holy Spirit, 183.
35 Of the occurrences of "pneuma" in the Gospels and Acts, the word refers to the Holy Spirit 6 times in Mk, 13 times in Mt, 17 times in Luke and 18 times in John, but 58 times in the Acts (cf. Kee, Good News, 28; 111; Moulton-Geden, Concordance, 819-821).

The Spirit is the promise (*epangelian*) of the Father (Ac 1,4) with whom the Apostles will be baptised (v.5) and he will bestow power on them so that they can witness to Jesus Christ in the whole world (v.8). This promise is fulfilled on the Pentecost day when the Spirit descends on the Apostles in a vivid and dazzling manner and fills them with unusual power and boldness to proclaim the marvels of the Lord in different languages (2,1-12) in accordance with the prophesy of Joel (3,1-5; Ac 2,17-21.33). All who repent and accept the Good News are to be baptised for the forgiveness of their sins and will also receive the Holy Spirit (2,38).

Under the influence of this Spirit Peter with unusual boldness accuses the Sanhedrin of having crucified Jesus by whose name a cripple is healed and in whose name all are saved (4,8-12). And as the persecuted apostles prayed to Jesus for help they were granted the fortitude of the Spirit to proclaim God's word fearlessly (4,31). The Spirit is God's gift to all who obey him, and he witnesses with the apostles to the Christ event (5,32).

In their missionary outreach beyond Hebrew-speaking Jews, the apostles lay hands on the seven selected men "filled with the Spirit and wisdom" to look after the welfare of the widows of the Greek-speaking Jews (6,1-3). One of them, Stephen, is characterized as "a man full of faith and of the Holy Spirit" (v.5). Later in his defense before the Sanhedrin, the Spirit witnesses to his teaching about God who grants him a glorious vision of Jesus standing at God's right hand (7,55-56). After Philip has evangelized the Samaritans, Peter and John lay hands on them and they receive the Holy Spirit (8,14-17). Philip is led by the same Spirit to baptize the Ethiopian eunuch and to evangelize the towns of Azotus and Caesarea (vv. 26-40).

At his conversion, the persecutor Saul (Paul) recovers his lost sight and is filled with the Holy Spirit (Ac 9,17). After a lull in persecution, the local Churches of Palestine are encouraged by the Spirit and continue to grow (v.31). At Jaffa the Spirit inspires Peter to receive the messengers from the centurion Cornelius (10,19). In his speech to the Gentile Cornelius and his friends about Jesus, Peter reminds them of how "God had anointed him with the Holy Spirit and with power" to do good, to cure and to heal and to exorcize demons (v.38). As Peter preaches to them the Spirit comes upon all the listeners to the astonishment of the Jewish Christian companions of Peter (v.44f.

This spirit-phenomenon is so similar to that of the Pentecost day (Ac 10,46f; 11,15) that it reminds Peter of the Lord's promise of the "baptism with the Holy Spirit" (11,6) to his apostles (1,5). So he declared before the Judaizers:

I realised then that God was giving them (the Gentiles) the identical gift he gave to us (Jews) when we believed in the Lord Jesus Christ: and who was I to stand in God's way? (11,17)

This is the event which Peter is referring to at the JC (15,8). His argument is that God has granted the Holy Spirit to the Gentiles just as he had earlier done to the apostles on the day of the Pentecost. It is the justification for Peter's admission of the Gentiles into the Church without imposing on their males the custom of circumcision or the observance of Mosaic or Jewish Law.

Soon afterwards, God also confirms the faith of other Gentile converts through Barnabas, "a good man filled with the Holy Spirit and faith" (Ac 11,24). Later on, the Spirit selects Barnabas and Saul for the mission to the Gentiles (13,2.4). With the power of the Spirit Paul strikes Elymas the magician blind (vv.9-10). At the end of their ministry in Pisidian Antioch, the Gentile converts are "filled with joy and the Holy" (13,52). The active operative presence of the Holy Spirit among the Gentiles is a sign that God has approved of their unconditional conversion to the Christian faith.

So right from the beginning the Acts presents the Spirit as the mover and animator of the apostolic preachers and evangelizers. After Paul's conversion and a lull in persecution the Church enjoys the peace and consolation of the Spirit who continues to open "the door of faith" to the Gentiles through the ministries of Peter, the persecuted Hellenists, Paul and Barnabas. The Spirit is the one who encourages the apostles to carry the Good News from Jerusalem to the ends of the earth. He is the one who empowers and guides the apostolic people in their mission.

The Spirit pronounces the divine judgement on those who resist the Good News like Elymas the magician and Simon Magus or live deceitfully like Ananias and Sapphira. And he is the one who confirms the membership of anyone or any group in the community of believers. He is the one who in a spectacular way has confirmed and still confirms the membership of the Gentiles in the Christian Church[36]. This is the import of Peter's saying in v.8.

4.5 No Distinction Between Jews and Gentiles (V.9a).

God has made no distinction between Jews and Gentiles. It is the Jews, the chosen people of God, who are making this distinction. Actively *diakrinein* means to evaluate, judge, recognize, discern; to separate, distinguish, differentiate, discriminate, make distinction (between persons); to consider or make

---

36   Cf. Kee, Good News, 30-41.

superior. In the *middle voice* it means to doubt, hesitate; to dispute, debate, take issue[37].

The NT uses the verb in both active and middle senses. But in its active sense here, it means making distinction between persons or making oneself superior to another, or discriminating against another. This meaning (though in middle voice) is brought out in Jm 2,1-4:

> My brothers, do not let class distinction (*prosopolempsiais*) enter into your faith in Jesus Christ, our glorified Lord. Now suppose a man comes into your synagogue, well-dressed and with gold ring on, and at the same time a poor man comes in, in shabby clothes, and you take notice of the well-dressed man, and say, 'Come this way to the best seats'; then you tell the poor man, 'Stand over there' or 'You can sit on the floor by my footrest'. In making this distinction (*diekrithete*) among yourselves, have you not used a corrupt standard?

Although James is talking of class distinction between the rich and the poor or the privileged and underprivileged, such a differentiation can be analogically applied to the distinction which the believers from the Pharisaic sect are making between themselves and the Gentile Christians who do not observe the requirements of Jewish Law.

Just as the poor in the community of James are not given the same respectful treatment as the rich, so also are such Gentile converts marginalised by the Judaizers in the new "christian sect". And just as James condemns such a discrimination against the poor as corrupt or immoral, so also should the discrimination against Gentile converts be condemned. Therefore, those of the circumcision party should not, because of their divine election, make themselves superior to the Gentiles whom God has now chosen as he chose the Jews in earlier times.

The dividing wall of hostility, "that is, the Law of commandments with its decrees" (Eph 2,15) separating Jews and Gentiles has been broken by God through Jesus Christ. Both races now form "a chosen race, a kingdom of priests, a holy nation, a people to be a personal possession to sing the praises of God" (1 Pt 2,9; cf Ex 19,5-6) who has brought them out of darkness into the light of the christian faith. Both races can now freely mix with one another, eat and drink together as the one, holy people of God who is not concerned with race but with *faith* (cf. Ac 10,28-29).

---

37   Of its 19 occurrences in the NT, the verb is found 3 times in the Gospels, 4 times in the Acts, 7 times in Paul's Letters, 3 times in James and 2 times in Jude (cf. Morgenthaler, Statistik, 87).

4.5.1 By Faith God Purifies Hearts of Gentiles (V.9b).

God, the knower of hearts, has purified the hearts of his Gentiles by faith (*te pistei katharisas tas kardias*). This may be an interpretation of God's message to Peter: "What God has made clean, you have no right to call profane" (Ac 10,15; 11,9). God has made it clear to Peter that he must not call anyone common and unclean. He has learnt and internalised that lesson. Now he imparts the lesson to his fellow Jews who are yet to understand that God has no favourites but loves any upright person from any nation. This is proved by his purification of the hearts of the Gentiles by faith.

Katharizein means to cleanse, to make clean, to purify; to declare ritually acceptable. It is found 31 times in the NT and it is used 18 times in the Gospels in contrast to only 3 times in the Acts. Its corresponding noun is *katharismos* (cleansing, purification; purification rites) and is found 7 times in the NT[38].

In the OT certain persons and animals are considered unclean, and any form of contact with them renders one ritually unclean (Lv 11). Hence the need for the rite of purification by a devout Jew. The devout Peter is referring to these unclean animals when, at the time of his vision, he lets us know that he has never eaten anything profane or unclean (Ac 10,14; cf. Ez 4,14).

In the Gospel narrative the parents of Jesus carry out the rite of purification in keeping with the Law of Moses (Lk 2,22; cf. Lv 12,2-4). Lepers or people with virulent skin-diseases are cleansed by Jesus or his Apostles[39]. Jesus himself orders a man cured of such a disease to observe the purification rites prescribed by Moses[40]. In fidelity to their religious tradition, the scribes and Pharisees attach much importance to the purification rites of washing of hands and of cleansing of cups and dishes[41]. But these external and showy rites draw a sharp condemnation from Jesus.

You Pharisees! You clean the outside of cup and plate, while inside yourselves you are filled with extortion and wickedness. Fools! Did not he who made the outside make the inside? Instead, give alms from what you have, and, look, everything will be clean to you (Lk 11,39-41; cf. Mt 23,25-26).

---

38   Katharismos is used 19 times in the LXX. The noun-form katharotes is found only once in Hb 9,13 while the adjective "katharos" occurs 26 times in the NT (cf. Morgenthaler, op. cit., 108).

39   Cf. Mt 8,2-3; 10,8; 11,5; Mk 1,40-42; 7,19; Lk 4,27; 5,12-13; 7,14; 17,14.17.

40   Mk 1,44; Lk 5,14; cf. Lv 14,1-32.

41   Mt 23,25-26; cf. Mk 7,1-5; Jn 2,6. The disciples of John the Baptist are also engaged in a discussion about purification (Jn 3,25).

Jesus thus places inner purification and works of charity above external cleansing. And this is Peter's emphasis in his Council speech. His stand is also supported by Paul's exhortation that "we should wash ourselves clean of everything that pollutes either body or spirit, bringing our sanctification to completion in the fear of God" (2 Co 7,1). This purifcation is done not by mere ritual observances and practices but by faith and spiritual washing (Ep 5,26) in the blood of Jesus which purifies "our conscience from dead actions" and "cleanses us from all sin" "so that we can worship the living God" (Heb 9,14; 1 Jn 1,7).

4.5.2   Hearts Purified by Faith.

With the phrase, "having purified their hearts by faith", Peter knocks out and reduces to absurdity the demands of the Judaizers that Gentile Christians, in order to be saved, should be circumcised and observe the Law of Moses. A Jewish or Gentile convert to Christianity is made clean not through physical circumcision but by faith in Jesus Christ.

The noun *Pistis* (faith, belief, trust) is used 243 times in the NT and is found 142 times in the Pauline corpus, 24 in the Gospels, 32 in Hebrews, 16 in James, 15 in the Acts, and the remaining 14 in other NT Writings[42]. The statistics shows that *pistis* is a major Pauline theme. Nevertheless it is an important theme in the Gospels and Acts.

Jesus demands faith from his followers and chides them either for their lack of faith or small faith (cf. Lk 18,8, Mk 4,40). But he does not hide his satisfaction and astonishment at the great faith of the gentile centurion at Capernaum who wants his sick servant to be cured and yet declares himself unworthy to receive the divine master under his roof: "In truth I tell you, in no one in Israel have I found faith as great as this" (Mt 8,10; Lk 7,9). By this faith his servant is healed (Mt 8,13). In the same way anyone suffering from any kind of disease, ailment or sickness but has faith in Jesus, has his sins forgiven or is healed of his infirmity[43]. With faith in God one can do what seems so impossible. With faith and prayer one receives his petitions (cf. Lk 18,7-8).

In the Acts Peter heals a cripple who has faith in the name of Jesus (Ac 3,16). Paul also heals a cripple who has faith to be cured (14,9). The Christian Religion is called "the Faith" (6,7; 13,8) and some apostolic people are described as being filled with the Holy Spirit and Faith and are therefore able to urge others to remain faithful to the Lord (6,5; 11,24). Also Paul and his com-

---

42   cf. Morgenthaler, Statistik, 132).
43   Cf. Mt 9,2.22.29; 15,28; Mk 2,5; 5,34; 10,52; Lk 5,20; 7,50; 8,48; 17,19; 18,42.

panions encourage their disciples to persevere in the faith (14,22; 20,21), and subsequently the Churches grow in faith in Jesus Christ through whom the members receive "forgiveness of their sins and a share in the inheritance of the sanctified" (26,18). It is noteworthy that in the Acts "the door of faith is opened to the Gentiles" (14,27)[44].

In Peter's thesis, it is this faith, and not circumcision and Jewish Law, which purifies the Gentiles from their sins, justifies them and guarantees their salvation in and through Christ Jesus. In the piercing words of Paul, it is through Jesus that "justification from all sins from which the Law of Moses was unable to justify is being offered to every believer" (Ac 13,38b-39).

A similar thought is expressed by the Roman Paul who goes on to emphasize that, since there is only one God for both Jews and Gentiles, Jesus "will justify the circumcised by their faith, and he will justify the uncircumcised through their faith" (Rm 3,30)[45]. In so doing the Law is not invalidated but placed on a surer footing (Rm 3,31). So then the hearts of the Gentile Christians are purified and justified not by Jewsish legal and ritual observances but by their faith in God and Christ Jesus.

4.6 Why Do You Now Tempt God by Imposing Insupportable Yoke? (V.10).

4.6.1 Why Do You Now Tempt God? (V. 10a).

This rhetorical question is the logical consequence of the Petrine argument in vv.7b-9. It is a direct response to the demand made on the Gentiles by some of the Christian Pharisees in v.5. If God himself has caused the Good News to be freely and unconditionally announced to the Gentiles (v.7b); if he as the knower of the hearts of every one has given the Holy Spirit to Jews and Gentiles alike (v.8); if he has purified the hearts of the Gentiles by faith and has shown no partiality in taking care of the spiritual welfare of both races (v.9), then to discriminate against the Gentiles by imposing on them burdensome legal observances as a necessary condition for salvation is to tempt God.

---

44 For a similar metaphoric expression in Pauline corpus confer 1 Co 16,9f; 2 Co 2,12; Col 4,3.

45 Note that here I am equating "justification by faith" with "purification of heart by faith" because the end-result of each of them is "salvation" (cf. Rm 4; 5; Ga 3).

Peirazein means to test, put to the test; to tempt; to try, attempt[46]. "To put God to the test" is an OT expression which means to posit a challenge to the manifest will of God (Ex 17,2; Dt 6,16). The one who tempts God is the one "held responsible for everything which cuts across the work of God and of Christ"[47]. So are the children of Israel who deliberately challenge God and are killed by snakes[48]. So is the devil or satan who tests Job (1,6f) or puts Jesus to the test[49]. So also are Ananias and Sapphira who agree "to put the Spirit of the Lord to the test" and are instantly punished with death (Ac 5,9).

Peter is thus arguing that the demands being made by the Judaizing party on the Gentiles is like the pernicious acts of the devil. It is similar to the rebellious acts of the forefathers of Israel who tried in the past to thwart God's plan. By asking the Judaizers why they are putting God to the test, Peter is insinuating that those people are behaving like the devil or satan whose stock in trade is to tempt and accuse the children of God for no just cause[50]. Thus in a friendly and clever manner, Peter uses a strong phraseology to refute the stand taken by the Judaizers in relation to the Gentile Christians and at the same time counsels submission to divine will and plan. By the reception of Cornelius and his friends God has made it clear and plain that he does not require the imposition of Mosaic Law on the Gentiles.

4.6.2 By Imposing Insupportable Yoke? (V.10b).

Peter says that by trying to impose the unbearable weight of Mosaic Law on the Gentile disciples (*mathetai*), Jewish Christians are putting God to the test[51]. They are tempting God who from the unfathomable depths of his wisdom first conferred the title *Christianoi*[52] to the Gentile followers of Christ. But *is the Mosaic Law with all its prescriptions really a burden (zugos) to the*

---

46   Newman, Dictionary, 138. Occurring 38 times in the NT, "peirazein" is used 13 times in the Gospels, 5 in Ac, 7 in Paul, 6 in Hb, 4 in Jm and 3 in Rv. Here the discussion of the verb is to be limited to its contextual usage.

47   NJB, 1613, footnote "4c".

48   Cf. Ex 17,2; (Nb 21,5f); Dt 6,16; Ps 78 (77),18; 95,9; 1 Co 10,9; Hb 3,7-10.

49   Mt 4,1f; Mk 1,12; Lk 4,1f.

50   Cf. Jb 1,6f; 1 Co 7,5; 1 Pt 5,8; Rv 12,10f.

51   Nolland, Fresh Look, 107f.

52   Cf. Ac 11,26. Before this title was given to the converts at Antioch, the common title for the believers in Jesus was "mathetai" (cf. 6,1.2.7; 9,1.10.19.25-26.38; 13,52; 14,20.22.28; etc). By calling the early Christians "mathetai", Luke continues the Matthean tradition in which Jesus sends out the eleven Apostles to go and make disciples (matheteusate) of all nations (Mt 28,19).

Jews? This question can be answered either positively or negatively depending from what perspective one looks at the Law.

In the LXX the term "*zugos*" is used in three senses: In the spiritual sense it designates the demands of the Covenant which binds Israel to her God, but which Israel in her infidelity has broken[53]. In the political sense it refers to the oppressive reign of a king over his subjects[54] or over a conquered land[55]. In the ordinary human condition, it refers to the human suffering that awaits every human person from birth to death (Si 40,1)[56].

Zugos (burden, yoke; in Rv 6,5: balance scales) is a rare NT word. It occurs only 6 times but only once in the Acts. The Matthean Jesus says in Mt 11,29-30:

> Come to me, all you who labour (*kopiontes*) and are overburdened (*pephortismenoi*), and I will give you rest. Shoulder my yoke (*zugon*) and learn from me, for I am gentle and humble in heart, and you will find rest to your souls. Yes, my yoke (*zugos*) is easy and my burden (*phortion*) light.

What is this easy "yoke" or light "burden" in the context of the Matthew's Gospel? Firstly it may refer to what many readers consider as a strict interpretation of the Law and the Prophets. Although its interpretation is strict and may not be easily put into practice, its exposition is succint and therefore not difficult to understand[57]. In this sense it may be regarded as an easy yoke and a light burden.

Secondly, it may refer to "the burden of the Law and of the additional Pharisaic observances"[58]. This is referred to by the Matthean Jesus as heavy burdens (*phortia barea*) laid on people's shoulders by the Scribes and Pharisees who will not even lift a finger to move them (Mt 23,4). This seems to be supported by the Galatian Paul who states that if Gentile Christians return to the practice of circumcision, they are only again fastening themselves to the *yoke* of the slavery (*zugo douleias*, Ga 5,1) of the whole Jewish Law from which the grace of Christ has liberated them (5,2-4).

Thirdly it may refer to the cost of discipleship of Jesus who demands that anyone who wants to follow him should practice self-denial and bear the daily suffering consequent on this discipleship (Lk 9,23-26; 14,26f)[59].

---

53   Jr 2,20; 5,5; cf.2,11.
54   2 Ch 10,4.9.11.14.
55   Is 14,5.15.29; 47,6; Jr 27,8.11; 30,8; 34,8.11.
56   Cf. Monsengwo, L'Inculturation, 129.
57   The Sermon on the Mount (Mt 5-7) is a typical example of the yoke of the Law which is heavy to carry but easy and light when carried "in Christo" as a cost of discipleship.
58   NJB, 1629, footnote "l" on Mt 11,28.
59   Cf. Mt 10,37-39; Mk 8,34f; Jn 12,25.

Fourthly, it may refer to the *Law of Love of God and neighbour* which the Lukan Jesus regards as the basic law for inheriting eternal life (Lk 10,25-28). The Matthean Jesus also says that the love of God is "the greatest and the first commandment" (Mt 22,38) of the Law, while the second is the love of neighbour as onself. And "on these two commandments hang the whole Law, and the Prophets" (v.40). The same is true of Markan Jesus (Mk 12,28-34) who praises a Scribe for wisely noting that the love of God and neighbour is "far more important than any burnt offering or sacrifice" (v.33). To attach such a weight to this law of love brings one nearer to the kingdom of God (v.34). For the Johannine Jesus love is an obligation of discipleship.

I give you a new commandment: love one another; you must love one another just as I have loved. It is by your love for one another that everyone will recognise you as my disciples (Jn 13,34-35).

Love is the characteristic mark of all those who carry the burden of following Jesus. This is the OT law (Dt 6,5; Lv 19,18) now actualised in the life and teaching of Jesus and made binding on all his disciples.

The above evidences do favour the understanding of Jesus' *easy yoke* and *light burden* in terms of his law of love which, though hard to observe, makes life easy and light for all his disciples who faithfully carry the cross of love daily and follow him (Lk 9,23f).

But it is good to remember that in the OT, infidelity to the Law of God or the refusal to serve him by not keeping his ordinances and walking in his ways is described by the Prophet Jeremiah as *breaking from one's yoke or bursting from one's bonds* (Jr 2,20; 5,5). On the contrary the ones who trust in God, search for him, and silently wait for his salvation are those who submit to his *yoke* which is good for someone to bear from a young age (Lm 3,25-27). The OT wisdom of Jesus ben Sira counsels people to put their necks under the yoke of "wisdom" which is sometimes taken as a synonym for the "Law" (Si 51,23.26f).

In rabbinic tradition a proselyte who has undertaken to keep the Law of Moses is said "to take up the yoke of the kingdom of heaven" which concretely means that he has taken upon himself the obligation to recite the "*Shema' Yisra'el*" (Hear O Israel...)[60].

Nevertheless it should be observed that not all Israel would agree with Peter that the Law is an unbearable *zugon*. Some take pride in the Law as a sign of God's special love for Israel. For example the composer of Ps 119 (which I have already cited) expresses delight in the Law and commandments of the Lord. Philo the Jewish Philospher states that the precepts are "not too numer-

---

60   Cf. Dt 6,4-5; Berakhoth, 2.2; Bruce, Book, 290-291.

ous or too heavy for the strength of those who are able to make use of them"[61]. Therefore for a Jew of the Pharisaic Sect, the Law is not an *unbearable yoke* but a *delight* (cf. Ac 15,1.5).

But from Lukan Peter's perspective, one can positively assert that the Law is a yoke which the Jews and their ancestors have found too heavy to bear[62]. And judging from the stories of the frequent lapses of some of the Jewish people into idolatory or their frequent infidelity to their covenant with Yahweh[63], one can affirm that the Law has been an *unbearable burden* for every Jewish generation. That may be the implication of Peter's generalization on the burdensomeness of the Law for the whole of the Jews.

As a simple Galilean Jew who observes the Law of cleanliness (Ac 10,14) and can under divine guidance readily fraternize with the Gentiles (Ac 10.28; Ga 2,11-14), Peter and those like him may find the details of the Pharisaic legal tradition too burdensome to observe. They would rather prefer the easy yoke and light burden of the Matthean Jesus' interpretation of the OT Law. Above all they would prefer the easy yoke and light burden of the law of love as found in the deutronomic code (Dt 6,5) to the minute details of the pharisaic scribal legislation.

4.7 Jews and Gentiles Saved Through Faith and Grace (V.11).

This verse refers to the teaching of the *tines* from Judaea who make circumcision a necessary condition for salvation (v.1). Peter states the means of salvation for everyone. Jewish and Gentile Christians believe (*pisteuein*) that they are saved (*sozein*) in the same manner through the grace of the Lord Jesus. *Pisteuein*[64] (believe in, have faith in, have confidence in) and *charis* (grace, kindness, mercy, goodwill favour, gift) are two strong bases for salvation and christian life and so they deserve our attention here.

---

61 Philo, On Rewards, 80.
62 Haenchen states that "it would be more correct to say that the Gentile Christian Luke, who is speaking here, has lost sight of the continuing validity of the Law for Jewish Christians (which he does not contest - cf. 21,21), because all that matters to him is to demonstrate Gentile Christian freedom from the Law" (Acts, 446). So held some other German Scholars, for example: Weiser, Apostelkonzil, 202; Conzelmann, Apostelgeschichte, 83; Schneider, Apostelgeschichte, 2, 181; etc.
63 Cf. Ex 32; Jg 2,11f; 3,7f; 4,1f; 6,1f, etc; 1 Kg 11,1f; 18,16f; Jr 7,16f; Ezk 14,1f, etc.
64 In the foregoing section, we considered the usage of the noun "pistis" (faith), in this section we focus on the verb "pisteuein".

In the NT, the verb *pisteuein* occurs 241 times[65] (2 times less than the noun *pistis* which occurs 243 times). This shows that it is a key theme of the NT. What is already said of "faith" above (cf. 4.5.1) is equally valid for "having faith". In chapter three (cf.3.2.3.3) *sozein* is introduced in a rather negative and derogatory manner by the Judaizers who made salvation depend on circumcision[66]. Here *Peter's* positive teaching which links salvation with grace and faith has made it imperative to discuss *sozein* in Luke-Acts in relation to other NT works.

4.7.1 Sozein.

As already noted the verb *sozein* is used 17 times in Luke and 13 in the Acts. Its cognates are *soterion* (twice in Lk and once in Ac), *soteria* (6 times in Ac and 4 in Lk) and *soter* (twice in each book). These three concepts taken together give the reader an idea of Luke's teaching on salvation.

In general salvation, as G. Walters defines it, is

> the action or result of deliverance or preservation from danger or disease, implying safety, health and prosperity. The movement in Scripture is from the more physical aspects towards moral and spiritual deliverance. Thus, the earlier parts of the Old Testament lay stress on ways of escape for God's individual servants from the hands of their enemies, the emancipation of His people from bondage and their establishment in a land of plenty; the later parts lay greater emphasis upon the moral and religious conditions and qualities of blessedness and extend its amenities beyond the nation's confines. The New Testament indicates clearly man's thraldom to sin, its danger and potency, and the deliverance from it to be found exclusively in Christ[67].

This long definition provides the reader with a basic understanding of the concept of salvation. It has a wide range of connotations as is also evident in Luke-Acts.

In the hymn (*Benedictus*) at the circumcision and naming ceremony of his son John the baptist, the Priest Zachariah blesses the God of Israel for visiting (*epeskepsato*) his people and setting them free (*epoiesen lutrosin to lao auto*,

---

65 Of this number 98 are found in Jn, 46 in Lk-Ac, 14 in Mk, 11 in Mt, 54 in Pauline corpus, and the remaining 18 in other NT Writings. From this evidence one can describe John as the "Gospel of Faith" (cf. Morgenthaler, Statistik, 132).

66 In 4.5.1, I considered the noun "pistis" which purifies the hearts of the believer. But here is a treament of the verb "pisteuein" which goes together with "charis" as means of salvation. In 3.2.3.3, I treated the theme of "sozein" from the Judaizers' perspective. The positive consideration of "sozein" here is in tune with its occurrence in Acts 15.

67 Walters, Salvation, 1126; cf. Marshall, Luke, 94.

Lk 1,68). The verbal expressions employed in this verse are among those which describe God's benevolent saving acts for Israel. Then follows a cluster of words which speak of God's salvific acts. According to his oath to Abraham and later patriarchs in the OT, God has raised up in the NT a "horn of salvation" (*keras soterias*, v.69) of the davidic dynasty as their deliverer (*soterian*, v.71) from the hands of all their enemies and haters, and from every fear (v.74). The *keras* refers to Jesus, the Messiah son of David[68].

"Horn" (*keras*) is a metaphor referring to the strength of a fighting animal, and the whole phrase is tantamount to a "mighty saviour", since a pesonal meaning is obviously intended. The reference to the house of David takes us into the realm of Messianism, with the hope of a Davidic Messiah. Here, therefore, the Messiah is identified as a Saviour through whom God delivers his people[69].

In this hymn Zachary describes the content of salvation in OT terms. It means deliverance from enemies and the opportunity to serve and worship God in "holiness and uprightness" throughout one's life (Lk 1,.74-75). The son of Zachary, John the Baptist, as the precursor of the mighty Saviour Jesus, is to give to the people of God the knowledge of salvation through the forgiveness of their sins (v.77).

Salvation in the context of *Lukan Jesus* begins with the meaning of his name. In Lk 1,31 the prophecy of the Archangel Gabriel to his mother, the Blessed Virgin Mary, informs us that her future son shall be named Jesus, a Greek name corresponding to the Hebrew *Yehoshuah* or *Yeshuah* which means "Yahweh saves".

So before his birth the son of the Most High is recognised by his name as the Saviour of his people. This is attested to by a parallel passage in which the angel of the Lord tells Joseph that her spouse Mary will give birth to a son whom he must name Jesus "because he is the one who is to save his people from all their sins" (Mt 1,21).

In Mary's thanksgiving hymn (the *Magnificat*, Lk 1,46-55), she calls God her "Saviour" (*soter*, v.47). God is Mary's redeemer because of the special favour shown to her, a poor handmaid, in fulfilment of the divine promise of deliverance to the patriarchs of Israel and their descendants (v.55).

In Lk 2,11 the Angels announce to the shepherds, "today in the town of David, a Saviour (*soter*) has been born to you; he is Christ the Lord". This Saviour-Christ-Lord is none other than Jesus the son of Mary. He is the Messiah (*Christos*) and the Lord (*Kyrios*) or divine Son spoken of by the Prophets and by the Baptist. He is the actualization of the personal presence of God

---

68   Cf. Lk 1,32; Ac 2,29f.
69   Marshall, Luke, 98.

who has promised to visit his people and redeem them. This resumes the contents of the *Benedictus* (cf. 1,68f). The effect of this divine presence is peace to all men and women who enjoy his favour (2,14). Hence for seeing the child Messiah the old Simeon prays,

"Now, Master, you are letting your servant go in peace as you promised; for my eyes have seen the salvation *(to soterion)* which you have made ready in the sight of the nations *(laon)*; a light of revelation for the gentiles *(ethnon)* and glory for your people Israel (2,29-32).

In this prayer the Lukan narrator presents the child Jesus as the saviour of the people of Israel and of all peoples or nations. The birth narrative as a whole tells the reader that God is the ultimate source of salvation and Jesus his son is born into the world to bring peace and salvation to the Jews and Gentiles. This promised salvation heralded by John the Baptist is in accord with the divine promises in the OT.

In the public ministry of the Lukan Jesus the verb *sozein* is used many times in the healing stories to describe his acts of healing the sick or delivering people from other threats to life and safety[70]. The healing is based on the faith of the invalid as is indicated in the use of the "faith formula" in a number of the healing stories, "your faith has saved you" *(he pistis sou sesoken se)*[71].

But in the passion narrative, physical healing merges with healing in the broader sense of deliverance. Hence the bystanders and the dying thief taunted Jesus to manifest his power as the Christ by saving himself from death on the cross, just as he has saved others *(allous esosen, sosato heauton,* Lk 23,35; cf.vv.37.39). *Sozein* here refers to rescuing oneself from danger to life. However, it takes on a spiritual meaning in the conclusion of the story about the sinful woman (7,50) who has no physical ailment or disability but spiritual incapacitation. She is forgiven because she has loved much, and she is saved from sin because of her faith: "Your faith has saved *(sesoken)* you; go in peace".

Thus one sees the link between the healing activities of Jesus and the spiritual salvation which he has brought to mankind. Jesus has the power to heal the suffering person and to save the sinner. As the Son of man he "has come to seek *(zetesai)* out and save *(sosai)* what was lost" (19,10).

In the *Acts* there is a similar usage of *sozein* and its cognates. It means healing (4,9; 14,9) and rescue from mortal danger (27,20.31). This latter is the meaning of the compound *diasozein* (27,43.44) and the noun *soteria* (27,34). We have noted that in 4,9 the use of the verb *sozein* to describe the healing of

---

70   Cf. Lk 6,9; 8,36.48.50; 17,19; 18,42.
71   Lk 8,48; 17,19; 18,42.

a cripple is followed in *v.11* by the description of Jesus as the only name and person in whom there is salvation (*soteria*) because "of all the names in the world given to men, this is the only one by which we can be saved" (*dei sothenai hemas*).

⁻ Thus salvation comes through the healing ministry of the Jesus and through the name of Jesus whom God has raised up as "leader and Saviour, to give repentance and forgiveness of sins through him to Israel (Ac 5,31). God grants to all the bodily and spiritual health through Jesus. Salvation is the gift of God the Father (2,39; 5,32; 11,18) but it is intrinsically linked with Jesus his Son and Saviour. According to the prophetic witnesses only through him shall all believing men and women receive salvation which comes to the individual through the forgiveness of one's sins[72].

᠊ Forgiveness of sins therefore is the content of salvation in *Luke-Acts*. The salvation comes first and foremost through divine initiative who sends out his Good News and selects his messengers to prepare the hearts of people for its reception[73]. Sometimes he directly and freely grants the opportunity to repent to both Jews and Gentiles (cf. Ac 5,31; 11,18). Although salvation is a gratuitous gift of God - because all are saved by his grace - yet the divine initiative demands appropriate **human response**. This response consists of repentance (*metanoia*), faith (*pistis*) and conversion (*epistrophe*).

Acts frequently summons everyone to faith, conversion and repentance from wickedness and sin. But the Lukan Peter's appeal to his pentecost audience summarizes what human response to the divine offer of salvation entails:

You must repent (*metanoesate*) and everyone of you must be baptised in the name of Jesus Christ for the forgiveness of your sins, and you will receive the gift of the Holy Spirit.... Save (*sothete*) yourselves from this perverse generation (2,38.40).

So despite the divine will and initiative to save all, the Acts stresses the importance of human effort for one's salvation. The Blessed Virgin's response in faith to the promise of God made her blessed (*makaria*, Lk 1,45). Salvation is therefore the result of divine grace and good human works.

Two passages in the Acts further buttress this point: God's favourites are only those who fear him and do what is right (10,34-35). Here the emphasis is on good works. In order to be saved, one must become a believer in the Lord Jesus (16,31). Here the emphasis is on faith. So the *Acts* demands the good works of repentance and faith as a condition for forgiveness of sins and salvation.

---

72 Cf. Ac 4,12; 10,43; Lk 1,77.
73 Cf. Ac 8,26; 9,10f; 10,19f; 13,1; 16,6f; 18,21; 20,22. In all these passages God himself calls, sends out, guides, and encourages his messengers.

4.7.2 Pisteuein.

·*Pisteuein* is one of the necessary conditions for salvation. The thousands of people[74] who believed in Jesus through the ministry of the apostles would have their sins forgiven through the name of the exalted Jesus (cf. Ac 13,38-39). He has made Paul a light to the Gentiles so that the salvation which he has brought may reach the ends of the earth (v.47). Hence all Gentiles destined for eternal life happily receive the Good News and become believers (v.48). Faith with repentance heals and saves holistically.

Some few examples from other *NT books* can help illumunate the Petrine teaching on the salutary power of faith: The Markan Jesus appeals to everyone to "repent and believe the Gospel" (Mk 1,15). He emphasizes that "everything is possible for one who has faith" (Mk 9,23).

Have faith in God. In truth I tell you, if anyone says to this mountain, 'be pulled up and thrown into the sea' with no doubt in his heart, but believing that what he says will happen, it will be done for him" (Mk 11,22-23; cf. Mt 21,21).

With this act of faith one obtains all he prays for: "I tell you, therfore, everything you ask and pray for, believe that you have it already, and it will be yours" (Mk 11,24; cf. Mt 21,22).·Faith in God the Father and in Jesus his Son is a guarantee of salvation or eternal life. The Johannine Jesus categorically asserts that whoever believes in God and in his Son has eternal life, but anyone who does not believe in him is judged already and will never see life[75].

I am the resurrection (and the life). Anyone who believes in me, eventhough that person dies, will live, and whoever lives and believes in me will never die (Jn 11,25-26).

Therefore "blessed (*makarioi*) are those who have not seen and yet believe" (Jn 20, 29). Since belief in God and Jesus is the necessary condition for salvation, those who believe in Jesus and in all about him are declared happy or blessed.

The Letter to Romans repeatedly stresses the salutary value of having faith in the Good News[76] which is

"God's power for the salvation (*soterian*) of everyone who has faith (*panti to pisteuonti*) - Jews first, but Greeks as well - for in it is revealed the saving justice of God: a justice

---

74 Cf. 4,4; 5,14; 8,12; 11,21; 17,12; 19,18; 21,20; etc. These massive conversions are described by the M. J. Cook as Luke's "Myth of the 'Myriads'" (cf. Mission to Jews, 102-123).
75 Cf. Jn 3,16.18.36; 5,24; 6,40.47; etc.
76 Rm 3,22; 4,3.5.11.18.25; 6,8; 10,4.9-11; Gl 2,15-21; and parallels.

based on faith and addressed to faith. As it says in scripture: Anyone who is upright through faith will live" (Rm 1,16-17).

Furthermore if anyone declares with his mouth that Jesus is Lord, and if he believes (*pisteuses*) with his heart that God raised him from the dead, then he will be saved (*sothese*) because it is by believing (*pisteuetai*) with the heart that one is justified and by confessing or making declaration with the lips that one is saved (*stomati de homologeitai eis soterian*) [cf. Rm 10,9-10)].

When scripture says: No one who relies on this will be brought to disgrace, it makes no distinction between Jew and Greek; the same Lord is the Lord of all, and his generousity is offered to all who appeal to him, for all who call on the name of the Lord will be saved (*sothesetai*) (Rm 10,11-13).

Jews and Gentiles are saved by their act of faith in God and in Jesus, and not by practising the Law (Ga 2,15-21). This faith goes together with the saving grace of God.

4.7.3 Charis.

Grace (*charis*) is used 155 times in the NT. Interestingly enough, it is not found in Mt and Mk, but occurs 8 times in Lk, 17 in Ac, 4 in Jn, 12 in Pt, and 100 times in the Pauline corpus. It is therefore right to assume that *charis* is basically a Pauline theological concept that is shared with Luke and Peter. But how is it used in Luke-Acts?

Luke reports that Mary the Mother of Jesus is full of grace (1,29) and finds favour with God (v.30)[77]. God's favour is also with her child Jesus (2,40.52)[78]. As he proclaims the Good News his audience are astonished by the gracious words (*tois logois tou charitos*) that come from his lips (Lk 4,22). His teaching emphasizes that it is an act of grace to love one's enemies and do good to them (Lk 6,32-34). Such an act of kindness is rewarded by God.

Like the Master Jesus the early apostolic community finds favour with the whole people (Ac 2,47; 4,33). Stephen works miracles and signs because he is filled with grace and power (6,8). The Church of Antioch is founded through the act of God's grace (11,23). And for their ministry Paul and Barnabas are commended by the grace of God (14,26). As they bear witness to the Good

---

77 In the OT, people whose deeds are pleasing to God are said to win his favour (cf. Ac 7,46).

78 In a similar way John's Gospel descibes Jesus the "Word of God" as one "full of grace and truth" (1,14.17). And "from his fullness we have, all of us received grace upon grace" (v.16).

News of God's grace (20,24), they urge their converts to remain faithful to the grace received from God (13,43). By signs and wonders the Lord attests to what they preach about his grace (14,3) through which Jews and Gentiles are saved (15,11).

Ac 15,11 is the epitome of what Peter has been taught by God through his experience with Cornelius. It is also the central insight that should guide the Jerusalem church in its decision[79].

'In Lukan Peter's thought, salvation is a free gift of God to mankind. It is an act of his grace which includes safety, peace, deliverance from evil, God's mercy, forgiveness of sins and eternal life. But it demands repentance, faith and good works from the individual beneficiary of this grace. Hence in his distinctly theological statement about salvation, the Lukan Peter teaches that God is at the helm of affairs. He draws his conclusions from his pastoral experiences in the Cornelius episode: God chose the Gentiles; he testified to his choice of them; he did not discriminate against them, but removed their uncleanliness and saved them by his grace in the same way as he saved the Jews[80].

The Pauline corpus adds to this teaching by stressing that salvation is a gratuitous loving gift of God for the sinful and fallen humanity. Since all are saved by grace through faith and not by human effort, nobody can claim credit for one's salvation (Ep 2,4-8). God is the saviour who "wants everyone to be saved and reach full knowledge of truth" (1 Tm 2,4). United and reconciled in Christ Jesus, all peoples are saved by his grace and by faith in him[81].

4.8 Significance of Peter's Speech.

What is particularly striking in this speech is the emphasis on *divine initiative* for the salvation of peoples. Salvation is brought about by God's grace (*charis*)[82]. Peter who in his earlier speech to the Gentile Cornelius and his friends laid much emphasis on good works - fearing God and doing what is right - (Ac 10,34.35) as a condition for being acceptable to God, now says in his speech to the leaders of the church that the believer is saved by the grace of the Lord Jesus. Good works (*Werke*) are no longer mentioned even if the *Acts* regards them as a prerequisite for salvation.

---

79   Tannehill, Narrative Unity, 2, 186.
80   Cf. Tannehill, Narrative Unity, 2, 184. Weiser, Apostelkonzil, 202.
81   Cf. Rm 5,2.15.17.20.21 for similar thoughts.
82   Cf. Nolland, Fresh Look, 111f.

Rather the grace of God through faith guarantees salvation for every believer[83]. Here the narrator comes closer to the Pauline teaching that "all have sinned and lack God's glory, and all are justified by the free gift of his grace through being set free in Jesus Christ" (Rm 3,23-24). But unlike the teaching of Luke-Acts, the Pauline gratuitous salvation is brought about by the *expiatory death* of Jesus (3,25-26).

The same thought is evident in 1 Tm 2,4 which says that God "wants everyone to be saved and come to the knowledge of the truth" through the *expiatory death* of Jesus, the only mediator between God and humanity (v.5). This atonement for our sins is the sign of God's love for all (1 Jn 4,10). It is noteworthy that the whole Gospel tradition and the Pauline corpus teach about the passion and death of Jesus, yet the Lukan tradition does not speak of his death in terms of expiation or atonement for the ransom of many[84].

Luke-Acts avoids any mention of the atoning death of Jesus for the salvation of humanity. Rather salvation is brought about, not by Jesus' expiatory death for the sins of mankind (cf. 1 Jn 4,10) but, by the whole *Christ event*: his birth (Lk 2,11), his ministry to the lost ones (19,10; by his lordly service (22,27), by the reception of baptism in his name (Ac 2,38; 10,48), by faith in his exalted name[85] which are all works of divine grace, and through the endurance of the daily tribulations of human life (Ac 14,22). This is the distinguishing mark of the Luke-Acts theology of salvation in and through Christ[86].

But despite this emphasis on divine initiative for salvation, it is important to note that the Lukan Peter's theocentric speech at JC is much conditioned by the question of *how one is saved*. Because the Judaizers are insisting that salvation depends on human activity (the observance of Jewish Law and customs), Peter stresses from his pastoral experience that salvation is a free gift of God to and for all peoples[87]. His experience at the meeting with the Gentile Cornelius and his friends has taught him to present Christianity as a Religion without frontiers, open to anyone from any nationality who fears God and does what is acceptable to him (Ac 10,34f). So through the mouth of the Lukan Peter the reader learns that the basic Lukan theology of salvation consists

---

83   Cf. Ac 13,39; 14,22.26.27.
84   Mt 20,28; cf. Jn 3,14f; Rm 3,25-26.
85   Lk 24,27; Ac 4,9-12; 5,31; 10,43; 13,38; 26,18.
86   Cf. Marshall, Luke, 94.
87   Salvation by faith and grace is typically Pauline (cf.Rm, 3-5; Ga 3-4), while salvation by faith and good works is typically Jacobian (Jm 2,14-26). But Paul does not exclude human striving after salvation since he exhorts christians to work out their salvation with fear and trembling.

of a harmonious blend of *divine* initiative and *human* response in the achievement of this salvation[88].

God freely offers the gifts of faith, grace and salvation to the individual who must respond by his/her personal faith, repentance and conversion. In reality it is God alone who saves sinful humanity through his incarnate son Jesus but he also wants everyone to work out his or her salvation with a holy fear and trembling. However the divine initiative takes precedence over human efforts[89] and this confirms the belief that Jews and Gentiles are saved not just by their good deeds but "through the grace of the Lord Jesus" (Ac 15,11).

The reader should also note that after this speech Peter is no longer mentioned in the apostlolic mission of the Acts. As the chief Apostle and pastor, and in line with his pastoral duty as described in the Gospels and particularly in the Acts[90], one can credit him with giving a sense of direction to a christian assembly engaged in dispute and wrangling over ethnic customs and practices.

His "disappearance" after his powerful theocentric speech seems to make it a valedictory or a farewell address to the leaders of Jewish and Gentile Churches. After his efforts to bring order into the chaotic assembly, no one hears of him any more in the Acts and so he seems to have left the pastoral stage when the ovation for him was highest. With the speech he bids farewell to his flock and lays out for later generations of Christians the guideline for the resolution of culture-bound problems in the Church.

Furthermore the cultural or inculturation significance of the speech should not be lost sight of. Peter, the chief apostle and leader of the Church, makes a thoroughgoing theological statement on the question of the relationship between Jews and Gentiles in the Church. In doing so he formulates the official apostolic policy[91] that remains valid for christians of every nation and every age. The christian faith is thus not culture-bound but a supra-cultural and transcultural faith that should be rooted in the culture and life of the individual who loves and fears God, irrespective of his nationality, culture or status in society.

---

88 In this the Lukan Peter is close to the Jacobian teaching that faith requires good deeds because faith without good deeds/works is dead (Jm 2,14-26).

89 For more on the theme of salvation in Luke-Acts confer, Marshall, Luke, 188-215; Bovon, Luc, 259-307; O'Toole, Unity, 33-61.

90 Cf. Brown et al., Petrus, 40-53. The pastoral role of Peter in the Acts shall be further discussed in our "theological reflection" on Ac 15,1-35.

91 Cf. Kee, Good News, 58. The effect of this speech on the audience shall be discussed in the next chapter.

Since this highly theocentric and yet deeply inculturation speech comes from Peter the chief pastor[92], it will not be superfluous to regard it as one of the basic teachings on the inculturation of the faith in the apostolic Church which also remains valid for the contemporary local Churches.

---

92   It is good to observe that in Matthew's Gospel the earthly Jesus entrusted the eminent pastoral care of the Church to Peter (Mt 16,17.19). In a similar way the risen Jesus asked Peter to take care of his lambs and sheep (Jn 21,15-17).

5. Chapter Five.

God's Wonders And Signs Among The Gentiles (15,12).

5.0 Greek Text of Ac 15,12.

12. Esigesen de pan to plethos kai ekouon Barnaba kai Paulou exegoumenon hosa epoiesen ho Theos semeia kai terata en tois ethnesin di' auton.

5.1 Narrative and Stylistic Features of V.12.

This chapter which consists of only one verse of the whole episode is the second real scene of the story (cf. 2.3.10). It is a scene because there is a change of time introduced by *"esigesen de pan to plethos"*. There is a change of character(s): from Peter to Barnabas and Paul and hence a *shift* in the scene. The action changes from Peter speaking to the assembly to the two Gentile missionaries narrating the marvels of the Lord among the *ethne*. Consequently there is a change of subject or theme. To the simple reader it may be at the outset too surprising that a single verse of an episode can make up *one chapter of a thesis*. But this element of surprise may not arise if the verse is read from the point of view of a story and a plot.

The verb *exegeisthai* (to tell, relate, explain, report; make known, reveal) occurs only six times in the whole of the NT (once in Jn, once in Lk, and 4 in Ac). So it is a Lukan terminology that qualifies the narrative (*diegetic*) nature of Luke-Acts. It describes well the report given to the assembly by the two missionaries to the uncircumcised Gentiles and adds flavour to the story form of our text.

As already pointed out in chapter two, one of the important features of the narrative method is the intrinsic relation between "narrative time" (= narrated time: *erzählte Zeit*) and "narration time" (*Erzählzeit*). This verse offers the reader a good example of how a concrete narrative is perused in a narration time of a few words. Here in v.12 the story of the first missionary work of Paul and Barnabas (which took them a long period of time from Syrian Antioch to Derbe and back again to Antioch, 13,4-14,27) is told in one verse. Here a long stretch of time is summarized in a narration time of one sentence. With one stroke of the pen the narrator artistically writes the story of a whole missionary journey with its ups and downs.

By assuming the voices of Paul and Barnabas, the narrator tells the story of their missionary enterprise in a free indirect discourse[1]. Although the narration time is normally shorter than the narrative time, their respective durations are very close to each other in this single verse. From the brevity of the story itself the reader can detect the choices of the narrator and the effects he wants to produce[2]. To detect these narrative choices and effects, let us compare the event reported here in 15,12 with the story of the conversion of Cornelius in 10,1-11,1-18 and the story of the conversion of Paul in 9,1-19; 22,4-16 and 26,9-18.

The Cornelius episode is narrated twice and is used by Peter in his speech (15, 7b-9) to plead for a Gentile Church free from the obligations of Jewish way of life. This means that the narrator focuses thrice on the Cornelius story and on the conversion of Paul respectively. There is then no doubt that these two episodes must have left a deep impression on the narrator. And this may be the reason for their triple repetition in the Acts.

On the contrary, it is very surprising that the author (or the narrator) does not deem it necessary to repeat, even in a summary form, the two-chapter story of the first mission of Paul and Barnabas to the Gentiles as he did in the case of the conversions of Paul and Cornelius. Rather he only makes a cursory mention of that mission in 14,27 and 15,4. So the iterative questions would be: *Why does the author not retell the key aspects of God's wonders and signs through Paul and Barnabas. Are they not as important and impressive as the ones he retold* in the same book?

The answer may be that the narrator has made his choices with a purpose in mind. It may be that the marvels of God among the Gentiles through the two missionaries do not seem to him to be the best "*pladoyer*" or apologia for the reception of law-free Gentiles into the community of Jesus Christ, rather the conversion of Cornelius is for him the *classic apologia* for their reception and a clear pointer to the divine will and intent over the Jewish/Gentile question in the Church. By extraordinary manifestation of the Holy Spirit and his decscent on the Gentiles before their baptism and even before the first gentile mission initiated by the Spirit, God has approved of the Gentiles and has certified their integration into the christian fold.

With this argument from the Cornelius story and not from the gentile missionary activity full of God's wonders and signs the narrator achieves the effect he intends to produce. The effect is reported in the words of v.12a: "*esigesen de pan to plethos*". Upon hearing that the Gentile mission was already a divine "*fait accompli*", the contentious *plethos* (15,7) is silenced and

---

1   Cf. Genette, Narrative Discourse 174-175.
2   Cf. Id., on "Duration", 86-112.

calmed down (v.12). Peter's speech has achieved the supposedly desired effect on his audience, namely, to call the quarrelsome "Church Leaders" to order and instil in them some measure of decent christian behaviour.

The silence after the brief theocentric speech is indicative of its effect upon the *plethos* among whom the narrator makes audible the opposition to the gentile mission[3].

Peter's speech puts an end to all conflict within the *plethos* - the assembly holds its peace and allows Barnabas and Paul to relate the signs and wonders God has wrought through them among the Gentiles. These experiences, in which God's will became visible, confirm the arguments of Peter[4].

In the account attributed to Paul and Barnabas, the voice of the omniscient narrator is quite prominent and audible. It can be described as a reported, council intervention in the voice of the narrator. His voice intrudes into the narrative and narrates the work of the missionaries in the third, instead of in the expected first, person narration. He does not allow them to tell the story of their work as they experienced it. But with his characteristic omniscience, he summarizes with *astonishing brevity* all those marvels performed by God through Paul and Barnabas. One wonders why these two were not allowed to speak for themselves? Does it mean that they were not present at the Council? Or is it part of the narrator's *artistic device*?

If the reader compares this episode with the event at Corinth where the narrator through the proconsul Gallio speaks for Paul before the hostile Jews who brought Paul to his tribunal (Ac 18,12f), and also with the Ephesian silversmiths' riot in which the narrator again through the town clerk speaks for Paul before an irrate crowd (19,35), he cannot but presume that the missionary report of 15,12 is part of the narrator's *story style* or *artistry* for coming in defence of Paul and the gentile mission and at the same time shielding him from the attacks of his opponents.

By even stating that the *plethos* kept quiet after Peter's speech, the narrator subtly introduces some element of agreement and harmony among the contentious groups and covertly begins to defend the two missionaries to the Gentile. The reported silence of the *plethos* makes it possible for the missionaries to give an account of their stewardship among the Gentiles by means of the voice of the narrator.

---

3   Cf. Haenchen, Acts, 447, footnote no. 3.
4   Id., 447.

5.2 A Silent and Attentive Assembly.

The word *plethos* has been mentioned several times in this work. It is now time to consider it in some detail. *Plethos* means "crowd; quantity, number; people, population; congregation; assembly"[5]. In the context of Acts 15, it is more appropriate to translate *plethos* as congregation or assembly[6]. In this sense one can state that the *plethos* comprises the three groups mentioned later in v.22: *Apostoloi presbyteroi syn hole te ekklesia*. These three groups are engaged in a riotous dispute and conflict until Peter's speech calls them to order and disposes them to listen with wrapt attention to the story of the signs and wonders performed by the Lord among the Gentiles through Paul and Barnabas.

From the narrative point of view, the silence among the *plethos* gives a first indication of a gradual break-through and consensus among the contentious assembly. From this the reader gets the impression that the story of Paul and Barnabas has begun to influence or convince the quarelling councillors. Here then the proverb, "*silence means consent*" can be applied to all who listened to the tale of the two missionaries. The silence of the *plethos* evokes a ray of hope that all is not yet lost for the gentile cause.

From this time on, a change of attitude is found among the assembly which gradually shifts from a state of dispute and disagreement towards an unanimous resolution of the problem that confronts it. By the *esigesen pan to plethos* the narrator seems to be stressing the corporate responsibility of all the delegates at the Council[7].

5.3 Signs and Wonders.

The expression "*semeia kai terata*" is found 3 times in the Gospels[8] and 9 times in the Acts[9]. The pair of words is the LXX translation of the MT Hebrew *'othoth umophethim* which refers mainly to God's miraculous acts of deliverance of OT Israel especially in the days of Moses. Luke uses the expression to describe the wonderful works performed by the apostolic people under divine power and influence.

5   Newman, Dictionary, 144.
6   Such is its translation by Haenchen, Acts, 440; by Barclay, Acts, 114; by NJB, 1824; by A. Weiser who translates it into German as "Versammlung" [= assembly, gathering], Apostelkonzil, 206.
7   Cf. Weiser, op. cit., 206-208.
8   Cf. Mt 24,24; Mk 13,22; Jn 4,48:
9   Cf. 2,19.22.43; 4,30; 5,12; 6,8; 7,36; 14,3.

Semeia is the plural of *semeion* with the following meanings: miraculous sign, miracle; portent, warning sign; mark, signal, sign, indication, that by which something is known or distinguished. *Terata* is the plural of *teras* which means a wonder, object of wonder; omen, something indicating a common event. Hence "*semeia kai terata* refers to God's miraculous signs and wonders for his creatures.

The Prophet Joel foresees a day when God will show portents (*mophethim*) in the sky above and signs (*'othoth*) on the earth below (Jl 3,3; cf. Ac 2,19). Jesus warns his disciples that "false Christs and false prophets will arise and produce signs and portents, enough to deceive even the elect, if that were possible" (Mk 13,22; Mt 24,24). To the court official at Capernaum who wants his very sick son to be cured, Jesus says: "Unless you see signs and portents you will not believe!" (Jn 4,48). The man believed without seeing the *semeia* and *terata* and his son was healed (vv.50-51).

In the Acts, Peter says that the outpouring of the Holy Spirit on the first disciples of Jesus is the fulfilment of the prophecy of Joel (Ac 2,19). He witnesses to Jesus as a man through whom God performed miracles and wonders and signs before the people of Israel (2,22). The apostles themselves work wonders and signs among the people (2,43; 5,12) and pray to God for the power to heal and work signs and wonders through the name of Jesus (4,30).

5.4 Signs and Wonders Among the Gentiles.

What are those signs and wonders worked by God through Paul and Barnabas? The narrator does not tell the reader in this verse what the two missionaries actually told the assembly. But if one follows the Acts story, especially from the first missionary journey up to this point (13,4-14,27), there is no doubt that the two were referring to the miraculous events which were performed in their mission from Syrian Antioch to Derbe and back to Antioch (see 5.1 above). It is not out of place to mention and present a summary of those marvels of the Lord which are here used as an argument for the confirmation of God's approval and acceptance of the Gentiles. Those narrated include the miraculous blinding of a Jewish magician Bar-Jesus or Elymas; the healing of a cripple at Lystra; the resurrection of Paul stoned to death.

5.4.1 Two Missionaries and Bar-Jesus (13,6-12).

As the Acts tells the reader, Bar-Jesus whose Greek name is Elymas (an Arabic word for the *skilful one*)[10] lived in Paphos, the capital of the Island of Cyprus[11]. He was a "dealer in magic, a false prophet and a Jew" and attended to the intelligent proconsul or governor of Cyprus, Sergius Paulus residing in the city of Paphos which was then "infamous for its worship of Venus, the goddess of love"[12].

These were intensely superstitious times and most great men, even an intelligent man like Sergius Paulus, kept private wizards, fortune tellers who dealt in magic and spells[13].

So was Elymas who confronted and resisted Saul[14] and Barnabas whom the proconsul summoned to preach to him. Elymas must employ all his fraudulent tactics to retain his client and prevent him from being converted to Christianity, otherwise he would lose his only means of livelihood. In the contest that ensued between Elymas and the missionary Saul filled with the Holy Spirit, the magician was struck temporarily blind and his evil powers were completely decimated by Saul's harsh words and mercilessness[15]:

> You utter fraud, you impostor, you son of the devil, you enemy of all uprightness, will you not stop twisting the straighforward ways of the Lord? Now watch how the hand of the Lord will strike you: you will be blind, and for a time you will not see the sun (13,10-11).

Elymas became blind and lost the battle for the faith and soul of Sergius Paulus who immediately became converted to the christian faith, having been overwhelmed by "what he had learnt about the Lord" (13,12) and by the miracle worked in his name. The new Greek name "Paul", which the narrator here gives to the Jewish Saul, lends credence to the transforming effect of this

---

10 Barclay, Acts, 100.
11 At that time Cyprus was a Roman province.
12 Barclay, Acts, 100.
13 Ibid.
14 Note that it is after this contest with Bar-Jesus that the narrator gives to Saul the Greek name "Paul" which is also the name of his first missionary convert (Sergius *Paulus*).
15 The justification for such harshness may be due to the seriousness of the opposition experienced by the young and missionary Saul from an apostate Jew. The zeal of Saul the Pharisee cannot tolerate such a Jewish religious renegade who has betrayed the faith of their fathers. Saul's words are an eloquent testimony of his burning zeal and anger.

incident on the life of the one chosen by God and sent on a mission to the Gentiles[16].

The narrator gives a new name to Saul. After the conversion of the gentile (Roman) official Sergius Paulus, the chief missionary to the Gentiles is given the name of his first convert. From now on he is not just the converted Jewish *"Shaul"*, but the Gentile missionary *"Shaul* Paulus"[17]. This additional name is a literary art with theological significance.

The OT Jewish tradition attaches much importance to the name of a person. For example, Adam named all beasts of the earth to demonstrate his authority and power over them (Gen 2,19-20). Nebuchadnezzar, King of Babylon, deposed the King of Judah Jehoiakim and replaced him with his paternal uncle *Mattaniah* (Gift-of-Yahweh) whose name he changed to *Zedekiah* (Yahweh-is-my-justice) [cf. 2 Kg 24,17]. Nebuchadnezzar has changed the name of his new appointee to show that he exercises authority over the kingdom of Judah which for him is an act of "divine justice" against the insubordinate vassal King of Judah, Jehoiakim. Jeremiah is called by Yahweh's name, indicating the power of Yahweh over him and his prophetic ministry.

Reflecting on this event from the perspective of Paul's divine mission to the Gentiles[18], W. Barclay writes:

> So Saul was also Paul. It may well be that from this time he so fully accepted his mission as the apostle to the Gentiles that he determined to use only his Gentile name. If so, it was the mark that from this time he was launched on the career for which the Holy Spirit had marked him out and that there was to be no turning back[19].

In a similar way the name Paul, which the narrator gives to Saul and which afterwards becomes his principal name both in the Acts and in the rest of the NT and up to our times, shows the authority exercised by the missionary Paul over his first gentile convert, and also the influence of the gentile mission over Paul. Here the name expresses a bilateral exercise of influence and power.

From this Elymas/Paul episode emerge some lessons for the reader of the story. Firstly, the evil powers of the magician are overpowered by Paul[20] with three actions: a sharp gaze of the eyes (v.9) parallel to the gaze of Peter before healing the lame man in the Temple (Ac 3,4) and Paul's intent gaze at the

---

16 This first wonder by Saul, accompanied by the conversion of the proconsul, must have made a deep impression on the missionary life of the Apostle. His new name "Paulus" insinuates this supposition.

17 Cf. Wildhaber, Paganisme Populaire, 78.

18 Ac 9,15; 13,2-3; 22,21; 26,17-18.

19 Barclay, Acts, 100.

20 Cf. Wildhaber, op. cit., 78-79.

Lystran cripple before healing him (14,9); an angry reproach and accusation (v.10), comparable to Peter's reproach of Simon the magician at Samaria (Ac 8,18-23) and a merciless but temporary curse of blindness (v.11) pronounced in the language style of the LXX.

By the temporary nature of this divine punishment reminiscent of events in the ancient miracle stories, the narrator leads the reader to think and hope that Bar-Jesus would later repent of his apostasy as did Simon Magus before Peter and John in Samaria (Ac 8,22-24). But in general the Bar-Jesus episode follows the pattern of some miracle stories in the Acts[21].

Secondly, the incident also highlights the fact that God is not a respecter of persons and has no favourites (cf. Ac 10,34). It shows that the soul of a superstitious Gentile pagan is as precious to God as that of a Jew. He loves the salvation of the Gentile as much as that of a Jew, and he even prefers a repentant Gentile (ready and willing to hear the Good News of his Son Jesus Christ and be converted) to a Jewish magician or apostate who indulges in idolatory.

Thirdly, the event clearly brings out the influential role of the Holy Spirit in the apostolic mission. Elymas is struck blind by the sentence pronounced on him by Saul/Paul filled with the Holy Spirit. The Spirit promised and sent by Jesus also sends Saul and Barnabas on their mission (Ac 13,4) and demonstrates his abiding presence and power by the miraculous blinding of Bar-Jesus (*son of Jesus*)[22]. The Spirit continues to act as the helper (*Beistand*) of his two messengers.

Fourthly, the narrator takes pains to tell the reader what in actual fact brought about the conversion of the Proconsul to the faith. Both the miracle of blindness and the Good News of the Lord struck him wonderfully. Their irrestible force moved him to believe and be converted (13,12).

Finally it is one of those many episodes that shows that Christianity enjoys the favour of the officials of the Roman Empire[23]. For if highly placed rulers like Sergius Paulus can be convinced of the christian faith and embrace it, then this religion is not a danger to the security and peace of the state. Christians

---

21 Cf. Weiser, Apg., 318.

22 This can be regarded as a *PUN*. The battle for the soul of Sergius Paulus is fought between the follower and attendant of Jesus, son of God, and Elymas son of Jesus, the attendant of the proconsul. When Saul conquered his spiritual opponent, he is given the name of S. Paulus, the master of Elymas, perhaps in order to demonstrate the Apostle's mastery and power over the master of his spiritual enemy, and above all, to show the superior power of his master Jesus Christ. In biblical parlance, the assumption of the name of an opponent shows that the one is overpowered, conquered, despoiled and reduced to nothing (cf. 2 Kg 2,17).

23 Cf. Ac 18,12-17; 19,35-40; 24,10-27; 25; 26.

should then feel free to worship the God and Christ proclaimed by the missionaries[24].

5.4.2   Paul Heals a Cripple at Lystra (14,8-18).

The healing of the lame man at Lystra is a strange but an interesting incident. Paul and Barnabas arrived at Lystra and began to preach. Among his audience sat a man "who had no power in his feet. He had been a cripple from his birth and he had never worked"[25]. Paul noticed that he had faith to be cured and said to him in a loud voice, "Get to your feet - stand up". Immediately the cripple jumped up and began to work (vv.8-10). The healing story contains elements of unexpectation, speed, surprise and astonishment.

There is no doubt that this is a great *semeion kai teras* and the story is told in such a way as to create a bewildering impression on the reader. The man's incapacitation is perfectly described by the adjective (*adunatos*). He is completely lame from his mother's womb (*cholos ek koilias metros auto*) and so was never (*oudepote*) able to lift up a leg for once and take one step. The narrator dwells so heavily on the man's disability and affliction[26] in order to enhance the greatness of the miracle. The cripple was indeed a man of faith and listened with deep faith to the preaching of Paul who also perceived the depth of his faith.

The narrator does not tell us the content of Paul's message to his audience but from the sentence, "Paul looked at him intently and saw that he had the faith to be cured" (*hoti echei pistin tou sothenai*, v.9), one may state that Paul must have been preaching on "*the healing or saving power of faith*". Faith is the condition for this miracle as it is for other miracles of Jesus and Peter[27]. It is this faith that restored power to the feet of the crippled so that he could leap and walk about like the others around him.

Then came the expected reaction from the people. Upon seeing this miracle the crowd took Paul and Barnabas for incarnate gods. In their Lycaonian language unintelligible to the missionaries they shouted, "The gods have come down to us in human form" (v.11). Perhaps, because of his noble appearance, Barnabas was named Zeus, the king of the gods while Paul the chief speaker was called Hermes, the messenger of gods. This appellation was based on the legendary history of Lycaonia about the incarnation of Zeus and Hermes in

---

24   Cf. Cassidy, Society and Politics, 91-116.
25   Barclay's translation, Acts, 108.
26   Cf. Haenchen, Acts, 173.
27   Cf. Mt 8,10; 9,2f.22.28-29; Mk 2,5; 6,5.6; Ac 3,6-8; etc.

that region[28]. When they came, only an old peasant couple, Philemon and his wife Baucis offered them hospitality. The rest of the population was later wiped out for not receiving the gods while the hospitable couple was made the guardian of a splendid temple and upon their death, they were transformed into two great trees[29].

From this legend the Lycaonians had learnt their lesson. They must not repeat the mistake of their ancestors with its evil consequences. This time they must show their hospitality to the two gods who have again come to them in human form. So the priest of Zeus and the crowd prepare to offer a sacrifice of oxen to Paul and Barnabas. But the two rend their clothes as a sign of their horror at the blasphemy against the true God. Then with an impromptu *"nature homily"* on the goodness of the provident God, they try to stop the sacrifice.

The two missionaries address the Lystrans as "friends" and tell them that they are not gods but mortal, human beings like themselves (*homoiopatheis*) who have come with the Good News to appeal for their conversion from the heathen idols (*ton mataion*) to the true, living God (*Theon zonta*)[30], the creator of the universe and everything in it[31]. In the past generations this patient God has let the Gentiles (*ta ethne*) go their own ways without revealing himself to them as he is now doing (cf. 17,30). This fact excuses their erroneous ways of life in the past[32].

However God has left evidence of himself to the Gentiles in his many providential good deeds and gifts for human beings. He sends them rain from heaven and fruitful seasons. He fills them with food and their hearts with merriment[33]. These blessings of nature are signs of God's love and acceptance of the Gentiles.

With this down-to-earth speech the missionaries succeeded only with difficulty in dissuading the Lystrans from offering sacrifice to them. This *teras* for

---

28 Cf. Wildhaber, Paganisme Populaire, 91.
29 Cf. Barclay, Acts, 109.
30 This is a summary of Paul's preaching to the Gentiles. This is clear from Ga 4,8-9: "But formerly when you did not know God, you were kept in slavery to things which are not really gods at all, whereas now that you have come to recognise God - or rather, be recognised by God - how can you now turn back again to those powerless and bankrupt elements whose slaves you now want to be all over again? (cf. 1 Th 1,9; Ac 26,18.20).
31 God is a "Τηεον ζοντα" because he created and upholds the universe and all in it (Ac 4,24; 17,24; Ex 20,11; Ne 9,6; Ps 146,6; Rv 10,6; 14,7).
32 In Rm 1,19-20 Paul says that the Gentiles are without excuse because they should have known God through the created things.
33 Cf. Lv 26,4-5; Jr 5,24; Pss 145,16; 147,8. So this theme of God's providence is a takeover from the OT.

a lame gentile believer made a profound impression on a pagan nature-bound folk who had not yet heard of the Good News of Jesus the Son of God who created them and pours down abundant blessings on all of them. It is a very interesting incident for demonstrating God's impartial love for all peoples and for inculturating the faith among non-Jewish and christian groups. W. Barclay rightly notes that

> this passage is specially interesting because it gives us Paul's approach to those who were completely heathen and without any Jewish background to which he could appeal. With such people he started from nature to get to God who was behind it all. He started from the here and now to get to the there and then[34].

If an uncircumcised lame man who had never know anything about Jewish Law and about Jesus could have the faith to be healed or saved (*sothenai*) and was in fact miraculously healed, then the Judaizers' demands for circumcision and the observance of Mosaic Law as necessary for salvation is nothing but absurd. This is the story of the second *semeion kai teras* which Paul and Barnabas told the Jerusalem assembly in order to back up their stand and that of Peter that God had already sanctioned the reception of the Gentiles into the Christian Church without the requirements of Mosaic Law.

5.4.3   Resurrection of Paul Stoned to Death (14,19f).

This is the third recorded *semeion kai teras* narrated to the Councillors. It takes place in Lystra, a Roman colony and an outpost famous for its corn produce and corn merchants. It is again a strange occurrence and shows the shallowness of the faith of the Lystrans immersed for a long time in polytheism. It is strange because people who have just acclaimed Paul and Barnabas as gods are easily stirred up against them by some Jews from Pisidian Antioch and Iconium.

These Jews may have been treading hard on the heels of the missionaries in order to undo their work (cf. 17,1-15), or they may have come to Lystra to buy corn. Whoever they are and whatever may be their aim, those unfriendly Jews successfully arouse and incite the feeble Lystrans who immediately unleash their anger and hatred on the two evangelisers.

Paul the chief speaker is the real target and has to pay with his dear life. He is stoned to the point of death and dragged out of the city by the people who have presumed that he is dead. Paul, a Roman citizen is murdered by the

---

34   Barclay, Acts, 109.

Lystrans who must account for their crime against the Roman Empire[35]. They are afraid of Roman justice and to escape the anger of the State, they drag Paul outside the city walls. There lies Paul sorrowfully and mournfully surrounded by his helpless disciples. But at that moment he rises up and surprisingly re-enters the city of his murderers. The next day he departs from Lystra and sets out with Barnabas for Derbe.

This is a *semeion kai teras* because according to the story, the Paul who is stoned to death suddenly rises up and comes to life and continues his apostolic work and journey without any rest or any medical treament of the wounds and bruises from the stones rained down on him by the angry Lystrans. Such a de-livery from death is miraculous for it goes beyond the explanation of human reason that a person so mortally stoned can rise up immediately and resume his duty. In the narrator's view, it is only by God's power and protection that such an occurrence is possible.

The outstanding feature of this story is the sheer courage of Paul. When he came to his senses, his first act was to go right back into the city where he had been stoned... There could be no braver thing than Paul's going straight back amongst those who had tried to murder him. A deed like that would have more effect than a hundred sermons. Men were bound to ask themselves where a man got the courage to act in such a way[36].

In this way the narrator shows that this sheer courage and bravery of the "resurrected" Paul among the hostile, gentile Lystrans is certainly another sign and wonder that confirms the authenticity of the divine mission *ad gentes.*

5.4.4   Miracles as Divine Guarantee of Law-free Gentile Mission.

There may be more *semeia kai terata* not mentioned but these are three of those which Paul and Barnabas must have recounted to the Jerusalem assem-bly in order to support Peter's position and their own demand for a Gentile Church free from the burdens of Jewish Law and practices[37]. In the case of the lame man, faith alone in the Good News preached by Paul effected bodily healing for him. The narrator makes no mention of the practice of Mosaic Law and customs as the necessary condition for his cure. Only his faith has made him whole (14,9) as is also indicated in the Gospel narratives.

---

35   Note that in Ac 22,25-29 the story is told that even the the tribune, a military officer was alarmed when he relised that he had put Paul, a Roman citizen, in chains. (Cf. Edward, Acts, 373-4).
36   Barclay, op, cit., 110.
37   Cf. Weiser, Apostelkonzil, 203.

Another important point to be noted here is the fact that the narrator does not allow Paul and Barnabas to speak for themselves. Rather he assumes the role of a spokesman and an advocate while summarizing their work in terms of God's wonders and signs through their agency. This is already a type of *theological apologia* for the missionaries even before they presented their case before the not-so-friendly assembly. It is similar to the episode at Ephesus where the silversmiths rioted in opposition to the mission of Paul and his companions (Ac 19,23-40). Here, the narrator refuses Paul to make a defence for himself (vv.30-31). Instead, he choses the *unnamed* town clerk to speak on Paul's behalf, to calm down the riotous assembly and to dismiss them (vv.35.40). The same is applicable to the way in which the narrator allows Gallio the proconsul of Achaia to speak in Paul's defence while totally neglecting the Jews who accused Paul of persuading the people to worship God contrary to the Law (18,14f).

These three episodes share one thing in common: they demonstrate the favourable attitude and disposition of the Roman officials to Christianity in general, and to the Pauline, Gentile mission in particular[38]. The narrator has skilfully "*shown*" this to the reader without explicitly "*telling*"[39] or saying it to him. Finally all the miracles of Paul and Barnabas, known and unknown, are decisive evidence of the authenticity of the law-free gentile mission authorised and sanctioned by God.

---

38   This is not to say that Luke wrote the Acts for political apologetic purpose, but rather that the author shows that the christian message preached by Paul and companions does not endanger the peace and well being of the Roman Empire as some of his opponents alleged (cf. Ac 16,19ff; 17,5ff; 18,12ff; 19,23ff; 21,27ff; etc). For more on this confer, Cassidy, Society and Politics, 145-155.

39   Cf. Ska, Our Fathers, 53.

.

6. Chapter Six

Speech of James: No More Hindrance to God's Gentiles, a People Chosen for His Name (15,13-21).

6.0   Greek Text of Ac 15,13-21.

13. Meta de to sigesai autous apekrithe Iakobos legon: andres adelphoi, akousate mou.
14. Symeon exegesato kathos proton ho Theos epeskepsato labein ex ethnon laon to onomati autou.
15. kai touto symphonousin hoi logoi ton propheton kathos gegraptai:
16. meta tauta anastrepso kai anoikodomeso ten skene David ten peptokyian kai ta kateskammena autes anoikodomeso kai anorthoso auten,
17. hopos an ekzetesosin hoi kataloipoi ton anthropon ton kurion kai panta ta ethne eph' hous epikekletai to onoma mou ep' autous, legei kyrios poion tauta
18. gnosta ap' aionos.
19. dio ego krino me parenochlein tois apo ton ethnon epistrephousin epi ton Theon,
20. alla episteilai autois tou apechestai ton alisgematon ton eidolon kai tes porneias kai tou pniktou kai tou haimatos.
21. Moüses gar ek geneon archaion kata polin tous kerussontas auton echei en tais synagogais kata pan sabbaton anaginoskomenos.

6.1   Narrative and Stylistic Features of Vv.13-21.

The mission report of Paul and Barnabas about God's *semeia kai terata* is sandwiched by Peter's speech in defence of the Gentiles and the speech of James which takes up from where Peter stopped[1]. Notice once more that James refers to Peter's speech as a story about God's choice of the Gentiles as his own People (*Symeon exegesato kathos proton ho Theos epeskepsato labein ex ethnon laon to onomati autou*). The reference to Peter's tale (which precedes the report[2] of Paul and Barnabas) continues to indicate the story form of the whole episode and the unity of its plot. Let us recall that the contribution of James is the third real scene of the story (2.3.11). It is both the climax and

---

1   It is strange that James does not take up his speech from where Paul and Barnabas stopped (as is expected), but from Peter. It may be that he is "diplomatically" trying to avoid supporting outright those whose work is apparently the cause of the dispute. By taking up from Peter the head of the apostles, James is using a type of "argument from authority" to make his point to the listening assembly (cf. also Bruce, Book, 293).

2   Notice the use of the verb exegesthai in v.12 for the mission wonder story or report by Paul and Barnabas, and in v. 14 for the reference of James to Peter's mission story.

the turning point of the whole story since it is the authoritative pronouncement of James, the leader of the Jewish Church.

6.2 James and His Speech.

Who is this James of the Acts? Without the aid of other NT and ecclesial sources, the person or figure of James cannot be easily deciphered from the Acts story alone. He is first mentioned in Ac 12,17 in connection with the miraculous deliverance of Peter from prison. Upon leaving the house of Mary the mother of John Mark for an unnamed place, the Lukan Peter requested those gathered there to tell James and the *adelphoi*. This first notice of James does not tell the reader much about him, but through the mouth of Peter the narrator has shown that he is an important person.

The second mention of him is here in 15,13f where he speaks authoritatively to the first crisis assembly of the christian Church. In this scene the narrator undoubtedly highlights his prominence and leadership role. He gives the final decision in the Jewish/Gentile controversy. The third and last information about James in the Acts is during Paul's last visit to Jerusalem (21,18-25). In this scene the narrator presents James as counselling Paul on what to do in order to avoid the wrath of the myriads of Jewish believers who are "staunch upholders of the Law". As in the JC episode James is again presented in this scene as one who seeks to resolve the problem about Jewish/Gentile relationship.

But these three informations about James are too little for his leadership role in the Acts. The narrator devotes many chapters to Peter and half of the book to Paul, but only a few paragraphs to James. How can one explain this to the reader? J. Jervell attempts to propose what I also consider to be a very probable answer in view of the Acts story. He notes that while many people are merely mentioned,

the reader is not in doubt that James, in spite of the silence surrounding his position, is actually a main figure for the writer of Acts, a kind of colourless celebrity. He is the only character in Acts whose authority no one questions. At the two of the most decisive points in Luke's account, he renders the final word in a controversy. In crisis and conflict he provides answers to which all submit without objection (Chapters 15 and 21)[3].

The events of these two chapters no doubt provide the clue to the significance of James in the Acts. In this way the narrator presents him as playing a role that is "not commensurate with the silence surrounding his person, power,

---

3   Jervell, Luke, 185-186.

and priority"[4] in the Jersualem Church. In the two episodes he is used by the narrator as a principal defender of Paul and his gentile ministry.

From other NT records one learns that James is the brother (cousin) of the Lord Jesus[5], and the leader of the Church of Jerusalem[6]. James is favoured with a special personal appearance of the resurrected Lord (1 Co 15,7) and according to Paul he was one of the three pillars of the early Church (Ga 2,9)[7]. James was such good a man that later ecclesial tradition referred to him as "James the Just"[8].

His knees were said to be as hard as a camel's because he knelt in prayer so often and so long... Further - and this was all-important - he himself was a rigourous observer of the Law. If such a man should come down on the side of the Gentiles, then all was well; and he did, declaring that the disciples should be allowed into the Church without let or hindrance[9].

From the literary point of view, this speech of James has both a retrospective and prospective significance within the Acts[10]. *Retrospectively* its interpretation of Scripture justifies and confirms the missionary enterprise among the Jews and Gentiles (Ac 2-14). The achievement of this mission fulfils the prophecies about Israel and the nations. *Prospectively* the proposed decree seeks to harmonize the relationship between the Jews and the Gentiles and then goes on to introduce the section of the Acts (15,36-28) which focuses mainly on Paul's mission and also determines the course of his missionary activity (16,4)[11].

The *reading position* of the Jacobian speech can be regarded as evenhanded for both the narrator and the reader who must have read the text of Am 9,11-12, the Cornelius story of Ac 10,1-11,18 and Peter's speech (15,7-11). The narrator shows his usual omniscience by telling the reader through the mouth

---

4 Id., 187.
5 Cf. Ga 1,19; Mt 13,55; Mk 6,3.
6 Cf. Ac 12,17; 15,13; 1 Co 15,7; Ga 2,9.12).
7 The other two are Cephas (Peter) and John.
8 Eusebius, Historia, 2.23.4.
9 Barclay, Acts, 115. Cf. Bruce, Book of the Acts, 292.
10 This idea is furnished by J. Jervell, Luke, 186.
11 The scene of Ac 21,15-26 where James receives and counsels Paul is also retrospective and prospective. **Retrospectively** it refers to the concluded mission of Paul (15,36-20,17ff) and the resulting crisis of relationship between him and the Judaizers (21,20ff). Part of the solution proposed by James to Paul goes back to the apostolic decree (v.25; cf. 15,29) while **prospectively**, it introduces the concluding, apologetic section which focuses on Paul and the Jews (21,27-28,31) [cf. Jervell, Id., 186-187].

of James a series of story about the divine election of the Gentiles in both the OT and NT times.

The *form and structure* of the speech consist of three main parts: Vv.13-15: Acquiescience to the theological principles enunciated by Peter. Vv.16-18: A citation from the prophecy of Amos to backup or support the formulated theological principles. Vv. 19-21: James' proposal of practical principles for the solution of the problem of Jewish/Gentile relationship. But R. Tannehill following J. Dupont deserves praise for pointing out the stylistic peculiarity of v.16 based on the future verbs beginning with the prefix "an-".

Acts 15:16 forms a neat chiasm built around four first-person singular future verbs beginning with the prefix *an-* (see Greek text of v.16 above)... Not only do the longer interior and shorter exterior lines balance, but also the verbs are placed in balancing positions within those lines[12].

Diagramatically the "**Neat Chiasm**" is as follows:

.... an-astrepso	A
.... an-oikodomeso ten skene	B
.... ta kateskammena an-oikodomeso	B*l*
.... an-orthoso auten	A*l*

The *captatio benevolentiae* of James, "men brethren, listen to me" (v.13), is an urgent appeal by a respected leader of the Jerusalem Church to the assembly to pay attention to his decisive speech and proposal which are based on arguments drawn from Peter's speech (v. 14) and from the OT Scriptures on the divine election of the Gentiles (v.15f). The first part of his OT sources are based on the Prophets[13] and the second on the Torah[14]. This is the employment of the "literary subform, called the '*testimonia*', which strings together OT verses to illustrate a common theme"[15].

The speech has been recognised as taking the form known as *y*e*lamm*e*dhenu* (let our teacher instruct us) response, in which an appeal is made to scripture as confirming what has been said or done already and what is about to be decided[16].

---

12 Tannehill, Narrative Unity, 2, 188; cf. Dupont, ϑε ρεβατιραι, 24-25.
13 Cf. Jr 12,15; Am 9,11-12 (LXX); Is 45,21.
14 Cf. Lv 17-18.
15 Fitzmyer, Romans, 51:35, p. 839.
16 Bruce, Book, 294; cf. Bowker, Speeches, 107-109.

By means of narrative *analepsis* or flash-back[17] James uses the divine interventions of the past to justify the inclusion of Jewish law-free Gentiles in the Church. The *prophetic* teaching taken mainly from Amos is a confirmation of God's call of the Gentiles as his people. The *torah* teaching is part of the prescriptions of the "holiness code" (Lv 17-18) outlining what a devout Jew must do in order to remain uncontaminated and holy. James takes from this code four minimal requirements for the communal and commensal coexistence of Jewish and Gentile Christians.

The inexact OT citation is from the LXX Amos and not from the expected MT text with which the traditional James would have been familiar. In the LXX, "in that day" is replaced by "after this I will return" (Jr 12,15) at the beginning of the quotation, and at the end, "who does this" is replaced by "who makes this known from of old" (Is 45,21). There is in general notable variation between the MT and the LXX text from Am 9,11-12. This has led some scholars to think that the quotation may have been taken from a "christian testimonia booklet, where words from Is 45,21 were added at the end"[18]. Others suppose that it is an evidence of Lukan composition[19].

But F. F. Bruce presents what may be accepted as a good interpretation of, and the reason for, the text differences.

More striking are deviations of LXX from MT, especially in the rewording of the clause "that they may possess the remnant of Edom". The primary sense of MT is that God will restore the fallen fortunes of the royal house of David, so that it will rule over all the territory which had once been included in David's empire, not only what is left of the Edomites but also "all the nations who are called by my name". The LXX rewording involves two variant readings, but the result is a complete spiritualization of the passage: "that they may possess the remnants of Edom" becomes "that the remainder of humanity may seek" (the Lord)[20].

As the story stands, Paul is present when James makes the proposal adopted by the assembly and then promulgated as the resolution of the Council (vv.22-29). Later in Ac 21,25 one learns from the narrative that Paul is absent and only hears of the Council decision for "the first time" through James himself, -

---

17   Cf. Genette, Figures III, 77-121 [English, 33-86]; Ska, Our Fathers, 8.
18   Dillon, Acts, in: NJBC, 44:83, p. 752.
19   The presence of loan words in this speech in particular tends to support this opinion. Such words peculiar to Acts and to this speech alone are: αλισγεμα; επαναγκεσ; πνικτοσ (cf. 21,25). Also the use of the LXX text of Amos here has led some scholars to think that the Jacobian speech was not a historical report but Luke's own creation (cf. Brown et al., Der Petrus, 50-51).
20   Book, 295. For a painstaking anaylsis of the key exegetical issues of this text, cf. Kaiser, Davidic Promise, 97-111.

an event that has given rise to questions about the historical authenticity of the Council[21].

The question is, *why must James tell Paul anew about the decision of the assembly if the Apostle was really present at the deliberations?* Is that due to the supposed Lukan "historical inaccuracy" or does it give a hint on Luke's use of another historical source in the composition of this part of his work? Or is it a literary device to stress once more the cause of the controversy between Paul and the Jews on the one hand, and the Jews and Gentiles on the other?

This last alternative may be a more probable solution to the problem of the supposed "new information" which James gave to Paul about the JC decree, otherwise it is hard to imagine that Paul will be a neophite in the Gentile/Jewish question which confronted him from the period after his first missionary journey until his arrival in Rome[22].

Nevertheless it should be noted that a comparison of Ac 15,20-29 (which presents Paul as being present at the Council decision) with 21,25 (which seems to indicate his absence during the decision) continues to be a *crux* of Acts-studies[23]. Yet a careful reading of the Greek text of 21,25 which is supposed to be the "first report" of the JC decree to Paul (*"peri de ton pepisteukoton ethnon hemeis epesteilamen krinantes"*) may be a pointer to Luke's "tacit admission" that the decree was drawn up after the Council agreement to which Paul himself was a party[24].

6.3   A People for His name (Vv.13-14).

The Greek phrase *eph' hous epikekletai to onoma mou* (on whom my name is called/invoked or pronounced) translated by the LXX from the MT *('asher niqra' shemi 'alekhem, Am 9,12)* is common in the OT. Here it is the "trigger phrase" that links the thought of James to the words of Amos. In the OT usage, something called by the name of God belongs automatically to him and comes under his dominion or jurisdiction - whether cities or temples or human beings. The same is true of what man calls by name. Everything which God or

---

21   Cf. Haenchen, Acts, 470; Weiser, Apg, 368f.

22   Cf. 15,1.5; Ga 2,12f; 5,1f. Rm 2,12f for Paul's efforts to resolve this problem of Law and customs vis-a-vis the Christian Faith. His last speech to the Roman Jews (Ac 28,23f) is indicative of his non-ceasing controversies with his fellow citizens over the Jewish/Gentile issue.

23   C. K. Barrett even goes as far as asserting that the decree "was not laid down at the Jerusalem Conference" but rather "originated from the Dispersion" (cf. Apostolic Decree, 53).

24   Cf. Dillon, Acts, in: NJBC, 44:110, p. 759.

man names is owned and protected by each of them[25]. To invoke the name of God over a people is to consecrate them to him. Thus to the faithful Israel Moses promised that "the peoples of the world, seeing that Yahweh's name is pronounced over you, will be afraid of you" (Dt 28).

Therefore when James, in accord with Peter (*Symeon*)[26], recalls to the assembly that God had earlier arranged (*epeskepsato*) to take from the Gentiles (*ethnon*) a people (*laon*) for his name, he is saying that God has already called the Gentiles unto himself in the same way as he elected the Jews. The consecration of the Gentiles is an ancient event (*aph' hemeron archaion*, v.7)) testified to by the OT Prophets but revealed first (*proton*, v.14) to Peter in the NT.

Like Amos, Isaiah also speaks of the eschatological ingathering of all *nations* upon the mountain of the Lord in order to learn his ways and paths (Is 2,2-5). And Zechariah 8,20f foresees the prospect of salvation for all peoples, Jews and Gentiles alike.

Yahweh Sabaoth says this, "In the future, peoples and citizens of many cities will come; and citizens of one city will go to the next and say: We must certainly go to entreat Yahweh's favour and seek out Yahweh Sabaoth; I am going myself. Yes, many peoples and great nations will seek our Yahweh Sabaoth in Jerusalem and entreat Yahweh's favour". Yahweh Sabaoth says this, In those days ten men from nations of every language will take a Jew by the sleeve and say: We want to go with you, since we have learnt that God is with you" (8,20-23).

This divine visitation (*episkope*) and election of the Gentiles thus form the suitable basis and point of departure for every other thing which James had to say or propose to the august assembly on the Gentile question. However God's visitation of the Gentiles is made through the Jews whom he elected before the non-Jews[27].

Episkeptesthai (to visit, care for, be concerned about; pick out, select, look for) is basically a Lukan term. It is used 11 times in the NT and is found 7 times in Luke-Acts alone[28]. It can refer to the divine providential care for his creatures, or to the visit or care of someone for another[29] or the selection of a person or group to care of others (6,3).

---

25   For such cities, cf. 2 Sm 12,28; Jr 25,29; Dn 9,18. For temples, cf. 1 Kg 8,43; Jr 7,10.11.14.30; 32,34; 34,15. For men and women, cf. 2 Ch 7,14; Is 4,1; Jr 14,9; 15,16.
26   Symeon is the semitic form of Simon Peter (cf. 2 Pt 1,1) whom Paul calls Cephas (Ga 1,18; 2,9.11.14).
27   Cf. Rm 9,1f.22f; 11,1f.
28   The noun "*episkope*" is found in Lk 19,44; Ac 1,20; 1 Tm 3,1; 1 Pt 2,12.
29   Mt 25,36.43; Ac 7,23; 15,36; Jm 1,27.

In three Lukan passages, *episkeptesthai* is understood in terms of God's favourable visitation (*episkope*) of his people. At the circumcision of John the Baptist, his father Zechariah blesses God because he has visited (*epeskepsato*) his people (*laon*) and has set them free (Lk 1,68; cf. 1,78). And when Jesus restored the son of the widow of Nain to life, the astonished crowd glorified God who "*has visited his people*" by sending them a great prophet (7,16; cf. 19,44).

So then in the NT as in the OT[30], God's visitation is understood in the favourable sense of his intervention for the welfare of his people. He has visited Israel his people by sending them the Messiah Jesus as their saviour.

When used of God, 'visit' implies an absolute right of scrutiny, judgement and punishment. His interventions in the destiny of individuals or peoples can bring well being[31].

So is his intervention in the destiny of the Gentiles who turn to him. From these Gentiles it pleased God to chose a people for his name. From the pagan peoples (*tois ethnesin*) immersed in polytheism, God called a special people (*laon*) to pay him homage. It is good to note here the distinctions between *ethnos*, *ta ethne* and *laos*[32].

Ethnos generally stands for any nation or people. *Ta ethne* refers to non-Jews, Gentiles, pagans, heathens, unbelievers. *Laos* means nation, people, crowd[33], but biblically it is often used of the Jews or the Church as the people of God. At Sinai God promised Israel that they would be his chosen people (*'am segullah*) if they remain faithful to him.

You have seen for yourselves what I did to the Egyptians and how I carried you away on eagle's wings and brought you to me. So now, if you are really prepared to obey me and keep my covenant, you, out of all peoples, shall be my special possession, for the whole world is mine. For me you shall be a kingdom of priests, a holy nation (Ex 19,4-6).[34]

Later on, Deuteronomy reminds Israel of this election:

---

30   Cf. The hebrew verb for "to visit" is "paqad". For paqad in the favourable sense, cf. Gen 21,1; 50,24-25; Ex 3,16; 4,31; Ps 65,9; 80,14; Ws 3,7-13; Jr 29,10. In the sense of divine punishment cf. 1 Sm 15,2; Ws 14,11; 19,15; Jr 6,15; 23,24; Am 3,2.

31   NJB, 85, footnote, "h".

32   For more on the distinction between "*laos*" and "*ethne*", cf. Dupont, *LAOS*, 41-50; Id., Un Peuple, 321-335.; Dahl, People, 319-327.

33   *Laos* occurs 141 times in the NT and is used 36 times in Lk and 48 times in Ac (Morgenthaler, Statistik, 116). So more than half of its NT usage is found in Luke-Acts, indicating that it is a beloved Lukan term.

34   Cf. Ex 23,22 LXX; Dt 7,6; 14,2.

You are a people consecrated to Yahweh your God, and Yahweh has chosen you to be his own people from all the peoples of the earth (14,2).

Being his people they are obliged to desist from idolatorous practices and to keep his commandments (14,1; 26,18-19). Prophet Zechariah's eschatological vision makes Jerusalem the religious centre of the whole world. "And on that day many nations will be converted to Yahweh. Yes, they will become his people" (2,15). In the words of James, that day has come by the conversion of the Gentiles who have joined the faithful remnant of Israel in the final constitution of the chosen People of God.

In the Acts *laos* is usually reserved to the Jewish people but here in 15,14 it is applied to the Gentiles as also in 18,10: "I have so many people that belong to me (*laos esti moi polus*) in this city". Hence in Rm 9,24 Paul boldy tells his Gentile faithful that he and they are that *laos*, called by God "not out of the Jews but out of the Gentiles too" (*ethnon*). Then he cites some prophetic texts to prove that this call has been foretold in the OT[35].

But the election of the Gentiles has been possible because of the infidelity of the majority of the chosen people to the Law. Their failure to fulfill the demands of the Law and gain justification thereof, makes it possible for the Gentiles, who are not looking for justification by law-keeping, to gain saving justice by faith (cf. Rm 9,25f). This leads J. Dupont to believe that in the Acts, the two applications of *laos* to the Gentiles brings out its full theological force. It implies that Gentiles can be God's *laos* in the full sense that Israel is[36].

Consequently one can say that it is right and logical for the narrator of *First Peter* to extend and apply the OT divine election of Israel as a *people* to non-Jewish Christians. Like God's Israel the Gentiles are also

"*a chosen race, a kingdom of priests, a holy nation, a people to be a personal possession* to sing the praises of God" who called them "out of darkness into his wonderful light" (1 Pt 2,9)[37].

What is striking is that before their call, these Christians were "*a non-people*" "outside the pity of God" but after their call, they become "the People of God" "who have received his pity" (v.10). The extension and application of Israel's special election to the *ta ethne* have a great inculturation value for all Christians. The reader learns therefrom that without being a Jew by birth,

---

35   Cf. Ho 2,1; 2,25; Is 1,9; 10,22-23.
36   Dupont, Un Peuple, 326-329; Tannehill, Narrative Unity, 2, 187; Dahl, A People, 323.
37   Cf. Rv 5,9-10; Is 43,20-21; Col 1,12-13.

anyone who accepts the Christian faith already belongs to the chosen People of God.

In the context of the Jacobian speech, God has chosen from the Gentiles a *faithful people, a laos* who have the same privileges, rights and obligations as the people of Israel chosen since the time of their exodus from Egypt. This choice is evidenced in a special way by his call of Cornelius and his friends through Simon Peter.

Now James describes the event as God's choice of a people, using language reminiscient of God's choice of Israel according to Scripture: "God visited to take from the nations (or 'Gentiles') a people for his name". God's choice pertains not only to Peter but to a people. The events directing Peter and Cornelius to each other and the subsequent coming of the Holy Spirit have the same meanings for the Gentiles as the election of Israel has for the Jewish people. The God who chose Israel continues to act in the same way, calling a people as special possession, now from non-Israelites also. This expansion of the people of God began when Peter and Cornelius were guided to their encounter[38].

6.4 That All Gentiles May Seek the Lord Accords With Prophetic Words (Vv.15-18).

Not only does James agree with Peter's interpretation of the Cornelius event, but what both of them are teaching is in accord with the Scriptures. The call of the Gentiles is in agreement with (*symphonousin*) the words of the prophets. *Symphonein* (to agree, agree with, be in agreement with)[39] occurs only six times in the NT[40].

In Mt 18,19-20, Jesus' teaching on common prayer is, "if two of you on earth *agree* to ask anything at all, it will be granted to you by my Father in heaven. For where two or three meet in my name, I am there among them". In 20,2 the landowner makes an *agreement with* the workers for a day's wage before sending them into his vineyard (cf. v.13). But Ananias and his wife Sapphira *agree* to put the Spirit of the Lord to the test (cf.Ac 5,9).

So then people can agree to do good or evil. Their way of life can be in harmony or disharmony with set norms. In the same way two or more things can be in harmony or disharmony with each other. The same applies to the teachings of Peter and James to the Jerusalem assembly. Their teachings are not contradictory but in harmony with the Word of God.

---

38   Tannehill, op. cit., 186-187. Cf. Bruce, Book of the Acts, 293.

39   When used of cloth "symphonein" means to match, to fit together (cf. Lk 5,46).

40   It is found 3 times in Mt, 2 in Acts and once in Lk (cf. Morgenthaler, Statistik, 145).

James cites from LXX Am 9,11-12 as a proof that what he and Peter are teaching are entirely in harmony with the Holy Scriptures. The time has come for God to return (*anastrephein*) and rebuild (*anoikodomein*) the fallen house or tent of David (*skene Dauid ptokuian*)[41]. It is already noted that the LXX deviates from the original Hebrew MT and thereby spiritiualizes the prophetic text. It changes the text on the prospects of the restoration of the fallen davidic dynasty or kingdom to a text on the election of a people (*laos*) from the Gentiles (*ethnon*).

Out of a prophecy of Israel's *conquest* of the Gentiles, the LXX makes a prophecy of the *conversion* of the Gentiles. This thematic change is however in harmony with Israel's avowed mission of trying to bring the knowledge of the true God to other nations or Gentiles. And with this textual change the way is paved for James to use the text in his defence of the Gentile mission of Paul and Barnabas.

6.5   Verdict of James Places No Obstacles to Gentile Christians (V.19).

James the respected leader has heard the disputes and debates from the time of the arrival of the Antiochian delegation in Jerusalem (v.4) up to the time of the reported joint council intervention by Paul and Barnabas. He has weighed the arguments of the opposing parties and has seen that the Gentile mission is in accordance with the divine will and purpose. As a just man he cannot but give a just ruling over the Gentile question. His verdict is simple.

Since it is God's purpose to unite the Gentiles with the Jews as the one chosen people, there is no need to make things difficult for those Gentiles who turn to God: "*Ego krino me parenochlein tois apo ton ethnon epistrephousin epi ton Theon*" (v.19). The words of his judgment are well selected and demand special attention.

The verdict is an authoritative interpretation of prophetic words, a decisive statement by the powerful respected president of the first Christian "crisis assembly". The words "*ego krino*" (which emphatically evoke different aspects of "decisive judgement": *I jugde best, pass judgment on; condemn; decide, determine; consider, regard, think; prefer*) say it all. In the words of Jervell,

most remarkable is the accentuation of James' authority in the opening remark of his interpretation of scripture: *dio ego krino* (15,19): *Ego* gives prominence to James, and *krino* points to an independent decision by him. Each time this verb appears in connection with

---

41   "Skene" reminds one of the tent which David's son, Jesus the Messiah, through his incarnation pitched among all men and women (eskenosen en hemin) in order to live with them and save them (Jn 1,14).

the decree, it has the meaning "resolve, decide" (16,4; 21,25)... What is decisive for Luke is that the main responsibilty for the decree is placed on James... whose dedication to the law can not be questioned[42].

The "*ego*" reinforces the personal, authoritative and forceful nature of the Jacobian judgment (*krisis*) not to trouble the Gentiles or cause extra difficulties *(parenochlein)* to those of them who turn *(epistrephousin)* to God (cf.v.3). The verb *parenochlein* is a loan word in Acts and it obviously refers to the Petrine protest against the imposition of any yoke on the neck of the disciples *(epitheinai zugon epi ton trachelon ton mathetai,* v. 10). The difficulties in question are the legal and customary demands (vv.1.5) made by the Judaizers on the Gentile converts. With the words "*dio ego krino*", "James is now speaking as forcefully of freedom from the law as Peter!"[43].

If the Gentiles have really abandoned their idolatrous way of life and have turned back *(epistrephousin)* to God, then there is no need troubling them any more by demanding the circumcision of their males and imposing on them all the obligations of Jewish Law and custom.

Out of its 36 occurrences in the NT *epistrephein* is found 18 times in Luke-Acts (11 in Acts and 7 in Luke)[44]. So it is primarily a Lukan word/theme. In the Acts *epistrephein* (as also its noun, *epistrophe*, cf. 15,3) is used mostly in the sense of conversion and it is applied to both Jews and Gentiles who repent of their evil ways or idolatorous lives and turn to the living and true God[45].

In Ac 3,19 Peter urges the Jews to repent *(metanoesate)* and turn *(epistrepsate)* to God so that their sins may be wiped out *(eis to exaleiphthenai hymon tas harmatias)*. Peter's miraculous cure of Aeneas the paralytic leads to many conversions at Lydda and Sharon *(hoitines epestrepsan epi ton kyrion,* 9,35). In Antioch the preaching by unnamed Hellenists (Greeks) is blessed with numerous conversions to the faith *(polus te arithmos ho pisteusas epestrephen epi ton kyrion* 11,21). At Lystra Paul appeals to the natives to turn from their empty idols to the living creator God (14,15).

The effect of this turning to the true God is the forgiveness of one's sins. This is well brought out in the narrator's description of Paul's mission during his apologetic speech before King Agrippa. Paul is sent to the Gentiles

---

42   Jervell, Luke, 190-191.
43   Haenchen, Acts, 449.
44   It is used 4 times each in Mt and Mk, once in Jn, 3 times in Pauline corpus, 2 times each in Jm, Pt, and Rv. (Morgenthaler, Statistik, 100). For our purpose I shall only consider its usage in the Acts.
45   See 3,19; 9,35; 11,21; 14,15; 15,19; 26,18.20 (cf. Is 42,7.16); 28,27 (cf.Is 6,10. In the remaining three usages epistrephein refers to the motion of turning to, or back from, somebody (Ac 9,40; 15,36; 16,18).

to open their eyes so that they may turn from darkness to light, from the dominion of Satan to God, and receive through faith (in him), forgiveness of their sins and a share in the inheritance of the sanctified (Ac 26,18).

This mission is decribed in the words partly borrowed from the prophecy of Isaiah (cf. 42,7.16). The *Lukan* Paul, like the Lord Jesus who called him, is to be a light to the Gentiles (Lk 2,32; Ac 26,23). In obedience to the Lord, Paul went about preaching to the Gentiles, "urging them to repent and turn to God, proving their change of heart by their deeds" (26,20). The turning to God is preceded by repentance from evil and followed by good deeds that show that one is truly converted to the Lord.

Such is expected of every Gentile convert to the christian faith. James proposes that the Council should allow the non-Jewish converts to live as truly converted Gentile Christians, but not as converted Jews. However the Council is to send Gentiles a letter and demand from them some minimal abstinences necessary for a harmonious, living relationship with Jewish Christians.

6.6   A Letter of Abstinence to the Gentiles (V.20).

"Alla episteilai autois tou apechesthai": "But rather to write to them a letter" telling them merely to abstain from anything polluted by idols (*ton alisgematon ton eidolon*), from illicit marriages (*tes porneias*), from the meat of strangled animals (*tou pniktou*) and from blood (*tou haimatos*) (v.20).

Let us first consider the issue of letter writing in the NT before going into the contents of the letter *ad Gentes*. Outside of the Acts (15,20 = 21,25), the verb *epistellein* occurs only in Heb 13,22[46]. The JC writes to the Gentile Christians to urge them to observe certain moral norms and diatary laws for good christian living and table fellowship with Jewish Christians. So the three NT uses of *epistellein* have to do with letters written to exhort the believers to live as good Christians.

The noun *epistole* (the effect of *epistellein*) is found 24 times in the NT[47] : 2 in Pt, 5 in Ac, 17 in Pauline works. In the Acts *epistole* is used of the letters which Saul (Paul) received from the High Priest and the whole council of Elders for the synagogues in Damascus (9,2; 22,5), and of the letter which Claudius Lysias sent to the Governor Felix (23,25.33).

---

46   The author of Hebrews also writes his *adelphoi* to exhort them to good christian living.

47   Morgenthaler, op. cit., 100.

The author of 2 Pt refers to it as *deuteran (second) epistole* (3,1) which presupposes a first Petrine letter[48]. The letter tries to reawaken in the Christians the knowledge of the contents of the prophetic teachings and the command of the saving Lord given by the apostles. And in 3,16 Peter refers to Paul's writings as "letters"[49]. Together with v.15, this important witness to the NT letters need be cited.

V.15 Think of our Lord's patience as your opportunity to be saved; our brother Paul, who is so dear to us, told you this when he wrote to you with the wisdom that he was given. V.16. He makes this point too in his letters as a whole (*en pasais epistolais*) wherever he touches on these things. In all his letters there are of course some passages which are hard to understand, and these are the ones that uneducated and unbalanced people distort, in the same way as they distort the rest of scripture - to their own destruction.

From the usage of *epistole* in the NT one finds that it is a means of giving official information to a ruler (Ac 23,25), a means of instructing either the Jewish faithful living far away from their religious leaders (Ac 9,2; 22,5) or as a means of instructing Christians far removed from their pastors as is evident in the Pauline, Petrine and other apostolic letters.

The letters are of three types (a) informatory (b) mandatory and (b) exhortatory or a combination of the two or all of the three together. This is well attested to in the Pauline letters which at the same time inform, encourage and admonish the faithful to authentic christian life. Some citations from the *Second Thessalonians* buttress this view:

"Stand firm, then, brothers, and keep the traditions that we taught you, whether by word of mouth or by letter (2,16)". "My brothers, never slacken in doing what is right. If anyone refuses to obey what I have written in this letter, take note of him and have nothing to do with him, so that he will be ashamed of himself, though you are not to treat him as an enemy, but correct him as a brother (3,13-15)"[50].

The contents of the *epistole* of the abstinence proposed by James to the assembly bear the stamp of a religious prohibtion, an admonition and a legal facilitation for the Gentile Christians. But the prohibitory aspect of the Jacobian clause seems to carry more weight as indicated by *apechesthai*[51] (to ab-

---

48   Cf. 1 Pt 1,1; 5,12.
49   Internal evidence from the pauline works refer to them as letters written either by Paul himself or by his assitants (cf. Rm 16,22; I Co 5,9; 16,3; 2 Co 7,8; 10,9-11; Col 4,16; 1 Th 5,27; 2 Th 2,2.15; 3,14.17).
50   Cf. 1 Pt 2,11f for a similar epistolary style. These are only two of the many examples.
51   In the NT *apechesthai* is used 6 times: Ac 15,20.29; 1 Th 4,3; 5,22; 1 Tm 4,3; 1 Pt 2,11. It is interesting that in the entire Luke-Acts, this prohibitory middle voice of the

stain from, avoid, keep free *from something*) which is the middle voice of the verb *apechein*. The prohibitions have both ritual and moral implications. To this effect the *NJB* comments:

> The ritual exceptions mentioned by James show clearly the sort of thing that was at issue and answer the question asked in Ac 11,3 and Ga 2,12-14: what gentile Christians must do for Judaeo-Christians to mix with them without incurrring legal impurity. James decides to keep only those prescriptions for purity that have a fundamentally religious meaning[52].

It is indeed surprising that James who in v.19 does not want to put obstacles to the Gentile Christians now turns in v.20 with a series of demands on them. However,

> the adversative connection of this to "trouble" (v.19), and the reprise of vv.10-11 in 19, demonstrate that the "decree" is a concession rather than an imposition, making common life and table possible without laying any onus on the newcomers[53].

The four prescriptions seem to be based on the Torah prohibitions made for Israel and the aliens resident among them (Lv 17-18). They form part of what is now known as the "*holiness code*" (17,1-26,46) because of the emphasis of this section on the *holiness* of Yahweh[54]. It is a compilation and codification of the earlier ritual and ethical laws. Yahweh's holiness forms the basis and model for the holiness of the people of Israel. In every aspect of their lives, they are to be holy as Yahweh is holy (Lv 19,2; 20,26). This holiness of life transcends mere *legal purity* and embraces *moral rectitude*. The holiness code also lays emphasis on the sacredness of blood (17,1-16), on sexual matters (18,1-30) and on priestly sanctity (21,1-24).

But the focus here is on the prescriptions parallel to the Jacobian four, mininal demands which the Gentile Christians must observe in order to gain access to the community of the chosen people kept sacred by the holiness code. These are the abstentions from strangled meat (17,15), from blood (17,10ff), from incest or sexual intercourse with blood relations (18,6ff). Abstention from idol meats goes back to the Decalogue (Ex 20,3f; 34,15). If the Gentiles faithfully observe these minimal but necessary requirements, then Israel can freely and reciprocally intermingle and celebrate with them without any fear of incurring ritual uncleanliness.

---

verb *"apechein"* (= receive in full, have back; be distant) is used twice only with reference to the Jacobian clause.

52 New Jerusalem Bible, 1825, footnote "v".
53 Dillon, Acts, in: NJBC, 44:83, p. 752.
54 Cf. Dt 12-26 for a similar holiness code.

6.6.1 Abstention from Pollutions of Idols (V.20).

The abstention from the pollutions of idols (*ton alisgematon ton eidolon*) is the first commandment of the Decalogue. Yahweh forbids Israel to worship or serve the false gods of other nations (Ex 20,3-6). Such a worhip is compared to prostitution[55]. This is equally the *first* prohibtion for the Gentile converts. They are to abstain from (*apechesthai*) the pollutions or defilements or contaminations of idols. *Alisgema* means "something polluted or defiled", a loan word occuring only in this verse. Its plural "*alisgemata*" means "things polluted or defiled". Barrett notes that

> *Alisgema* is a rare word. The noun does not occur in the LXX; the cognate verb, *alisgein*, occurs very seldom, but always in the sense of defilement incurred by idolatory, at least by contact with paganism. The phrase was probably taken by the author of Acts to be very nearly, perharps quite, synonymous with *eidolothuta* (food offered to idols)[56], but its effect is to make clearer that the essential concern is to avoid any contact with idolatory[57].

So the defilements from idolatrous practices are referred to as "pollutions of idols". If *alisgema* is a loan word[58], *eidolon* is not because it occurs twice in Acts and is used 11 times in the NT. The problem of eating food or meat offered to idols and the defilement that may be incurred by a Christian who eats of it, is an important theme of Paul in 1 Corinthians and Romans[59]. He lays down general principles of conduct for the Christians who are divided over the question of eating or not eating the meat offered to idols[60] (*eidolothuta*, 8,1).

At that time in the Corinthian community, when a heathen sacrificed to the gods, part of the food or meat went to the priests and part to the offerer to make a "sacred meal" for his friends either in the temple precincts or in his own house. The rest was sold in the markets or shops for ordinary use. This obviously created problems for the Gentile Corinthian converts whose new faith stood in opposition to any form of contaminations with pagan deities. Should they as Christians continue to eat food offered to idols or not?[61]

---

55 Cf. Ex 34,15; Ezk 16; 23; Ho 1-3; Rv 17.

56 The words in brackets are inserted by me.

57 Barrett, Apostolic Decree, 51-52.

58 Its cognates are: *eidolon* 11 times; *eidolothuton*, 9 times; *eidololatres*, 7 times; *eidololatria*, 4 times. Prohibition against idols and idolatory is a principal OT theme (cf. Ex 20,3-5; 32,1f; Lv 19,4; Dt 4,15f; 5,7f; 1 Kg 18,20f; Is 10,10f; 44,9f; Jr 2,26f; Ps 115,4-8 etc).

59 Cf. 1 Co 8 and 10; Rm 14-15.

60 Instead of the word *alisgema*, Paul uses *eidolothuton* (Co 8,1) as is in Ac 15,29. Their similarities and differences shall be discussed in the next chapter.

61 Cf. Barclay, Acts, 116.

Paul came in to resolve this dilemma. In *principle* there should be no compromise with idolatory, hence sacrificial meat and feasts must be avoided at all costs (1 Co 10,14). But in *practice* a Christian can freely eat what an unbeliever presents to him/here without qualms of conscience (10,26). Also the *eidolothuta* sold in butchers' shops can be bought and eaten by a Christian with thanksgiving to God, provided that such an act does not give scandal to the conscience and life of another Christian (vv.25.28).

Therefore the Christian must *"never be the cause of offence, either to Jews or to Greeks or to the Church of God"* (v.32). So then the principle that the Christian must abstain from all pollutions of idols remains valid at all times.

6.6.2 Abstention from Sexual Immorality (V.20).

Second, the Gentile converts are to keep away from *porneia* which is variously translated as illicit marriage[62], fornication, incest (1 Co 5,1), unchastity, sexual immorality. Which of these then suits the context of the Jacobian proposal? If it is understood in the light of Lv 18, *porneia* will correspond to the hebrew term "*zenut*" or incestuous fornication[63]. In the NT *porneia* occurs 25 times and refers mainly to "sexual immorality"[64]. But in 1 Co 5,1 *porneia* means *incest*:

> It is widely reported that there is sexual immorality (*porneia*) among you, immorality (*porneia*) of a kind that is not found even among gentiles (*ethnesin*): that one of you is living with his stepmother.

But if, according to Paul, *porneia* as incest is not found even among the Gentiles, then there is no need for James to propose that the Gentiles abstain from it. This implies that *porneia* in the Jacobian speech may be referring not just to incest but to sexual immorality among the Gentiles.

In *First Thessalonians*, *porneia* as sexual immorality is clearly brought out in Paul's exhortation of the people to holiness and purity. The same verb (*apechesthai*) used by James to urge the Gentile converts to abstain from sexual immorality, is also employed by Paul in his exhortation to the Thessalonians to purity and holiness of life.

---

62 In the context of Lv 18, porneia refers to incestuous marriages considered illicit, but since neither *porneia* nor its cognate appears in this chapter, it may not be proper to translate *porneia* here as "illicit marriage" as th NJB does (cf. p. 1825, footnote, "u").
63 Cf. Dillon, Acts, 44:83, p.752.
64 It can be translated as unfaithfulness in Mt 5,32; 19,9.

God wills you all to be holy. He wants you to keep away from sexual immorality (*apechestai hymas apo tes porneias*), and each one of you to know how to control his body in a way that is holy and honourable, not giving in to selfish lust like the nations (*ta ethne*) who do not acknowledge God (1 Th 4,3-5).

Furthermore, the verb *porneuein* means "to commit sexual immorality", while a *porne* is a "prostitute", usually a prostitute in a holy place. It is then evident that

> *Porneia* is an obstinately ethical word. The family of words to which it belongs denotes various aspects of prostitution... In addition to the simple meaning of dealings with a prostitiute (e.g. Gen 38,24) it could be used as a metaphor for unfaithfulness to God (e.g. Jer 3,2.9), so that to some extent it doubles with idolatory[65].

The *Torah* forbids sexual intercourse between blood relatives. It strictly forbids the Jew to marry, or have sexual intercourse with one's mother, other wife of one's father, a sister, a mother's sister, an aunt, a daughter-in-law, a sister-in-law (Lv 18,6-16) or a mother-in-law (Dt 27,23). Lv 18,21 condemns adultery as an instance of ritual impurity. V.22 condemns homosexualism as "*a hateful thing*", while v.23 forbids sexual relationships with animals (*bestiality*). Such an evil practice renders one unclean before God and draws down divine punishment on the offender (vv.24-25).

Scholars uphold the view that the Jacobian demand for abstention from *porneia* is referring to the levitical prohibition[66]. On the basis of Lv 18, *porneia* can mean the sexual immorality of incest (vv.6-16) or adultery (v.21), or homosexuality (v.22) or bestiality (v.23), and not just incest alone. However the long list of forbidden incestuous unions tends to support the understanding of *porneia* as incest or marriages within the forbidden degrees of kindred[67]. Since James says that his motion is a necessary requisition from the Gentile Christians to facilitate their social relationship with Jewish Christians, then the Gentile converts must do away with their incestuous unions if they are to belong to the same people of God as Israel.

It is true that the mention of *porneia* as a specific type of sexuality disturbs the sequence of the *dietary* ruling laid down by James. Nevertheless the command to refrain from *porneia* sets the moral tone of that dietary prescription. Therefore, it may not be contextually right to regard the Jacobian proposal as a merely ritual ruling for the Gentile Christians. It is equally a demand for moral

---

65   Barrett, Apostolic Decree, 52.
66   See the reference to Lv 17-18 as a parallel reference text for the Jacobian clause in the Nestle-Aland greek text, Novum Testamentum, 366.
67   Cf. Omanson, Gentile Palaver, 279--280. Strack-Billerbeck, Kommentar, 1, 694; 2, 376 & 729.

rectitude and sanity among the Gentile Christians. Just as abstinence from incestuous union is binding on every Jew, so also is the Gentile convert bound by such a prohibition. In a gentile world of sexual immorality, the Christian convert is required to avoid strictly every form of sexual promiscuity that militates against the virtues of his/her calling.

6.6.3   Abstention from Strangled Meat (V.20).

The third requisition for Gentiles is abstention from the meat of a strangled animal (*tou pniktou*). This demand is also based on OT/Jewish dietary laws which forbid the eating of the blood[68] of an animal. In the whole of the NT, the adjective *pniktos* occurs only three times in the Acts (15,20.29; 21,25) - and all in the context of the Jacobian provisions. It is a very technical and unfamiliar word derived from the verb *pnigein* (to choke, strangle, suffocate)[69] which is also found only thrice in the NT[70].

Pnigein is used for the *drowning* of the pigs possessed by unclean spirits from the Gerasene demoniac (Mk 5,13). Jesus uses it in the context of the parable of the seeds to describe the *choking* of the seeds which fell and germinated among thorns (Mt 13,7). It also describes the cruel act of the unforgiving debtor-servant who seized his fellow-debtor-servant on the throat and began to *throttle* him to pay his debt (18,28). From the NT usage of the verb, it becomes easy to infer the full meaning of *to pnikton*, namely: what is strangled or throttled or suffocated or choked. The plural *ta pnikta* then means "things strangled".

Many scholars have subscribed to the interpretation of *ta pnikta* in terms of the prescription of Ex 22,30:

You must be people consecrated to me. You will not eat the meat of anything in the countryside savaged by wild animal (*basar basadeh terepah lo' to'khelu*); you will throw it to the dogs[71].

---

68   Cf. Gen 9,4; Lv 17,10.13; Dt 12,16.23-25.
69   In the LXX *pnikton* does not occur at all, but *pnigein* occurs only in 1 Sm 16,14.15 where it is used of the evil spirit that afflicted *(ba'at)* King Saul. In Si 51,4 *pnigmos* is used of the stifling heat of fire.
70   Cf. Morgenthaler, Statistik, 133.
71   Josephus, Antiquities, 3.260 defines *pnikton* as "*kreos tou tethnekotos automatos zoou ten brosin diekolusen*". Strack and Billerbeck say that *pnikton* "befasst beides unter sich, sowohl was das AT (OT) nebelah, als auch was es terepah nennt" (Kommentar, 2.2730).

In rabbinic usage *nebelah* refers to any beast which is not subjected to the process of correct ritual slaughtering (*sehitah*) while *terepah* refers to any beast, dead or alive with a disqualifying blemish[72]. In *De Specialibus Legibus* Philo condemns people who

> desire novel kinds of pleasure and prepare meat unfit for the altar (*athuta*) by strangling and throttling (*agchontes kai apopnigontes*) the animals (*4.122*).

It is then clear that both the Jewish Torah and religious tradition are opposed to the stangling of animals for meat. But in the Levitical prescription,

> anyone, whether Israelite or resident alien, who hunts and catches game, whether animal or bird, which it is lawful to eat, must pour out its blood, and cover it with earth. For the life of every creature is its blood, and I have told the Israelites: You will not consume the blood of any creature, for the life of every creature is its blood, and anyone who consumes it will be outlawed (Lv 17,13-14, cf.vv.10-12).

Thus the law against the strangulation of an animal for food is based on the fact that its blood is its life, and if that blood is not drained away, it is like eating it alive and consuming its life which belongs to God alone (cf.Lv 17,10). If any Jew who ate such a stangled animal was outlawed, so should a Gentile who enters into a relationship with a Jew by becoming a member of a Christian Church originally considered as a Jewish sect of the Nazarenes (cf. Ac 24,5). Therefore the meat of a stangled animal must not be eaten by both races because its blood has not been (ritually) drained away. The Gentile Christian must kill and eat an animal in a Jewish way so as to have fellowship with a Jewish Christian.

6.6.4   Abstention from Blood (V.20).

This is the fourth and last demand of the Jacobian motion. *Haima* occurs 97 times in the NT. It is the LXX translation of the MT Hebrew word, *dam* (plural, *damim*) which means blood, bloodshed or murder. As "*bloodshed*", *haima* can be equated with the rabbinic *sepikut damim* which regulary forms a trio with *abhodah zarah* (idolatory) and *gilluy karayot* (incest).

Primarily *haima* is that red fluid which flows in the veins and arteries of human beings and animals. Here it refers to animal blood[73] which must be drained off and poured away when the animal is slaughtered for food. Blood is

---

72   Cf. Strack-Billerbeck, Kommentar, 2.730-734
73   For this reason we limit our brief study to biblical/Jewish attitude to the blood of animals.

the life of every animal and the loss of blood means the loss of life. The consumption of blood is strictly and explicitly forbidden by the OT, especially by the Torah. To Noah God gives this pre-Abrahamic ruling or law,

> Every living thing that moves will be yours to eat, no less than the foliage of the plants. I give you everything, with this exception: you must not eat flesh with life, that is to say blood, in it (Gen 9,4).

This precept is repeated in the Levitical sacrifical rules:

> Wherever you live, you will never eat blood, whether it be of bird or of beast. Anyone who eats any blood will be outlawed from his people (Lv 7,26-27).

In Lv 17,10-12 this rule is expanded to embrace both Jews and resident aliens (cf. vv.13-14):

> If any member of the House of Israel or any resident alien consumes blood of any kind, I shall set my face against that individual who consumes blood and shall outlaw him from his people. For the life of the creature is in the blood, and I have given it to you for performing the rite of expiation on the altar for your lives, for blood is what expiates for a life. That is why I told the Israelites: None of you will consume blood, nor will any resident alien consume blood.

In the context of sacrifice Deuteronomy tightens the rule by stressing that abstention from blood must be carefully and meticulously observed (Dt 12,15-16.23-24). So *dam* or *haima* is "life" and has an expiatory power and must not be eaten by anyone who simply kills an animal for food or offers it in sacrifice. This is an irrevocable divine ruling in the Torah, the most respected part of the OT. In later Judaism up to the time of Jesus, the abstention from blood remained in force according to the prescriptions of the Torah[74].

From the perspective of the holiness code, the Jacobian proposal to abstain from blood does not strictly deal with matters of faith and practice but mainly concerns ritual and moral demands to facilitate social relationship between Jews and Gentiles. Nevertheless the abstention from *alisgema* and *porneia* argues for matters of faith and morals as part of the *minimal demands* of the Torah and the Prophets[75].

---

74 Against this background one can then understand the reason for the big dispute that arose between Jesus and the Jews when he taught that his blood (*dam* or *haima*) is true drink. For this unbearable teaching many of his disciples abandoned him for ever (cf. Jn 6,60-61.66).

75 Cf. Ex 20,3f; Lv 19,4; Dt 4,15-20; 5,7f; Ho 13,2f; Is 44,9ff; Jr 2,26-28; 10,11ff; etc.

6.7 No More Disputes over Moses (V.21).

If the assembly were to accept the Jacobian motion, there should be no more commotion over Moses (= *hattorah*), and there should be no need for imposing the observance of the Mosaic *ethos* on the Gentiles. On every Sabbath, Moses is read aloud and preached in all the synagogues in the Jewish and Gentile environments. He has had enough preachers to proclaim his Law or custom in all towns[76]. This had been an age old practice (*ek geneon archaion*).

So there is no need to make a legislation on the Mosaic *ethos* for Gentiles who must have regulary heard of it in their various localities. The universal proclamation of Mosaic *ethos* had for long ensured the influence of the Torah among the Gentiles, and in this way it has partly supplemented for the demands being made by the Judaizers on the Gentiles.

The believers from the Pharisaic sect who zealously want to enforce the teaching of the whole Torah among the Gentiles should therefore calm down, because neither is the Jacobian proposal detrimental to Israel's mission *ad Gentes*, nor does the Mosaic tradition suffer any loss if it does not obtain the allegiance of those who had never kept it from the time of its promulgation[77].

One may infer from this v.21 that James is stressing that to continue to bother the Gentiles about the Jewish Law so well entrenched among them for many ages, is quite absurd and uncalled for. One is also tempted to think that James is trying to tell the assembly that the Gentiles have the prophets or preachers in the synagogues to tell them all about Mosaic Law or customs. If they fail to listen to what they are preaching neither will they practice what they have been taught even if someone should rise from the dead and force them to do so (cf. Lk 16, 27-31).

6.8 Significance of the Jacobian Speech.

Three things are especially significant in the speech: *First*, the question of circumcision of the male Gentiles is never mentioned by James. In this way the demand of the *tines apo tes Ioudaias* (15,1) is totally neutralized and nullified through neglect and silence by a highly respected "pillar" of the Jerusalem Church. Like the speakers before him, circumcision is a "*none theme*" for James. *Secondly*, it is an authoritative judgemental speech that wins the approval of the opposing parties to the dispute. The *third* is his use of the text of

---

76   Cf. Schwartz, Futility of Preaching Moses, 276-280.
77   Cf. Bruce, Book, 296.

LXX Amos 9,11-12 to support his *thesis* of God's election of the Gentiles as a people for his name.

One cannot overestimate the significance of the Jacobian use of what may be described in scholarly circles as the "*corrupt text of Amos*" to convince the contentious orthodox Christian Pharisees that God had long ago elected the Gentile Christians and sanctioned their integration with the chosen Jewish race into the one People of God.

This "corrupt text" is the *LXX Amos* which has wrongly translated the prophecy of Amos from the Hebrew MT, and in so doing, converts an oracle on the restoration of the royal house of David to a prophecy on the divine election of a people for his name from the Gentiles. The resultant spiritualized LXX links up christology with mission.

> The rebuilt Davidic house is the ground upon which the rest of men may seek God. Gentiles who are called by God's name may come. Acts 15,11 describes the offer of salvation as coming through the grace of the Lord Jesus in Peter's remarks, to which James adds assent with his citation of Amos. James regards this text as fulfilled in the current activity of the Church... He is also portrayed as citing a particulary hellenistic version of the passage, possibly to show good will, as well as to make use of a particulary explicit text where christiology and mission are placed in one locale[78].

From the perspective of the informed reader, it is astonishing that *James the Just*, a strict orthodox Judaist, would dare to quote from an *incorrect* prophetic text of the LXX Amos[79] (instead of citing from the authoritative Hebrew MT) in order to pass a critical but an acceptable judgement on the disputed Gentile question. In doing so he "canonizes" the *wrong* LXX translation which eventually becomes, so to say, a "*felix culpa*" that justifies and gives divine backing to the admittance of the Gentiles into the Church without requiring them to carry on the burden (*zugon*) of having their males circumcised or to observe the Jewish *ethos* outside those four proposed by James.

Whatever may be the arguments for or against the use of the LXX Amos, the fact remains that James did have his way because his verdict was immediately welcomed by all present at the Council (Ac 15,22).

---

78   Bock, Use of the OT, 508.
79   This is one of the points used by scholars to argue that the speech is put into the mouth of James by Luke. That is, Luke composed the speech attributed to James (cf. Haenchen, Acts, 459).

7. Chapter Seven.

Inspired Letter with a Decree: No Unnecessary Yoke On Gentile Brothers (15,22-29).

7.0 Greek Text of the Letter (Vv.22-29).

22. Tote edoxe tois apostolois kai tois presbyterois syn hole te ekklesia eklexamenous andras ex auton pempsai eis Antiocheian syn to Paulo kai Barnaba, Ioudan ton kaloumenon Barsabban kai Silan, andras hegoumenous en tois adelphois,

23. graphentes dia cheiros auton: "Hoi apostoloi kai hoi presbyteroi adelphoi tois kata ten Antiocheian kai Syrian kai Kilikian adelphois tois ex ethnon chairein.

24 Epeide ekousamen hoti tines ex hemon exelthontes etaraxan hymas logois anaskeua-zontes tas psychas hymon hois ou diesteilametha,

25. edoxen hemin genomenois homothymadon eklexamenois andras pempsai pros hy-mas syn tois agapetois hemon Barnaba kai Paulo,

26. anthropois paradedokosi tas psychas auton hyper tou onomatos tou kyriou hemon Iesou Christou.

27. apestalkamen oun Ioudan kai Silan kai autous dia logou apangellontas ta auta.

28. edoxen gar to pneumati to hagio kai hemin meden pleon epitithesthai hymin baros plen touton ton epanankes,

29. apechesthai eidolothuton kai haimatos kai pnikton, kai porneias, ex hon diaterountes heautous eu praxete. Errosthe".

7.1 Textual Criticism of the Decree (V.29).

Acts is particulary notable for the divergence between the so-called Old Uncial text (represented by, for example, **B** and **aleph**) and the so called Western text (represented by **D** and **E**, the OLd Latin, and the margin of the Harclean Syriac). Perharps the most notori-ous divergence between these two text types is found in the Apostolic Decree of 15,29[1]. The two forms of the Decree are often referred to as the ceremonial, or cultic (that of the Old Uncial), and ethical (the Western)[2].

This observation by C. K. Barrett may perharps serve as a very appropriate insight to the textual problem of the decree of the Apostolic Letter. The Greek text of B reads: "*apechesthai eidolothuton kai haimatos kai pnikton kai porneias, ex hon diaterountes heautous eu praxete*". This is exactly the same

---

1   Compare this verse with 15,20 and 21,25. Cf. Barrett, Apostolic Decree, 58, footnote, 1.

2   Barrett, Id., 50. This footnote embraces all in *1* and *2* of this paragraph.

reading in the current *Nestle-Aland, "Novum Testamentum Graece"*. The text of D reads: *apechesthai eidolothuton kai haimatos kai porn[e]ias, hosa me thelete heautois ginesthai hetero me poiein aph' hon diaterountes heautous eu praxete pheromenoi en to hagio pneumati.*

The two texts are different and so require some comparison and comment for a better understanding of the decree. First the *pnikton* of **Codex B** is omitted in **Codex D** which in turn contains some additions and expansions not seen in **B**.

These additions in **D** are: The negative form of the Golden Rule, *"kai hosa me thelete heautois ginesthai hetero me poiein"* (Do not do to another what you will not have done to youselves). This is a simple but an important distillation, not only of "the Law and the Prophets", not only of Jewish and Christian morality, but also, of morality in general[3]. The *"Pheromenoi en to hagio pneumati"* implies first, that one needs the assistance of the Holy Spirit to fulfil even such an elementary command for christian life, and secondly that the christian life requires spiritual direction[4].

These two text variants also differ from the draft of the decree proposed by James in 15,20 where *porneia* comes before *pnikton* and *haima* and *alisgematon ton eidolon* is used in place of *eidolothuton* (v.29).

The omission of *pnikton* from codex **D** is said to have created some changes in the meaning of the decree. First, it removes the explicit reference to the improper slaughtering of an animal for meat in accordance with the OT law and later Jewish legislation. Second, it changes the sense of *haima* from the "slaughtered animal blood" to *bloodshed* by infliction of injury and above all through *murder*. Third, it sets a moral tone to the decree[5]. From this, one may deduce that in the text of **D**, the decree forbids even the mildest form of idolatory, bloodshed and fornication (*porneia*), but enjoins the practice of the Golden Rule which one can achieve with the help of the Holy Spirit. Consequently Acts-research tends to support the view that the text of **D** or the later Western text is *ethical*, while the original **B** or Old Uncial[6] text is *ceremonial*.

But from the language of what is considered as the original text itself, I prefer to state that the decree has both moral and ceremonial overtones and imports because three of what the Genitles are required to avoid (*eidolothuton,*

---

3   Cf. Mt 7,12; Lk 6,31; Rm 13,8-10; and in OT: Tb 4,15.

4   Cf. Barrett, op. cit. 50-51.

5   Cf. Boman, Das textkritische Problem, 27f; 31f.

6   Following one of the rules of textual criticism that the "shorter text is earlier than the longer text", scholars have regarded the longer and more expanded *D text* as being later than the shorter and therefore original *B text*.

haima, porneia) for the sake of commensality with the Jews are also proscribed by the moral precepts of the Decalogue[7].

7.2 Narrative and Stylistic Features of Vv.22-29.

Here begins the fourth real scene and the resolution (*Auflösung*) of the plot of our story (2.3.12). There is a change of time indicated by "then" (*tote*); a change of characters: from James alone to *all who are present*; a change of action: from James talking to a listening (perhaps skeptical) *andres adelphoi* (v.13) to an assembly deciding unanimously (*homothymadon*, v.25) on the gentile question; a total change of attitude: from a negative posture towards Gentile Christians to giving them a hand of fellowship as *adelphoi* (v.23), and finally a practical change of subject: from the plea not to burden the Gentiles to the concrete action of lifting up any unncessary burden (*baros*) from them.

Thus this narrative unit shows that the speech of James did bring some harmony within the rank and file of the assembly of apostles, elders and the whole Church (v.22). Its effect is comparable to Peter's speech (vv.7-11). It is a speech of plot-resolution or "*peripeteia*" which here produces the reverse action engendered by the reconciliatory four-point motion. The initial tension begins to ease off as the assembly acquiesces to the proposal and agrees to use it as a "working paper" for the resolution[8] (at least temporarily) of the Jewish/Gentile problem at hand.

The omniscient narrator's voice rings and sounds throughout this narrative unit. He starts afresh to tell the reader what has already taken place in Antioch and Jerusalem and what he retells is known both to the characters and readers of the story. He accompanies them, sees, hears, perceives and feels with them. He is telling the events of the scene from internal point of view or "internal focalization"[9]. The reading position of this unit is evenhanded, because in vv.20-21, the narrator has already notified the reader about the basic contents of Letter and its recipients.

---

7   Cf. Ex 20,3-5.13.14.
8   Cf. Ska, Our Fathers, 27.
9   This is one of the three major angles of vision or focalizations in telling a story. The other two are "vision from without" or external focalization and "vision from behind" or zero focalizazion [cf. Genett, Figures III, 205-207; Id., Nouveau Discours; 43.52; (English, 186-190); Ska Our Fathers, 66-67].

7.3 Structure of the Letter.

The structure of this Letter should be carefully noted by the attentive reader. Preceded by the resolution to send the Letter through selected delegates (vv.22-23a) its structure follows the ancient Hellenistic Letter form which consists of three major parts typical of the contemporary, Graeco-Roman letters: The *Opening Formula* or the *praescriptio* (v.23b), which is an elliptic sentence that gives "the name of the sender (nominative case), the addressee (dative case) and a short greeting (usually *chairein*, an infinitive with the stereotyped meaning, 'Greetings!')"[10]; the *Message* (24-28), which is the body of the letter; the *Final Greeting*, usually *erroso* (plural *errosthe*) which means goodbye or farewell (v.29). Its latin equivalent is *vale, valete*[11]. Thus scholars affirm that the prescript of the Letter is in keeping with Hellenistic letters and with the literary style of a historian influenced by Hellenistic convention[12].

A further breakdown of the three main parts of this Letter are: the senders of the Letter with its opening greeting (v.23b); the statement of its occasion (v.24); the mention of the four delegates Paul, Barnabas, Judas Barsabbas and Silas (vv.25a.27); official recognition and praise of the missionary witness of Paul and Barnabas (vv.25b-26); the decision to impose only necessary burden on Gentile Christians made in union with the Holy Spirit (v.28); the decree of four abstentions and exhortation to observe them (v.29a); the closing greeting (v.29b). Thus the decree (which is the most important statement of the letter) is placed not at its beginning but at its end. The exegetical study of this pericope follows the outline of the Letter.

7.4 Decision to Send Ambassadors to Antioch (v.22-23a).

The motion of James has commended itself to the assembly of the apostles and elders and it seems acceptable to the whole (Jerusalem) Church. So they resolve to select and send to Antioch, two Christian leaders, Judas Barsabbas and Silas. These will go along with Paul and Barnabas[13] and report the decisions of the Council to the Gentile Church. What then is the profile of each of these two "leading (*hegomenous*) men among the brothers?" (v.22).

---

10 Fitzmyer, J. A., Introduction, in: NJBC, 45:6, p. 769.
11 Cf. Id., ibid. For similar final greetings confer, 2 Mac 16,21.33.38.
12 Cf. Dillon, Acts, in: NJBC, 44:84, p.752.
13 Paul and Barnabas are chosen by the Holy Spirit as missionaries to the Gentiles (AC 13,2-4). Their role as protagonists of law-free gentile Christians is obvious in the Acts (cf. 9,26f; 11,27f; 12,25; 13-14; 15,12.36f). So we need not repeat the description of their profile here.

In the Acts *Judas Barsabbas* is mentioned only in the context of this ecclesial embassy to Antioch (15,22.27.32). And so not much is known about him
from the NT. His other name Barsabbas has led some to think that he may
have been the brother of Joseph Barsabbas (1,23) and may also have been one
of the leaders of the Hebrew group of the Jerusalem Church (6,1). But there is
no evidence to support these suppositions. The narrator only says that Judas is
one of the leaders of the Christian Church (15,22) and a "prophet" (v.32). This
is the much the reader knows of him.

More is known about the co-delegate *Silas* who is mentioned 12 times in
the Acts. Like Judas, he is a prophet (Ac 15,32) and an important missionary
companion of Paul (15,40-18,5). After the sharp disagreement that separated
Paul and Barnabas (15,37-39), Paul choses Silas to accompany him in his second missionary journey (v.40). At Lystra Paul recruits Timothy as another
(second) companion. While at Philippi, Silas and Paul are flogged and imprisoned (16,19ff), but are miraculously delivered and set free (v.35f) by the
frightened magistrates on account of their Roman citizenship (v.37f).

Leaving Philippi, Silas goes to mission with Paul in Thessalonica (17,1ff)
and in Beroea (vv.10ff) from where the *adelphoi* escort Paul to Athens while
Silas and Timothy stay back in Beroea (v.14) with the hope to rejoin Paul later
at Athens (v.15). However they rejoin him at Corinth and help him in evangelizing the city (18,5ff).

Sacred Tradition and biblical scholars identify Silas with the *Silvanus* mentioned in the Pauline corpus and in a Petrine letter[14]. If this is true, then Silas
is the one who, in the company of Paul and Timothy, proclaimed the Lord Jesus Christ to the Corinthians (2 Co 1,19). He is one of the *"trio"* who sent two
letters to the Thessalonians (1 Th 1,1; 2 Th 1,1), and he is the *"trustworthy
brother"* and scribe of *First Peter* (5,12). So these NT letters, like the Acts,
present Silas as a Christian Leader[15], a prophet, a devoted missionary preacher
and an apostolic writer. In the phraseology of the Letter to the Hebrews, the
four delegates chosen by the JC are some of those examplary Christian Leaders whose life, faith and preaching are worthy of emulation (13,7.17).

What is evident from v.22 is that Paul, Barnabas, Judas and Silas are well
qualified and equipped to carry the Council's Letter to the Christians of gentile
birth. Here the narrator *shows* that the unanimous agreement of the assembly
of the apostles and elders with the whole church (*syn hole te ekklesia*) to write

---

14   Cf. 2 Co 1,19; 1 Th 1,1; 2 Th 1,1; 1 Pt 5,12. See also NJB, p. 1825, footnote "x".
      Footnote "k" on p. 1913 affirms that "Silvanus is the disciple called Silas in Ac".
      Then Silas is his *greek* name, while Silvanus his *latin* name.
15   As a leading man and a Hellenist, he must have represented the interests of the helle-
      nist Christians in Jerusalem.

a letter to the Gentiles is balanced by a corresponding unanimous choice of the delegates to deliver its message to the addressee. Here is the narrator at his *artistic* best, painting a glowing picture of an assembly of early Christian Leaders whose initial contentious deliberations are giving way to a mature agreement for a harmonious resolution of the problem of social relationship facing the two major racial blocks of the *brethren*.

7.5 Greetings from Brethren to Brethren (V.23b).

"The apostles and the elders, your brothers (*adelphoi*), send greetings to the brothers (*adelphois*) of gentile birth in Antioch, Syria and Cilicia". Now let us analyse this *captatio benevolentiae*. The letter *ad Gentes* begins with the senders' greetings (*chairein*). In the whole of NT, this formula is used here, then in Ac 23,26 and in Jm 1,1. It is an opening formula of salutation that follows the standard prescript (*praescriptio*) of the ancient Hellenistic letters[16]. So from the outset the councillors address their gentile brothers in a form very familiar to them.

Both the senders and the receivers are brothers or fellow christian men and women. It is a message from brethren (*Geschwister*) to brethren. The addressee include not only the inquiring Church of Antioch, but also those of Syria and Cilicia[17]. Thus the scope of the destination of the Letter is expanded giving room for the inference that it is addressed to the gentile cities or areas evangelized by Paul and his companions (14,22; 15,41).

7.6 Disclaim of Unauthorized Disturbing Group (V.24).

The polite introduction of the Letter is immediately followed by unalloyed disapproval of the activities of the unauthorized free-lance preachers, the *tines* who came from Jerusalem to Antioch demanding the circumcision of male Gentile converts as a condition for their salvation (cf. v.1). With their unsettling preaching and demand they have disturbed (*etaraxan*) the minds or consciences of the new converts and caused a lot of disharmony among the christian community. These trouble-makers were the Judaizing Pharisees (Ac 15,5) who did not have the mandate of the apostles and elders for their disturbing mission (cf. Ga 1,7).

---

16 See, for example, 1 Mac 10,18.25; 11,30.
17 Compare this opening address with that of James to "the twelve tribes of the Dispersion" (Jm 1,1).

The disapproval of the circumcision party is put in unmistakable terms: *hois ou diesteilametha*[18] (we did not issue instructions to them). So the Judaizing party are evangelizing without apostolic mandate. In other words, they are preaching their own mind without the backing of appropriate ecclesial authority. This is a dangerous precedent which the Jerusalem authorities are quick to annul. They dissociate themselves from such a discreditable conduct and teaching. The Gentiles need not adhere to the false and unauthorized teaching of the circumcision group because they have not been mandated to teach in that manner.

7.7 Unanimous Decision to Send Delegates (Vv.25-27).

These three verses hark back to the resolution of vv.22-23a (see 7.2 above). There is a unanimity (*homothymadon*, v.25) in the selection of the four emissaries to Antioch. *Homothymadon* is a peculiar Acts word found 10 times in Acts out of its eleven occurrences in the NT[19]. It may be a pointer to the narrator's desire for the continuation of the primordial unanimity, unity and consent (2,46; 4,32; 5,12f) in the young Church often "visited" with divisions, dissensions, contentions and disagreements (6,1; 15,1-2.5-6.39).

Paul and Barnabas are singled out as men "who have committed their lives to the name of our Lord Jesus Christ" (*tou onomatos hemon Iesou Christou, v.26*)[20]. Rendering the apostolic service of preaching, teaching, baptizing, exorcizing and praying "*in the name of Jesus Christ*" or "*calling upon his name*" is a favourite theme of the Acts. Only in the name of Jesus is the apostolic task successful and salvation made possible because anyone who invokes or calls upon his name is saved (Ac 2,21).

The apostolic people have carried out their mission in the name of Jesus and are glad to suffer humiliation for his name (Ac 5,41), but Paul and Barnabas are given a special praise and recognition for their heroic mission in the name of the Lord Jesus. In a special way Saul (Paul), who wanted to arrest everybody who invoked the Lord's name (9,14) and indeed fiercely opposed his name (26,9), now fulfils the words of the Lord Jesus that the converted Saul is his chosen instrument to bring his "name (*onoma*) before gentiles and kings and before the people of Israel" (9,15).

---

18 *Diastellesthai* (to issue instructions, order) is found 5 times in Mk, once in Heb, and only here in Luke-Acts (cf. Morgenthaler, Statistik, 88).

19 Cf. Morgenthaler, op. cit., 125.

20 The variants of this phraseology in the Acts are: *en to onomati Iesou, eis to onomati tou kuriou Iesou, pros to onoma Iesou* (cf. 2,38; 3,6; 4,10.18.30; 5,40; 8,12.16; 9,27; 10,48; 16,18; 19,5.13.17; 21,13; 26,9).

Paul has suffered so much for his name as the Lord said (9,16; 21,13). For the councillors, he and Barnabas are the beloved (*agapetoi*) apostolic pair who have risked their lives for the sake of the Good News of Christ (v.26). For their hazardous tasks they now enjoy the special affection and esteem of the apostles and elders of the Church as missionaries found worthy of ecclesial glory.

Two delegates are to accompany Paul and Barnabas as oral witnesses to the apostolic Letter. They are Judas and Silas, the leading men (v.22) who will inform (*apangellontes*) the Gentiles by word of mouth (*dia logou*) the contents (*ta auta*) of the Letter already known to the reader (and so reader-elevating position, cf. v. 20) but not yet known to the recipients. Their function is well described by the use of the verb *apangellein* (to tell, inform; proclaim; acknowledge, confess; call upon, command).

They are to *tell* the Gentiles about the events of the JC, *inform* them about the decision and demands of the assembly, *acknowledge* their faith irrespective of their gentile background, *call upon* them to remain steadfast in the faith, *confess* that the Judaizers have erred in their unauthorized teaching, *proclaim* to them the demands of their christian liberty as contained in the apostolic Letter, and *command* them to keep its prescriptions.

One can then deduce from the *seven meanings* of *apangellein* that the narrator has chosen the *verb* to describe in a picturesque manner the comprehensive assignment of Judas and Silas as the oral witnesses of the decision of the JC before the Gentile Christians.

7.8 Inspired Leaders Impose Only Necessary Burden (V.28).

"For it has been decided (*edoxen*) by the Holy Spirit and ourselves not to impose (*epitithesthai*) on you any burden (*baros*) beyond these essentials (*epanankes*)"[21].

This is the sentence that introduces the Council's decision. It begins with *edoxen* and so resumes the resolution of v.22 (*edoxe*). It stresses again the role of the Holy Spirit[22] in the apostolic mission in general and in this decision in particular. The Spirit is mentioned first in the first chapter of the Acts as the powerful mover of the apostolic action and witness (cf. Ac 1,8). Now he is inspiring and guiding the decision of the Leaders for the good of the apostolic Church.

---

21 Cf. Catchpole, Paul, James, 429-444.
22 Now refer to Peter's speech in *Chapter Four* where we discussed the role of the Holy Spirit in the Acts.

The primacy of place given to the Spirit shows that the Church leaders are quite conscious of their being possesed, inspired and controlled by him. They are the vehicles of the Holy Spirit and operate in union with him in their collegiate deliberations. The decision of the leaders is the decision of the Holy Spirit and vice-versa. Their collegiate pronouncement under the conscious influence of the Spirit does not seem to have a biblical precedent. W. L. Knox aptly points out that "there is no parallel for such a phrase to pronounce a corporate decision by a deliberative body"[23].

What comes closer to this, but not exactly like it, is the apostles' response to the Sanhedrin that they all together and the Holy Spirit are witnesses to the Christ event (Ac 5,32). As "God's gift to all who obey him" (5,33), the Spirit directs the judgments and utterances of those who are obedient to his inspirations[24]. The mention of the Spirit here suitably accords with the JC deliberations which have all along emphasized the divine initiative in the call of the Gentiles to the christian faith (15,7-10; 14-18).

The inspired decision states categorically the mind of the councillors. They have resolved never to impose (*epitithesthai*) any unnecessary burden (*baros*) on the Gentiles. This is like the resumption of Peter's speech which is against any imposition (*epitheinai*) of an unbearable yoke (*zugon*) on the gentile disciples (Ac 15,10). So the Leaders want the Gentiles to observe the barest minimum that is necessary for their communal and commensal christian living with the Jews. They are therefore not expected to observe what is not necessary (*epanankes*) for such a life.

Epanankes is a Lukan loan word used only here in the whole of the NT[25]. Though not suggested in the narrative, one could infer that its occurrence only in this verse (which introduces what the leaders of the Church deem necessary for Gentile Christians) is the narrator's device to draw the attention of the reader to the necessity and importance of the inspired apostolic ruling. The four requirements of the decree are *epanankes* for the Gentile Christians.

But why are those requirements *necessary*? Ac 15,21 gives credence to the view that the four necessary requirements come from Moses or from that section of the Torah that must be observed by the Gentiles or strangers (*goyim*) living among the OT Israel[26]. This fact makes them also necessary for the Gentile Christians who are *goyim* to the Jews.

---

23   Acts, 50, no. 1.
24   This agrees with Christ's promise of the Holy Spirit as the instructor and guide to his witnesses (cf. Jn 7,39; 15,26f; Ac 1,8).
25   Cf. Morgenthaler, Statistik, 98.
26   Cf. Lv 17,8.10.13; 18,6ff.

What links these four prohibitions together, and at the same time distinguishes them from all other 'ritual' requirements of 'Moses', is that they - and they only - are given not only to Israel but also to strangers dwelling among the Jews. Whereas in other respects the law applies solely to the Jews, it imposes these four prohibitions on *Gentiles also*![27]

Once the Gentile converts observe the prescriptions of the Mosaic Law as laid down in the decree, they have done what is *necessary* for a harmonious relationship between Jews and Gentiles in the Church. This demand is a *burden* but it is a *necessary burden* to remove barriers and tensions in the christian community. Any demand beyond the mentioned four is an unnecessary burden on the Gentile Christians.

It should be noted, however, that the JC's directives to the Gentiles are not conveyed by any of the Greek verbs of commanding. Yet the form of words used for the prohibitions is authoritative enough. "*It has been decided*" (*edoxen*) is a paraphrase used in the wording of government or imperial decrees. And the four abstentions are "necessary" and obligatory not optional. So even without the verb of commanding, the Leaders of the Church give out their inspired prohibitions in an imperative manner, thereby providing the future Church with an example of how to exercise power forcefully and yet amicably.

7.9 The Four Abstentions Revisited (V.29a).

Apechesthai eidolothuton kai haimatos kai pnikton kai porneias... (v.29).

Compare this order and formulation of the official decree in v.29 with the Jacobian order and formulation in v.20:

...Tou apechesthai ton alisgematon ton eidolon kai tes porneias kai tou pniktou kai tou haimatos... (v.20).

The formulation of the abstentions in v.20 has been discussed in chapter six (**6.5**) as a proposal from James through the narrator's voice. But here they are presented as an official resolution or decree of apostolic Leaders led by the Holy Spirit and acting in union with him (v.28). A new dimension is thus added to the Jacobian four-point proposal, thus prompting the resumption of its discussion here from a new perspective without in any way detracting from what is already said about it in the former chapter.

---

27   Haenchen, Acts, 469.

Although the narrator says that the decree issues from the Holy Spirit and the apostolic Leaders, yet the reader has been informed that it was James who made the four-point proposal of what is now an inspired decision by the Leaders of the Church. Both the narrator and the reader evenhandedly know already the main contents of the decree. But the four prohibitions are formulated in a slightly different order from the Jacobian motion of abstention in v.20.

Now I shall try to present my *insight* into the varied order of the prohibitions in the two verses, if only to show that their variation is not a mere literary accident or device but has some *theolgical implication* in each case.

The language of the decree varies from the Jacobian formulation in terminology and in the ordering of terms. First, the definite article preceding the infinitive *apechesthai* in v.20 drops out in v.29. The *ton alisgamaton ton eidolon* of v.20 is reduced to *eidolothuthon* in v.29. The definite article placed before each of the terms of the prohibitions of v.20 is dropped out entirely in v.29. But why is this curious literary variation in an issue that is directed towards the resolution of a deep-seated conflict between two racial christian groups?

The answer is not easy to come by, but I suggest that it may be a simple literary device by the author. This may be more evident if the two versions are again placed side by side and compared from the literary perspective.

V.20 tou apechesthai ton alisgematon ton eidolon kai tes porneias kai tou pniktou kai tou haimatos.

V.29 apechesthai eidolothuton kai haimatos kai pniktou kai porneias.

V.29 or the decree proper is *shorter* and *simpler* and seems adapted for easier memorization by the christian neophite. It also reduces the weight (*baros*) of the Jacobian prohibition from "*pollutions of idols*" to a specific abstention from meat or *foods sacrificed to idols*.

The meaning of the word *eidolothuton* is not in doubt. The synonym *hierothuton* was more common, but to Jews and Christians heathen gods were idols and the pejorative word was obviously appropriate for food that had been offered in sacrifice to non-existent deity. The worship of such gods was simply forbidden; no worshipper of the one true God could take part in it[28].

So while adopting the Jacobian principle, the leaders specify what the "pollutions of idols" really refers to. By using the term *eidolothuton* they pin down the meaning of *alisgematon ton eidolon* to "foods offered to idols" which they consider to be the most insidious and persistent form of contact

---

28   Barrett, Apostolic Decree, 51.

with idolatory. By their new call, the Gentile Christians are expected to have abandoned all forms of idol worship which they practised before their conversion.

But it may not be easy for them to give up their habit of eating foods sacrificed to those empty idols as is the case among the Corinthian Christians (1 Co 8,1ff; 10,14ff). Such a habit would obviously pose a big problem for relationship between them and the orthodox Jewish Christians who strongly repudiate any form of idolatory. Hence the specific decretal demand of abstention from idol foods.

Despite this prohibition by the Jerusalem leaders, is the eating of such foods forbidden at all times? The narrator of Acts seems to say that the decree implies that there is no exception to the ruling, whereas Paul who is also a party to this decision makes some exception to the ruling for the Gentile Christians of Corinth. Although the *"Corinthian"* Paul does not agree that to eat foods offered to idols (*eidolothuta*) is in all circumstances idolatory (vv.25.27), yet he affirms that idolatory must be avoided at all costs (1 Co 10,14). Eating *eidolothuta* in the context of pagan worship is idolatory because in the words of Paul,

> when pagans sacrifice, what is sacrificed by them is sacrificed to demons who are not God. I do not want you to share with demons. You cannot drink the cup of the Lord and the cup of the demons as well; you cannot have a share at the Lord's table and the demons' table as well (1 Co 10,20-21).

Eating it and causing scandal to fellow Christians with little knowledge or weak consciences is sinful. Hence the Christian should refrain from eating what is dedicated to a god (8,1-13; 10,23-29). So despite the Pauline exception which however proves the rule, the decree's prohibition of eating *eidolothuta* remains the basic principle[29] for the Gentile Christians. This is also true of the prohibitions from incest, strangled meat and blood.

Next is the order of the formulations of the two verses. In v.20 the *Jacobian order* is abstention from: (a) pollutions of idols (b) incestuous fornication (c) stangled meat (d) blood. In v.29 the *decretal order* is abstention from: (a) food sacrificed to idols (b) blood (c) strangled meat (d) incestuous fornication.

While (a) idolatory and (c) stangled meat retain their positions in both verses, incestuous fornication and blood exchange their positions with each other. That is, the no. (b) of the Jacobian order becomes the no. (d) of the decretal order, and the no. (d) of the Jacobian order becomes the no. (b) of the decretal order.

---

29 Here one must note that the most elementary principles of christian law rule out completely ordinary idol-worship, as also ordinary fornication.

A closer observation shows that in the *Jacobian order*, idolatory and fornication which is biblically a form of idolatory[30], are placed close to each other,
while strangled meat and blood which are similar to each other are placed together. Here the like is placed close to the like or likes are paired together.
Idolatrous prohibitions which are ethico-moral in character come before food
prohibitions which are ritual and social in character. The reader may infer that
this may be a pointer to their order of importance and seriousness as viewed
by the narrator because in the question of moral offence, idolatrous practices
are graver than offences against food laws.

But in the *decretal order*, the food prohibitions (a) and (b) are placed at the
centre and are then rammed in by the prohibitions from idolatory (a) and incestuous fornication (d) which are placed at opposite extremes. Here the food
regulation is "fenced" by the moral regulation. But it should be noted that
idolatory here is specified: it has to do with "foods sacrificed to idols".

However from the decretal positioning of the prohibitions, the reader may
be led to deduce that the ruling on commensality is encircled by the ruling on
morality. In other words, social relationship is determined by sound moral behaviour. In this way the framing of the decree seeks to face up squarely to the
question of commensality and social relationship between Jewish and Gentile
Christians. The bases for this relationship is a minimal sound moral behaviour
which the decree fraternally demands of the Gentiles.

7.9.1   Do Well to Avoid these Things (V.29b).

Since the decree aims at prescribing what will facilitate social and religious
harmony between the two racial groups in the Church, its concluding section
urges the Gentile addressee to observe the prohibitions (*ex hon diaterountes
heautous eu praxete*). Diaterein is a peculiar Lukan word occuring only twice
in the NT[31] : here in Ac 15,29 and in Lk 2,51 where it is reported that the
Mary the mother of Jesus "stored up all these things (about Jesus) in her
heart".

Here the participle of *diaterein* (to keep safe/free, to avoid) is used conditionally: If the Gentiles would treasure the contents of the decree and avoid
those things forbidden by it, they would be doing what is right. Their abstention from forbidden foods and marriages puts them on the right track as good

---

30   Cf. Nb 25,1-3; Jr 3,2.9; Rv 2,14.20. For the prophets commiting adultery is a common
     figure of speech for idolatory or religious infidelity.
31   Morgenthaler, Statistik, 88.

Christians[32]. They should therefore do well to abide by the terms of the decree. The brotherly message fittingly concludes with a courteous plea to the Gentiles to accept what is required of them.

7.9.2   Farewell (Errosthe).

With the familiar ancient formula *errosthe*, the letter closes with good wishes for the recipients. The Jerusalem assembly has come to an end. The agenda have been debated and discussed by the participants. The initial tensions have given way to a united action (*homothymadon*) to settle the issues at stake. The members have come up with a "communique" that may hopefully resolve the areas of conflict between Jewish and Gentile Christians. The impact of the assembly's decision on the Gentile recipients is the theme of the next chapter. But first what is the import of the Council's Letter with its decree for the Church?

7.10   Significance of the Apostolic Letter.

This is the first and the only recorded Letter written together by the Leaders of the Church (apostles and elders) to a racial group (Gentiles or Greeks) in the Church. Pervo notes that in antiquity "letters create a warm and personal atmosphere, and they serve as a kind of documentation lending verisimilitude to the situation"[33]. So also is this Council's Letter which is framed in the style or form of a royal or state letter. There is a very personal warmth about it, for it has a friendly tone from its beginning to the end with a lot of good wishes for the gentile recipients. "By such means Luke has given the decree more weight and has painted the early Church with glowing colors"[34].

The Letter portrays the Jewish Church as being very understanding and conciliatory towards the Gentile Christians. The Jewish apostles and elders who had earlier protested to Peter for visiting and eating with the uncircumcised Gentiles (11,2f), now regard the Gentiles as brethren in the faith (v.22). This is an unprecedented milestone in the Acts story about the relationship between Jewish and Gentile Christians. Surprisingly too, the Letter is completely silent over the question of circumcision which ignited the long debates and contentions (Ac 15,1). One may then infer that the assembly did not con-

---

32   Cf. Catchpole, Paul, James, 430.
33   Pervo, Profit, 77.
34   Ibid.

sider circumcision as an issue what discussing or including in the Letter to the Gentiles whose males are not required to undergo the ritual.

The abstentions demanded of the Gentiles are both *ritual* (stangled meat and blood) and *moral* (idol foods and incest), and their observance will pave the way for socio-religious exchange between Jews and Gentiles. But the Letter in no way indicates that the four abstentions guarantee salvation for any Gentile who observes them. This is not surprising if the reader remembers that the Petrine speech stresses that salvation comes through faith and grace of God (15,11). So the Letter is not out to state what is necessary for salvation as one would have expected (v.1), but rather seeks ways and means to repair the damage done by the Judaizers (v.24) by prescribing minimum, ritual and moral requirements for harmonious life between Christians of two different races and cultures (v.29).

8. Chapter Eight.

Antioch Joyfully Receives JC's Letter (15,30-35).

8.0 Greek Text of Ac 15,30-35.

30. Hoi men oun apoluthentes katelthon eis Antiocheian, kai synagagontes to plethos epedokan ten epistolen.
31 anagnontfes de echaresan epi te paraklesei.
32 Ioudas te kai Silas kai autoi prophetai ontes dia logou pollou parekalesan tous adelphous kai epesterixan,
33 poiesantes de chronon apeluthesan met' eirenes apo ton adelphon pros tous aposteilantas autous.
[34 edoxe de to Silas epimeinai autou, monos de Ioudas eporeuthe eis Ierousalem].
35 Paulos de kai Barnabas dietribon en Antiocheia didaskontes kai euangelizomenoi meta kai heteron pollon ton logon tou kyriou.

8.1 Textual Criticism of Vv.30-35.

In the Nestle-Aland NT Greek text, v.34 is placed in the footnote with a sign indicating that it can be inserted between vv.33 and 35. V.34 says that after their mission Silas remained in Antioch while Judas alone returned to Jerusalem. Haenchen considers this verse as

> an interpolation of the Western text, obviously intended to mend the inconsistency with v.40, where it is implied that Silas remained in Antioch[1].

But if v.34 were really to follow up v.33 which tells the reader that after Silas and Judas had spent some time in Antioch, the Christians sent them back in peace to those (in Jerusalem) who commissioned them, then the inconsistency still becomes more glaring.

How can one reconcile the reported departure of Silas in v.33 with his staying back in Antioch in v.34? That may not be just resolved by citing v.40 where Paul takes Silas as his companion. It is more logical to think that Silas and Judas returned together to Jerusalem to report their mission to the Leaders who sent them to Antioch, and later on Silas left Jerusalem for Antioch where Paul and Barnabas continued their evangelical duties before they disagreed

---

1   Acts, 454-455; Cf. Bruce, Book, 300, footnote no.82.

and parted company (v.39). Then Paul found in Silas a suitable companion to replace Barnabas in his missionary journey (vv.40-41).

Again employing the text critical principle that *a shorter text is more reliable than a longer text*, one can assert that the addition of v.34 is an elongation of the text and the longer version of the pericope of *five* verses is less reliable or preferable to the shorter text of *four* verses. All these may be a more plausible explanation for regarding v.34 as an "interpolation" by a redactor.

8.2   Narrative and Stylistic Features of Vv.30-35.

This is the final scene or *dénoument* of our story, the conclusion of our narrative, the epilogue of the story describing the final state of affairs (2.3.13). There is a change of character - from the Jerusalem assembly to the four envoys: Paul, Barnabas, Judas and Silas. There is a change of action: from the assembly composing a Letter to the delegates carrying and presenting the Letter to the Christians of Antioch. There is a change of place: from Jerusalem to Antioch. There is change of time: the decision and the Letter of the JC are followed by the later events at Antioch.

The narrator does not tell the reader the duration of time taken to travel from Jerusalem to Antioch. Here again an event which takes place over a period of days or weeks (narrative time) is summarized in two sentences or in one verse (narration time). The return to Antioch completes the cycle of the journey which narratively and stylistically places Jerusalem at the *center* and *highpoint* of the assembly.

After hearing the message of the apostolic Letter the Gentile Christians of Antioch were comforted and filled with joy. The initial dispute, tension and suspense (Ac 15,1-5) have completely disappeared, giving way to a full joy and consolation for the neophites in the christian faith. The reading of the Letter by the delegates gives a binding force of its contents on the addressee.

The Gentiles are now aware that they are free from male circumcision and from the observance of all other Mosaic presciptions (Ac 15,1.5). Once they observe the injunctions of the apostolic decree (v.29), they can freely and quietly practice their christian faith. The initial conflict is at last happily resolved and peace and calm return to the Church of Antioch, the original seat of the conflict.

8.3 Delegates Bring the Letter to Antiochians (V.30).

"Then having been sent off" (*hoi men oun apoluthentes*, v.30a) reminds the reader of the escorting or seeing off (*hoi men oun propemphthentes*, v.3) of the Antiochian delegates (comprising Paul, Barnabas and others) who were initially sent off to go and confer with the apostles and elders in Jerusalem. Having successfully conferred with the Jerusalem Leaders, Paul and Barnabas along with Judas and Silas are now seen off and sent back to inform the Antiochians of the result of their Jerusalem conference. The message for the Antiochian community is embodied in the brotherly, warm Letter of vv.23-29. The delegation arrives, gathers the community (*plethos*) and hands over the consoling Letter (*epistolen*) to them.

8.4 Antiochians Read the Letter and Rejoice (V.31).

Let us note that the narrator does not say that the delegates read the Letter. Rather it is read by the Antiochians themselves. The Letter is addressed to them and it is their duty to read it. The reader is not told how it is read - whether someone is appointed to read it or whether it is placed on a "notice board" for everyone to read. The fact remains that the Christians read the Letter as indicated by the aorist participle *anagnontes* (having read).

The verb *anaginoskein* (to read, to read in public worship) occurs 3 times in Luke and 8 in the Acts[2]. Except for the reference to the reading of the Letter from the military tribune Claudius Lysas to the governor Felix (Ac 23,34), *anagnoskein* in the Acts refers mainly to the reading of the Holy Scriptures especially the Law and the Prophets which may be carried out either individually or collectively[3]. In a similar way the apostolic Letter is read before an assembled christian community of Antioch.

One may then infer from the Lukan context and usage that the Letter has some divine authority behind it and those who read it might have regarded it as having a binding force similar to that of the *Holy Scriptures*. This supposition is supported by the fact that the narrator says that the Church Leaders affirmed that they were united with the Holy Spirit as they issued the decree of the Letter (v.28).

---

2   It occurs 32 times in the whole of the NT and is found 7 times in Mt, 4 in Mk, 8 in Pauline corpus and once in John and Revelation respectively (cf. Morgenthaler, Statistik, 72).

3   Cf. Ac 15,21; 8,28.30.32; 13,27; Lk 4,16; 6,3; 10,26.

The people rejoice (*echaresan*) for the encouragement or comfort (*paraklesis*) which the Letter gives them. *Chairein* (to rejoice, be glad) is used 12 times in Luke and 7 in Acts[4]. Two of the usages in the Acts are found at the openings of two different letters (15,23; 23,26). In the other five usages, the Acts annouces the joy of the apostles who suffer for the name of Jesus (5,41); the joy of the Eunuch who is baptised in the name of Jesus (8,39); the joy of Barnabas at the grace given to the Gentile converts (11,23); the joy of the Gentiles at hearing that the Lord's salvation is also for them (13,48). In the same way the Letter to the Gentiles which opens with greetings of joy (*charein*) really brings this joy to the recipients.

The joy derives from the *paraklesis* (encouragement, comfort, help, appeal) of the Letter which can be compared to the "word of encouragement" (*logos parakleseos*, Ac 13,15) which the presidents of the Pisidian synagogues requested from Paul and Barnabas (Ac 13,15). Here it is noteworthy that Barnabas or the "son of encouragement" (*huios parakleseos*, 4,36) is one of the bearers of the consoling Letter. His spiritual talent for encouraging and exhorting the Gentile Christians to fidelity in their faith (11,23) must have added a more joyful mood to their consolation. In relation to Lk 2,25 the Letter may also be regarded as a *paraklesis* (or a setting free) of the Gentiles since it sets them free from the yoke (*zugon*) of Mosaic Law and customs.

8.5 Judas and Silas Encourage Gentiles (Vv.32-33).

Now Judas Barsabbas and Silas carry out their assignment from the Jerusalem assembly. They are the two leading men in the brotherhood chosen to deliver and confirm the contents of the letter by word of mouth (15,22.27)[5]. The narrator also calls them *prophetai*. This reminds the reader of the group of charismatic christian prophets who came from Jerusalem to Antioch (11,27) and of the prophets in the Antiochian community from which Paul and Barnabas were selected by the Holy Spirit for their mission to the Gentiles (13,1-3).

As prophets, Judas and Silas should have some knowledge of the divine will and possess some power of inspired utterance. *Paraklesis* is a spiritual, prophetical gift for strengthening people in the faith. As *First* Corinthians teaches, "someone who prophesies speaks to the other people, building them up and giving them encouragement and reassurance" (1 Co 14,3). Thus the narrator summarily presents the two prophets as being engaged in a prolonged

---

4   It occurs 74 times in the NT but 29 times in Pauline corpus alone (cf. Morgenthaler, op. cit., 155).

5   Cf. Kaye, Acts Portrait of Silas, 14-16.

work of encouraging (*dia logou pollou parekalesan*) the Gentile Christians. In this way their activity resembles the earlier work of Barnabas (the son of encouragement) at Antioch (11,23-26).

It was a wise thing for the Leaders to have sent Silas and Judas as oral emissaries and guarantors of their Council decision. For had Paul and Barnabas alone returned to Antioch to tell the people about the JC ruling on a Jewish-law free Gentile Church, their opponents might have doubted their message or might have regarded it as a farce.

> The Church was wise in sending a person as well as a letter... A letter could have sounded coldly official; but the words of Judas and Silas added a friendly warmth that bare reception of a letter could never have achieved. Any amount of trouble might be avoided many a time if only a personal visit is paid instead of someone being content with sending a letter[6].

It is therefore proper that Silas and Judas went to Antioch as oral witnesss to the apostolic Letter and above all to strengthen (*episterizein*) the Christians.

In the NT *episterizein* occurs 3 times and only in the Acts alone (14,22; 15,32.41)[7]. Each occurrence has to do with the strengthening or confirmation of the faith of the Gentile Christians. Here *episterizein* signifies the spiritual reinforcement of the Antiochian Christians by Judas and Silas. The narrator makes their pastoral activity resemble that of Paul and Barnabas (14,22), and the later gentile mission by Paul and Silas (15,41). From the narrator's report on the joy and consolation of the Antiochians, one can certainly infer that the encouraging mission of Silas and Judas did succeed in strengthening the faith of the formerly unsettled and anxious disciples (15,2.24) and in renewing their spiritual lives.

Silas and Judas did not leave immediately after delivering the joyful message from Jerusalem. They sojourned for some time in Antioch. But the reader is not told how long they stayed. Again as in v.32 the narrator summarizes the narrative time of their activity in a narration time of few words. The summaries may be an indication that the narrator is not so much interested in the details of their work as in its effect on the people.

After spending some time with the happy Gentiles, the two messengers return to the Jerusalem community who sent them out. It is normal and proper that a messenger gives a feedback to his sender(s). So have Silas and Judas

---

6   Barclay, Acts, 117-118.
7   Cf. Morgenthaler, op. cit., 100.

done as an example for future missionaries[8]. The lesson from it is that none may forget to report the success or failure of his or her mission to the ones who sent him/her.

The two Leaders leave for Jerusalem with good wishes of peace (*met' eirenes*) from the Antiochians. *Eirene* occurs 91 times in the NT. Of this number, 7 are found in Acts and 13 in Luke. In the Acts it is only here that *eirene* is used in the context of a farewell send off by a christian community for its two Leaders. In Lk 7,50 and 8,48 Jesus is presented as sending away those whom he has healed *in peace*. So also does the gaoler at Philippi report to the imprisoned Paul and Silas that the magistrates have asked them to leave the city *in peace* (Ac 16,36).

Sending Judas and Silas off with the "kiss" of peace indicates a cermonial send off with fraternal blessing. This gives a special meaning to the peaceful "send off party" organised for the two delegates who were leaving Antioch for Jerusalem. They have brought peace and harmony to the Church of Antioch. The same peace now follows them back to the Jerusalem Church and her Leaders.

8.6 Teaching and Evangelizing in Antioch (V.35).

While Judas and Silas returned to Jerusalem, Paul, Barnabas and some others stayed on (*dietribon*) in Antioch and continued to teach (*didaskein*) and proclaim (*euangelizesthai*) the word of the Lord to the people. This is an interesting verse which summarizes the customary activity of Paul and companions in the Acts.

In the NT *diatribein* (to stay, remain) occurs once in John and 8 times in the Acts[9]. So it is a typical Acts verb. Except for Ac 12,19 (where it refers to Herod staying or residing in Caesarea) the narrator uses it to describe the sojourn of the apostolic people in the cities where they carry on their work for a given period of time.

In Iconium Paul and Barnabas stay for some time, (Ac 14,3) preaching fearlessly in the Lord who attests to their proclamation by allowing signs and wonders to be peformed by them. After their first misssionary journey the two apostles return to Antioch where they stay for some time with the disciples (v.28). A similar sojourn is reported here in 15,35. In Philippi Paul and Silas

---

8   This is another reason for regarding as an interpolation the reading of the Western text which says that Silas decided to stay back in Antioch (v.34). We shall therefore skip this verse and go to v.35.

9   Cf. Morgenthaler, Statistik, 88.

stay a few days before going to preach to a group of the faithful women gathered at a place of prayer by the riverside (16,12). Finally at Troas Paul and a few companions stay for a week and minister to the Christians (20,6ff). So then *diatribein* describes the act of apostolic sojourning in a place so as to proclaim the good news to the people[10].

Even the inner context attests to the purpose of sojourning at Antioch. The narrator says that Paul and his companions are teaching (*didaskontes*) the Christians. The participial verb points to a continuous and repeated teaching activity. Their evangelical sojourn at Antioch reminds the reader of the prophets and teachers (*prophetai kai didaskaloi*) who witnessed and taught in the city even before the first missionary journey (Ac 13,1). It is interesting to observe that Paul and Barnabas are among those teachers mentioned in Acts 13, and it is from their ranks that the Holy Spirit selected them for their present task (v.2).

In the NT *didaskein* occurs 95 times of which 17 are found in Luke and 16 in the Acts[11]. So teaching is a prime task of the apostolic people. Before the appearance of Paul on the mission scene, the apostles, despite all threats to their lives (Ac 4,18; 5,28), were frequently engaged in "teaching the people the resurrection from the dead and proclaiming the resurrection of Jesus" (4,2). They did this both in the temple and in private houses[12]. In doing this they were faithfully following the practice of the Lord Jesus and carrying out his command of witnessing to him from Jerusalem unto the ends of the earth (Ac 1,8).

Paul and Barnabas following in the footsteps of the Twelve Apostles made Antioch the base for their teaching. Initially they taught for a whole year in the Church of Antioch (11,26). Their success earned the disciples of Antioch the title of *Christianoi* or followers of Christ. Thus one can assume that after their return from the JC, their teaching activity in the Antiochian Church is a faithful continuation of their original task. Acts does present Paul as continuing his teaching about the Lord even as a prisoner in Rome[13].

In Antioch *teaching* pairs up with the *preaching* of the good news. Again the narrator uses the participial *euangelizomenos* to show the continuous nature of the preaching activity of Paul and his companions. This reflects the

10   This is the sense in which the narrator of John uses the same verb: "Jesus went with his disciples into the Judaean countryside and stayed (*dietriben*) with them there and baptised (Jn 3,22).

11   It is used 14 times in Mt, 17 in Mk, 9 in Jn, 15 in Pauline corpus, 2 in Heb, 2 in Rv etc (cf. Morgenthaler, op. cit., 88).

12   Cf. 5,21.25.28.42.

13   For other references on the teaching activity of Paul confer, Ac 18,11; 20,20; 21,21.28; 28,31.

practice of the Twelve who daily and ceaselessly taught and proclaimed the Good News of Christ Jesus publicly and privately (Ac 5,42). The verb *euangelizein* (to bring the good news, preach the good news; preach, proclaim) is used in the middle voice "*euangelizesthai*" but with no change in meaning from the active voice. It occurs 54 times in the NT (10 in Luke, 15 in Acts and 21 in Pauline corpus)[14]. But the middle voice is more commonly used in the Acts[15].

In the Lukan Gospel, *euangelizesthai* describes the Angel's proclamation of the Good News of the future birth of John the Baptist (1,19); the Angels' procalmation of the great joyful news of the birth of Jesus (2,10); the Good News proclaimed by John the Baptist (3,18); the Good News of the Kingdom proclaimed by Jesus himself[16] and by the Twelve Apostles (9,6). So preaching is the fundamental task of Jesus, the Baptist, the apostles and the apostolic people.

In the Acts, the Twelve taught the people and proclaimed Jesus in the temple and in private homes (5,42). The Hellenists who escaped from Jerusalem to avoid persecution preached the Good News from place to place (8,4). Philip preached to the Samaritans and converted many of them (v.12). Peter and John also preached the Good News to a number of Samaritan villages (v.25). After preaching to the Ethiopian Eunuch and baptising him (v.35), Philip proclaimed the Good News to the towns lying between Azotus and Caesarea (v.40).

In the same Caesarea, Peter preached to Cornelius and his friends and also informed them that through Jesus Christ God preached the Good News of peace to Israel (10,36; cf. Is 52,7). The Hellenist disciples from Cyprus and Cyrene proclaimed the Good News of Jesus to the Hellenists of Antioch (11,20). In Pisidian Antioch Paul and Barnabas told the Jews about the fulfilment of the Good News promised to their Fathers (13,32). The same Good News was preached to the Gentiles in the towns of Lycaonia (14,7.15.21). It was later carried over to Macedonia (16,10) and to Athens (17,18).

So then *euangelizesthai* describes the apostolic preaching of the Good News which centres on the person and life of Jesus Christ and on the kingdom of God. That is the mission received from Christ himself (cf. Lk 9,1-6). Paul is very devoted to this task of preaching the name of Jesus to the Gentiles *(ta*

---

14 Cf. Morgenthaler, op. cit., 101.
    Note that among the Evangelists "euangelizein" is used only once in Mt (11,5); the rest is in Luke; it is not found in Mk and Jn. Is it not very surprising that this verb is lacking in the writings of those who are called "Euangelistes" - the noun of the verb?
15 Cf. 5,42; 8,4.12.25.35.40; 10,36; 11,20; 13,32; 14,7.15.21; (15,35); 16,10; 17,18.
16 Cf. Lk 4,18.43; 7,22; 8,1; 16,16; 20,1.

ethne). After his return from the JC, it is therefore not surprising to see him stay in Antioch in order to continue the work of evangelization.

But Paul and Barnabas are not the only teachers and preachers at Antioch. There are many others (*prophetai kai didaskaloi*, 13,1) who perform this task with them and look after the Antiochian community in their absence. Hence the two can confidently go on their missionary journeys without anxiety about the pastoral care of their local community.

With the resolution of the conflict between Jewish and Gentile Christians, the narrator tells the reader that peace and harmony have returned to the Antiochian community and so the apostolic preaching of the Good News to the people continues as usual. But only the community of Antioch receives and reads the Letter that puts fresh hearts in them. The reader is then moved to make an important observation on the destination of the letter. It is addressed to the Christian brethren of Antioch, Syria and Cilicia (v.23). Why then is it not despatched to the three communities at the same time? Why does the Antiochian Church alone read it before the other two communities?

It may be because Antioch is both the seat of the Gentile Church (11,26) and the seat of the controversy over the Jewish/Gentile question, and for that reason the Letter is first taken to that community in order to establish the fact of a Jewish-law free Gentile Church. Once that has been done the message can then be sent to the other Churches.

This opinion is supported by the internal evidence of the Acts where, at the onset of the second missionary journey, the narrator reports that Paul and Silas "travelled through Syria and Cilicia, consolidating the Churches" (15,41)[17], and later on as they "visited one town after another, they passed on the decisions reached by the apostles and elders in Jerusalem, with the instructions to observe them" (16,4). The result is a Church that is reportedly growing strong in faith and increasing daily in numbers (v.5).

8.7   Significance of the Reception of the Letter.

The narrator tells the reader that delegates sent out to Jerusalem by the Church of Antioch (v.3) have now returned to the commnity of Antioch. Their journey is completed and their assignment successfully carried out. The conflict/resolution structure of the unified plot of the Jerusalem assembly is well delineated[18]. The plot is unified not only by the succession of an event that

---

17   Here the Western text adds *"passing on to them the injunctions of the elders"*, thereby presupposing the report of 16,4.

18   Cf. Ska, Our Fathers, 19-20.

leads to the other but by the journey that moves forwards and backwards with a definite purpose by the travellers.

The Antiochian delegates arrive at Jerusalem, successfully perform their task and return to Antioch. In the same way the Jerusalem delegates arrive at Antioch, successfully perform their task and return to Jerusalem. Such a unified narration cannot but draw the attention of the reader to a profitable, delightful reading of the adventurous events of the missionary journey to, and from, Jerusalem[19].

At last the initial conflict is now resolved. Every controversy is brought to an end. The problem of the admission of the Gentiles into the Church is now solved. The desire of the Gentiles not to be burdened with circumcision and the keeping of Mosaic *ethos* is fulfilled. The yoke (*zugon*) being placed on their necks is removed. The obstacles on their way to christian living are taken away. The initial sorrow of the Antiochian community (vv.1-2.5) is now turned into joy. The dissension (*stasis*) and debate (*zetesis*) give way to emotional rejoicing (*echaresan*), encouragement (*paraklesis*) and enlivenment.

There is a complete return to the old, peaceful unanimity[20] of the Church of Antioch (15,35; cf. 14,27-28) before the Judaizers came in with their disturbing demands on the people (15,1). So the narrator paints an ideal picture of a post JC ecclesial harmony which, however, will soon expose its fragility and cracks by the report of the ensuing acrimony (*paroxusmos*) between Paul and Barnabas, the chief leaders of the Gentile Church (15,39).

The narrator also shows that the Judaizers are subdued at least for the moment. But the rest of the Acts story shows that they are only temporarily silenced, for they will reappear again and again in the Acts as fierce opponents of Paul and his companions. They resurface in 21,20-25 as stunch upholders of the Law and hostile to Paul's Jewish-law free Gentile mission. Here again James is presented as the defender of Paul and as the mediator between the Judaizers and the Pauline Gentile mission[21].

The narrator demonstrates that human conflict may temporarily succeed in disturbing the preaching of the Word of God but will not be able to stifle it forever. The initial conflict caused confusion among the Christians and upset (*etaraxan*, v.24) their inner peace. It tended to falsify the Gospel message of salvation by binding it intrinsically and conditionally to the practice of circumcision and the observance of the Mosaic Law (15,1.5).

But the message of the apostolic Letter which repudiates the unauthorised preaching and burdensome demands of the Judaizers reinstates the place of the

---

19   Cf. Pervo, Profit, 40-41.
20   Cf. Weiser, Apostelkonzil, 207-208.
21   Cf. Jervell, Luke, 193-196.

Word of God in the early Christian community. This Word remains for ever and the apostolic people continue to proclaim it without allowing it to be subjected to the legal and socio-cultural demands of the Judaizers. Such a Gospel message transcends Mosaic Law and customs and enlivens the faith of the Gentile Christians.

Conclusion to Chapters Three to Eight.

I have so far demonstrated from chapters three to eight that Acts 15,1-35 can be exegetically studied as a story and a plot of conflict/resolution of conflict between the christian faith and the Jewish and Gentile cultures. The plot of resolution centres on the question of the conditions for admitting Gentiles into the Christian Church.

Should male Gentiles be circumsised before being received into the Church or not? Should all baptised Gentiles observe the whole Torah or Jewish Law and customs in order to become Christians?. In other words, must all Gentiles first become Jews in order to be Christians and be saved? The Judaizers or Pharisee Christians insist on total Torah obedience and observance as a necessary condition for the salvation of the Gentile Christians.

But the two missionaries to the Gentiles, Paul and Barnabas, insist on a Gentile mission and Christianity free from Torah observance. Peter, James, all the apostles and elders at the JC throw in their lot with a Torah-free Gentile Church because this accords with divine will and purpose attested to by the Holy Spirit and the Holy Scriptures. However four minimal abstentions are deemed necessary for the Gentile Christians in order promote peaceful coexistence with the Jewish Christians. With this decision, the JC sets a seal on the free and unconditional admission of Gentiles into the Christian Church.

Part Three.

Theological Reflection on Exegetical Study And Correlation.

From the exegetical part (chapters 3-8) the study moves into the theological section divided into two chapters (9-10). The *ninth chapter* shall be concerned with a reflection on the inculturation theology of the Jerusalem Council (**JC**). The *tenth chapter* shall deal with the correlation of the inculturation theology to the Igbo Church today. While keeping in mind the narrative study of the exegetical section, this theological section is to be treated mainly with the basic method or approach of missionary inculturation with some tinge of the narrative method[1]. This is also the reason for commencing chapter ten with a brief "story" of the pristine socio-cultural situation of the Igbo and the general prevailing situation of the oncoming missionaries.

The method in this section is therefore diachronic and contextual: diachronic because it focuses on the apostolic missionary event in Acts 15 in relation to the Igbo Church; contextual because it is oriented to the Igbo audience. This method is appropriate here because the faith-culture conflict resolved at the JC is generated in the context of the mission of the apostolic people to both Jews and Gentiles.

---

1   The reader is again reminded that the basic method of this work is narrative-inculturation. 'Method' or 'approach' should be understood in the inclusive sense of any efficient way of presenting a theological teaching to the modern person as demanded by the SVC (cf. GS, no. 62). See "methodological procedure" in "General Introduction".

9. Chapter Nine.

Christian Message In Conflict With Jewish And Gentile Cultures.

This chapter concentrates on the inculturation theological questions raised by the whole JC story by focusing on the conflict arising from the meeting between the early christian message and its Jewish and Gentile carrier-cultures. Such a meeting was brought about by the missionary activity of the apostolic people. Hence the theological reflection shall take into account the inculturation import of the roles of the characters of the story and its narrator. Since the JC takes place within the context of the mission of the apostolic Church *ad Gentes*, this reflection is also to be situated within the context of that mission in Luke-Acts[1]. Where necessary, it will be supported by appropriate biblical parallels and references.

The theological reflection is meant to provide a unified holistic theology of the JC especially to the reader who may not be conversant with the narrative exegetical analysis based on the original Greek text of the JC. It is hoped that this reflection on the theology of the JC shall prepare the way for its *hermeneutical correlation* to the areas of faith-culture conflict in the Igbo Church today. To streamline our reflection in the context of Luke-Acts, it may be necessary to pose some relevant questions here:

What is the broad context of the JC in Luke-Acts? What is the implication of the conditions for salvation placed by the Judaizers to the Gentile Christians?. What is the inculturation role of Peter's pro Gentile Christian speech followed by the support of James the leader of the Jerusalem Church? What is the inculturation significance of the narrator's brief report of the mission of Paul and Barnabas to the Gentiles. What is the inculturation importance of the Jacobian intervention and proposal in favour of a Jewish-law free Gentile mission? What is the inculturation effect of the JC decision on ecclesial worship and relationship between Christians of Jewish and Gentile cultures? What is the special impact of the decision on its immediate Gentile audience and on the post JC mission to the Gentiles? What is the inculturation import of the JC for its narrator and its readers? How has the post apostolic Church received and applied the JC decision in proclaiming the faith to Jews and Gentiles? In

---

1   I say Luke-Acts and not Acts alone because the understanding of mission and inculturation in Acts requires a holistic knowledge of the Lukan teaching on mission in his two volumes.

other words, what is the missionary message of the JC in the first century Church?

In my opinion these nine questions posited in the context of Luke-Acts underline the theological-cultural issues raised by the JC story and a brief discussion of them shall hopefully highlight for the reader the elements of inculturation or the inculturation theology of the JC[2].

9.1 Broad Context of the JC: From a Purely Jewish Christian Church to a Multi-Culture Ecclesia.

(This is a reader's inculturation reflection on the general background to the JC episode. It situates the episode in its remote or broad narrative context for better intelligibilty of the faith-culture conflict in the JC proceedings).

From the beginning the Christian Church was completely Jewish in personnel and culture. Its founder, Jesus, was Jew born of a Jewess (Lk 2,1-20) circumcised and named on the eight day in accordance with Jewish Law (v.21) and brought up according to Jewish Law and customs (vv.22f.39f.41f). His twelve apostles and disciples were all Jews (9,1f; 10,1f) and his ministry was first and foremost to the Jews. But he had also a place for the non-Jews or Gentiles. He healed the dying servant of the Roman centurion whose great faith he admired and praised (Lk 7,1f). He warned about the destruction of Jerusalem and the captivity of its inhabitants by the Gentiles (Lk 21,24).

After his death and resurrection the pattern of mission changed. Before his ascension, the *risen* Lord directs his remaining eleven apostles to embark on a world mission that moves gradually from Palestine (Jerusalem, Judaea, Samaria) unto the ends of the earth (Ac 1,8b; Lk 24,47). This programmed world mission is to be undertaken only after the apostles have been fortified by the power of the Holy Spirit (Lk 24,49; Ac 1,8a). Despite all these directives, the apostles behaved as if Christianity was a movement destined for the restoration of the kingdom to Israel (Ac 1,6).

9.1.1 Christianity in Jewish Environment and Culture.

At their reception of the promised Holy Spirit on the Pentecost day (Ac 2,1f), the apostles commence their evangelisation of the Jews. The wonders and

---

2   In order to refresh the memory for a better grasp of the subsequent discussions, the reader is now advised to refer to the exposition of the title of the work in chapter one and also to the narrative concepts and terminogies explained in chapter two.

signs of the Pentecost form the basis of the apostolic proclamation of the marvels of the risen Lord. Peter's preaching to Jews and proselytes from all nations of the known world brings about the conversion of about three thousand people to the christian faith (Ac 2,41). It is striking that these initial thousands of converts were Jews from and outside Palestine, thus depicting the Jewishness of the early Church.

So the new believers and their pastors followed the normal Jewish way of life. Acts reports that the converts remained faithful to the teaching of the apostles, to the christian fellowship, to the breaking of bread and to prayers (2,42).

Each day, with one heart they regularly went to the Temple but met in their houses for the breaking of bread; they shared their food gladly and generously; they praised God and were looked up to everyone. Day by day the Lord added to their community those destined to be saved (2,46-47; cf. 3,1; 4,1; 5,42).

Note that the new christian community did not immediately break away from their former Jewish way of life and worship in order to become Christians. Rather they retained their Jewishness and tried to integrate it into their christian faith. In the language of inculturation, the new Jewish christians sought to integrate their culture and tradition in their new faith. The typical initial Jewishness of the young christian Church was to continue until an inner discontent gave rise to the choice of the the "seven men of good reputation" (6,3f) whose ministry was to transform the original Jewish face and stamp of the Church.

The first of the "seven" men was Stephen accused by a bribed mob of disparaging the holy place and the Law (6,11.13). He refuted the accusation and then reproached the Jews for failing to observe the Law given through ministry of the angels (7,53) and containing the words of life (7,38). He also disparaged the Temple by stressing that the "Most High does not live in a house that human hands have built" (7,48).

The persecution following upon the murder of Stephen engenders the preaching of the good news to the Samaritans (8,1b-25), to the Ethiopian Eunuch (vv.26-39), to peoples of Azotus and Caesarea (v.40), and to the Gentiles, Cornelius and his friends (10,1-11,18) which was for the circumcised Jewish believers a clear sign that God had granted to the Gentiles the repentance that led to life (11,18). Next the Gospel was proclaimed to the peoples of Antioch (11,19-26).

From Antioch the faith spread to all the other Gentile cities thus confirming the prophecy of Simeon that Jesus the Saviour is "a light of revelation for the Gentiles and glory for (the) people Israel" (Lk 2,32). This implies that God's salvation is "a public disclosure in view of all the Gentiles but redounding to

Israel's glory"[3]. It implies that in Christ God's salvation is for all peoples, Jews and non-Jews alike as prophesied by Isaiah in the OT[4]. Despite the Lukan presentation of the universality of salvation[5], Luke-Acts

"was and remains a story of God's determined purpose to redeem Israel and even to restore Israel's glory of bringing the light of God's reign to the Gentiles"[6] through Christ in whom "God's *boule* (Ac 2,23) of salvation has been and is being fulfilled of, by, and for Israel"[7].

For this reason, the Jewish Christians everywhere retained their Jewishness in Christianity. Even Peter is very anxious to continue his observance of the demands of Judaism (Ac 10,14). The disciple Ananias sent to minister to the converted Saul (9,10f) is described as "a devout follower of the Law" (22,12). Paul and Barnabas attend synagogue services (13,14; 14,1;17,2) during which they proclaim the christian message. And after his missionary journeys James, the leader of the Jerusalem Church, proudly tells brother Paul about the "thousands of Jews who have now become believers", yet all of them are staunch upholders of the Law (21,20) which guided the Jewish way of life at that era.

Paul himself, the Jewish apostle to the Gentiles who fought tenaciously for a Gentile Church free from the yoke and burdens of the Jewish Law and customs[8], did remain faithful to his observance of the prescriptions of that Law. He took the nazirite vow (cf. Nm 6,9-18) and shove his head as a result of that vow (Ac 18,18). He went to the Temple, joined Jewish men who took a similar vow and purified himself with them in order to refute the accusation of Jewish zealots that he was teaching the Gentiles to abandon circumcision and other customary practices of the Jews (Ac 21,21-26). He introduced himself to the Sanhedrin as "a Pharisee and the son of the Pharisees" who was on trial because of their hope on the resurrection of the dead (23,6).

---

3 Tiede, Glory to Thy People Israel, 27.
4 Cf. Koet, Simeons Worte, 1553-1557. From the comparative study of the biblical parallels of the Servant of Yahweh as "the light of the peoples or nations" in Deutero-Isaiah 42,6 and 49,6, Koet opines that Luke uses both texts as the background to a universalistic theology of salvation embracing Jews and Gentiles (Lk 2,31-32; Ac 13,47; 26,17-18) through the mission of Jesus, the servant of Yahweh: "Damit geht es in Jes 42 and 49 darum, daß die Mission des Knechtes nicht nur Israel allein betrifft, sondern auch die Volker miteinschließt" (Koet, ibid., 1555). Cf. Roloff, Kirche, 193-194.
5 Cf. Lk 2,30.32; 3,6; Ac 28,28.
6 Tiede, op. cit., 21.
7 Moessner, Ironic Fulfilment, 48.
8 Ac 15,2; Ga 3; 5,1-12; 6,11-13.

Forcefully defending himself before the govenor Felix against the false accusations of some Jews, Paul said: "I have committed no offence whatever against the either Jewish Law, or the Temple, or Caesar" (25,8). Paul observed the demands of Judaism and made sure that some converts observed the same out of deference to Jewish sensibilities. So he circumcised Timothy (the son of a Greek Father and a Jewish mother) who is considered Jewish by Jewish Law (16,1-3).

What is clear from the Acts story is that in the Jewish evironment, the first Jewish christians converted from Judaism did not renounce their Jewishness for the sake of their christian beliefs but rather continued to live according to their socio-cultural and religious traditions[9] in such a manner that Christianity appeared to its opponents as one of the Jewish religious sects (*hairesis*) called the Nazerene (6,14; 24,5). However because of their varying cultural backgrounds and different religious attitudes to the Holy City of Jerusalem, the Jewish Law and customs and the Temple, Jewish Christians who spoke Hebrew were also in conflict with the Greek-speaking or Hellenist Jewish Christians (Ac 6,1).

Even within the rank and file of the Hellenists, there were varying religious attitudes to Judaism and Christianity probably arising from the extent of the influence of Hellenist culture and civilization on them. There were staunch and conservative observers of the Law like Saul before his conversion[10] and there were also those with liberal religious views like Stephen (6,8-7,60). Unconverted "Hellenist Jews were the most active opponents of Christian propaganda"[11] just as the Hellenist Christians were the most active promoters of the missionary work[12]. The liberal Hellenist Christians were very critical of the Jewish Law, traditions, the Temple and the Holy City as testified in the false accusations brought against Stephen by his opponents from the Synagogue of Freedmen:

This man is making speeches against this Holy Place (*tou topou tou hagiou*) and the Law (*tou nomou*). We have heard him say that Jesus, this Nazarene, is going to destroy this Place and alter the traditions (*ta ethe*) that Moses handed down to us (6,13-14; cf.v 11).

Stephen's critique of Jewish religious Law and customs at his trial before the Sanhedrin (Ac 7,1-60) resembles that of Jesus presented partly in the form

---

9   Cf. Weiser, Zur Gesetzes- und Templekritik, 231.
10   Cf. Ac 23,6-7; 22,3; 26,4-5.
11   New Jerusalem Bible (NJB), Acts, 1815, footnote no. "n". Cf. Ac 6,9f; 7,58; 9,1; 21,27; 24,19.
12   Cf. Ac 8,3-40; 11,19-21.

of antithesis in the Sermon on the Mount[13] and partly in his anti-Temple sayings[14] and indirectly through the false accusations against him during his
trial[15]. As the NJB notes,

> the 'false witnesses' at the trial of Jesus similarly brought the accusation that he 'would
> destroy the Temple'. There is also a similarity in the climax of the two trials (Ac 7,56-57;
> Mt 26,62-66). The allegations concerning Mosaic practice will be made in Paul's case also
> (Ac 15,1.5; 21,21.28; 25,8; 28,17)[16].

Stephen's response to the accusations brought against him by the staunch
Hellenist Jews could be regarded as a typical representation of the critical religious attitude of the liberal Christian Hellenists towards the cherished religious places, objects, traditions, laws, customs and values of the Jews. In his
apologia before the Sanhedrin, the Hellenist Stephen played down the importance of the Temple as the house of God (7,48-50) and also accused his opponents of resisting the Holy Spirit (7,51) and of failing to keep the Law given
through the angels (7,53). At the same time he confessed his faith in Jesus as
the Messiah (7,55-56).

For such an "anti Jewish" *apologia* Stephen had to pay the price with his
life (7,56-60). And the leader of his persecutors and murderers was the young
unconverted Hellenist Saul (Paul)[17], himself a strict Pharisee who, after his
conversion (Ac 9,1-25) also became a critic of the Jewish Law and customs as
Stephen had done[18].

So despite the fact that Jewish Christians were living their faith according
to their socio-cultural context, there were still internal tensions and conflicts
arising from the contact and dialogue between Christianity and Jews brought
up within the different variants of Jewish culture. Through the Hellenist Jews
who were critical of traditional Jewish religious attitudes and practices, the
Good News spread to the Gentile environment where the cultural conflicts
deepened as the Gospel came into contact with non-Jews or Gentiles[19].

Thus in a refined and intelligent manner, Luke incorporates into the Acts
story, traditions circulating around Jewish opposition to the missions of Jesus,
his apostles and Paul, and at the same time reworks and changes them in order

---

13 Cf. Lk 6,20ff; Mt 5-7.
14 For the critique of Jesus against the Temple or his sayings against it cf. Mk 14,58f
   and Mt 26,61; Mk 15,29 and 27,40, Jn 2,19. Compare them with the accusations
   against Stephen (Ac 6,13f).
15 Cf. Lk 22,66-71; Mt 26,59-66.
16 NJB, op. cit., 1809, footnote, no. "j".
17 Cf. Ac 8,1-3; 22,1-5; Ga 1,13-14; Phil 3,6.
18 Cf. Ac 9,29; 15,2; cf. Ga 1,23.
19 Cf. Dumais, Church, 5-8 for more on this theme.

to highlight his story of the faith-culture conflict in the Jewish socio-cultural environment[20]. The internal faith-culture conflict between Jews of different religious attitudes and shreds of culture (Ac 6-7) later explodes into a faith-culture conflict between the Jewish-law Christians and the Gentile Christians.

9.1.2 Christianity in Gentile Environment and Culture.

Peter brought the Good Gews to the Gentile Cornelius and his household (10,24-48), anonymous Hellenist Christians to Antiochian Jews and Gentiles (11,19-21), and then Paul and Barnabas preached to Jews and Gentiles within the reach of their first missionary journey (11,22-14,28). None of these Jewish evangelizers required the Gentiles to be circumcised and to live like the Jews, nor did they set any condition for their conversion and salvation. Just as the Jewish Christians worshipped God and his Christ as converts to Christianity, so did the Gentile converts wish to worship God and his Christ as converts to Christianity.

The conversion of Gentiles went *pari-pasu* with the geographical movement of Christianity from the Jewish environment and culture to the Gentile world and culture. At the same time the racial composition of the Church changed. What follows is a socio-cultural and religious conflict typical of a weak human nature at the service of religion.

The conflicts are caused by extremist Jewish Christians or Judaizers[21] who are strongly opposed to the unconditional inclusion of the Gentiles in the Christian Church. This group criticised Peter for his free commensality with uncircumcised Gentiles (11,3). Although for a while they were compelled by Peter's sound theological argument to concede to the obvious fact that God has granted to the Gentiles the repentance that leads to life (11,18), yet they continued to oppose and to thwart the mission of Paul and Barnabas to the Gentiles. The two missionaries were then forced to turn their backs on their Jewish brethren while fully directing their attention to Gentiles willing to embrace the christian faith[22].

The Acts shows that the opposition from the circumcision party is borne out of prejudice and culpable ignorance of the Holy Scriptures. For if the Judaiz-

---

20   For more details on Luke's fusion and change of traditions in the Acts story, confer Weiser, Zur Gesetzes- und Tempelkritik, 231-243.

21   In this work, Christian Pharisees, converted Pharisees, Pharisee converts, Judaizers, Jewish Law Chritians, circumcision party or those of the circumcision, Jewish zealots and the like, are to be understood as referring to the same group of people opposed to a law-free Gentile Church.

22   Cf. Tannehill, Rejection, 83-101.

ers use the Scriptures to assert their special and exclusive prerogative to salvation and glory brought about by Jesus the Jew (Lk 2,30.32), it means that they have also failed to take cognizance of the same Scriptures which consider the same "*Jewish*" Jesus as "a light of revelation for the Gentiles" (Lk 2,31-32). If Jesus is the saviour and glory of the Jews, he is also the saviour of the Gentiles (Ac 4,11-2) and it is through *Him* that they glorify God[23] for granting them his mercy and salvation (Ac 26,17-18) in fulfilment of the scriptural promises[24].

Whatever may be the reservations and protestations of the Judaizers or the Pharisee Christians, the Acts story shows that even before the JC, the membership of the young *ecclesia* has already changed from a Jewish dominated Church clinging fast to Jewish religious customs and traditions to a Church that incorporates and accomodates every non-Jew who believes in the Good News of Jesus Christ preached by the Jewish evangelizers. Before the JC, the Church was no longer a Church of the Jews alone or for a privileged Jewish *haireses* but a large community of Christians made up of distinct Jewish groups and many races of the Gentiles living in the various cities of the Graeco-Roman imperium[25]. It has become a multi-racial and cultural *ecclesia* with the obvious tensions, obstacles and conflicts which characterise an assembly of different peoples and cultures.

9.2 Implications of the Cultural Obstacles Placed by Judaizers to Gentile Christians (Ac 15,1.5-7a).

(This is a reader's inculturation reflection on the exposition, the inciting moment and the complication of the JC episode. It presents to the reader the origin, cause, course, and the "dramatis personae" in the faith-and-culture conflict to be addressed and resolved by the first christian Council).

The insistence of the Christian Pharisees on the circumcision of the Gentile converts and on their observance of the whole Torah as a necessary condition for their salvation is an unbearable yoke and burden (15,10; cf. v.28). Such a demand generated a big palaver or crisis which almost divided the early Church along racial lines. The reader of Acts knows that Paul and Barnabas are totally against circumcision as a means of salvation. But he does not have before him the contents of their hot debates with the Judaizers at Antioch and Jerusalem (15,1-2.5). What they must have said in both cities may be gleaned

---

23 Cf. Benhayim, Jews, 49-60.
24 Dt 32,43; Is 11,10; Ps 18,49; Ps 117,1; Rm 15,8-12.
25 Cf. Ac 10,1-11.18; 11,19-26; 13,5.14f.46f; 14,1-27.

from the Pauline writings on circumcision and the Law where he categorically states that neither the Law nor circumcision can save the Jews or Gentiles. A citation from *Romans* may give some insight into the teaching of the Judaizers and the ensuing debates.

Circumcision has its value if you keep the Law; but if you keep breaking the Law, you are no more circumcised than the circumcised. And if an uncircumcised man keeps the commands of the Law, will not his uncircumcised state count as circumcision? More, the man who, in his native uncircumcised state keeps the Law, is a condemnation of you, who, by your concentration on the letter and on circumcision, actually break the Law. Being a Jew is not only having the outward appearance of a Jew, and circumcision is not only a visible physical operation. The real Jew is the one who is inwardly a Jew, and real circumcision is in the heart, a thing not of the letter but the spirit. He may not be praised by any human being, but he will be praised by God (Rm 2,25-29)[26] .

In the thoughts of the Galatian Paul, only those who want to cut a figure by human standards force circumcision on Gentile Christians in order to boast of their outward appearance and to escape persecution for the cross of Christ (Ga 6,12-13). What matters then is not circumcision or uncircumcision but a new creation in Christ Jesus (cf. Ga 6,15). Since the mere observance of the Law and the practice of circumcision can save neither the Jew nor the Gentile, why then did the Judaizers insist on them as necessary conditions for the salvation of the Gentile Christians? (Ac 15,1.5).

Firstly, circumcision is the characteristic mark of the fidelity and commitment of a Jewish man and his household to Yahweh's covenant with Abraham (cf.Gn 17,11f). Any male who fails to have himself circumcised has broken Yahweh's covenant and the Torah prescribes that such a man shall be cut of from the people of Israel (Gn 17,14). Circumcision is therefore basic to belonging to the tribe or family of Israel and hence to the People of God. It is both a covenantal and tribal mark. It is the easiest and surest way of integrating the Gentiles into the Abrahamic covenant.

Circumcision is the gate way to Judaism and the most essential act for the reception of a Gentile into the People of God[27] . Through it a Gentile becomes a Jewish proselyte, a full member of the Synagogue, and is fully incorporated into the Jewish people. After this full incorporation, he enjoys the rights and privileges of a Jew and assumes the obligations of keeping the whole Torah.

On the contrary, uncircumcision is a mark of a Gentile or of Jew banned from having a share in the inheritance of Israel. Hence in the eyes of the Circumcision Party, the uncircumcised Gentiles cannot have a share in the inheri-

---

26   Cf. also Ga 3; 6,11-15.
27   Cf. Lake, Proselytes, 76-79.

tance of salvation promised to Israel from of old (Lk 1,55.71). Therefore they must be banned from the salvation offered by the *Christian movement*, the new *hairesis* of Israel.

So by making circumcision and the Torah necessary conditions for salvation of the Gentiles, those Jews of the pharisaic sect who had become Christians were unequivocally stating that the Gentiles could not, and cannot, be saved unless they first become Jews and live exactly like the Jews. After all, Jesus the founder of Christianity was a Jew and lived faithfully like a Jew. He did not abolish the Jewish Law and the Prophets but actually observed all that was written in the whole Torah, Prophets and Psalms (Lk 24,44)[28]. So the Gentiles would do well to follow the footsteps of their divine master Jesus who was circumcised according to Abrahamic covenant (Gn 17,10f) and Mosaic Law (Lk 2,21) and observed and fulfilled the entire Torah.

Secondly, in the Jewish culture, circumcision is linked with the Law of cleanliness and purity (Lk 2,21-27). Hence every male is circumcised on the eight day (1,59; 2,21). An uncircumcised male is unclean and impure and contact with him also makes the Jew unclean and impure. Did not, for exmaple, the mortally wounded King Saul prefer to be killed by his circumcised armour-bearer to being alive and made fun of by the uncircumcised Philistines? (1 Sm 31,4). Did not the Jews consider as an abomination of the Maccabean era the prohibition of circumcision by King Antiochus Epiphanes and his subsequent execution of the Jews who circumcised their children? (1M 1,44-48). Was not the term *akrobustia* an insultive epithet for an "unclean" Gentile?[29]

So then to cleanse the Gentiles and make them worthy of the membership of the new Jewish sect of the Nazerenes and the salvation accruing therefrom, the Judaizers presumably thought that the best way out was to get rid of their foreskin (*akrobustia*) which makes them perpetually unclean and then impose on them the whole obligation of the covenantal Torah. In this way they hoped

---

28 Cf. Lk 2,22f.41f; 4,21; 24,44; Mt 5,17f.

29 Here a supporting footnote comment from extra Lukan sources would be helpful. Does not biblical tradition personalise the terms uncircumcised (*akrobustia*) and circumcision (*peritome*) and use them in opposition to denote the Gentile and Jewish races respectively? (Ga 2,7-9; Eph 2,11). Did the Matthean Jesus not forbid his apostles to mission to the Gentiles and to Samaritans who were half-Jews and hence unclean? (10,5-6)? Did not the same Jesus use the terms children/house dogs (*tekna/kunaria*) to express the unfortunate distinction between Jews and Gentiles respectively? (Mt 15,24). Nothing could be more humiliating to the Gentiles than such an attitude ingrained in the Jews by the deep consciousness of their special divine election (Cf. Ex 19,3f; Dt 4,1-8; 6,1ff; 7,1ff; 9,1ff).

that the ageold "revelation of his (God's) will would be integrated with belief in Jesus and the total be presented as what is required for salvation"[30].

This attitude to what is necessary for salvation has many *false* implications. It implies that it is not Jesus alone who saves. Neither does faith in his name save nor does the keeping of his commandment of love save. Belief in Jesus alone and in his saving grace does not save the Christian. What alone saves is compulsorily living like a Jew and practising the obligatory religious characteristics of Judaism such as circumcision, Temple worship and observance of purity laws. Thus the Judaizers are deliberately set on uprooting the foundations of christian soteriology. Their "Gospel" cuts at the root of the Acts theology of salvation based firstly on belief in the name and power of the grace of Jesus (Ac 13,38)[31] and secondarily on the observance of Jewish Law (*nomos*) and customs (*ethe*)[32] which are concretely expressed in the believer's good works (10,34-35).

The Christian Pharisees are thus making erroneous sectarian demands that are completely contrary to the letter and spirit of the Good News preached by Jesus and his apostolic witnesses. It is a dangerous heresy couched in a simple conditional sentence that appears to proclaim a salutary message to the Gentiles. It is a total falsification of the saving Gospel which the Galatian Paul calls "another gospel" preached by false brethren (Ga 1,16) insisting on justification through the Law of Moses (Ac 13,38).

By so preaching the Judaizers have negated the true Gospel of Jesus and his witnessess, placed circumcision and the Torah above faith and salvation in Jesus and set themselves up as the determinants of salvation. The means of salvation in the christian pharisaic dispensation are no longer faith in Jesus[33], repentance and baptism in the name of Jesus Christ or the Trinity[34] and the love of God and neighbour which is the fulfilment of all the Torah and the Prophets (Mt 22,40). Rather salvation is gained only by the practice of male circumcision and the observance of Jewish "*ethe*".

It is indisputable that the Lukan Gospel story shows that Jesus actually fulfilled all that is contained in the Law, the Prophets and the Writings (Lk 24,44), but while fulfilling the OT prescriptions, he did not teach that circumcision and Mosaic Law are necessary conditions for the salvation of his followers. Neither did he send out his apostles to preach circumcision and Torah observance. Rather he mandated them to be his witnesses to all nations and

---

30   Kilgallen, Brief Commentary, 121.
31   Cf. also 4,11-12; 10,43; 15,11; 16,31.
32   Cf. Ac 6,13.14; 26,3; 15,1; Weiser, Zur Gesetzes- und Tempelkritik, 227-229.
33   Cf.Lk 7,50; 8,40; Ac 4,11-12,
34   Cf Ac 2,38; 8,16; 10,48; 19,5; 22,16; Mt 28,19, etc.

peoples from Jerusalem unto the ends of the earth (Ac 1,8). All who believe in their teaching will be saved through faith in his name (Lk 24,47)[35]. So the Gospel evidence shows that Jesus clearly laid out the necessary means and conditions of salvation for his witnesses and their audiences.

Therefore to teach or preach otherwise is an erroneous deviation from the salutary message of Christ and a deliberate opposition of oneself to his saving good tidings. If male circumcision and the observance of the whole Jewish Law *qua* Law is the only means to salvation, then Jesus died in vain and christian life would be nothing more than a return to the primordial "*tohu-wabohu*" (cf. Gn 1,2).

But if for the sake of argument one accepts that the rightful observance of the whole Torah would save the Gentile Christians, such a tenet immediately poses some disturbing questions about the salvation of both female Jews and female Gentile Christians excluded by the Torah from the obligation of the Abrahamic covenant of cirumcision (cf. Gn 17,10-14.26-27). Now if it happens that the Jewish females as integral members of the covenant are *indirectly* saved through their ceremonial and ritual participation in the circumcision of their husabands and sons, what happens then to the female Gentile Christians who have no claim to the *salutary* benefits of the Abrahamic covenant? On what then depends their salvation? If the Judaizers or the circumcision party have discovered a way of assuring the salvation of the female Jews, then they should also invent a means of saving the female Gentile Christians. Does this not really expose the emptiness and absurdity of the teaching on circumcision as a necessary condition for salvation?

Still there is another problem. Since in Jewish eyes an uncircumcised Gentile is in the permanent state of ritual uncleanliness, does it also mean that he remains unclean even after his conversion to Christianity?. If it is so, then it means that the Jewish Christians must desist from every form of table-fellowship with the Gentile Christians lest they (Jews) also incur ritual uncleanliness.

Against this background one can better understand the reason for the indignation of "*those of the circumcision*" against Peter's lodging and commensality with the converted Gentile Cornelius and his friends (Ac 11,3; cf. 10,48). But through his vision of clean and unclean animals, Peter underwent socio-cultural and spiritual transformations before he mustered some courage to commensalate with the Gentiles. His passionate defence for his conduct (cf. Ac 11,4-17) shows that he overcame his racial prejudice against non-Jews.

The question of the *cleanliness or uncleanliness* of the Gentile converts does not in any way augur well for authentic christian life. It threatens the very

---

35   Cf. Ac 1,8; Mk 16,15; Mt 28,19.

communal life of the followers of Jesus. It means that Jewish and Gentile Christians cannot eat nor worship together as believers united in Christ. It implies that the Church must institute and promote "*Eucharistic apartheid*" in order to take care of Jewish sensibilities to the detriment of christian love and unity. The breaking of bread in memory of Jesus will thus become a racist partisan meal of two opposing christian peoples, a schismatic celebration instead of a loving *koinonia* in Christ as a community of believers.

This brief reflection on the implications of the Judaizers' teaching on Law and circumcision (Jewish *ethe*) reveals that it is not consonant with the Gospel of Jesus Christ and the teaching of his witnesses on salvation. Rather the Judaizers' teaching is a heresy, an erroneous attempt to replace the Good News of salvation with socio-cultural and religious observances that only sow and nurse the seeds of discord, disunity and schism in the christian community of Jesus.

Inculturationally the Judaizers embarked on a wrong course of trying to root the Gospel into the lives of the Gentile Christians by first seeking to make Jews out of them. To force the Gentiles to lose their "Gentilesness" in order to become Christians is a perversion of the Gospel message. But since grace builds on nature, the Gospel of grace must build on the nature of the Gentiles just as it builds on the nature of the Jews to prepare them for Christ.

Such a situation cannot be allowed to persist in an *ecclesia* that claims to witness to the name of Jesus who purifies the hearts of both Jew and Gentile by faith (Ac 15,9) and saves them through his grace (v.11). Therefore something must be done to restore the unity and love being disrupted by the heresy of Judaizers. Providential is the timely intervention of the Church leaders to settle the problem.

9.3 Inculturation Role of Peter's Pro Gentile Speech (Ac 15,7b-11.14-18).

(This is a reader's reflection on the inculturation role of Peter's Council intervention. As a combination of the first real scene and the first part of the third real scene of the JC episode, it stresses divine impartiality to Jews and Gentiles).

When the "whole" Church has gathered to resolve the dispute caused by the demands of the Christian Pharisees, Peter makes an intervention that axes the roots of their heretical teaching. In opposition to the Pharisee Christians, Peter teaches that the impartial God had through his own ministry granted his Holy Spirit, grace and salvation to devout Gentiles in the same way as he did to Jewish believers without any preconditions or differentiations (15,7-9). This is because grace and salvation are unmerited divine favours granted gratuitously and equally to every believer in Jesus Christ irrespective of his/her ethnic origin or nationality (v.11). To place conditions on the way of Gentiles called by God is to oppose the divine will. It is a heresy which tantamounts to a temptation of God (v.10).

The speech stresses God's initiative in the vocation of the Gentiles to the christian faith and his impartiality in granting salvation to Jews and Gentiles alike. It emphasizes the fundamental equality of all races before God and underlines the equality of all believers in Jesus Christ. It highlights the universal offer of salvation to everyone who fears God and lives uprightly.

As already noted in the exegetical section, Peter's teaching is a flash-back to his missionary experience in the conversion of the Roman *Gentile* centurion Cornelius and his circle of friends. And because Peter anchores his Council intervention (Ac 15,7-11) mainly on the reminiscences of his missionary encounter with Cornelius (cf. Ac 10,1-11,18) which is also supported by James, the respected leader of the Jerusalem Church (15,13-15), *much space* will be given to that Cornelius episode in this section.

9.3.1 Cornelius Episode and Peter's Speech.

The visionary expriences of Cornelius (Ac 10,1-8) and Peter (vv.9-16) prepare them for the important trans-cultural encounter between Jewish Christians and God-fearing Gentiles sympathetic to Judaism[36]. The visions are a necessary preparations to help Peter overcome his Jewish scruples and prejudice against social intercourse with Gentiles. While a pious and God-fearing (*eusebes kai phoboumenos ton Theon*) Gentile Cornelius will easily and without any objection mix up with the Jews, even a moderately orthodox Jew would be unwilling to enter the dwelling of such a devout Gentile.

Such a Jew would require some special divine revelation to convince and move him on to accept an invitation from a Gentile. That revelation did come as the messengers sent by Cornelius in obedience to his own vision and divine guidance were approaching Peter's seaside residence at the house of Simon the tanner. The mission from Cornelius perfectly clarifies the strange vision to Peter. He must go and "present the Gospel to the Gentiles on exactly the same terms as to Jews"[37]. He had no other option but to readjust himself and his lifetime of habits to his new vocation[38].

---

36 Cf. Lukasz, Evangelizzazione, 68-69.
37 Guy, Missionary Message, 55.
38 Cf. Lukasz, op. cit., 90-91.

In Peter's vision of clean and unclean animals[39] (Ac 10,12; 11,6), reminiscient of the Torah pericopes on such creatures[40], he is admonished to regard all animals as clean because God has cleansed them all. He is also commanded three times to slaughter ritually (*thuson*) and eat (*kai phage*). Despite such a triple divine revelation, Peter the orthodox Jew, remonstrates and refuses to slaughter and eat, lest he defile himself and contravene the Torah prescriptions against eating certain creatures designated as unclean[41].

But what precisely made these animals clean or unclean? The animal world is divided into three groups or spheres: the flying, the walking, and the swimming spheres. Each group has its peculiar mode of movement and its characteristic behaviour. The clean animals conform to the nature of their species. But the unclean do not conform to the set standards of their species or group[42]. They rather transgress the proper nature of the standard pure types.

The lists of animals in Peter's vision basically correspond to the terrestial animals created on the sixth day (Gn 1,24.30) and the birds of heaven on the fifth day (vv.20-22)[43]. By this correspondence of the lists, the narrator seems to be suggesting that the clean and unclean animals of the vision are representative of the whole animal world created by God. It is important to note that from the beginning (*b^ereshith*) of creation, no creature was considered unclean. Rather God their creator found them all *very good* (Gn 1,31). How does it then come about that some of these *very good* creatures were later regarded as unclean?

Biblically the enumeration and distinction between clean and unclean animals are attested to for the first time during the deluge (cf. Gn 6-9). In 7,2 God asks Noah to take with him and his family into the Ark seven pairs of clean animals (*apo ton ktenon ton katharon*) and one pair of unclean animal (*apo ton ktenon me katharon*). However in 7,8-9 Noah takes with him a pair of each animal species[44], a male and a female either from the clean (*apo ton ktenon katharon*) or from the unclean (*apo ton me katharon*). But the issue is not whether he takes seven pairs of the clean and only one pair of the unclean, or just equal pairs of both clean and unclean animal species. The emphasis is

---

39 Unlees otherwise stated, "*animals*" here stand for land, air and sea creatures.
40 Cf. Gn 7,2f.8-9; 8,1.17.19; 9,1-3; 9,10; Lv 11,1-47; Dt 14,3-21. (cf. Gn 6,19-20).
41 The unclean species of larger animals, birds and reptiles are enumerated in Lv 11,1-47 and Dt 14,3-21.
42 Cf. Wenham, Theology, 7-10.
43 The two lists in Ac 10,12 and 11,6 vary by the addition of "*ta Theria*" (wild-beasts) in 11,6. Cf. Lukasz, Evangelizzazione, 75.
44 Scholars explain that the variations are due to different traditions or sources used in the composition of the book.

on Noah's selection and accomodation of both clean and unclean animals in the protective and saving Ark.

After the flood, Noah kept, reared, ritually slaughtered and ate all the clean and unclean species of animals. In the same way Peter is ordered in his vision to do like Noah by slaughtering and eating the animals without bothering about their ritual cleanliness or uncleanliness. In this sense, Peter's vision harks back to the Noachide practice[45].

Again the Noachide selection of animals shows that God did spare both clean and unclean animals for the repopulation of the earth after the deluge. This may also symbolically mean that God loves and takes an impartial and equal care of all his creatures. If God equally cares for every animal or beast (cf. Mt 6,26), moreso does he take an impartial care of every human being created in his very image and likeness (cf. Gn 1,26-27). God's equal care and love for all animal species can therfore be symbolically correlated to his impartial and providential care and love for "every race, language, people, nation" (Rv 5,9) of the earth.

What is particularly striking is that the division of animals into clean and unclean took place in the Noachide era (cf. Gn 6,5-10,32) before ever the Jewish people were specially elected by God in the person of Abraham (cf. Gn 12-17). Yet the Noachide lineage, representing the new human race after the deluge, slaughtered and ate all species of animals irrespective of their classifications (cf. Gn 9,1-5). It is only later on in the religious history of the Jews, the descendants of Abraham, that the Torah prescriptions of Lv 11,1-47 and Dt 14,3-21 makes the abstention from unclean animals[46] a ritual law to be observed by every Jew faithful to the Judaistic religion.

This brief reflection on Peter's vision of animals in the Acts in relation to the Torah show that from the time of Noah up to the apostolic times, the biblical story classified the animal world into clean and unclean species. The Jews later incorporated and integrated this classification into their purity laws, perhaps as a help towards purity of life. This is because "holiness requires that individuals shall conform to the class to which they belong"[47]. The failure of a Jew to conform to his/her race by eating unclean animals makes him/her unclean and unholy.

Peter's protest against eating unclean animals (cf. Ac 10,14) shows his preknowledge of the Torah prohibitions of Lev 11 and Dt 14. It testifies to his

---

45   Cf. Derret, Clean, 216f; Lukasz, Evangelizzazione, 76f.

46   Besides abstention from unclean animals, the law also forbids the eating of "clean animals" that died naturally or were slain by savage beasts or were ritually tainted by what is unclean (cf. Lv 17,15; Dt 14,21).

47   Douglas, Purity, 53.

strict observance of this religious taboo which is also a sign of his religious orthodoxy. His protest parallels that of the Prophet Ezekiel (4,9-17) who also refuses to eat what Yahweh offers him to eat because he considers them defiled[48]. But while Ezekiel's vision symbolically shows him how the exiled Israel/Jews would have to eat their food defiled (v.13), Peter's vision invites him to rethink his protest against eating *unclean animals* which are part of God's *very good* creatures and which the same Torah has permitted him to eat in his "unclean" situation at the Tanner's home at Joppa. For in the sacrificial laws of Dt 12,13ff one reads:

"...whenever you wish, you may slaughter and eat meat wherever you live - as much as the blessing of Yahweh affords you. Clean or unclean may eat it as though it were gazelle or deer. You will not however eat the blood, but will pour that like water on the ground (Dt 12,15-16; cf.vv.22-23).

If this deuteronomic food regulation did not help Peter overcome his religious scruples, he should have used the Master Jesus' pronouncement of "all foods clean" (Mk 7,19)[49] as a justifying excuse for slaughtering and eating the unclean animals without qualms of conscience. Or he should have remembered that cleanliness does not consist in a wicked person's cleaning of the outside of the cup and plate, but consists of giving alms from one's possessions (Lk 11,39-40).

However Peter's lodging with Simon the Tanner arouses some curiousity about his strict adherence to the Torah ritual observance. By lodging at the house of a man whose leather trade had consigned to a "permanent state of uncleanliness", Peter had already compromised or even relaxed his strict observance of the purity laws of the Torah[50]. Therefore even if he had never eaten "what is common and unclean" (Ac 10, 14), he could no longer claim to be free from defilement by an "unclean" person or house.

Why then was he protesting against eating unclean animals while he was cohabiting with a traditionally unclean person? It is hard to explain. But from the point of view of the narrator, the explanation may be due to the program of

---

48   See Ezk 4,14: "Then I said, 'Lord Yahweh, my soul is not defiled. From my childhood unti now, I have never eaten animal that has died a natural death or been savaged; no tainted meat has ever entered my mouth'".

49   Cf. Cf. Bruce, Book of the Acts, 206; Mk 7,1-5.14-23; Mt 15,1-2.10-20 for the teaching of Jesus on the "clean and unclean". This teaching is not found in the Gospel of Luke, but it is found in the Acts. The probable reason for its absence from the Gospel may be due to Luke's plan of a two-volume work in which he programatically narrates the cleansing and gradual integration of the unclean Gentiles into the community of clean Jews.

50   Cf. Barclay, Acts, 80-81.

the gradual revelation of God's will to Peter in order to manifest his purpose of gradual inclusion of the Gentiles in the Church. The Gospel stories of Mark and Matthew have already pronounced all foods clean (Mk 7,19,) but in Luke's story, God is yet to pronounce them clean. The pronouncement comes later in the Acts as the apostolic mission programatically moves from the Jewish World to the unclean Gentile environment.

The divine cleansing of the food in Acts metaphorically and symbolically marks the first step towards the divine cleansing of the "common and unclean Gentiles"[51]. So the triple command to eat unclean meat and the triple protest by Peter help to emphasize the gradual unfolding of divine will and purpose to him. At the same time, Peter's triple demural portrays him as one either lacking the moral courage to listen to the heavenly voice and change his narrow religious views or as being oblivious of the dietary permission of the Torah and of Jesus' teaching which has fulfilled and superceded the Torah dietary laws.

Nevertheless after his protest and bewilderment at such a vision which was urging him to act against his religious scruples, the arrival of the "*unclean*" messengers from the uncircumcised and "unclean" Gentile Cornelius begin to clarify the meaning of his vision. His hospitality to those messengers marks the reversal of his Jewish prejudice and the beginning of his social conversion that initiates a new stage in Jewish/Gentile relationship (cf. Ac 10,23). By following the messengers to Cornelius, Peter strikes a death-blow to Jewish religious exclusivism and cultural prejudice against Gentiles and then unlocks the "door of faith" to those considered to be "dogs" (cf. Mt 15,26-27).

From then on it is no longer *atemitos* or improper for Peter and the other Jews to mix up socially with the Gentiles (Ac 10,28). The vision of Cornelius and his own vision have taught him a big lesson. Now he regards the Gentiles in the same way as he regards the Jews. He is not only socially but also spiritually converted and enlightened to see the impartial and just design of God in the call of the Gentiles to the christian faith.

Peter's open acknowledgement before the Gentiles of God's equal love for both Jews and Gentiles can be regarded as the "*punctum puncti*" of his social and spiritual conversion. He has at last come to realise that God does not love the Jews more than the Gentiles. Rather both races are pleasing and acceptable to him so long as they fear him and do what is right (10,34-35). And to please God, one must not be a Jew or Jewess nor must one live like the Jews. All that

---

51 To this effect Rolof says: "Das Ineinander von Rein und Unrein, das Petrus zugemutet wird, verweist auf seinen zukünftigen Umgang mit reinen und unreinen Menschen innerhalb der gleichen Gemeinde" (Apg., 170).

is necessary is one's pious and God-fearing life irrrespective of one's qualities and origin.

Put in inculturation language, it means that God does not love or favour a person because of his/her natural beauty, intelligence, wealth, titles, honours, prestige, social class, colour, race, language, nationality, or for any of one's personal and artificial make-ups and or qualifications. After all, those endowments and make-ups are God's gratuitous gifts to his creatures. Rather God loves, accepts, and saves someone because of his/her piety and good works which are performed with faith in the saving grace and name of Jesus Christ for *"all who believe in Jesus will have their sins forgiven through his name"* (Ac 10,43)[52].

In the same way, physical circumcision or the observance of the requirements of Jewish Law plays no role in making one pleasing to God. This is also attested to by the descent of the Holy Spirit on the unbaptised and uncircumcised Gentile Cornelius and his friends (Ac 10,44-46) in a similar, manifest and dramatic manner as he descended on the Jews (15,8f) on the Pentecost day (2,1-12).

Since those Gentiles were not yet baptised, their reception of the Spirit is still more amazing than that of the baptised Jews. It is totally an unprecedented event that uncircumcised and unbaptised Gentiles could be favoured by God with his pentecostal gifts of the Holy Spirit, thereby placing them on a par with the Jews, and moreso indicating a greater favour for the Gentiles since the Jewish disciples, unlike the Gentiles, were prepared and disposed aforehand for the descent of the Holy Spirit (Ac 1,4-5.8).

The wondrous, dramatic outpouring of the Holy Spirit upon the devout Gentiles do overwhelm Peter and his Jewish companions of the circumcision party. It has superceded the stunning, heavenly voice of his vision declaring the end of the Jewish, legal and ritual distinctions between "clean and unclean". It reveals to them clearly that the promise made to Israel (Ac 2,33.38; 5,31) is now openly extended to the Gentiles. It leads Peter to remember the word of the Lord Jesus (11,16) and to give an authoritative and convincing interpretation of the event which damped and stilled the objections of the circumcision party (11,18; 15,12) both before and during the JC (11,3;15,1.5). So he orders the Gentiles to be baptised as formal admission of their divine initiation into the christian fold (10,47-48; 11,17).

If God himself, through his Holy Spirit, has manifestly approved the Gentiles and granted them his forgiveness, mercy, grace and salvation as he exactly granted them to his chosen people, the Jews; if God has spoken and acted marvellously through his Holy Spirit, who then are the Jews to raise ob-

---

52   Cf. Ac 2,38; 3,16; 4,11-12; 15,11.

jections against God and thereby resist the Spirit and his divine will and purpose? Peter's argument and defence before the Judaizers (11,4-17) and the Councillors (5,7-11) are clear and incontrovertible. All could not but keep quiet (15,12a) or give thanks to God for granting the Gentiles repentance unto life (11,18).

All in all, the descent of the Holy Spirit on the Gentiles remains the most vivid and undeniable revelation and proof that God has accepted them into the community of believers in Christ and granted them his salvation without first of all requiring them to observe any of the prescriptions of the Jewish Torah. It is a confirmation of the scriptures that God has gratuitously called them and saved them through his grace[53] (cf. Ac 13,47; 15,13-18).

9.3.2   Cornelius Episode and Jacobian Speech.

The scriptural confirmation of the Petrine interpretation of the Cornelius episode is supported by James (Ac 15,14). The Prophets from the ancient days (*aph' hemeron archaion*, 15,7) had witnessed the initial, irreversible, divine choice of the Gentiles. This election firstly refers to Cornelius and his friends, but the Jacobian citation of the Prophet Amos as a back-up to that call (15,15f) may well justify its *hermeneutical extension* to God's choice of the Gentiles in the OT times and NT times.

Some examples are urgent: In time of drought and famine God sent the Prophet Elijah to the widow of Zarephath whose hospitality was rewarded by the Prophet's raising of her dead son to life[54]. Also Elisha healed the Syrian leper Naaman by instructing him to wash himself in a river for his cleansing[55]. At the preaching of Jonah the Ninivites repented and did penance for their sins and were converted to the Lord[56]. And the queen of Sheba travelled a very long distance just to listen to the wisdom of King Solomon[57]

Early in his ministry Jesus used these Elija-Elisha miracles and the episodes of Jonah and the queen of Sheba to prove the fact of God's special visitation of the Gentiles (cf. Ac 15,14) to his hostile Jewish brethren[58]. Later he praised

---

53   God "saved us and called us to be holy - not because of anything we ourselves had done bur for his own purpose and by his own grace. This grace had already been granted to us, in Christ Jesus, before the beginning of time, but it has been revealed only by the appearing of the saviour Christ Jesus (2 Tm 1,9-10a).

54   Cf. Lk 4,25-26; 1 Kg 17,7-24.

55   Cf. Lk 4,27; cf. 2 Kg 5,1ff.

56   Cf. Lk 11,29-30.32; cf. Jon 3,1-10.

57   Cf. Lk 11,31; cf. 1 Kg 10,1-13.

58   Cf. Lk 4,24-27; 11,29-32.

the Roman centurion for his faith that was greater than that of anyone in Israel (Lk 7,10). There are other examples[59] but these are enough to show that God's favours had been granted to the Gentiles long before the JC[60].

Before and after the Council, one reads that these favours are passed on to the Gentiles especially when some Jews appeared to have rejected the Good News. On two occasions Paul had to address the opposing Jews thus:

"We had to proclaim the word of God to you first, but since you have rejected it, since you do not think yourselves worthy of eternal life, here and now we turn to the gentiles. For this is what the Lord commanded us to do when he said: '*I have made you a light to the nations, so that my salvation may reach the remotest parts of the earth*[61]' (Ac 13,46-47)". And "your blood be on your heads; from now on I will go to the gentiles with a clear conscience (18,6)".

However the mission to the Gentiles was not just patterned on the Jewish rejection of the Gospel message[62]. It was/is rather an integral part of God's will to save all peoples (Ac 13,47) as expressed in the commission of the *risen Jesus* to his disciples (1,8) and to Paul in particular (9,15; 22,21). It is a further proof of God's equal love for Jews and Gentiles. Christ's universal imperative of mission "unto the ends of the earth" connotes in itself the universal offer of salvation to all Jewish and Gentile believers in him.

All these constitute the *inculturation role* of Peter's pro Gentile speech. God's unpreconditoned and gratuitous offer of his Holy Spirit and grace to Cornelius and his friends is the best *apologia* for an unconditional proclamation of the Good News to the Gentiles and for their unconditional integration into the Church. The Cornelius episode then becomes the *classic symbol and model* for the vocation of the Gentiles as a people of God on a par with his Israel[63].

In Cornelius is symbolised God's call of the Gentiles and the Church's unrestricted openess to all peoples and cultures. In Cornelius are all Gentiles

---

59 Other extra Lukan examples are: the Matthean genealogy (1,1-17) recalls the inclusion of two Gentile women, the impious Rahab and the devoted Ruth (v.5) and also two impious or adulterous (unclean), Tamar and Uriah's wife (v,3.6) in family tree of Jesus. Rahab was elected for saving Israel's spies and for her confession of faith in Israel's Yahweh (Jos 1,1-21; 22-25), and Ruth for her fidelity to her Jewish mother-in-law (cf. Rt 1-4).

60 Cf. O' Toole, Unity, 109-148; Cassidy, Society, 2-5: these provide a good summary of Jesus affirmation for less regarded groups like Gentiles, Samaritans, women, tax collectors and sinners.

61 This citation in italics is taken from Is 49,6.

62 See Tannehill, Rejection by Jews, 83-101, for the exposition of this pattern of Paul's mission in the Acts.

63 Cf. Bovon, De Vocatione, 118-129; 212-219.

symbolically called, blessed, cleansed, and saved (11,18). In Cornelius is salvation symbolically actualised for every devout Gentile in an equal, impartial and gratuitous manner as for a devout Jew. Thus did Peter set the principle and pace for the Council and for the continued ecclesial mission *ad Gentes*[64].

9.4 Inculturation Significance of God's Marvels for the Gentiles (Ac 15,12).

(This is a reader's reflection on the inculturation import of the mission report via the narrator's voice. As the second real scene, the marvel story depicts God's gratuitous election of Gentiles in the same way as he chose the Jews).

The previous section has presented some examples of God's marvels for the Gentiles in the OT and in the ministries of Jesus and his disciples especially Peter. Here are more examples of these divine wonders and signs in the Acts that further confirm the vocation of the Gentiles. The marvels are worked both before and after the JC as Paul himself glowingly testifies during his defence before King Agrippa. The Lord Jesus who appeared to him in a vision and called him also promised him these saving marvels:

I shall rescue you from the people and from the nations to whom I am sending you to open their eyes, so that that they may turn from darkness to light, from the dominion of Satan to God, and receive, through faith in me, forgiveness of their sins and a share in the inheritance of the sanctified (26,17-18).

These two verses present a five-part summary of the Lord's marvels worked for the Gentiles through the agency of Paul and his companions. The Peoples' eyes are opened through the powerful operation and influence of the Good News. Before hearing it, they were like blind people, but after hearing and accepting it, the scales of the blindness drop away from their eyes. The marvels turn them away from the darkness of error to the light of grace and life coming from Christ, the way, the light, and the life. The meeting with Christ redeems the Gentiles held under the sway of evil. Then they break away from their sinful past and receive forgiveness of their sins. A new life in Christ is finally offered to them[65]. So this passage goes to indicate that the marvels of the Lord are not only miracles but also the converting, transforming and sanctifying effect of the Good News on its audience or recipients. More of these marvels are worked through Paul in his second and third missionary journeys.

---

64   Cf. Guy, Missionary Message, 52-56.
65   O'Toole, Unity, 192-193.

Urged in a vision, Paul crosses over to Macedonia to "help" the Gentiles with the preaching of the Good News (Ac 16,9). In this second mission, Lydia, the wealthy woman of Thyatira is won for Christ (16,13-15). A possessed slave-girl is exorcised to the chagrin of her master who profited much from her soothsaying (16,16-24). A gaoler with his household is converted to the faith after the experience of a miraculous earthquake that freed the imprisoned Paul and companions from the jail (16,25-40). Dionysius the Areopagite, Damaris and some others are converted after Paul's preaching to the Athenian philosophers (17,34). At Corinth, Paul receives a vision of the Lord encouraging him to stay on in the city with so many believers (18,0-10).

These marvels continue in Paul's third missionary journey and and in his travel from Jerusalem to Rome via Malta. At Ephesus he instructs, baptises, and imparts the Holy Spirit on the twelve disciples of John the Baptist. The men speak in tongues and prophesy (19,4-7) as the apostles spoke on the Pentecost day (2,1-4) and as Cornelius and his friends spoke even before being baptised (10,44). Paul spends two years in Ephesus preaching to both Jews and Greeks.

So remarkable were the miracles worked by God at Paul's hands that handkerchiefs and aprons which had touched him were taken to the sick, and they were cured of their illnesses, and the evil spirits came out of them (19,11-12).

Here again is a summary report of God's marvels which attest to his choice and acceptance of the Gentiles.

Furthermore the city of of Ephesus is swept clean of its superstition, magic and spells as evidenced in the despoiling of the quack exorcists - the seven sons of Sceva (19,11-16), in the many conversions and the burning of magic books of costly sum (vv.17-20) and in the subsequent riot of the silversmiths whose trade of making images of the goddess Diana is grounded by the great success of Paul's Ephesian mission (vv.23-40).

At Troas Paul raises the dead young Eutychus to life (20,7-12). In his sea voyage to Rome, God saves him and all the travellers from the ferocious storm and shipwreck (27,14-44) as earlier revealed to him in an angelic vision (vv.23-26). Being miraculously delivered from the expected deadly bite of a viper in the Island of Malta, the natives think that Paul must have been a god (28,4-6). As their guest, Paul cures the father of chief Publius and many Maltese of their various sicknesses and ailments (vv.8-9).

All these are God's signs and wonders for and among the Gentiles at different stages of Paul's mission. These miracles worked through Paul are seen to correspond to Peter's miracles for and among the Jews, thus showing how

Paul's authority is confirmed by the same wonders and signs as Peter's[66]. Paul's many miracles, the routing of magical powers and the conversion of many Gentiles do confirm God's election of the Gentiles as a people for his name on an equal footing with the Jews. All these manifestations of God's love and election of the Gentiles highlights the inculturation significance of the Council report of Paul and Barnabas.

9.5 Inculturation Import of Necessary Torah Burden for Gentiles (Ac 15,19-20; 29).

(This is a reader's reflection on the inculturation import of the four abstentions decreed for the Gentiles. As a combination of parts of the third and fourth real scenes of the JC episode, the decree links the Gentile Chrisitans to the Noachide covenant, to the scriptural visionary elections of the Gentiles, and reminds them of their Torah obligations as non-Jews).

Of the whole Torah prescriptions, only four are imposed upon the Gentiles as a necessary burden (cf. Mt 11,28; 20,28) for the Gentiles. Two are ethical in nature and prohibit them from idolatory and incest respectively. The other two are ritual and forbid the eating of strangled animals and blood which symobilses life belonging to God alone. These four prescriptions proposed by James (15,20) and adopted with a slight amendment by the Council (v.29b) were already stipulated by the Torah in order to facilitate Jewish/Gentile social relationship on equal terms. The Gentiles would have done well by abstaining from them (v.29c).

Does this mean that the rule of christian life is reducible to only four minimal prescriptions for social behaviour? By no means. The whole of Torah as fulfilled by Jesus (Lk 24,44), the founder of Christianity, is binding on every believer (Lk 16,17; cf. Mt 5,17). So the JC with all its powers from Christ cannot simply exempt the Gentiles from the obligation of keeping his commandments which are necessary for christian life and eternal life[67]. So it is obvious and presumed that the Gentile converts are bound by the commandments of God and of the Church. What is not acceptable to them, or rather what constitutes an obstacle to their christian living, are the minute details and

---

66 For the correspondence of Peter's miracles with Paul's, compare: Ac 3,2-8 with Ac 14,8-10; 5,15 with 19,2; 5,16 with 16,18; 8,18-24 with 13,6-11; 8,17 with 19,6; 9,36-41 with 20,9-12; 12,6-11 with 16,25-34. Cf. Bruce, Acts (1990), 26, for a summary of the seven corresponding miracles of Peter and Paul.

67 Cf. Lk 18,18-22; 10,35.

elongations of those commandments in the form of ritual purity laws[68] or what the Judaizers describe as the custom (*ethos*) or the Law (*nomos*) of Moses (cf. 15,1.5).

Should a Gentile convert be subjected to Jewish social and dietary laws in order to be a Christian or be saved?. An orthodox Judaizing Christian would answer affirmatively while a Gentile would outrightly reject such laws. This would put a stalemate to any form of social intercourse between both races, and since human nature is not disjunctured, the resultant social problems would also be carried over to the religious sphere - to the practice of christian faith.

A compromise must therefore be worked out so that no one feels cheated or disadvantaged. That may be the purpose of the four minimal demands on the Gentile Christians - *a placatory gesture to the Judaizers* - otherwise the Gentiles are not being obliged to do anything more than what the Torah and the christian message require of them[69].

Common sense also shows how impossible it would be for Gentile converts to be introduced to Christianity by way of observance of all Jewish ethical and ritual laws[70]. How can a Gentile who, in his socio-cultural background, has no atom of knowledge of the Torah, begin to be catechized in Jewish Law as a necessary prelude to christian life? How can such a Gentile neophyte be indoctrinated with Jewish rules about clean and unclean foods that are prejudicial to his/her very culture in order to christianize the Gentile and open the way of salvation to him/her? (15,1.5).

And even if the Gentile accepts that indoctrination as necessary for his faith and salvation, will it be possible for him to change suddenly and completely his old eating habits in order to be received into the Church with her difficult and apparently *strange message* about "Jesus and resurrection" or about "outlandish gods" (Ac 17,18), or "about a dead man called Jesus whom Paul alleged to be alive" (25,19)? If the Jews were in the place of the Gentiles, would they accept such a condition for a religious exchange for eternal life?. It is hard to reply affirmatively. For this reason the least that can be demanded from the Gentiles are certain minimal observances common to both Judaism and Christianity in order to assuage the unpleasant feelings of the Judaizers

---

68 Cf. Lv 11,1ff; Dt 14,3ff.
69 Cf. Gn 9,4; Ex 20,3-6; Lv 17,10-14; 18,6-25; Dt 12,15-16.23-24; 27,23; Mt 5,17-48; 1 Co 5,1; 10,14; etc.
70 The same common sense demands that a painful physical operation of circumcision should not be performed on male Gentile believers as a necessary condition for their salvation. That would not only make the acceptance of the Good News very painful, but would make its content empty, absurd and ridiculous to the Gentile audience.

and also throw the gate open to all levels of contact bewtween Jewish and Gentile Christians.

Although there are only four minimal abstentions, the JC still considers them as a burden (*baros*) on the Gentiles. But they are slight burdens with a difference (Ac 15,19) - different because they are necessary (*epanankes*, v.28), not because they guarantee the type of salvation preached by the Christian Pharisses (15,1.5), not because they would guarantee the salvation of the Gentiles as would do baptism, faith in Christ and the grace of God, but because they are a *compulsory requisition* in order to legitimize the baptismal cleanliness or purity of the Gentile Christians before a traditionally uncompromising Jewish Christian sect that is yet to do away with its prejudice of regarding the Gentiles as being in a permanent state of ritual uncleanliness despite their conversion to Christianity. In this sense the inspired apostolic command is *epanankes* - a compromisory *sine qua non* for social exchange and peaceful co-existent with the turbulent Judaizers. So the Gentiles are to observe only four "inspired" *compulsory* things from which circumcision and the whole Mosaic Law are totally excluded.

By observing the four requirements, the Gentile Christians even though uncircumcised, are, so to say, *symbolically* cleansed and made worthy of entry into Christianity which the Judaizers still regard as a *Jewish hairesis*. The Gentiles are then bound to keep some of the Torah regulations of Lv 17-18 which concern both Jews and resident aliens. This is the basis of the compromise founded on authentic Mosaic (also *Judaistic*) Law and custom. This may account for the unanimous acceptance of the Jacobian proposal by all parties at the JC.

R. L. Omanson has bequeathed to Acts-studies a summary of the legal and theological relationship between the Jacobian initiated Council prohibitions and Lv 17-18:

The first prohibition - "abstain from food sacrificed to idols" - comes from Leviticus 17,8-9 which refers to sacrifices which are non-Jahwistic and therefore idolatrous sacrifices. The second - "abstain from blood" - comes from Leviticus 17,12, which prohibits eating blood. The third - "abstain from the meat of strangled animals" - comes from Leviticus 17,14-15, prohibiting eating the flesh of an animal that was strangled with its blood still inside. The last regulation - "abstain from illicit marriages" - comes from Leviticus 18,6-18, prohibiting incestuous marriage[71].

In the light of Lv 17-18, the four prohibitions of the JC thus equiperate Gentile Christians with "resident aliens". This is far from being a complimentary equiperation because Gentile Christians are in no way the same as *pagan*

---

71   Omanson, Gentile Palaver, 280.

foreigners living among the Jews. But the disputes that have been raging over a Jewish-law free Gentile Christianity were more disturbing and disparaging than a wrong classification of the Gentile converts. So it seems better to nominally classify the Gentile Christians as "resident aliens" in order to pacify the Judaizers and then freely admit the Gentiles into the Church than to give them their rightful and suitable titles which may block their free entry and integration in the Church. Thus tactics and play on terminologies may have contributed in forging the unanimous agreement by the opposing parties to the four minimal prohibitions.

But however minimal the prohibitions may appear to the reader, they are basically a summary of the Mosaic preconditions for the integration of the non-Jews into the *community and "commonwealth"* of Israel. While the renunciation of idolatory alone suffices to bring a Gentile closer to Judaism, the observance of all the four prohibtions intimately links the uncircumcised Gentile Christians with the uncircumcised Noachides who ate both ritually clean and unclean animals (Gn 9,1-3) but were required to abstain from eating animal flesh with "life" or blood" (v.4) and from idolatory, blasphemy, murder, robbery, sexual deviation[72]. In the same way Gentile Christians are bound to abstain from those things which link them to the Noachides[73]. Thus the JC decree, though taken from the Torah, harks back to "God's primordial covenant with Noah, to which Mosaic 'legislation' was only a provisional exception[74]".

The pre-Mosaic nature of the content of the prohibitions later made obligatory by the Torah for Jews and non-Jews also justifies its consideration as a necessary burden for the Gentiles. The decree is partly based on Peter's missionary integration of the Gentiles in the Church and partly on an appeal to Prophet Amos who foresaw the purity of the new People of God whom he has chosen for his name.

By accepting to observe them, the Gentiles will no longer be considered as "separate from Christ and excluded from the membership of Israel, aliens with no part in the covenants of the Promise, limited to this world, without hope and without God" (Ep 2,12) but as integral members of Israel, Christ and the Church who also hear the Mosaic *ethos* proclaimed in the synagogues within their environemt (Ac 15,21). All these demonstrate the inculturation import of the four abstentions as a necessary Torah burden for the Gentiles.

---

72   Gn 4,8f; 6,1f.12-13; 9,6.20-25.
73   Cf. Derrett, Clean, 211.
74   Ibid., 217.

9.6 Inculturation Effect of JC Decision: A Spirit-Guided Christian Fellowship of Equal Jews and Gentiles (Ac 15,22-28).

(This is a reader's reflection on the inculturation effect of the JC decision on the Christians of both races. As a part of the fourth real scene of the episode, it streeses the equality and unity of all the people of God irrespective of their nationality or position in the Church and denounces the false Judaizers).

In their Letter to the Gentile Christians represented by the Churches of Antioch, Syria and Cilicia, the Leaders of the Jerusalem Church (apostles and elders) addressed them as "brothers *(adelphoi)* of gentile birth". This implies that the Leaders regard the Gentile Christians as equals by virtue of their common belief in Jesus Christ. Thus the Christian Church of Acts is no longer a Jewish *hairesis* belonging only to the members of Jewish commonwealth. Rather at the time of their writing, she has already become an *international community* of believers in Christ, a community in which class distinctions are done away with and in which members are *adelphoi (Geschwister)* or brethren with equal rights, duties and privileges[75].

This is the logical consequence of the recognition and acceptance of the fact that God loves the Jew and Gentile equally and impartially. It is the ultimate consequence of the divine abolition and transcendence of all racial and national distinctions and of every religious sectarianism. It is the spiritual result of belonging to Jesus Christ through faith, baptism and the reception of the Holy Spirit.

So the Letter *ad Gentes* does well in emphasizing the unity of the Leaders with themselves (cf. *homothymadon*, 15,25a), their christian fellowship with the Genitles (cf. *adelphoi*, v.23) and their love and fellowship (cf. *agapetoi*, v.25b) for Paul and Barbanas who have risked their life in the mission *ad Gentes*. In this way the Leaders demonstrate a great understanding for the meaning and challenges of the life of all believers in Christ. Baptism, faith and the new life in the Spirit have broken down all class and racial distinctions. All are united by the Holy Spirit in the name of Jesus. All are equal in the international community of believers. There is no more room for the discriminatory attitude of the circumcision party or the Judaizers, no more place for anyone who proclaims oneself clean and despises the other[76].

Now the Jewish and Gentile Christians are true brothers in all respects irrespective of their ethnic origin, ethnic marks, language, traditional religion and the general of way of life. Through their Letter the Jerusalem Leaders are try-

---

75   Cf. Weiser, Gemeinde und Amt, 319-320.
76   Cf. Id., Basis und Führung, 71.

ing to restore the primordial brotherly unity (cf. *homothymadon*, Ac 2,46), love or oneness of heart and soul (cf. *kardia kai psyche mia*, 4,32) characteristic of the first group of believers in Christ[77].

The equality of christian fellowship extended to the Gentiles stems from and goes back to the awareness of the Council members about God's earlier choice and favours to the Gentiles as reported by Peter (Ac 15,7-11) Paul and Barnabas (v.12) and acknowledged and confirmed by James with scriptural quotation (vv.13-16). The Jewish Christian Leaders humbly recognize the Gentile Christians as *brethren* because God has called them as his own people through baptism, purified their hearts by faith in Jesus Christ and granted them his Holy Spirit. All these entitle them to all the duties and benefits, spiritual and material, which accrue from their brotherhood and christian fellowship (cf. Ac 2,42.44-46). No one is a slave in the Church of Christ. All have equal social status and enjoy the liberty and privilege of believers in Christ whose needs are taken care of by the community (cf. Ac 4,32.43-35). Therefore no more uncessary burden is to be led on the Gentile converts or brethren. The demands and challenges of their christian status are already a sufficient yoke and burden for them.

The recognition of the Gentiles as brethren and equals fosters love and unity between Jewish and Gentile Christians, and by implication, between Christians of different races and cultures. So once the Jewish Christians do away with their national and religious superiority complexes and respect the sound ways of life of the Gentile converts, then there will be no more obstacles to a unity of heart and soul between Christians of both races. Unity is in turn fostered by love and mutual respect among all believers and by a recognition of the dignity of every one in the believing community. The failure of the one group to recognize the dignity of the other group engenders tension, disrespect, discontent, and finally disunity in the christian community (cf. Ac 6,1).

But the councillors are aware of the fact that the unity of Jewish and Gentile Christians is not a mere human unity for the sake of commensality. Rather it is a unity and fellowship granted and fostered by the Holy Spirit[78]. Hence their humble Letter of brotherly fellowhsip with its necessary burden on the Gentiles is decided and written in union with the Holy Spirit who has made them overseers of the People of God (20,28) and is the prime mover of all apostolic decisions and activities (16,6-7) throughout the Acts from the "beginning in Jerusalem" (1,2.8) to "the end in Rome" (28,25)[79]. The Spirit is also the bond

---

77 Cf. Ac 2,42-47; 4,32-35; 5,12-16.
78 Cf. Ac 4,32; 5,12; 15,28.
79 Cf. Kee, Good News, 35-41; Guy, Missionary message, 57-64; Bruce, Holy Spirit, 166-183.

of love and unity between the Leaders themselves and between them and the Gentile Christians.

By declaring that they and the Holy Spirit have issued the decree of four abstentions, the Leaders are openly telling the Gentiles of the seriousness of their decision which is inspired, empowered, guided and directed by the Spirit of love and unity. It is not merely a decision of Jewish Christian Leaders but an authoritative divine-human decree issued with brotherly affection for Gentile converts.

> The Holy Spirit had overruled all the disputing, all the discussion, all the declarations, all the details of the conference. He had allowed the matter to a head... He had engineered the whole thing to settle once and for all the questions of faith, freedom, and fellowship in the church[80].

The Leaders speak as the vehicle and mouthpiece of the Holy Spirit. The Gentiles need not become Jews first in order to become Christians and gain salvation. They need only to keep the four abstentions demanded by the inspiring Holy Spirit and all will go well with them. This is why they would do well to accept and observe them very carefully and faithfully as necessary regulations (Ac 15,29c).

But the stress on brotherly unity and equality under the influence of the Spirit of love and grace does not mean that heresy shall be condoned. Hence the Jerusalem Leaders did condemn the troublesome false teachings of the Judaizers *(tines... apo tes Ioudaios* (15,1) coming from their very midst (v.24). This shows that though love reaches out to the good and bad in the christian community, it does not condone error and falsehood among its members.

> Love reaches out to everyone, it is true, but love does not embrace error. There comes a time when those who propagate false and divisive teachings must be confronted, their false teachings denounced, and their errors exposed. And when they use the names of their more orthodox brethren to lend credence to their beliefs, the deception must be exposed[81].

This is precisely what the Judaizers set out to do. Without any authorization they went to Antioch to preach a false gospel in the name of the apostles and the elders. They embarked on making Jewish culture a gospel of salvation for the Gentiles (15,1.5). They engaged themselves in an erroneous inculturation of the christian message among the Gentiles and received the ecclesial condemnation due to their false evangelistic inculturation. In this way the Leaders saw a way out for settling the burning issue of the conditions for the faith and salvation of the Gentiles.

---

80 Phillips, Exploring Acts, 73; Cf. Weiser, Apostelkonzil, 208-209.
81 Phillips, op. cit., 71.

The Holy Spirit has approved that it is possible for one to be at the same time a Christian and a Gentile by birth and culture just as it is possible for one to be at the same time a Christian and a Jew by birth and culture. The Christian community is thus a fellowship of equals from the Jewish and Gentile races gathered together in the unity of the Holy Spirit. These are the inculturation effect of the JC decree.

9.7 Joy for Gentiles Free from the Yoke of Law (Ac 15,30-35).

(This a reader's reflection on the inculturation significance of the abundant joy of the Gentiles upon hearing the favourable decision of the JC).

Throughout the period of the JC meeting, the Gentiles must have been anxiously waiting for its outcome. Their anxiety is understandable because the practice of their new faith hangs much upon the outcome of the Council. If the assembly decides in favour of the Judaizers and obliges them to painful circumcision and to the observance of the heavy burden of the whole of Torah, then a very impossible condition is placed before them and it may well mean *adieu* to the christian faith. But if the decision favours their preference of a Jewish-law free Gentile Church, then is all in order for their continued life as Christians. The latter preferable alternative took place. The apostles and elders decide in favour of Gentile Christians free from the yoke of the Jewish law and customs and the non-Jews rejoiced.

The Gentiles have every reason to rejoice at hearing the contents of the inspired Letter brought to them by Paul and Barnabas, and the two witnesses, Barsabas (Judas) and Silas. By their free admittance into the Church, the inspired JC is now doing for all Christians, what the inspired Peter had already done for the first group of Gentiles represented by Cornelius and his friends. The difference however is that while the former Gentile converts were not bound by any necessary Council requirement, the latter are bound by four compulsory burdens two (*pnikton* and *haima* 15,29) of which are peculiar to Jewish cultural rituals.

However all Gentile Christians (past and present) and all Jewish Christians (past and present) are compulsorily bound by the commandments of God and the Gospel precepts taught by Jesus and his apostolic witnesses. What is more important for the Gentiles is that the four emissaries from the JC have brought them the Good News that all distinctions between Jewish and Gentile Christians have been abolished.

The accredited witness of Judas and Silas becomes the oral endorsement of the Council's decision in accordance with Jewish Law which requires the evidence of two or three witnesses to confirm such matters (cf. Mt 18,16). Here the two witnesses testify to the truth of a Law-free Gentile Church (Ac 15,32). Set free from the troublesome legalist doctrines, the Church of Antioch has now a new lease of life giving Paul and Barnabas more time to teach and preach to the enthusiastic converts (v.35).

The news of comfort and joy to the Gentiles shows that the promise made to the people of Israel, believed to be nearer to God, is now extended to the very Gentiles considered afar off but called by the same God to conversion and faith (Ac 2,39). This is consonant with the OT revelation which summons all nations and Gentiles to praise the God of Israel.

"Let all the children of God pay him homage! Nations, rejoice with his people, let God's envoys tell of his power" (Dt 32,43). "Praise Yahweh, all nations, extol him, all peoples, for his faithful love is strong and his constancy never-ending" (Ps 117,1-2).

This is also in harmony with the NT revelation in which the saints sing a hymn to the lamb of God for buying

people for God from every race, language, people and nation and made them a line of kings and priests for God to rule the world (Rv 5,9).

In accordance with the scriptures, the Gentiles are to glorify God for his love and mercy (cf. Ps 18,49) because their integration into the Church has evoked their complete trust in Jesus "the root of Jesse" who now reigns over them and the Jews (cf. Ps 11,10). They can now rejoice because they are *officially recognized* as sharing with the Jews the repentance unto life (Ac 11,18), as being purified like the Jews by the Holy Spirit through faith in Jesus (Ac 15,8-9.10) and not by the Jewish cultural and covenantal circumcision and Torah (15,1.5). They can rejoice because Jewish Law and customs are no longer necessary for their salvation and a new era is ushered for them as a People of God.

The Gentiles can rejoice and be glad for the grace of unhindered worship of God who has granted to them the marvels of faith and salvation in Jesus. They can rejoice that they are now christians without the fear of losing the sound aspects of their time-honoured cultural heritage that are not opposed to the the Good News and their new life in Christ. They can rejoice because they can live their faith according to their culture and traditions as the Jews do[82].

---

82   Cf. Dumais, Church, 11-12.

9.8 Inculturation Import from Omniscient Narrator's Point of View.

(This is a reader's attempt to understand the inculturation import of the JC from the narrator's perspective. It is the first corollary to the inculturation reflection on the JC proceedings).

It is the omniscient narrator who alerts the reader to the official outbreak of the socio-cultural conflict between the Judaizers and Gentile Christians. The conflict had its roots in the opposition of the circumcision party to Peter's first mission to the Gentiles (Ac 11,3) and in the opposition of some Jews to the mission of Paul and Barnabas which led to their turning to the Gentiles (13,46-47). The opposition gradually builds up and blows out into an open conflict spearheaded by Christian Pharisees who could not come at terms with their cultural prejudice against Gentile converts. So they want all Gentiles to become *artificial Jews* through circumcision and observance of the Jewish Laws in order for them (Gentiles) to have a share in the salvation which is believed to be reserved to Jews alone (15,1.5).

The narrator calls in the Church Leaders of both camps and races to put out the flame of ecclesial discrimination based on cultural superiority complex (15,6-7a). The Leaders muster arguments to brush aside the gospel of conditional salvation proclaimed by the Judaizers (15,7b-29). By emphasizing the unanimous decision (*homothymadon*, v.25) of the Leaders to opt for a Gentile mission free from the yoke of Jewish law, the narrator cleverly reduces to absurdity the contentious Judaizers and their prejudiced culture-bound gospel. The narrator lays emphasis on the operation of God and his Holy Spirit. The leaders themselves see their decision as guided by "*divino afflante Spiritu*".

The narrator replaces the impossible conditions demanded by the Judaizers (Ac 15,1.5) with the Council's four minimal necessary abstentions (15,20.29) also prescribed by the Torah for Gentile believers (cf.Lev 17-18). By thus weakening the standpoint of the Judaizers, he opens the way for a future cross-cultural Gospel message that facilitates social, ethical and religious togetherness between Jewish and Gentile Christians. The narrator's announcement of the joy of consolation of the Gentiles at the conclusion of the story (Ac 15,31) shows that the resolution of the conflict by the Church Leaders has achieved the desire effect of allowing the faith to be rooted in the culture of the Gentiles without disturbing their sound ways of life. Thus the narrator views the JC as a complete success.

The narrator's story also indicates that he sees every character in the JC as contributing in some measure, either negatively or positively, to its inculturative decision. *Negatively* the heresy of the Pharisee Christians incites the conflict which leads to the convocation of the Council in which the leading figures *positively* express their candid views and put forward proposals that eventually help the whole assembly arrive at a final decision that resolves the problem of Jewish and Gentile socio-religious relationship. In this way the narrator presents a perfect plot of a conflict and its resolution.

9.9 Missionary Message of the JC Decision.

(This is a reader's attempt to understand the message of the JC for the later apostolic mission "ad Gentes". It is the second corollary to the inculturation reflection on the JC story).

Whether its decision is accepted or not, the JC has enunciated once and for all the basic principle of unconditioned and unconditional evangelisation for the salvation of both Jews and Gentiles within their socio-cultural milieu. So no race or people has any ecclesial authorization (*ou diesteilametha*, Ac 15,24) to impose its culture on the other - all in the name of spreading the Good News of salvation (cf. Ac 15,1-2.5-7a). While observing the Torah or the Mosaic *ethos*, the Jewish converts should not compromise their faith in Christ. And while resisting the Mosaic *ethos* in preference to their own *ethos*, the Gentile converts should not compromise the principles of the Gospel proclaimed to them.

Each racial group should try to respect the sensitivities of the other as equal partners or *adelphoi* in their new faith in Christ. Each should not lose its socio-cultural identity which is not at variance with the Gospel message. While retaining their authentic cultural values each people or nation should live authentic christian life and seek to save themselves through grace and faith in the name of Jesus, the Saviour of all (cf. Ac 15,11). The JC

called on Jews as well as Gentiles to put their faith in God's Messiah and to join the company of His people. For the Gentile this would be a conversion to the new faith; for the Jew it would be, in an important sense, conversion within the faith in which you had been nourished, and of which Christ was the summit and goal. But the shock of it would be as great for the Jew, or even greater, than for the Gentile[83].

The principle enunciated by the JC calls for a simultaneous cultural accomodation of the Good Gews and the Gospel accomodation of all races, peoples and cultures[84]. This basic message of the JC did prevail in the post-

---

83   Green, Evangelism, 147. Cf. Guy, Missionary Message, 61.

84   This is similar to Paul's "being all things to all peoples in order to save some (*tois pasin gegona panta, hina pantos tinas soso*, 1 Co 9,22).

Council mission of Paul and his companions. For as they visited one town after another, they instructed the Gentiles and their Jewish neighbours to observe the teachings (*ta dogmata*) of the Jerusalem apostles and elders (Ac 16,4).

Their observance did result in the daily increase of the early Church in faith and numbers (Ac 16,5), so much so that by the end of Paul's mission, the Church has become a mixed community of myriads (*myriades*)[85] of Jews zealous for the Law (21,20) and of greater myriads of Gentiles[86] converted to Christ. And although the orthodox Jewish Christian myriads continued to press for the Gentile observance of the Mosaic *ethos* (21,21-24), the JC's principle of Jewish-law free Gentile Christians has become an irreversible teaching of the Church of the Acts (cf. 16,4).

9.10 Strengths and Weaknesses of the JC.

This critique is carried out by a reflection on the internal (synchronic) evidence of the Acts in comparison with the external (diachronic) evidence from the Pauline corpus.

9.10.1 From Internal Evidence of Acts.

Positively the use of the Cornelius episode to argue for a divinely approved Gentile mission and Church is the highest achievement of the JC in general and of Peter who makes good use of his pastoral experience to bring order and harmony among his flock at a very critical time (cf. Jn 21,15-17). His intervention at the Council remains a good example (*Vorbild*) and an inspiration (*Anregung*) for pastors and pastoral workers today. Again the Jacobian use of the LXX text of Amos to settle faith-culture conflict between Jewish and Gentile Christians shows the reader the important role played by the OT in the apostolic kerygma[87].

Nevertheless the JC has some weak points. It is convoked to address the issue of circumcision and Torah observance as necessary conditions for the salvation of Gentile Christians (15,1-2.5-6). But it is astonishing that circumci-

---

85   Cf. Ac 2,41-47; 4,4; 5,14; 6,1.7; Cook, Mission to Jews, 102-123.

86   Though Acts does not use the word "*myriades*" to describe the conversion and large influx of the Gentiles to the faith, the many reports about the conversion of Gentiles from Ac 16-21 lends credence to the assumption of greater number of Gentiles than Jews at the end of the Pauline mission.

87   Cf. Bock, Use of OT, 494-511; Richard, Creative Use of Amos, 40f.

sion which sparked off the disputes and contentions in Antioch (15,1.5) is not even mentioned or referred to in the Council debates and interventions. And the Judaizer's demand for the Gentile observance of the whole Torah is generally referred to as unbearable yoke (v.10) or burden (v.28) which should not be imposed on the Gentile converts.

Perhaps the Council inadvertently omitted its very basic, vital *agendum*, or perhaps for the councillors, the issue of circumcision as a necessary means for salvation had to be silently neglected. The JC ends up with a decree on minimal abstentions from idolatory, incest and from eating ritually unclean meat[88]. It appears then that the councillors met in order to regulate table-fellowship or commensality for Jewish and Gentile Christians without making any definitive statement on what is necessary for salvation which is the *status questionis* of the meeting.

Peter's categorical teaching that "*it is through the grace of Jesus Christ that we (Jews) have been saved in exactly the same way as they (Gentiles) too have been*"[89] (Ac 15,11), is regrettably absent from the Council's final statement or decree. The reader may not be unjustified to ask for the inclusion of that Petrine teaching in the "*Letter ad Gentes*" (vv.23b-29). He may be rightly disappointed at the omission of that important teaching by the leader of the "Twelve".

The Council story gives the impression of a unanimous decision that resolves the conflict once and for all (15,25) and this decision is passed on by the delegates to its Gentile Christians first at Antioch (v.30) and later on by Paul himself to other local Churches (16,4). But the later part of the Acts story contradicts the earlier impression of a harmonious resolution of the dispute. The reader continues to learn that Judaizers did not cease to press on for the Gentile observance of the Jewish Torah.

The cicumcision of Timothy out of deference to the Jewish inhabitants of Lystra (Ac 16,1f), the hostilities of some Jews of Thessalonica (17,5f.13), Corinth (18,6f.12f), and the uproar of Jewish zealots against Paul accused of preaching to "everyone everyhwere" against the Jewish people, the Law and the Temple (21,27f) are but some of the glaring evidences of unresolved problems and disputes between Jewish and Gentile Christians. So then the JC's decision might have silenced the Judaizers only for a while but it did not succeed in satisfying their demands once and for all. They employed all their energy opposing and thwarting Paul's law-free Gentile mission despite the protection given to Paul by James (21,20-21), the Jewish Christian leader par excellence.

---

88   Cf. Wilson, Gentiles, 175-176.
89   This citation is from Barclay, Acts, 114.

Moreover, one who reads in between the lines can still detect the presence of three different groups of Christians holding fast to their points of view in the post JC Acts. These are: the intolerant and extremist Pharisee Christians or the Judaizers persecuting Paul and companions (Ac 17,5f; 21,27f); a Jewish Christian group tolerant of the Gentiles and ready to accommodate the terms of the decree. James is a typical representative of this group (21,25); a mixed group of Jewish and Gentile Christians who freely observe the Torah without imposing it on the Gentiles. Paul is a typical representative of this group (21,23-24).

One can then suppose that the presence of these groups at the JC was responsible for the hot debates that raged on before Peter made his "passionate" speech and appeal to the contentious assembly. Taking into account the conflicts that led to the convocation of the Council, the narrator's use of the rare word "*homothymadon*" to describe the unanimous agreement of the Councillors leaves the critical reader with the impression of an insinuated temporary unity existing among the three groups of Jewish/Gentile Christians with different attitudes to the Torah observance[90].

Another weakness of the JC is the non-mention of women in the proceedings, as if the whole apostolic *ecclesia* was only a masculine christian movement[91]. It is true that women are included in the *adelphoi* (Ac 1,15f; 15,23), but they are also usually mentioned explicitly in the Acts story and are called by the Greek noun, *gyne/gynai*[92]. So it is serious to have omitted them from a Council that claims to be a gathering of the apostles and presbyters with the whole Church (15,22). Certaintly "*the whole Church*" is not a male Church but a community of men (*andres*) and women (*gynai*) in Christ.

Although circumcision is not binding on the women within Jewish Law, they are all bound by the whole Torah and by the JC's four minimal prescriptions (Ac 15,29). The Council's silent attitude to women is therefore strange and remains, in my opinion, one of its regrettable omissions and weaknesses because, even without intending it, the Council seems to have made women an unimportant group in the *ekklesia* of Christ, yet all those male councillors were born of women.

But if the Council neglected the women, the Acts story fortunately does recognize them and their positive roles in the spread of the Good News before

---

90   For more on these groups presented in a slightly different way cf. Omanson, Gentile Palaver, 274; Brown/Meier, Antioch, 1-9.
91   Note that I am not in the least advocating a feminist "theological movement" in the Church, but only merely making a critical evaluation of the weaknesses and strengths of the Council proceedings.
92   Cf. 1,14; 5,1; 9,2.26f; 16,14; 17,12.34; 18,2 etc.

and after the Council[93]. Some are noted for their faith and hospitality and others for their apostolic zeal[94]. Their important contributions go to confirm the fact that the JC left a regrettable *lacuna* by its, perhaps, unintended silence on the womenfolk during its proceedings[95]. So far for the critique from internal evidence. Now let us look at the Council from the external evidence of the Pauline Writtings.

9.10.2 From External Evidence of Pauline Corpus.

The Acts portrays Paul as being present at the JC and as participating fully in its deliberations and in the execution of its decisions[96]. But some of his Writings tend to contradict his positive stance at the Council.

Ga 2,1-10, generally considered as a parallel to the JC story[97] paints the picture of a Paul totally uncompromising to the Jewish/Gentile question. The *Galatian* story does not present a Paul who went up to Jerusalem to settle the uproar at Antioch with the apostles and the elders (Ac 15,2.6.12) and to win support and approval for his Jewish-law free Gentile mission (vv.23-29).

Rather *Galatians* portrays a Paul who is almost recalcitrant and unwilling to submit to the supreme authority of the Jerusalem Church and her leaders. It presents a Paul who is audaciously asserting his independence from the "important people" and the "pillars" of the Jerusalem Church - James and Cephas/Peter and John (Ga 2,6). It introduces a Paul boldly stating and emphasizing his divinely appointed mission to the uncircumcised Gentiles just as Peter was divinely elected to minister to the circumcised Jews (vv.7-10)[98].

Such an assuming attitude of Paul in a letter personally written by him (Ga 6,11) cannot but bewilder the reader well-acquainted with the JC Paul and Barnabas who were almost relegated to the background but were introduced in the third person through the narrator's voice (Ac 15,12). It also cast a big

---

93   Cf. Ac 1,14; 1,15-26; 2,1f; 9,36f; 16,13f; 17,34 18,1f.26; etc.

94   Cf. Ac 9,16f; 16,13f; 18,1f.26. In his greetings and good wishes to the church of Rome, Paul calls Prisca and Aquilla her husband "my fellow workers in Christ Jesus, who risked their own necks to save my life". The apostolic zeal of the couple is attested to by the "church at their house" (Rm 16,3-5; cf. 1 Co 16,19; 2 Tm 4,19).

95   Cf. Kee, Changing Role of Women, 228-238.

96   Cf Ac 15,2.4.12.22.25-26.35; 16,4.

97   Cf. Haenchen, Acts, 464-468; Bruce, Book, 283-285; Fahy, Council, 232-342; Parker, Once More, Acts and Galatians, 175-182; Sanders, Peter and Paul, 138ff; Barrett, Apostles in Council, 27f.

98   Cf. Sanders, Peter and Paul, 134; Catchpole, Paul, James, 443; Verseput, Paul's Gentile Mission, 38-58.

doubt on the historicity of the Council story[99]. But it may be plausible to think that the "historical roots" of Pauline mission and the Churches may have influenced his "curious ambivalence" towards the Jerusalem Church.

He (Paul) employs the story of his own independent calling and career... to support the validity of his converts' salvation without incorporation into the ranks of Jewish Christendom[100].

Paul's divine call and independent Gentile mission may have in fact determined his ambivalent attitude to the Jerusalem authorities, but this explanation does not reconcile all the conflicting accounts of the Acts and Galatians. The correlation of the two accounts remains "one of the most difficult exegetical problems in the NT"[101] as A. Fitzmyer has noted. But their contradictions may be explained by noting the differences of authorship and situations.

In the Acts, the author/narrator is telling the story of faith-culture conflict and its resolution, but in Galatians, the author/narrator is engaged in a fierce apologetic defence of his ministry against disparaging hostile Judaizers. His polemical stance may have accounted for his apparent defiance of the Jerusalem authorities whom the narrator of the Acts presents as being in harmony with the zealous loyal Paul and Barnabas (Ac 15,2.4.22.24)[102].

But if the Galatian story presents the reader with a defiant Paul (cf.Ga 1,13-24) who fiercely withstands any attempt to *judaize* the Gentiles (cf. 2,11-21), the same story also presents a Paul whose Gentile mission is confirmed by the Jerusalem Leaders (cf. 2,1-10)[103]. However, it is not my intention here, nor is it within the scope of this work, to delve into the solution of one of the most *difficult cruces* of the NT (so Fitzmyer). Rather I only point out this *crux* as a way of pinpointing one of the weaknesses of the JC.

However, Paul's claim of independent divine mission did not prevent him from succumbing to the pressure from the Circumcision Party of the Jerusalem Church. That pressure forced him to circumcise his missionary companions, the Gentile Titus (Ga 2,3f; 5,11) and the half-Jew Timothy (Ac 16,3). In each case Paul shows that concession and compromise had to be made for the sake of the spread of the Gospel[104].

---

99 Cf. Brown et al., Der Petrus, 49-51.

100 Verseput, op. cit., 38.

101 Fitzmyer, Galatians, in: NJBC, 47:17, p.783.

102 Paul's language and teaching in Rm 14; 1 Co 8,1-13 and 10,14-22 indicates that he is loyal to the apostolic decree and is at pains to explain its implications to his audience.

103 Cf. Verseput, op. cit., 44-58.

104 Cf. Fahy, Council, 236-240. Fahy argues in defence of Paul's action by saying that he yielded to their circumcison, "not because the Pharisees ordered it, but because the preaching of the gospel demanded it" (239).

To the Jews he made hiself a Jew, to win the Jews; to those under the Law as one under the Law (though he is not) in order to win those under the Law; to those outside the Law as one outside the Law though he is not outside the Law but under Christ's Law... for the sake of the gospel (cf. 1 Co 9,19-23).

So despite Paul's strong objections to circumcision as a necessary condition for the salvation of Gentile converts, the integrity of the Gospel and the salvation of souls did at times oblige him to permit or accommodate the circumcision of a Gentile who would be his missionary companion to both Jews and Gentiles (Ga 2,3f; 5,2f).

Next is the evidence of 1 Co 8 and 10. Paul's teaching on the eating of idol foods (*eidolothuta*) differs from that of the JC. While *eidolothuta* are strictly forbidden by the Council (Ac 15,29) and Paul himself teaches that there should be no compromise with idolatory and sacrificial feasts (1 Co 10,14-22), yet he makes moral exceptions to that prohibition. In practice, he is somehow *indifferent* to the eating of food sacrificed to idols. One may eat of such oblations without losing or gaining anything from it (8,8).

Foods offered to empty idols are unreal offerings. But if eating such foods goes against ones's good conscience or will scandalise another Christian, then one should desist from eating them out of deference to the weak conscience of the fellow christian[105]. So while upholding the basic principle of the JC prohibition against idol meats, Paul makes subtle moral distinctions in order to give practical solutions to the question of eating or abstaining from *eidolothuta*. Paul's pastoral attitude to the JC teaching brings out for the reader the difference between theory and practice, between ecclesial teaching and pastoral life, and between an ecclesial law and its actual observance[106].

But all the weaknesses of the JC nothwithstanding, it cannot be denied that the Council took a decisive step in laying the basic foundation for the proclamation of the Good News in the apostolic period and in the later times.

Summary and Conclusion of Theological Reflection.

The originally Jewish Christian Church later becomes a Church of myriads of Jews and Gentiles with the expected cultural shock and religous conflict characteristic of a meeting of different races, peoples and cultures. The conflict is hinged on a deep-seated Jewish prejudice against Gentiles considered by the Jews as unclean contaminants. Hence the hard line Jewish converts require from the Gentile converts a ritual purification through male circumcision and the compulsory observance of the whole Torah in order to make them worthy

---

105   Cf. 1 Co 8,10-13; 10,23-32.
106   Cf. Barrett, Apostles, 26-31.

of social exchange with Jewish converts and also worthy of the salvation coming from the originally Jewish Christianity. Such a spite is too much for the Gentiles to bear. This gives rise to "a conflict-ridden situation provoked by strife and disunity"[107] between the Christians of both races.

In the meeting that followed, the apostles and elders wade into the crisis in order to settle the matter and avert an impending schism in the early Church. Their inspired decision lays down the basic principle for relationship and commensality between Jewish and Gentile Christians. This principle is echoed in Paul's ministry and letters in which he stresses the salvation and the unity of all believers in Christ without any distinction between Jews or Greeks, between the socially advantaged or disadvantaged[108].

But while the Christian message accomodates all peoples and cultures, neither the Jewish nor the Gentile culture is to be identified with the Good News and neither of them is a guarantee of salvation. Each of these cultures can be a veritable vehicle of the message of salvation which transcends them. The Gospel is transcultural, trans-Jewish and trans-Gentile. None should be constituted into a condition for the salvation of believers in Christ.

From narrative exegesis to theology I have tried up to this point to highlight the elements of inculturation patent or latent in the JC episode. Is the theology of the JC still topical in the Church today? Does it have perennial and universal validity for the Church? Does it serve any theological purpose in the current Igbo Church? This logically leads to the issue of correlation in chapter ten.

---

107 Arrington, Acts, 150.
108 Cf. Rm 2-5; 1 Co 8; 10; Ga 2-3; 6,11ff; Ep 2,11ff; Col 2,16ff.

10. Chapter Ten.

Evangelisation and Conflict: A Hermeneutical Correlation of the Jerusalem Council Theology to the Igbo Church Today.

10.0.0 Formulation of the Problem and Procedure.

Now comes the end purpose of the work - the correlation of the resolution of the faith-culture conflict by the **JC** to a possible resolution of a similar faith-culture conflict arising from more than a century of the Euro-American[1] and native evangelisation of Igboland. It is an attempt at a practical application of the results of the theology of the JC to the life of the Igbo Christians today.

The correlation is very difficult because the Jewish/Gentile question (namely circumcision and Torah observance on which the convocation and decision of the Council was based), is no longer the problem confronting the contemporary Local Churches. After nearly two thousand years of christian mission and ecclesial life, does the **JC** still have any relevance to the Igbo Church? Does it provide this Church with any clue to the solution of her problems of faith and culture?

By the end of the first century A.D. the Church had ceased to be a Jewish *hairesis*[2], and had broken off from the synagogue and from much of her early Jewishness and became a believing community made up of an overwhelming majority of Gentiles living in the Graeco-Roman or Euro-Asian world. In such an environment in which the Jews were in the minority, one could not really expect the Gentiles with their own religious cultures and traditions to observe Jewish ethical and ritual laws which were not necessary for the christian life. To oblige them to do so would be expecting too much. It was therefore logical for the JC's proscription of strangled meat and animal blood to be easily neglected or gradually forgotten.

While the patristic documents of the first six centuries bore witness to the observance of the JC decree in the Graeco-Roman Church with varying degrees of emphasis being given to the ethical and ritual aspects of the decree in different places and times[3], the ritual aspect did finally give way to the ethical

---

1   I say "Euro-American" because the missionaries who evangelised Igboland were peoples from Europe (mainly Holy Ghost missionaries from France, Germany, Ireland and England) and later some missionaries came from the United States of America.

2   Cf. Addison et al., A History of Israel, in: NJBC, 75:181-188, pp. 1251-1252.

3   Cf. Barrett, Apostolic Decree, 54-58, for a summary of the Patristic witnesses to the decree and its observance; Klijn, Pesudo-Clementines, 305-312.

aspect or became interpreted in terms of the ethical or fell in abeyance in the later centuries[4].

But if the ritual requirements of the JC became meaningless in a Gentile ecclesial environment, that does not mean that its ethical demands of abstention from idol meats and incest were equally invalidated or nullified. Nor does it mean that the intentions, aims, ethical and pastoral implications of the JC decision were not valid then and today. After all, idolatory and incest are for ever condemned in unmistakable terms by the Jewish and Christian Holy Scriptures.

So, even if the new composition of the membership of the Church and the changing historical circumstances had made void the observance of the ritual aspect of the JC decree, it is undeniable that its ethical teachings still remain biblically and ecclesially an obligatory moral precept for Christians of the age and of our times. If the "*letter*" of the JC decison is ever considered *dead*, at least the "*spirit*" of its teachings (*ta dogmata*, Ac 16,4) cannot be considered dead.

It is in the spirit of those living teachings that I embark upon a *hermeneutical correlation* of the Council's handling of the faith-culture crisis with a possible handling of a similar crisis facing the Igbo Church today. By this, I mean, not a very literal and rigid application of the Council's provisions in the local Church, but rather an **interpretative application** of the Council's teachings to the current Igbo Church.

In those days the conflict took place first between the Christian message and Jewish culture, then between the Gospel on the one hand and Jewish and Gentile cultures on the other, and finally between the original Jewish carrier-culture of the Good News and the receiving Gentile culture. But today, the situation of the conflict has completely changed. Now it is firstly between the European carrier-culture of the Good news and the Igbo culture, and secondly between this culture and the Christian message.

How then can the Igbo Church truly free herself from the yoke of Euro-Americanism and become really an autonomous, local Church delivered by the authentic Gospel from the power of

darkness to light, from the dominion of Satan to God, and receive, through faith in Christ, forgiveness of their sins and a share in the inheritance of the sanctified (Ac 26,18)?[5]

---

4   Cf. Barrett, op. cit., 57f; Haenchen, Acts, 471.

5   This citation should be understood in the metaphorical or hermenetical sense whereby both "darkness" and "Satan" import the conflicts arising from the missionary enterprise.

In order to respond to this question, there is need to discover the main areas of conflict between a *Euro-American acculturated* Christian message and the culture of the Igbo audience. To do this I shall discuss, from the point of view of evangelisation, conflict and resolution of the conflict, the missionary situation in Igboland to which the JC theology is being hermeneutically correlated.

The discussion begins with a very brief analysis of the original life-situations of the Igbo and foreign (white) missionaries[6]. This shall be followed by the discussion and evaluation of the principal foreign and Igbo missionary methods (1885-1994).

The third step shall discuss the *enduring* areas of faith-culture conflict in the Igbo Church which logically leads into making suggestions and recommendations for the resolution of the faith-culture conflict in the Igbo Church today. Each of the four steps shall constitute a section in this chapter.

The principal white missionary methods are the Christian village method under the Prefectures of Frs. Joseph Lutz and René Pawlas (1885-1900) and the catechetical schools method initiated by Fr. Lejeune (1900-1905). These two methods were employed when the Igbo mission was directed by the French Spiritans. The third was the literary education method under the pastoral leadership of Bishop Shanahan (1905-1931) and Bishops Heerey, Whelan, McGettrick (1931-1970) and the four Igbo Bishops[7] ordained between 1958 and 1965. This method was dominated by the leadership of the Irish Spiritans[8].

From 1970 the two main Igbo pastoral methods are: adaptation (inadequately called *indigenization*) or incarnation method (1970-1981) and inculturation method (1982-1994)[9].

Section One: Pristine Situation of the Igbo and Foreign Missionaries.

10.1.0 Igbo Socio-Religious Background.

Let us recall, as I pointed out in chapter one, that the term "Igbo" refers to the people and language of one of the three major ethnic groups in Nigeria. Al-

---

6   Inculturation study begins with an analysis of the situation. Cf. Sarpong, Evangelisa-
     tion, 4-6; Schineller, Handbook, 61-72; Hesselgrave, Communicating Christ, 72-78.

7   The four Bishops are Nwedo (1958), Okoye (1961), Ayiogu (1961), Arinze (1965).
     More shall be said about them as the work progresses.

8   Cf. Anyika, Missionary Enterprise, 50.

9   The words adaptation, indigenization, incarnation and inculturation express different
     forms and grades of the same reality of trying to make the Christian message relevant
     to the situation of the people (cf. Schineller, Handbook, 16ff; Hering, Evangelisierung
     15-24).

though colonialism and missionary enterprise did introduce a lot of changes into the Igbo way of life, yet "the metaphysical mentality of the Igbos has not been basically altered either by colonization or by the introduction of Christianity"[10]. There is no doubt that the texture and substance of the traditional culture, customs and practices still exercise much influence over the religious convictions of Igbo Christians. It is against this background of *continuity* in change[11] that I make a brief presentation of the main aspects of the traditional situation as the receiver of the message of oncoming missionaries.

10.1.1 Birth of a Child and Initiation Rite.

The birth of a child is always marked by a loud rejoicing and merriment within the family and kindred unit. Gifts keep pouring in for the maintenance of the lucky mother and her child who is initiated into the society through the naming ceremony (*ikpo/igu aha*) on the 28th day of birth. Usually Igbo names reflect the feelings of the parents or the circumstances of a person's birth[12].

10.1.2 Marriage and Family Life.

The Igbo attach primary importance to the human person, human life (*Ndubuisi* = life is first), hence procreation and progeny (male and female) are very much cherished as reflected in such names as *Ginikanwa* (what is more/greater than a child?), *Nwakaego* (a child is more precious than money), *Nwabugwu* (a child gives/is dignity), *Nwadiuko* a (child is dear), *Nwadinobi* (a child is the heart's treasure) *Nwadiuto* (a child is sweet) and so on[13]. The patrilineal nature of Igbo society gives preference to the male child.

The family (*ezi-na-ulo*), as the first unit of Igbo society, is made up of a man, his wife, children and dependants. The dynamic process of Igbo marriage[14] is not just a private affair between two couples but involves the whole exogamous agnetic community of families called *Umunna*[15]. Polygamy is

---

10   Cf. Edeh, Igbo Metaphysics, 152.
11   Cf. Nwoga, Focus of Igbo, 1984 Ahiajoku Lecture, 64.
12   Cf. Mbiti, Introduction to African Religion, 87-90.
13   Cf. Nwedo, Christianity, 27; Uka, African Family, 191.
14   Parrinder, West African Religion, 104-106; Bujo, Mehr als ein Vertrag, 95-96; 1980 Synod of Bishops, Selected Interventions, 40-49.
15   Cf. Mbah, Building Up, 10.

both a legitimate form of marriage either for social prestige or as a consequence of childless first marriage[16].

As wife and mother the Igbo woman is the centrepiece of the family life and harmony[17].

She is a being that surrounds the child with meticulous care, she caresses, nourishes, protects and shelters, she helps, she is patient and affective... she is always present, she welcomes and discovers what is delicate[18].

The Igbo woman is very much loved by her children. This is evidenced in such names as *Nneka* (mother is greater), *Nnediuto* (a mother is sweet), etc. This love is symbolically expressed in the cultural homage paid to the earth-goddess or mother, *Ala*[19]. Children's respect for their father is also reflected in such names as *Nnaka* (a father is greater) *Nnabugwu* (father gives dignity), Nnaemeka (father has done much), etc.

The first son (*Okpara*)[20] as the holder of the *Ofo*, a religious symbol of justice, power and authority, law and order[21] has a special place and role in the circle of *Umunna*. While the males continue the family lineage, the females leave the lineage after marriage and are integrated into the lineage of their various husbands. The daughters (*Umuada/Umuokpu*) of the *Umunna* are a strong force in the maintenance of peace and order among the *Umunna* circle.

Old age is a horror to a couple without a male child[22]. Even a family with an only son lives in constant fear of the possibility of suddenly losing the one who will continue the family lineage. While a malessless woman may be disconsolate, a *childless* woman suffers humiliation in public (cf. Lk 1,25).

10.1.3 Rites of Initiation and Passage.

Besides the rites after child birth, other rites of passage or initiation include the social puberty or marriage fatherhood rites (*iwa akwa*), the masquerade (*mmanwu*) or cult rites, (*ima mmuo*), the rites for higher social status, for oc-

---

16 Cf. Archbishop (Cardinal) Arinze's intervention on "Marriage and Polygamy" at the 1980 Synod of Bishops, op, cit., 97-99.
17 Njoku, Mother the Centerpiece, 25-32.
18 Nyamiti, African Sense, 98.
19 Cf. Ibid.
20 Cf. Uchendu, Igbo of Southeast, 41.
21 Cf. Ejizu, *Ofo*, Igbo Ritual Symbol. The whole book is an exposition of the socio-religious import of *Ofo*; Osuji, Concept of Salvation, 45-56; Edeh, Igbo Metaphysics, 62-63.
22 Uchendu, Igbo, 57.

cupational specialization and the death or funeral rites[23]. These rites though good in themselves are often connected with sacrificial offerings and homage to the family gods, ancestral spirits or the personal *Chi*[24].

10.1.4 Food and Drinks.

Main food crops are yam *(ji)* or "dioscorea rotundata", cassava *(ji akpu* or *abacha)* cocoyam *(ede)*, maize, beans and rice. To be a successful yam farmer *(Ezeji*, king of yam) is prestigious while the religious yam festival is the people's prime and central feast[25]. Igboland is blessed with an abundance of tropical fruits and palm produce throughout the seasons of the year[26]. Raffia and oil palm wines are the beloved drinks in the service of commensality, the marriage process and the funeral cermonies. To offer a visitor palm wine and the bitter kola nut is a symbol of friendship and hospitality[27].

10.1.5 A Monistic World View.

The pristine Igbo world view does not accommodate the typically Graeco-Roman christian dichotomy between the sacred and profane, the religious and the secular. The Igbo like many other Africans live in a religious universe where all living is religion and all religion is living[28]. Being an Igbo means being a believer[29]. A. G. Leonard testifies that the Igbo

are, in the strict and natural sense of the word, a truly and a deeply religious people, of whom it can be said, as it had been said of the Hindus, that they "eat religiously, drink religiously, bathe religiously, dress religiously, and sin religiously". In a few words, the religion of these natives, as I have all along pointed out, is their existence, and their existence is their religion[30].

---

23   Cf. Metuh, Comparative Religion, 197f; Anochie, Impact of Igbo Women, 18-22.
24   Ezekwugo, Chi the True God, 108-112.
25   Cf. Anigbo, Commensality, 73-88; Okigbo, Plants and Food, 1980 Ahiajoku Lecture, 13-21.
26   Cf. Okigbo, Plants and Food, 39-42.
27   Cf. Anigbo, op. cit., 139-140; 156-170.
28   Cf. Isichei, History of the Igbo, 24.
29   Cf. Shorter, African Christian Spirituality, 14.
30   Leonard, Lower Niger, 429.

This does not mean that every Igbo person is holy, but it demonstrates the monistic nature of the Igbo world-view[31] in which there is no clear-cut opposition or distinction between the temporal and non-temporal, visible and invisible, sacred and profane but rather a continuous exchange, between the material (human beings and objects) and the spiritual universe (Supreme Being, deities, ancestral spirits). This cosmic oneness makes it possible for human beings and spiritual beings to exercise reciprocal influence on one another[32].

10.1.6 Village and Town Festivals.

Socio-religious festivals in honour of the deities or ancestral spirits are common phenomena in Igbo villages and towns. The feasts with their rituals take place at different times or seasons of the year. They are centred "around the New Yam Festival (*Ahiajoku*) which, itself, is at the centre of the ritual year"[33]. The festivals provide special occasions for relaxation, much merriment and commensality among families and friends. They help to maintain law, order, peace and respect for one another. In some of these feasts, girls entertain the people with new songs and colourful dances[34].

10.1.7 Socio-Political Organization.

The levels of Igbo society are the family, the extended family (*Obi*), the kindred (*Umunna*) or a larger group of consanguine families, the village unit (*Ogbe*) or a group of consaguine kindreds and the town unit (*Obodo*) which is a component of several villages[35]. Socio-political life is basically ultrademocratic and egalitarian organised around the village group as the basic political unit with authority vested on the family and lineage heads (*Ndichie*). In this village unit everyone has the right and freedom to speak his mind in all the affairs of the polity[36]. "Strong individualism" is balanced by "fierce loyalty to the village and community"[37].

But the larger society (town or a group of towns) is

---

31   Cf. Agu, Secularization, 222-224; 228..
32   Cf. Metuh, Comparative Studies, 61-63.
33   Nwoga, Focus of Igbo, 1987 Ahiajoku Lecture, 62.
34   Cf. Onwubiko, African thought, 43-56; Leonard, op.cit., 434-436.
35   Cf. Edeh, Towards Igbo Metaphysics, 62-64.
36   Cf. Green, Igbo Village Affairs, 107; Forde - Jones, Ibo and the Ibibio, 50.
37   Okigbo, Towards a Reconstruction, 14.

a plural one comprising various groups... The sub-groups are marked apart from each other by differences of dialect, customs, political organization, occupation, outlook... the relations between the members of a village or village group, and between one village group and another are marked by social discord... None is prepared to accept the leadership of the other. Everyone is king to himself[38].

In the village, the ideals of communal life are cherished and enhanced. Each person has a sense of belonging to the nuclear and larger family unit. Commensality acts as a control to social mechanism in the village life in which the allotment and possession of the natural material object "land" is the key stone to unity among the villagers[39].

And that is why, in the thickening and thinning sense of blood relationship which each Igbo person feels with regard to units of social action, there is also a deepening and awakening sense of loyalty and commitment... The corporateness of the community unit means that somebody belongs to the next higher unit of the community on the basis of his membership of the smaller unit... with all its implications in group lobbying...[40].

Igbo egalitarianism and ultrademocratism led to many achievements and much progress[41], but it also did generate much discord and disorder[42] in a society where every one tended to be "a king unto himself", hence the saying: the Igbo have no kings (*Igbo enwe eze*)[43]. However the society is hierarchically graded according to the people's age and achievements. Respect for elders and people in authority is emphasized. But an elder or someone in authority may lose his/her prestige by any act of impropriety[44].

The elders are democratic gerontocrats while the titled men (*Ndi nze na Ozo*) command social influence and respect and perform religious services for and on behalf of the people[45]. Brotherlinees, hospitality, kindness, justice, truthfulness and respect for all are customarily unwritten values and norms for every Igbo[46].

---

38   Nwabueze, Igbos, 1987 Ahiajoku Lecture, 11-
39   Cf. Anigbo, Commensality, 18-22; 24-27.
40   Nwoga, op. cit., 27; cf. p. 2.
41   Cf. Agu, Secularization, 236.
42   Cf. Nwabueze, op. cit., 11-23; Achebe, Trouble, 47-48; Ojukwu, Because I am Involved, 95-103; 128-139.
43   Cf. Uchendu, Igbo, 20; Agu, Secularization, 235-237.
44   Cf. Onwubiko, African Thought, 28-29.
45   Cf. Arinze, Sacrifice, 91.
46   Uchendu, Igbo, 71; Onyenemegam, Pastoral Care, 24-25; Okafor, Africa, 14-24.

10.1.8 Religous Beliefs and Practices.

Igbo traditional religion acts as a cohesive and integrating force in the society[47]. It teaches that every one has his own *Chi*[48]. "*Chi*" is described variously as a "spiritual double" associated with one's personality at birth[49], "the guardian spirit allotted to him by God at the moment of his creation"[50] as a "personalized providence[51]", as "the guardian Spirit and the idea of Destiny or fortune"[52]. This religion believes in a pantheon of deities or minor spirits who are either worshipped or feared[53]. The people are very close to their "living dead" or ancestral spirits and venerate them[54].

The pantheon comprises the earth or earth-goddess (*Ala*), the sky/sky god (*Igwe*), thunder/god of thunder (*Amadioha*), sun/sun god (*Anyanwu*). Above the pantheon is the mysterious Supreme God (*Chi-ukwu/Chukwu*) or creator God (*Chineke/Chi-na-eke*)[55]. The Igbo names of God[56] or of deities and spirits and many other such names[57] are indicators of the presence of the Supreme Being and other divinities in the people's religious culture[58]. For example: (*Chukwudi*, God exists), *Chukwuemeka* (God has done much), *Chidiebere* (God/god is merciful), *Agbarakwe* (if a deity or spirit permits), *Muodebe* (let the spirit preserve), etc. So the concept of God "runs from extreme theism to extreme deism"[59].

It follows then that in Igbo religion, no one is an atheist since each one has a personal *Chi* and admits the existence of other divinities. These deities have cultic devotees (priests or consecrated *osu*) who offer to them sacrifices of expiation to remove abomination, or of prevention to ward off the harassment

---

47 Cf. Shorter, African Culture, 76-77.
48 Cf. Ezekwugo, *Chi* the True God, 179-248.
49 Cf. Basden, Niger Ibos, 37; Ilogu, Christianity, 36.
50 Agu, Secularization, 233.
51 Isichei, History, 25.
52 Metuh, God and Man, 22.
53 Cf. Ezekwugo, op. cit., 147-152; 166-169; Parrinder, West African Religion, 26-59. Metuh, Comparative Studies, 161-173; Idowu, African Traditional Religion, 137-178.
54 Zahan, Religion, 50; Parrinder,op. cit., 115-127; Metuh, Comparative Studies, 145-150; Id., God and Man, 95.
55 Cf. Ezekwugo, op. cit., 68-91; Parrinder, op. cit., 13-25; Metuh, Comparative, 103-123. Cf. Edeh, Igbo Metaphysics, 118-140. These pages demonstrate Igbo's belief in Chukwu and the seven ways of naming him.
56 Cf. Ezekwugo, op. cit., 114-116; The names with *Chi* as prefixes or suffixes are found in 307-310; Arinze, Church, 21.
57 Cf. Ezeanya, A Hand Book of Igbo Christian Names; Port Harcourt (Nigeria) 1967.
58 Cf. Shorter, African Culture, 54-57.
59 Id., 56.

of evil spirits, or of petition for their needs, or of thankfulness for favours such as childbirth and good harvest and other blessings received from the deities[60]. Salvation in Igbo religion is not individualistic but communalistic. It is centred around the relationship with the *Umunna* and the ancestors[61]. It has to do with the perpetuity of the family stock and the everlasting union with the circle of the kith and kin (*Umunna*) through the observance of the traditional *ethos* or customs (*omenala*).

The traditional Igbo had their own evangelisers and ritualists who wielded much power and influence in the society. The Nri missionaries as "agents of *Chukwu*" roamed about "propagating new religio-cultural forms".

They crowned kings, conferred and installed the highest title-holders, consecrated the vital staff of office (*Ofo*), imposed taboos and cleansed abomination, made peace (*Igbu Ogu/Ikpe Udo*), and above all collected tributes from individuals and communities[62].

Igbo traditional prayer forms are drawn from different life situations - regular ritual, passage rites, public worship, wills, death and burial, etc. are determined by the occasion, the mood of the situation and the dialect area of the one praying[63]. The quasi stereotyped features of the prayer include invocation, presentation of the existential, personal and communitarian situation, petition, and vertical-horizontal or God-man direction[64].

Much of the material consists of religious poetry or hymns... Texts which are spoken by an official while a ritual is in progress tend to be short and succint[65].

Since there are no written texts, "the prayer is always spontaneous, read out of the head and heart rather than out of a book"[66]. These rhetorical features of prayer still remain alive among the Igbo Christians today[67].

---

60   Cf. Arinze, Sacrifice, 34-36; Ilogu, Christianity, 65; Isichei, History, 26; Metuh, Comparative, 213-216; Id., Theological Basis, 78f.
61   Cf. Osuji, Concept of Salvation, 66-67.
62   Ejizu, Religion, 113.
63   Cf. Echiegu, Sacral Igbo, 34.
64   Cf. Echiegu, op. cit., 76-84; Metuh, Theological Basis, 76f.
65   Shorter, Prayer in the Religious Traditions, 19-20.
66   Echiegu, op. cit., 76.
67   Cf. Id., 19-20; 118.

10.1.9 Strict Moral Code.

The Igbo have a strict moral code with its totems and taboos about human persons and creatures[68].

As man's moral life is paramount in keeping the cosmic equilibrium, all norms of conduct, including taboos, even those which might appear mechanical, must be strictly complied with. In case of doubt or infringement, the services of diviners would be readily availed so that things could be promptly set aright[69].

There are three main groups of moral faults: bad behaviour (*ajo omume*) such as dirty habits and gossips, etc; bad deeds (*ajo oru or njo*) such as insults to parents or elders, theft, adultery or fornication, etc; taboos of the Earth-deity or abomination (*nso ala, aru*) such as murder and incest, etc.

To the culprits are meted out appropriate expiatory sanctions or punishmemts varying in severity according to the gravity of their offence[70]. This is because every form of misfortune, sickness or sudden death is believed to be a punishment coming from evil spirits or the offended deities or due to the flouting of traditional moral norms or the upsetting of social order by an individual or group of persons. Such evils must be expiated through divination, prayers, sacrifices[71].

10.1.10 Death and Funeral Rites.

The death of a family member or a relative, especially the young, is a very sad event for the Igbo. The whole kindred or village rally around the bereaved to console and help them. Because of the decomposing power of the tropical heat, the disposal of the corpse usually takes within twenty four hours after death.

The funeral rites for children and unmarried people are simple. But for the married or old people the rites are varied and complex according to the social status of the dead. But those who committed suicide or murder or die "abnormal" death, notorious brigands or thieves are denied funeral rites[72].

The elaborate and complex funeral rites carried out meticulously are symbolic of the physical separation from the living brethren and of the hope in life

---

68   Cf. Parrinder, West African Religion, 172-186.
69   Ejizu, Edurance of Conviction, 133.
70   Cf. Metuh, Comparative Studies, 250-252; Onwubiko, Facing the Osu, 55-58.
71   Adibe, Faith and Morality, 34-36.
72   Cf. Mbiti, Introduction to African Religion, 113.

after death[73]. Their proper performance is absolutely necessary for the reunion of the dead with the ancestral spirit and for his reincarnation among the living[74]. The burial is usually followed by songs of mourning and feasting by all present.

The *Umuada* group use to spend several days to console the family of the deceased and to pay their last respects to the "brother" or "sister". On appointed days other groups also take their turns in bidding their last farewell to a former colleague and friend. For the next one year the immediate relations usually wear black or white clothings as a sign of mourning for their beloved one.

10.1.11 Points of Pristine Contact with Christianity.

The *sensus religiosus* of the Igbo culture and religion has points of contact with Christianity[75]. Both religions believe in a supreme invisible, benevolent Being or creator God, in good and bad spirits, in the existence of good and evil and in the existence of human soul and the after life. Both have sacred persons, sacred objects and places for prayer and worship[76]. Both uphold, at least *conceptually* if not *identically*[77], a moral sense of justice and truth, respect for human life, great love and care for children, respect for parents and elders, good family life, brotherly love, virginity before marriage, care for the needy, reciprocal hospitality, life after death, hope for salvation, etc.[78]

I shall refer to these points of contact as "the seeds of the divine word" (*semina verbi*)[79], as the *positive elements* or as the *salvific values*[80] of Igbo

---

73   Cf. Metuh, op. cit., 271.

74   For more on death and after life cf. Mbiti, op. cit., 113-125; Metuh, op. cit., 261-271. Parrinder, West African Religion, 106-114.

75   Cf. Arinze, Answering God's Call, 6-7. Mbefo, Towards a Mature, 55-60; Onwubiko, African Thought, 94-98.

76   Cf. Onwubiko, op. cit., 59-64.

77   Some of these points of contacts are also understood differently. For example sacred places, life after death, spirits, are not exactly the same in the two religions but their traditional understanding facilitates the acceptance of their import in christian religion.

78   Cf. Ezeanya, Adapatation, 42-43; Arinze-Fitzgerald, Pastoral Attention, 49. Osuji, Concept of Salvation, 66-77.

79   Cf. Ac 17,27; Rm 1,19-20; Vatican II, AG, 6.9.15; LG, 13.16-17. These are some of the teachings on, or related to, the "semina verbi".

80   Cf. Kalilombe, Salvific Value, 141-143; PACT, Statement, 125-126. Arinze/Fitzgerald, op. cit., 49.

traditional religion and culture. They were to act like steppping-stones or preparation for the missionaries' Gospel message (*praeparatio evangelica*)[81].

10.1.12 Areas of Pristine Conflict with Christianity.

The traditional religion is bound with idolatory and superstition. Before the advent of Christianity, human sacrifices were offered to placate the anger of the deities and spirits; twins were killed as "miscreants being reincarnated to pay for the crimes of their former lives"[82] and their mothers were humiliated as bearers of human disorder. The people permitted serfdom or slavery and sanctioned polygamy as a remedy for a childess marriage or even for social prestige[83].

They consulted oracles, spirit-mediums and diviners and practised magic and medicine[84]. Their priests and the *Ozo* titled men performed the consecration of the *Osu* as a "living sacrifice"[85] for the service of a deity/spirit or as "living victims paying for the crimes of the community or family"[86]. The *Osu* were strictly excluded from marriage with the free-born (*diala*)[87].

> *Osu* is a caste system ritually instituted by paganism in some form of human sacrifice. It is believed that a person or the person's descendants are for ever consecrated to the service of a particular pagan god. (Hence) other people regard them as taboo for all purposes especially for marriage[88].

Traditional burial rites are bound with superstition while the reincarnationist or cyclic notion of immortality and after-life contradicts the christian notion of death, resurrection and eternal life. These socio-religious evils and contradictions characterized the pre-christian Igbo society. They were also to confront the oncoming missionaries.

---

81   Cf. Eusebius of Caesarea, *Euangelikes Proparskeues*, Liber 1-15, P.G. 21; Arinze, Church, 14.

82   Onwubiko, African Thought, 124.

83   Cf. Ndiokwere, Prophecy, 23-26; 257-258.

84   Cf. Parrinder, 137-171; Metuh, Comparative Studies, 221-234.

85   Cf. Arinze, Sacrifice, 91-92.

86   Onwubiko, African Thought, 124-125.

87   Cf. Atado, African marriage, 23-25.

88   Jinehu, Osu Caste, 4-5.

10.2.0   Socio-Religious Environment of the Oncoming Missionaries.

The 19th century environment of the white misionaries were equally characterized and oriented by the socio-political and ecclesial events that preceded or
surrounded them. It was separated in time and space from the culture of the
Graeco-Roman or Euro-Asian Gentile missionaries[89] and from the cultures of
their own peoples in the intervening centuries. It was completely different
from the pristine situation of the Igbo audience. It is on record that before they
ever set out for Igboland and other parts of Africa,

> questions concerning the human personality, rational ability, culture and the religious
> civilization of the black man, had been raised and hotly debated in parliaments, churches
> and lecture rooms. All this, against the background of the bloated ideas of racial superior-
> ity, scientific progress, industrial revolution and the widespread doctrine of social evolution
> which intoxicated many Europeans[90].

Some European anthropologists went on to assert that the African is "a
child of nature. He had no historical background outside the fact that he had
been a slave in history"[91]. Others continued to wonder if the

> black man was really a human being, if he had a soul, and if his conversion to the
> Christian life was likely to modify his spiritual capacity and destiny[92].

Magery Perharm's reports to her British Government stated among other
things that the 'barbarous' people of South-Eastern Nigeria (mainly the Igbo)
were

> a people of beastly living, without a god, laws, religion or commonwealth,... born and
> bred villains. A man of integrity is as rare among them as a white falcon[93].

Some missionaries certainly sipped a large dose of this classic example of
prejudicial "scientific racism"[94]. The consequence, as Ex-president Nyerere of
Tanzania put it,

---

89   In this work, the common terms for these missionaries are "the white people" or "the
     white pastors" or "the white preachers" "the white man" or simply "the whites". Their
     pastoral work shall be qualified as "westernised" or "western".
90   Ejizu, Decolonizing, 219-220. Cf. Nyerere, Church, 221-222.
91   Azikiwe, Renascent Africa, 179.
92   Von Rosen, *Le Ghetto Biafrais*, 156.
93   Perham, British Problem, 21.
94   Curtin, Scientific Racism, 40-51. For more on this scientific prejudicial racism, cf.
     Perham, British Problem, 638-639.

was that Christianity, as well as education and health services, came to Africa and other parts of the Third World in a European form. They came with all the cultural accretions of two thousand years of European history and developement: The reformation and counter-Reformation of the sixteenth and seventeenth centuries..., hostility between different christian sects; the relations developed between Church and State... and ealier feudal practices dating back to the Roman Empire... The Missionary had all these ideas - and many more - incorporated into the mode of operations[95].

But some like Fr. Francis Libermann, tried to counter the prejudice against the black person by emphatically telling the *Propaganda Fide* that Africans were/are also images of God in exactly the same way as the Europeans. He advised his white brethren to eschew every form of racial prejudice and adapt their mission to the material conditions and capacities of those *black* images of God:

> Make yourselves black with the blacks and you will judge them in the way they ought to be judged. Make yourselves blacks with the blacks in order to train them they way they ought to be taught, imposing nothing from your own point of view, but conceding them that which is proper to them[96].

With this spiritual counsel, the Spiritans set out to evangelise the Igbo people and their neighbours.

Section Two: Foreign and Local Missionary Approaches to the Evangelisation of Igboland.

10.3.0 Arrival and Initial Problems.

In 1885 the first group of missionaries - Fathers Joseph Lutz and Johann Horne, and Brothers Hermas and Jean Gotheau[97] - arrived at Onitsha as the fourth party to the white man's scramble for the lands, treasures, lives and souls of the Gentile Africans[98]. It was in the first place nothing but a *meeting*

---

95 Nyerere, Church, 221-222. Cf. Ela, African Cry, 14-27; Iwe, Christianity, 21-47; Mbefo, Theology and Inculturation, 57-62.

96 Carbon, *Notes et Documents*, IX, 330. This is nothing but a repetition and an application of the Pauline theology of cultural accomodation (cf. 1 Co 9,19-23). It is also in line with the directives issued in 1650 by the SCPF to missionaries to China and Indo-China (cf. Collectanea, vol. 1, no. 135, p. 42).

97 Mr. Townsend, a British trader personally acquainted with King *Obi Anazonwu* of Onitsha, navigated the two priest from Brass (21st November) to Onitsha (5th December) (cf. Obi, Hundred Years, 15; Nnabuife, History, 100-102).

98 Before them were the white traders colonial administratiors, and protestant missionaries (Cf. Agu, Secularization, 241-256).

of the strange with the strange. So Fr. Lutz[99] and his team[100] strove to convince King Obi Anazonwu of Onitsha of their good intentions to live near the Igbo and to teach all who are willing to "learn from the white men of Europe"[101]. Consequently the King gave them every possible assistance to settle down to work[102].

In trying to win over the people to the catholic faith, Fr. Lutz at first "adopted the practical expedient of approaching the inhabitants via the charitable provision of medicines and other material needs"[103]. Then guided by the missionary spirituality[104] of their Holy Ghost Congregation and the directives of Pope Leo XIII, they began to evangelize through the christian village method.

10.3.1 Christian Village Method under Fr. Lutz (1885-1900).

The aim of the christian villages established at Onitsha and Aguleri was to protect the ex-slaves from the unscrupulous traders and merchants and also to prevent the converts from blacksliding to idolatory within the natural Igbo village[105]. But the bulk of the inmates was

drawn from the poor, the needy, and the rejected: mothers of twins, women accused of witchcraft, those suffering from diseases such as leprosy which were seen as abominbale. Finding little satisfaction in the world around them, they turned to Christianity with a single-minded devotion which astonished all who beheld it[106].

As a separate settlement centred around the priest's house, the daily life of the converts was organised in a quasi-monastic form. They must be monoga-

---

99 He was made Prefect of the Lower Niger on April 1, 1889 with headquarters at Onitsha. This area stretches South from Port Harcourt-Calabar axis along the Atlantic coast, and goes Northwards up to the Benue River. It corresponds to the colonial administration's "Southeast Nigeria" or the present Eastern States of Nigeria plus Benue, Kogi, Tabara and part of Adamawa States in the North East (cf. Obi, Hundred Years, 38).

100 In the same 1889 four Sisters of St. Joseph of Cluny: Mother Clothilde, Sisters Mary Claver, Thierry, and Charles, joined the Igbo mission (cf. Nnabuife, op. cit., 124).

101 Ekechi, Missionary Enterprise, 74.

102 Nnabuife, op. cit., 108.

103 Ekechi, Op. cit., 74.

104 Nnabuife refers to this as "the missionary ideology of the Holy Ghost Fathers". Cf. History, 43-58.

105 Cf. Oputa, Bishop Shanahan, 67-68.

106 Isichei, History, 162.

mous, make a total break with the traditional religion and natural village way of life and observe strict christian discipline.

The inmates had a modest accomodation and basic facilities for elementary education and training, agriculture, health-care, worship and christian instruction[107].

Catechism classes, prayer and daily assistance at mass with regular general communion on feast days were the rule-of-life of the village. Labour at the village's plantation was a law and whoever was not hard-working was regarded a bad christian[108].

Being immune from all the obligations of the natural village, the two Christian villages "attracted law-breakers seeking refuge from retribution"[109]. Their inmates thus formed the nucleus and bastion for the evangelisation of the people. Chief Idigo of Aguleri was an examplary convert and an exceptional member of the Christian village[110].

10.3.2 Positive Results of the Village Method.

In 1885 there was no single Igbo Catholic[111]. Between 1885-1888 there were only 180 catholics[112]. But by 1900 there were 1,322 Igbo catholics[113]. The christian village also protected young girls from being forced into marriages. It saved the lives of criminals and innocent twins exposed to wild beasts[114]. Although "missionary growth was slow and painful"[115], yet credit must be given to Fr. Lutz and his companions for their missionary courage and efforts in trying to adapt the Gospel message to a non-Christian people.

---

107 Cf. Engel, Die Missionsmethode, 127.
108 Nnabuife, History, 160. Cf. Ozigbo, Igbo Catholicism, 6-7.
109 Jordan, Bishop Shanahan, 30.
110 Cf. Obi, Hundred Years, 47-50; Walker, Holy Ghost Fathers, 78f; Nwosu, Evangelization, 249; 250; Ozigbo, Igbo Catholicism, 7-8.
111 There were however Christians from other denominations. Cf. Nnabuife, History, 32-35.
112 Obi, op. cit., 36.
113 Cf. Obi, Hundred Years, 99. At this time there were already ten thousand Igbo Protestants many of whom, overwhelmed by the self-sacrifice and charity of Holy Ghost missionaries, later crossed over or were converted to the Catholic Church (cf. p. 74).
114 Twins were killed in those days because the Igbo perceived such a phenomenon as an irruption of disorder in the human society.
115 Ozigbo, Igbo Catholicism, 8.

10.3.3 Main Areas of Conflict with Igbo Culture.

The fewness of converts in the Lutz era was due to the fact that from its inception, the Christian village system did not take into account the organizational pattern of Igbo natural village life[116]. It introduced the profane-sacred mentality in a society with a monistic world view (10.1.5).

For once converted to the faith, the fervent converts practised iconoclasticism by destroying the idols and objects of their traditional religion[117]. From then on, they became for the many non-converts the "Church people" (*ndi uka*) or the children of the "christian village" (*ndi ogbe uka*)[118] while they regard the non-converts as "worshippers of deities or spirits" (*ndi ogo muo*) or "pagan" villagers (*ndi obodo*).

While the village system could not accomodate all who were willing to come and learn about the new faith and its school novelties[119], it also distanced the missionaries from the cream of the population in the natural village[120]. Added to all these the faith preached by the misionaries was completely foreign[121] to the people because it was

in general fully steeped in Western personnel, Western culture, Western philosphy, Western theology and Western psychology and cultural values - as monogamy, institutional celibacy, flowing garments reminiscent of the Roman toga or Medieval Europe, Western patterns of prayer and incantations, rituals and cermonials, and Western names and concept of authority[122].

The completely different christian forms of life and worship[123] failed to take into account the Igbo monistic and spiritual view of the universe and life (10.1.5)[124]. The language barrier and cultural differences were great set backs in the missionary endeavours. It led some to assert that "everything in native life from cradle to the grave bore the stamp of false worship"[125]. Hence

---

116 Cf. Anigbo, Commensality, 24-33; Nwosu, Evangelisation, 250.
117 Cf. Munonye, Only Son, 57-58 & 90; Achebe, Things Fall Apart, 161 & 168; Id., No Longer at Ease, 151; Id., Arrow of God, 47.
118 Cf. Nnabuife, History, 160.
119 So commented Fr. Lutz in *"Bullettin de la Congregation"*, XIV, 13 (1888) 442.
120 Cf. Nwosu, Laity, 28.
121 Cf. Onaiyekan, Christianity, 4-6.
122 Iwe, Christianity, 79; cf. Uzukwu, African Personality, 27-31.
123 Cf. Shorter, African Culture, 122-154.
124 Cf. Shorter, African Christian Spirituality, 9-14.
125 Jordan, Bishop Shanahan, 29.

elements in the traditonal culture not found in the foreign (missionaries') culture were labelled as devilish and uncivilized: they were earmarked for annihilation or replacement with the "superior, civilized, and saintly" elements of the foreign culture[126].

The identification of the Christian village with slaves and social outcasts (the *osu* or *ohu*) and refugee criminals simply caused a lot of stir and disaffection among the free born (the *diala*)[127] and alienated them from "the white man's religion". It made Christianity look like a religion fit only for social outcasts, and by implication, as inferior to the Igbo traditional religion. Igbo custom at that time could not accomodate the fact of slaves or social outcasts as the "pillars" of a religion to which they should belong[128].

As a safe haven for the "rejects" of society, not all the ex-slave inmates were true converts to Christianity. When some had a better alternative, they simply deserted the quasi-monastic village life.

All the negative effects of the Christian village accounted for much of the people's initial apathy to the christian (catholic) message in the era of Fr. Lutz.

10.4 Catechetical School Method under Fr. A. L. Lejeune (1900-1905).

As the fourth Apostolic Prefect[129] of the Lower Niger Fr. A. Lejeune first restructured the infrastructures for work and made radical administrative changes in the Vicariate[130]. He initiated the catechetical school method as a more effective means of penetrating and evangelising the Igbo heartland[131]. This method combined doctrinal instruction with basic elementary lessons in reading, writing and calculation.

---

126 Edeh, Igbo Metaphysics, 150.

127 Cf. Achebe, Things Fall Apart, 142; Jinehu, Osu Caste, 4-5.

128 Cf. Ekechi Missionary Enterprise, 89.

129 After Fr. Lutz, the second was Fr. Joseph Reling (1896-1898) and the third was Fr. Rene Pawlas (1898-1900). Their prefectures were an interregnum. Due to ill health, Reling could not take up his his seat at Onitsha and so resigned. But the energetic Rene died shortly after taking up his seat (cf. Obi, Hundred Years, 59-60).

130 Cf. Nnabuife, History, 178-185; Ozigbo, Igbo Catholicism, 9. Anyika, Missionary Enterprise, 57-58.

131 Cf. Nnabuife, op. cit., 180-182; Anyika, op. cit., 58.

10.4.1 Teacher/Catechists under Lejeune (1900-1905).

Suitable persons were trained as teacher/catechists for the stations erected in selected villages and towns[132]. From the Onitsha headquarters, the priests paid regular pastoral visits to the stations and celebrated the liturgy and sacraments with the people[133]. To facilitate the catechetical instructions in the native tongue, Fr. Lejeune employed the services of some of the Catechists in the production of the first Igbo catechism arranged in the form of questions and answers[134]. To improve communication he also supervised the publication of the first English-Ibo-French dictionary[135].

An examplary convert in this era was King Samuel John Okolo Okosi of Onitsha (1900-1931). He personally disengaged himself from all the immoral and idolatorous aspects of Igbo culture of his era[136], promoted the spread of the catholic faith and received papal honour for his evangelical services. In a letter of gratitude to Pope Leo XIII, the King informed him that "all the towns and communities in the Lower Niger are now disposed to receive the Gospel"[137]. But there was not a little opposition to the King's religious favour from the staunch adherents to the traditional religion.

The threats and dangers posed by the mafia-like Aro syndicates and their notorious *Chukwu* oracle could not allow the missionaries to penetrate the Igbo hinterland. Really

the Igbo did not regard Aro civilisation as a blessing. It was indeed a retrogressive civilisation, because the slave trade brought into Igboland slave raiding, depopulation due to instigated wars, family disorganisation, ritual cannibalism, human sacrifice, and the development of *osu* system[138].

So in separate British punitive, military expeditions of 1901-1902 the pernicious syndicates were swept off[139] and the most dreadful deity, the *Ibinukpabi* or the *"Long juju"* of Arochukwu, and its oracle were despoiled, thereby

---

132 Cf. Nwosu, Laity, 28; Nwosu, Evangelization, 271-273.
133 Anyika, op. cit., 58.
134 Cf. Igboko, Teaching Methods, 99-100.
135 Cf. Obi, Hundred Years, 81; Igboko, Teaching Methods, 99-100.
136 Cf. Nwosu, Laity, 5-8.
137 *Annales Apostoliques*, 6 (1902) 139-140. Quoted in Obi et alii, op. cit., 78.
138 Onwuejeogwu, Evolutionary Trends, 56.
139 Cf. Afigbo, Aro Expedition, 7-27; Anyika, Military Force, 28-33;

pacifying the Igbo heartland and the neighbouring Ibibio and Efik enclaves[140] for the mission work[141].

But some catechists reassigned by Fr. Lejeune to go and teach the teeming converts in the hinterland refused their appointment and instigated a riot against him[142]. The riot led to the apostasy of many new converts. At the end of the riot, Fr. Lejeune reorganised the catechetical system for a more effective evangelisation.

10.4.2 Evaluation of the Catechetical Method

The catechetical method made it possible for the Gospel to reach the interior areas of Igboland. Through it Fr. Lejeune proved to the Igbo that christianity was not just for the social outcasts but a religion concerned with the interests and welfare of every human person.

To his credit, there was now a local church founded on the grassroots as well as notables of the society, numerous children eager to go to school and the local population now trained in self-help[143].

Before Fr. Lejeune left the missionary scene to die in France at the age of 45, his method had yielded much fruit in the Prefecture[144]. He and his companions deserve accolades of praise for their catechetical initiative. It is not surprising that Msgr. Le Roy said of late Fr. Lejeune:

By his death the mission has lost a zealous priest, one who attains his avowed goal inspite of odds and difficulties and who seem to thrive best by the very obstacle he meets[145].

But Lord Lugard's[146] discriminatory and denegatory specification for missionaries underscored Lejeune's method. So wrote Nigeria's First Governor Lugard[147] to Lejeune:

---

140 Cf. Anyika, op. cit., 33-41.
141 This had a negative consequence for the missionaries who were often suspected by some wary villagers as another arm of British or European colonialism.
142 This is comparable to the riot against the apostolic missionaries (cf. Ac 13,45ff; 16,19ff; 17,17,1ff; 19,23ff etc).
143 Obi, Hundred Years, 93. Cf. Nnabuife, op. cit., 208-211.
144 Cf. Obi, op. cit.,99, for the statistics of personnel, structures, infrastructures and progress of evangelisation from 1900-1904.
145 Le Roy to the Propaganda Fide, Rome. Cited in Obi, op. cit, 117. Le Roy was the Spiritan General Superior at the time of Lejeune's death.

Missionaries are not to preach the equality of Europeans and natives at this stage, which however true from a doctrinal point of view is apt to be misapplied by the people in a state of developement and interpreted as an abolition of class distinction[148].

This prejudicial injunction[149] of the British Lord did exercise a measure of unhealthy influence on the pastoral attitude of some of the missionaries.

10.5 Schools Method under Shanahan (1905-1931).

The Irish[150] Fr. Joseph Ignatius Shanahan's ministerial leadership consisted of two major phases: Shanahan the Apostolic Prefect (1905-1920) and Shanahan the Bishop and Vicar Apostolic of Southern Nigeria (1920-1931)[151]. His first report to *Propaganda Fide* noted that

there were 11 priests, 8 brothers, 7 sisters, 25 local catechists, 4 church buildings, 15 school-churches, 18 schools, 3 nursery schools, 3 hospitals, 7 dispensaries, 3 refugee camps, 4 workshops, and 2 sewing workshops for girls[152].

This is what he inherited for the pastoral service in the vast area of the Prefecture[153] with about 2,000 Catholics, 8,000 Protestants and future converts from the 8,000,000 inhabitants[154]. Shanahan's experience under Lejeune helped him to choose *literary education* method as the best way of reaching the people through the younger generation[155]. His appointment to the Nigerian

---

146 The British government had passed on to him the duties of the Royal Niger Company (RNC) who were very often at loggerheads with the missionaries and at war with the Igbo.

147 In 1914 Northern and Southern Regions were amalgated to form the present Nigeria with Lord Lugard as its first Governor General (cf. Nwedo, Christianity, 12).

148 Congregation du Saint-Esprit, B/192/A/03, Letters: Lower Niger, 1886-1920, Lugard to Lejeune.

149 The subsequent riots in Dekina in the Northern part of the Lower Niger and the burning down of the Holy Ghost mission station in 1904 and 1905 were eloquent testimonies to Lord Lugard's maladministration and unpopular policies.

150 Recall that From Shanahan onwards, most of the missionaries to the Vicariate of Southern Nigeria were from Ireland.

151 Note that the Vicariate was territorially the same as the former Prefecture of Lower Niger.

152 Cf. Obi, op. cit., 122.

153 He also trekked a thousand miles from Onitsha to Cameroon as an Apostolic Visitor to the the German Pallottine mission. Cf. Obi, Hundred Years, 148-149.

154 Cf. Ibid.

155 Cf. Oputa, Bishop Shanahan, 68-69.

Education Board in 1906 "afforded him the opportunity of pushing forward his educational projects"[156].

As time went on, there was need for more and better qualified teachers commensurate with those of the Protestants. So Shanahan decided to build the St Anthony's Teacher Training College (TTC) at *Igbariam* (1912-1919) to off-set the educational imbalance. Before many difficulties led to its closure in 1919, it has produced some respected catholic teachers who were also helping in the apostolate[157].

The site of the *Igbariam* College was later converted to St. Paul's Seminary (1924). The Seminarians attended lectures together with the students of the newly founded St Charles' TTC, Onitsha (1928)[158], a beehive for future Igbo catholic elite. In 1930 John Cross Ayiogu[159] was ordained (by Bishop Shana-han) as the first fruit of the Seminary and the first Igbo priest East of the Ni-ger[160].

10.5.1 Local People and Schools Method (1905-1931).

With the help of the town Chiefs and village Elders[161], the missionary team erected a network of schools and stations as centres for literary and religious education[162]. For the siting of these centres, the people usually but not always freely donated the large acres of the "evil forests" (*ajo ohia/ofia*) either dedi-cated to the deities and spirits or used for the burial of twins, criminals and social outcasts. This was done to see if the divinity preached by the white man was more powerful than those of the traditional religion.

If the white man and his co-workers died after encroaching or settling on any of the portions of land, then is his divinity powerless before the Igbo di-vinity and should be ignored. But if he survived, then is his divinity more powerful and should be adored[163]. Fortunately for the evangelisers, the latter

---

156 Cf. Anyika, Beginnings of the Bishopric, 31.
157 Cf. Eke, Priestly and Religious Vocations, in : Obi op. cit., 306-307.
158 For more details, cf. Onwubiko, Catholic Church, in: Obi, op. cit., 224-264.
159 In 1957 he was made Auxiliary Bishop of Onitsha and later first Bishop of Enugu in 1962.
160 In general, the first Igbo priest was Fr. Paul Obodechine Emecete ordained in 1920. But he comes from the small Igbo town of Ezi, West of the Niger (cf. Isichei, History, 171).
161 Cf. Nwosu, Laity, 1-25.
162 Cf. Obi, Hundred Years, 144-145 for statistical data from 1917-1920 and 1929.
163 Cf. Achebe, Things Fall Apart, 135-136.

prevailed and their message began to win more converts which necessitated the erection of more stations and the recruitment of trained personnel. The experience of the advantages of literary education, led the people to hanker after it. As time went on, more

schools were established, some by communities, some as joint ventures between communities and missions, some by missions and other individuals... to "show the light" so that "the people will find the way"[164]

Initially sons rather than daughters were sent to learn, partly due to the prevailing cultural mentality of limiting the woman's role to domestic chores[165] or to devotion to her personal gods or *Chi*[166], and partly due to the people's reservations against a free mixture of males and females in the schools. But in 1925 the colonial government's policy made education compulsory for females.

The Native Teaching Staff should be adequate in numbers, in qualifications, and in character, and should include women. The key to sound sytems of education lies in the training of teachers, and the matter should receive primary consideration[167].

However Bishop Shanahan respected the cultural separation of both sexes and erected schools and Colleges for the female pupils and students entrusted to the care of the Holy Rosary Sisters[168] which he founded in Ireland in 1924.

10.5.2 School Teachers (1905-1931).

The teachers were graded and located according to their qualification and experience. In the primary schools, pupils were taught English, Writing, Reading, Arithmetic, and elementary vocational arts. But as the emphasis was laid on Catholic religion, the teachers also gave the children "a Christian outlook on what constituted the essence of paganism - juju worship, cannibalism, slavery, polygamy" and also taught them "to practise the christian virtues in their

---

164 Ohuche, *"Ibu anyi Danda"*, 1991 Ahiajoku Lecture, 30.
165 Cf. Onochie, Impact of Igbo Women, 16; Adigweme. Bishop Shanahan and the Advancement of Igbo Women, in: Okoye, Bishop Shanahan, 52; Kunambi, The Place of Women in the Christian Community, in: Shorter, African Christian Spirituality, 151.
166 Basden, Niger Ibos, 208.
167 Cited in Nwosu, Laity, 33.
168 Cf. Ochiagha, Bishop Shanahan, 21-22; Onwubiko, Catholic Church, in: Obi, Hundred Years, 234-235.

daily lives, even while living in the midst of paganism"[169]. Bishop Shanahan was full of unreserved praises for them.

> The catholic teachers are men of whom the mission has every right to be proud. They are men of sterling honesty. They help preach the Gospel without cost. If it has not been for their devotion, their zeal and their self-sacrifice, the Fathers would have achieved very little[170].

10.5.3 Catechists (1905-1931).

At this time there were three grades of catechists: the central catechist who assisted the parish priest and was in charge of all other catechists within the parish; the vernacular teacher-catechist who lived in a remote outstation and also taught in an ordinary town or village school; the 'assisted' school teacher-catechist who also taught in a school approved by the government[171]. They were given basic catechetical and liturgical formation and monthly refresher courses to equip them for their task[172].

The Catechists supplemented in a big way the work of the small team of priests and religious, vitually playing the role of 'native priests'[173]. While some also taught in the elementary schools, all were teachers of the christian doctrine. They held prayer services on Sundays and weekdays[174]. Bishop Shanahan calls them "wonderful fellows".

> They were real apostles of the people. There would be no Church in the country if they had not done their work so well. They never spared themselves and everyone of them was a catechist as well as a teacher[175].

They were poorly paid humble men of sacrifice who really brought the "Christianity into the villages"[176]. But their insufficient education and knowledge of English language sometimes made some of them nauseous interpreters for the white preachers[177].

---

169 Ochiagha, Bishop Shanahan, 18.
170 Jordan, Bishop Shanahan, 71; Isichei, History, 174.
171 Cf. Nwosu, Laity, 27-28.
172 Cf. Nwosu, Evangelisation, 222.
173 Cf. Nwosu, Laity, 36-43.
174 Cf. Okoye, M., Catechist, 67-71.
175 Jordan, Bishop Shanahan, 146.
176 Isichei, History of Igbo, 164f.
177 Nwosu, Laity, 54.

10.5.4 Lay Apostolate (1905-1931).

Group lay apostolate within and outside the school environment is comparable to the Igbo communal way of life[178]. So Bishop Shanahan cultivated the native fondness for social life to promote group apostolate[179]. The fewness of parish centres and the people's ardent desire for the Holy Eucharist helped in popularising the apostolate of devotion to the Sacred Heart of Jesus. Other clergy-inspired group apostolate include the Congregation of the Blessed Virgin Mary for the care of children, the society of St Vincent de Paul for the poor and needy, and the choral society of St Gregory for music[180].

10.5.5 Church Committee (1905-1931).

This body usually made up of the older and proven members of the Church were charged with the administrative functions in the stations. The committee looked after the Church schools, mission lands and property and the priests' daily maintenance. It settled land disputes and questions of inheritance, tried to resolve marrrage problems and defended the rights of the weak, especially widows. The catechist was usually an *ex-officio* member of this committee[181].

10.5.6 Health/Welfare Centres (1905-1931).

These centres (hospitals, clinics, orphanages, workshops, leprosaria) usually directed by the missionary Sisters and Brothers served not only for the bodily health of the people but also for their spiritual welfare[182]. An ideal catholic hospital was also a place to teach or learn the christian doctrine and the general demands of the christian faith. Sometimes the willingness to submit to the faith was a basic requirement for the non-baptised who applied to work or serve in any capacity in these catholic health or welfare centres.

---

178 Cf. Lwasa, Traditional and Christian Community in Africa, in: Shorter, African Christian Sprituality, 144-145.
179 Cf. Jordan, Bishop Shanahan, 80.
180 Cf. Nwosu, Laity, in: Obi, Humdred Years, 341-342.
181 Cf. Ikeme, 61-66; Nwosu, Laity, 45-54.
182 Cf. Obi, Hundred Years, 142-146.

10.5.7 Appraisal of School Evangelism (1905-1931).

Though the missionary Annals report that the Bishop personally tried to respect Igbo culture and tradition and taught others to do the same[183], yet his educational policy was "the spearhead of his attack on Igbo paganism"[184]. The increase in the number of catholics from 2000 in 1906 to 47,000 in 1925 bear witness to the success of his educational evangelism[185]. As he left the pastoral scene in 1931,

there were 81,285 Catholics, 88,288 Catechumens, 37,275 Pupils, 1,947 Teachers and 1,043 Primary Schools and Churches. There was a Teacher's Training College (St Charles) and a Seminary[186].

E. Isichei rightly observed that "Bishop Shanahan was a masterly strategist (who) recognised and exploited to the full... the Igbo people's thirst for education..."[187]. But the people's heroic sacrifices, religiousity, hospitality and receptivity[188] to a profitable novelty were also factors in their conversion to Christianity[189].

10.5.8 Main Areas of Conflict with Igbo Culture (1905-1931).

The decision or resolution of the first Catholic Congress (1915) in Shanahan's era provides an insight into the key areas of conflict between the Christian message and the Igbo culture of Shanahan's era. It prohibited Christians from the rites of initiation or participation in *Muo* (spirit) masquerade society and in *Muo* public dances and processions. It forbade them from taking the *Ozo* title and other chieftaincy titles because they were bound with traditional worship

---

183 Cf. The Missionary Annals of the Holy Ghost Fathers, Vol. XX, no. 11 (November 1938) 245-246.
184 Jordan, Bishop Shanahan, 27.
185 Cf. Obi, op. cit., 167; 171-172, for the statistics.
186 Cf. F. E. Okon, Expansion and Consolidation, in: Obi, op. cit., 177-178. Here Okon cites data from pp. 131 and 239 of J. P. Jordan's "Onitsha-Owerri: Une Grande Epogee Spirituelle" in: *Bulletin de la Congregation* (Paris), 1953.
187 Isichei, History, 173.
188 Cf. Leonard, Lower Niger, 429; Isichei, op. cit., 163.
189 Uchendu, Igbo of Southeast, 36.

and superstitions[190]. It did not permit Christians to marry in the traditional way[191].

While these prohibitions attested to the real existence of idolatory or religious syncretism among Igbo Catholics[192], their framing was too general and partly revealed the missionaries' lack of understanding or appreciation of the importance which the people attached to the social and festive aspects of the masquerades, traditional chieftaincy titles and the traditional marriage process (cf. 10.1.3 and 4)[193]. Hence automatic excommunication from all the affairs of the community faced any Igbo who abjured these titles and values for the sake of the Christian faith and practice[194].

Therefore the three prohibitions were bound to alienate those who regarded the Catholic religion as a "destabilizer" of the traditional way of life. These either apostasized or fell back to their pristine traditional convictions[195]. Nevertheless Shanahan's educational evangelism had succeeded in transforming the Igbo way of life[196]. The transformation was to continue under his successors.

10.6 Schools Method under Archbishop Heerey (1931-1970).

This was the era of expansive and intensive literary educational evangelism. It was the period when the traditional village way of life was rapidly integrating the western type of cities or urban life[197]. A major part of the area covered by the Vicariate of Southern Nigeria politically became the Eastern Region of Nigeria[198]. It was the era of strong native involvement in the political, religious and educational issues. It was equally the "golden period" of missionary enterprise. Archbishop Heerey's two main objectives were

---

190 Cf. Arazu, A Cultural Model for Christian Prayer, in: Shorter, African Christian Spirituality, 114-115.
191 Cf. Obi History, 147-148; Jordan, Bishop Shanahan, 70.
192 Cf. Onyeocha, Faith and Practice, 7.
193 Cf. Onwubiko, Facing the Osu, 68-69; Adibe, Faith and Morality, 20-24; 38.
194 Id., Onwubiko, op. cit., 69.
195 Within the time of Shanahan (1908-1923) there were ten more christian sects added to the existing six. These sects also found adherents among the Igbo (cf. Obi, op. cit., 155-156).
196 Cf. Ochiagha, Bishop Shanahan, in: Okoye, Shanahan, 29.
197 Cf. Coleman, Nigeria, 75.
198 Only the Benue Area was politically Northern Nigeria. The region west of the Niger is Western Nigeria which would later give birth to Mid-west Region (between West and East).

"to reach the relatively few Igbo towns that were yet to be evangelized" *and* "to exploit and perfect the mission strategies and gains of the earlier administrations. While consolidating the Catholic school system of Bishop Shanahan, a serious attempt was made to revive the medical strategy of the Lutz era"[199].

Heerey's ecclesial leadership could be divided into three phases. In the first phase (1931-1947) the Vicariate was reconstituted into Onistha-Owerri Vicariate and two Prefectures, Benue and Calabar in 1934. The Onitsha-Owerri Vicariate gave birth in 1938 to Ogoja Prefecture[200].

In 1937 Heerey founded the Congregation of the Sisters of the Immaculate Heart of Mary and in 1946 the Congregation of the Brothers of St. Peter Claver later known as the Marist Brothers of Schools[201].

In the second phase (1948-1962) he and his larger missionary team of Bishops, priests, religious, and lay people were engaged in education rivalry with other christian denominations and the colonial Government of Eastern Nigeria. In 1948 Onitsha and Owerri became two autonomous Vicariates. Fr. Joseph B. Whelan was the first Bishop of Owerri Vicariate and later Diocese of Owerri (1950) while Onitsha was elevated to an Archdiocese (1950)[202].

In 1951 the fledging, provincial St. Paul's Seminary was transferred to its permanent site at Enugu and renamed "Bigard Memorial Seminary" in honour of the two French foundresses[203] of "The Society of St. Peter the Apostle" who provided the funds for its establishment[204]. Until 1976, this Seminary alone was the hub of the formation of Igbo priests and others from several neigbouring African countries.

In 1955 the *partly* Igbo diocese of Ogoja[205] was entrusted to Bishop T. McGettrick. In 1958 Owerri gave birth to the diocese of Umuahia under Bishop Anthony G. Nwedo (1958), and to the *partly* Igbo diocese of Port Harcourt under Bishop Godfrey M. P. Okoye (1961). Both are foundation members of Igbo Spiritans. In the same 1961 Bishop Nwedo founded the Congregation of the Daughters of Mary Mother of Mercy (29th December) to boost

---

199 Ozigbo, Igbo Catholicism, 15.

200 Benue, Calabar and Ogoja Prefectures later on became dioceses. Calabar also gave birth to Ikot-Ekpene Diocese. Of these four only about half of Ogoja was an Igbo area. That part has since become the diocese of Abakaliki.

201 Cf. Eke, Priestly and Religious Vocations, in: Obi, Hundred Years, 322-325.

202 Cf. Okon, Expansion and Consolidation, in: Obi, Hundred Years, 175-187.

203 They were *Mesdames* Stephanie and Jeanne Cottin Bigard. Cf. Obiefuna, Archbishop Charles Heerey's Missionary Efforts, 1-3.

204 Obiefuna, op. cit., 6.

205 The partly Igbo dioceses of Ogoja and Port Harcourt are made up of many ethnic groups. The Igbo part of Ogoja later became the diocese of Abakaliki in 1973.

the work of evangelisation. In 1962 the Archdiocese of Onitsha gave birth to the diocese of Enugu under the pastoral care of Bishop John Cross Ayogu[206].

The third phase (1963-1967) was the gradual hand-over of the ecclesial leadership to the few Igbo Clergy and Religious. Meanwhile, the Second Vatican Council was taking place (1962-1965) and as it ended in 1965, it had introduced radical changes in the life and ministry of the Church. Archbishop Heerey and his team were faced with the implimentation of the new directives of the Council before his death in 1967 when the leadership of the Local Church in the Onitsha Ecclesiastical Province[207] fell on the young Archbishop Francis Arinze.

This phase was closed by two happy events in the thick of the Nigeria/Biafra civil war[208]: the profession of the members of Bishop Nwedo's Congregation on December 8, 1968 and Bishop Okoye's foundation of the Congregation of the Daughters of Divine Love on July 16, 1969[209].

The war violently disrupted both socio-political life and the dismembered local Church could only render basic pastoral services (celebration of the sacraments and relief work) to the millions of helpless refugees and victims[210].

10.6.1 Local People and Schools Method (1931-1970).

The creation of Dioceses, Vicariates and Prefectures from the one vast Vicariate helped the evanglisers to penetrate deeper into the rural areas. The love and quest for literary education engendered among the Igbo towns and villages a healthy competition and desire to progress or "get up" faster than the rest. From their meagre resources the people eagerly erected more primary schools that also served as station churches (church-schools) and paid for their running costs[211].

The people's enthusiasm also made it easier for missionaries to pay more attention to building Junior Seminaries and other post-primary institutions in order to catch up with the rival Protestant missions[212]. The Church's greater

---

206 Cf. Eke, Creation of More Dioceses, in: Obi, Hundred Years, 277-287.

207 This was the ecclesial nomenclature for the Eastern Region of Nigeria at that time. Now it is divided into Onitsha, Owerri and Calabar Provinces.

208 Among the flood of literature on the Nigeria/Biafra war (July 6, 1967 to January 12, 1970), cf. Madiebo, Nigerian Revolution, Gbulie, The Fall of Biafra; Forsyth, Emeka.

209 Cf. Eke, Priestly and Religious Vocations, in Obi, op, cit., 321-322.

210 Cf. Ozigbo, Igbo Catholicism, 25-29.

211 Isichei, History, 172.

212 Cf. Abernethy, Political Dilemma, 166; Ozigbo, Igbo Catholicism, 96; Uchendu, Missionary Problems, 114-115.

emphasis on post-primary education also coincided with the colonial Government's 1944 Ten Year Development Plan which required

the type of education most suitable to the needs of the country; better conditions of service for teachers employed by the missions and other voluntary bodies; more financial aid to the missions and other voluntary bodies and to native administrations[213].

In 1947 the Nigeria Government officially joined in the struggle for the ownership and control of schools "taking up from where the misionary stopped"[214].

To meet State requirements, the Council of Onitsha-Owerri Vicariate appealed for, and received qualified personnel from the Superior of the Holy Ghost Fathers in Ireland. The Nigerian Government also gave some grants for the improvement of the schools system. Some priests were appointed school managers who were sometimes compelled by circumstances to give more attention to schools than to pastoral work[215].

By mid-1950s the Catholics were proprietors of about half the region's primary schools and they were expanding rapidly the secondary and teacher-training fields where they had previously been weak[216].

The rival Protestant Churches, especially the Church Missionary Society (CMS), tried to counter the growing catholic influence by erecting more schools. Igbo nationalists joined in the rivalry and complicated the education question all the more.

10.6.2 Parishes and Schools (1931-1970).

As the number of converts increased and schools were being erected in towns and villages, the people requested for new parishes and donated generously towards the building of infrastructures at the selected centres. They provided for the daily maintenance of the resident priests and took their turns in doing

---

213 Okeke, Background, 7.
214 D. C. Osadebay, Easter Reflection, 290.
215 This was consonant with the official church policy at that time. The Apostolic Delegate to East Africa was reported to have advised missionaries in 1928 that *"where it is impossible for you to carry on both the immediate task of evangelisation and your educational work, neglect your churches in order to perfect your schools"* (cf. Waliggo, Acts, 37).
216 Id., 169.

free manual labour for the general cleanliness of the parish environment[217]. The parish offered a good opportunity for an intensified catechesis, communal worship and evangelisation of the community[218].

10.6.3 Lay Apostolate Groups (1931-1970).

Between 1931-1970 it was common to find, students, teachers and other lay people as zealous promoters of the Legion of Mary, the Sacred Heart Society, St. Jude's Society, St. Anthony's Guild, Vincent de Paul Society, Confraternity of Christian Doctrine, Pioneer Total Abstinence, etc. These were either devoted to the apostolate of prayer or to teaching catechism to converts and neophites, or to the visitation and provision of relief to the poor and afflicted[219].

For example, in the mid 1960s a good number of my colleagues and I were enrolled into two or more of these apostolate groups. By teaching catechism and visiting the homes of the poor and needy, we helped to facilitate the work of the white priests and catechists in our locality.

10.6.4 Catechists (1931-1970).

The catechists according to their qualifications and grades continued to be the prinicipal teachers of christian doctrine and the intrepreters for the white priests before the ecclesial community. But being less educated than the school teachers, the socio-political changes and the growing number of lettered people seemed to play down their earlier importance as public relations officers in the Church[220].

But their zeal for a faith and life free from superstition was incontrovertible. This sometimes led some of them into condemning the time-honoured Igbo customs and practices as "heathenish". Some used to warn the faithful "under pain of excommunication against participation in many community organizations and activities"[221]. Such catechists were regarded as cultural iconoclasts

---

217 Cf. Mbah, Group Laity Activities, 76-78.
218 Ojo, Significance of the Parish, 42-43.
219 Cf. Nwosu, Laity, in: Obi, Hundred Years, 344.
220 Cf. Eneja, Catechist, 46-54.
221 Ekechi, Missionary Enterprise, 160.

by some of the disturbed audience[222]. But in general the local Church regarded them as models for the faithful[223].

10.6.5 Teachers (1931-1970).

As the years passed by and many more people and agencies became involved in the schools system, the earlier collective influence of teachers began to wane. They were expected to teach christian doctrine in schools but their dissatisfaction with their conditions of service affected their faith and the quality of their teaching[224]. To offset their lukewarmness, the Confraternity of Christian Doctrine (CCD) was formed to teach catechism to the ever increasing number of converts[225].

10.6.6 Church-State Conflict (1931-1970).

Within this period the school system ran into crisis due to increased financial burden, few qualified personel for the post primary institutions and the opposition of nationalists to denominational schools seen as tools of colonialism. The Eastern Nigeria Government Universal Primary Education (UPE) policy of 1953 was directly aimed at curbing the socio- educational influence of the Catholic Church[226]. The policy was in fact spearheaded by all non-catholic denominations who altogether had a fewer number of schools than the Catholic Church alone[227] but wielded greater political power[228].

Faced with such a crisis and rivalry that tended to overshadow the principal task of evangelisation, the Church leaders had to act. Summarily restating the traditional teaching of the Church on christian education as the corporate duty

---

222 Cf. Ekechi, op. cit., ibid; Ejizu, Religion, 116;
223 Cf. Eze, Catechist as a Model, 56-58.
224 Cf. Onwubiko, Catholic Church, in. Obi, op. cit., 239.
225 Nwosu, Laity and the Growth, 35-36.
226 Cf. Eastern Region, Policy For Education (Sessional Paper No. 6 of 1953); Azikiwe, Renascent Africa, 178-192); Onwubiko, Catholic Church, in: Obi, Hundred Years, 258-259; Ozigbo, Igbo Catholicism, 96-97.
227 In 1960 Catholic mission had 2,446 primary schools, while all the non-catholic missions had 1,897 (cf. Nwosu, Laity, 79; Ozigbo, Igbo Catholicism, 96).
228 For tables of these statistics, confer, Nwosu, op.cit., 78-79. The data show that in 1952 and 1956, only one Catholic was in the cabinet of the Eastern Nigeria Government.

of the Church, the State and the Family[229], the Bishops called upon the people to resist the State's plan to monopolise and secularize education so as to forestall a "great tragedy" for the nation[230].

The faithfuls' response to the appeals[231] led to the formation of the largely para-political Eastern Nigeria Catholic Council (ENCC)[232]. Through mass rallies, demonstrations, protests, enlightenment campaigns and press releases, the various laity groups were able to induce the Government either to withdraw, or modify or change some aspects of its plans to take over the Catholic Schools. In reaction, the Protestants set up the Convention of Protestant Citizens (CPC) to counterbalance the ENCC and the increasing influence of the Catholic Church[233].

10.6.7 Positive and Negative Results of School Evangelism (1931-1970).

Numerically, literary education method was very successful. By 1964 "the Catholic Church alone owned about half of all the Voluntary Agency schools"[234] used for evangelisation. This implied that more than 50% of Igbo Christians at that time were Catholics. One needs to compare the situation of the Catholic Church in 1970 with the time of the arrival of the first missionaries in 1885 when there was no single Catholic in Igboland in order to be convinced that God has blessed their evangelical work.

But the education method did create the loophole for mass submissions to the faith without a true conversion of heart. Also the paucity of priestly and religious vocations at the end of Archbishop Heerey's pastoral era continued to question the extent of the evangelical success of the educational method. Nevertheless the missionaries should be extolled for using the method in inserting the Gospel message into the Igbo way of life[235].

---

229 Cf. Pius IX, Divini Illius Magistri. AAS 22 (1930) 49-86; Ozigbo, Igbo Catholicism, 103f.
230 Cf. Archives of Archdiocesan Secretariate Onitsha: "The Bishop's Joint Circular on Education of 1953".
231 Cf. "Catholic Bishops on the UPE", in: The Leader, Assumpta Press, Owerri, (June 1956), 9; Editoral on "Catholic Stand on the UPE", in: The Leader (September, 1956), 8.
232 Ozigbo, op. cit., 98.
233 Cf. Nwosu, Laity and the Growth, 76-116; Id., Laity, in: Obi, Hundred Years, 348-350.
234 Cf. Onwubiko, Catholic Church, in: Obi, op. cit., 271.
235 Cf. Ekandem, Church, 12-13; Nwedo, Christianity, 14-16.

10.6.8 Summary and Critical Evaluation of Missionary Enterprise (1885-1970).

The period from 1885 to 1905 dominated by French missionaries employed both the Christian village system (1885-1900) and the catechetical schools method (1900-1905). The missionaries started from the scratch with a small nucleus of redeemed slaves and social rejects as the foundation of the local Church. The initial apathy to the village method later gave way to a more fervent response to the catechetical method and quicker spread of the faith.

The literary education method (1931-1970) drew massive response from the people and led to a "conversion boom" and a the full blossoming of the Igbo Church. Such a progressive phenomenon of response to the three methods of evangelisation points to the fact that the Igbo have a preference for a faith "tutored" by education[236] because "depending on ignorance for the advancement of Catholicism is surely against every principle of our faith"[237].

The whole epoch (1885-1970) reveals the great importance of devout teacher/catechists in the evangelisation of the local people. It spotlights the evangelical role of traditional Chiefs, some titled men, elders and pious lay persons in the "infant" Igbo Church. It highlights the ardent zeal of some of the missionaries in implanting the faith among the people.

But as one appreciates the good works of the expatriate missionaries[238], one may not be oblivious of the "*Achilles heels*" of their missionary enterprise. Isichei points out that even the missionary era of the revered Bishop Shanahan had also "certain grave limitations". The Bishop

expected public penance for certain offences, and opposed the baptism of unmarried girls living in "corrupt towns" - a policy which led to much inquietude among his colleagues[239].

The charity works of the missionaries were also punctuated with "stories of patients left on the steps of mission hospitals, unable to pay the fees, and of brilliant boys sent away from school for the same reason"[240].

The immediate post Second Vatican Council Igbo Church (1965-1970) remained a *black* Church in a *white* missionary garb. In terms of inculturation, the white missionary epoch (1885-1970) only nurtured a *partial* local Church

---

236 Cf. Agu, Secularization, 276.; Meek, Law and Authority, 15.
237 Isichei, History, 172.
238 These were expelled by the Federal Military Government of Nigeria (1970).
239 Isichei, History, 174.
240 Id., 173.

with four Igbo Bishops[241], very few native clergy and religious and a great majority of foreign priests and religious who could not speak the native language. Despite the official use of the vernacular in the Liturgy, they continued to use interpreters to communicate their message[242]. Their inability to minister in local language, the vehicle of culture[243], remained one of the greatest weaknesses of their mission because avoidable pastoral mistakes were made due to this language barrier.

The exit of the white missionaries opened the eyes of the Igbo to the major pitfalls of the *eighty five years* of evangelisation. What went wrong? people asked. Did the missionaries ever think of handing over to the native clery and religious or were they bent on remaining in the Igbo scene for ever? Why were there few vocations after so many years of evangelisation? Archbishop Heerey gave the reply:

If our number of native priests is already not much greater, it is because we put them through a long course of preparation. This is not because they do not give sufficient promise in the Seminary. On the contrary, the general comment of those in charge of the Seminary is that they are too keen on their studies and are over-examplary in conduct. But these young men have only just emerged from centuries old pagan tradition and habits[244].

Fr. D. Kennedy, the fourth Rector of St. Paul's (later Bigard Major Seminary), also confirmed the Archbishop's doubts when he spoke out the musings of many missionaries:

We often asked ourselves, could we ordain to the priesthood, boys who were only baptised as teenagers, whose non-Christian parents expected to be faithful to the family and take part in the family? They were very good under supervision in school, but ordained and sent out alone on ministry in the bush, what would happen? How could celibacy succeed in such an environment? Would they resist the temptation to divert the funds of mission to their relations and friends?[245]

These musings and sayings from the two missionary leaders partly reveal that they were pastorally very anxious to form good *celibate* priests for the

---

241 The four Igbo Bishops were A. G. Nwedo (Umuahia), J. C. Ayiogu (Enugu), G. M. P. Okoye (Port Harcourt), F. A. Arinze (Onitsha). Only Joseph B. Whelan (Owerri) was Irish.
242 Cf. Isichei, op.cit., 173. As a Seminarian I acted as an interpreter even for our Rector who made more effort than his missionary colleagues to learn Igbo language. The reader can then imagine how helpless were the missionaries who did not speak the language of their audience.
243 Cf. Hesselgrave, Communicating Christ, 67-69.
244 Cited in Isichei, Entirely for God, 35.
245 Id., 26.

Igbo Church[246]. But it is also a pointer to the "ethnocentric ignorance of the missionaries and even racial arrogance"[247], otherwise one cannot grasp the reason for much anxiety over a group of "very good", "over-examplary" and industrious students.

If one recalls that the Igbo attach much importance to the family, progeny and also to virginity before marriage (10.1.3) and if one recalls that in the early missionary days, many Igbo parents were opposed to the idea of their children, especially the only sons, embracing priestly or religious life[248], one should readily accept those "very good" ones who had "left all things" to follow Christ as people of great faith[249]. So despite the desire to raise up a skilled native clergy and religious, the personnel crisis in the early 1970s arose more from the missionaries' prejudice to blacks becoming priests[250]. With Cardinal F. Arinze,

we must... admit that not every missionary from Europe has been able to achieve the best results in the planting of Christianity amidst our people's culture. Many of our customs were not understood and so were condemned. There is no surprise if a European missionary brings to Africa Christianity such as he knew it in Europe[251].

Vocations could hardly flourish in an atmosphere where ecclesial leaders were very skeptical about the true conversion of their "very good" Seminarians on the verge of priestly ordination. These suspicions and prejudices plus the severity of the esoteric "tridentine" seminary formation were largely responsible for the fewness of vocations in the first eighty five years of the Igbo mission[252].

As already pointed out, the successful literary educational evangelism had the disadvantage of blurring the distinction between true conversion to the Christian faith and the simple quest for the white man's wisdom and knowledge[253]. This is confirmed by the nefarious activities of the anti-Church teach-

---

246 Cf. Eke, Priestly and Religious Vocations, 309.
247 Eke, op. cit., ibid. Cf. Agu, Secularization, 257-260.
248 For example, late Fr. Michael Cyprian Tansi (later a Cistercian monk) was the son of a poor widow ordained in 1937. He died in St Bernard Abbey, England, in Jaunuary 1964 (cf. Obi, Hundred Years, 306; 308). The process for his beatification is now happily going on (cf. Isichei, Entirely for God, the Life of Michael Iwene Tansi, Ibadan 1980).
249 Cf. Nwosu, Evangelisation, 271.
250 Cf. Ekechi, Missionary Enterprise, 226; Nwosu, op. cit., 269-270.
251 Arinze, Church, 14-15 Cf. Paul VI, Africae Terrarum, no. 24, p. 23; Sarpong, Emphasis on Africanizing, 107.
252 Cf. Eke, Priestly and Religious Vocations, 308-309; Isichei, History, 174-175.
253 Cf. Uchendu, Igbo, 90; Achebe, Arrow of God, 189-190.

ers and nationalists who were the ex-students of the Catholic or Protestant schools or even former household servants of some of the missionaries. Their anti-Church operations kept the few Igbo pastors and religious wondering if they were ever Christians[254]. As Ozigbo noted,

> the Heerey regime had both the benefits and advantages of longevity... The Heerey regime, like those of his predecessors, was essentially a foreign regime which, given its inherent limitations, could hardly hope to effectively indigenize (or better **inculturate**) Catholicism in the Vicariate. That was to be the function and, indeed the primary task of an indigenous clergy[255].

The critical diagnosis of the failures of the past and the stock-taking of the problems of the present were followed with a purposeful action in order to rectify what went wrong in the local Church and rejuvenate it once again.

10.7 Igbo Missionary Epoch (1970-1994).

10.7.1 Crisis of Personnel and Rehabilitation.

One can imagine the confusion and despair that beset a post war Church deprived of most of her pastoral workers, manpower, material and almost all her means of evangelisation. How can one rebuild and rehabilitate with bare hands all the Churches and institutions in ruins? How can one proclaim the Gospel anew to a people already five years behind the reforms and renewals of the SVC Church? Some statistical data from the four main Igbo dioceses reveal much of the chaos that reigned in 1970 after the war and the exit of the missionaries.

---

254 Cf. Agu, Secularization, 303-307; 317-323, especially 318 and 321; Sarpong, Emphasis on Africanizing, 106.
255 Ozigbo, Igbo Catholicism, 15.

Culled from Annuario Pontificio 1971.

Dio	TP	CP	Pa	Dpr	PR	MS	MR	WR
Enugu	?	?	?	5	?	?	?	?
Onitsha	1,291,800	380,000	(4)	35	15	61	16	5
Owerri	2,000,000	615,319	50	31	75	55	111	78
Umuahia	?	327,032	27	19	38	55	62	35

Dio = Diocese; TP = Total Population; Pa = Parishes; DPr = Diocesan Priests; MS = Major Seminarians; MR = Men Religious; WR = Women Religious; (4) = Incorrect; ? = Not given.

Bishop J. C. Ayiogu of the diocese of Enugu died in 1967 few days before the outbreak of the civil war. The 30 month's war and refugee situation and the *Sede Vacante* must have been responsible for the non-submission of the Enugu data to the Vatican. But the five priests labouring desperately must have managed to register their pastoral presence in Rome.

Onitsha under Archbishop F. Arinze had many parishes but the incorrect number *(4)* inexplicably appears in both *1971 and 1972 Pontificio Annuario*[256]. Owerri's Irish Bishop J. B. Whelan had left and his successor Bishop M. Unegbu, ordained on September 20, 1970, was able to submit a working data for Owerri. Umuahia under Bishop A. Nwedo provided the basic data without knowing the total population of the diocese.

Surprisingly no datum was given on the catechists who were infact the mainstay of the Church in the hundreds of "quasi-parishes" without a priest[257]. They were either forgotten or neglected by the post SVC "Church of the Clergy". So these gaping and yawning diocesan data are indicative of the chaotic situation of the pastoral ministry in 1970.

The 1971 *Annuario* shows that within 1970/71, there were on record only 90 Diocesan Priests, 118 Priests Religious, 189 Men Religious, 158 Women Religious and 171 Major Seminarians. The total would not make much different if the figures from Enugu and the *partly*-Igbo dioceses of Port Harcourt and Ogoja were added[258]. This small number of pastoral workers took care of the millions of people in those hard times.

---

256 Unfortunately the big error in the 1971 Annuario was not rectified in that of 1972.

257 The Annuario Pontificio (1971) notes that, Onitsha had 30; Owerri 568; Umuahia 445. Enugu had probably a proportionate number of "quasi parishes".

258 Bishop G. M. P. Okoye and most of the few Igbo Priests in the diocese of Port Harcourt had to pack over to Enugu diocese because they were unfortunately refused entry into Port Harcourt by the Rivers State Goverment. Igbo priests in the diocese of

Often menaced by armed ex-soldiers and bandits, the few clergy and religious had to convince the suffering people that they were still good and trustworthy shepherds of their flock[259]. They had to teach and re-evangelise a people whose moral and spiritual fibres were broken by the violence of war. Initially assisted by the Vatican, some local and foreign benefactors, the impoverished dioceses embarked on an aggressive reconstruction and rehabilitation of the remaining structures and infrastructures that either lay in ruins or were not confiscated by the State Education Edict 1970[260] as a preamble to pastoral revival and renewal.

10.7.2 Adaptation Method (1970-1981).

This age-old ecclesial pastoral approach (cf. 1 Co 9,19-23)[261] was employed by the white missionaries. But its impact in Igboland seemed to have been blurred by much emphasis on the literary educational evangelism. Adaptation at this time is a modified form of Fr. Lejeune's catechetical method (10.4). It demanded from the pastoral workers the critical process of rethinking, reshaping and assimilating the old missionary approach in order to address the problems of the moment[262]. The presence of indigenous pastors facilitated communication in the Christian communities.

The priests and the parish centres or stations became the hub of religious activities. There the liturgy and sacraments are celebrated either in Igbo or Latin or English or in a mixture of all the three languages. There the people assemble on fixed days and hours to learn christian doctrine or memorize the questions and answers on the mysteries of the faith. There gather the lay apostolate groups and councils to pray or plan their work. There old and young meet and are guided to pious living by the pastor and devout persons appointed as patrons and matrons.

Ogoja were very few. It is not possible to know their exact number since the Annuario does not indicate the ethnic origin of indigenous priests.

259 Cf. Agu, Secularization, 325.

260 Cf. ECS, Public Education Edict 1970, in: East Central State of Nigeria official Gazette No. 3, vol. 2, Enugu, 21st January, 1971. A8, par.3 (1) (a) & (b), (4).

261 Collectanea SCPF, Instructio, vol. 1, no. 135, p.42; Pius XII, Summi Pontificatus. AAS (1939) 429; Id., Evangelii Praecones. AAS 43 (1951) 497-498; John XXIII, Princeps Pastorum. AAS 51 (1959) 833-864; Paul VI, To SECAM., AAS 61 (1969) 573-578; Vatican II, AG, nos. 10-15; 20-21; GS, nos. 43-44; Hering, Evangelisierung, 15-28.

262 Cf. Mbefo, Reshaping, 39f; 60f; 82ff.

Since religious instructions were no longer mandatory in the State schools or at best reduced to a formal one hour "religious lecture" per week[263], the religious upbringing of the children and the Youth devolved mainly on the parish priests, the catechists and some devout volunteers from the Lay Apostolate[264]. The priests' sporadic school apostolate tried to supplement for religionless education and to check the subsequent moral dangers[265].

10.7.3 Men and Women Religious (1970-1981).

The Igbo Religious can be described as "silent wonder workers" in the parishes, schools, hospitals, clinics, maternities and leprosaria and other institutes of benefices. They are comparatively well educated and more numerous than the priests[266]. They are not heard but seen wherever they are, wearing their habits in the heat of the day and the cool of the night and answering the call of duty to the point of wearing themselves out. Since their task is not to preach the divine word to the Christian assembly, their important role as healers of soul and body may sometimes pass unnoticed.

But their special pastoral contribution in the local Church is undeniable. Upon reflection, many do ask: What could have happened to the Igbo Church if some of her Bishops did not found the indigenous Congregations? (10.6). Despite their normal human weaknesses and initial difficulties posed by the State's seizure of their means of apostolate, the Igbo Women Religious proved within a decade to be capable pastoral workers and a missionary force within and outside Nigeria[267].

10.7.4 Apostolic Role of the Laity (1970-1981).

The directives of the *Apostolicam Actuositatem*[268] provided the guideline for pastoral role of the laity. Under the guidance of their chaplains, they revived and reorganised the pious assocations, organisations and councils and established new ones at the station, parish, diocesan, national and even international

---

263 Cf. Agu, Secularization, 318.
264 Cf. Ojo, Role of the Layperson, 24-26; Kaigama, Role of the Catholic Youth, 89-90; Nwosu, laity, 133-135.
265 Cf. Nwedo, Christianity, 25-27; OJo, Laity and the New Era, 90.
266 Cf. Ozigbo, Igbo Catholicism, 42f.
267 Cf. Anochie, Impact of Igbo Women, 59-66.
268 Cf. Vatican II, AA, 2; 6-10.

levels[269]. The reorganised Catholic Women Organisation (CWO), Laity Councils, Mary League Girls and Catholic Youth Organisation became powerful arms of the lay apostolate. Their regular business meetings are nourished with either devotional Holy Masses or prayer session. Pious sodalities multiplied and found large followings from the zealous faithful directed by priest chaplains[270].

In their parishes and communities, they made heroic sacrifices in setting up magnificent places of worship separate from the church schools seized by the State. They built nursery, primary and secondary schools which were run either by the State or the Church. They initiated profit-making projects in order to help them carry the burdens of parish administration[271]. Many put up a firm and concerted action for the return of the mission schools to their proprietors. Not a few engaged themselves in trying to combat the increasing godlessness and moral decadence among the Youth and adults brought up with a religionless education[272].

Even people without basic musical and liturgical formation exhibited wonderful initiative and talents in composing Church music in the traditional tongue, tone, tune, and rhythm[273]. Native musical instruments blended most of the liturgical celebrations. Members of the Bible Society devoted enough time to the reading of the divine word now available to them in the mother tongue[274].

The CWO and the Mary League deserve special mention as epitomes of lay apostolate and the mainstay of Igbo Church. The CWO in particular happily consider their "christian motherhood as a vocation"[275] and so they regard the whole clergy and religious as their "sons and daughters". For this reason their

---

269 Cf. Ojo, Laity, 33-38.
270 Cf. for example, Diary and Calendar of Pastoral Events, Diocese of Orlu (Nigeria), 1984 passim; 1994 passim.
271 Cf. Ojo, Significance of the Parish, 33-46.
272 Cf. Onotu, Individual Activities, 62-64; Mbah, Group Laity Activities, 78-79. But for financial reasons and better condition of service, the Nigerian Union of Teachers (NUT), many of them Catholics, generally favoured the Government control of schools while those lacking in moral fibre were openly against their return to the Church.
273 Cf. Carroll, Practical Inculturation, 89-90; Van Theil, African Religious Music, 179-180.
274 In St. Mary's Parish Umuowa (Diocese of Orlu) where I served from 1981 to 1985, I was privileged to inaugurate the society in 1981. It has since proved itself to be one of the strongest arms of the Lay Apostolate in the Parish.
275 Njoku, Mother the Centrepiece, 21ff. Cf. John Paul II, Mulieris Dignitatem (MD), 18-19; Nyamiti, African Sense, 98f.

material and spiritual support for these "children" is simply proverbial and spectacular[276].

10.7.5 Church Councils (1970-1981).

In fulfilment of the demands of the SVC, the pastoral, parish and laity councils were set up in the dioceses as the assistants and coordinators of the pastoral activity[277]. At the diocesan level is the pastoral council made up of the Bishop, parish priests and lay persons selected from the parishes. A lay person is the chairman of this council while the Bishop is the president.

The same pattern holds for the parish council in which the priest is the president. The station councils function without the physical presence of the priest but is under his jurisdiction. The Laity Council is entirely the affair of the lay persons directed by a chaplain.

All these *consultative* councils are entrusted with the organization and coordination of pastoral and social activities in their respective areas of influence. But "they have several functional weaknesses such as mutual rivalries, leadership struggles and personality clashes"[278].

10.7.6 Vital Role of Catechists.

With the State seizure of Catholic schools, many teachers were no longer interested in the apostolate of giving religious instruction as in the Shanahan-Heerey era. Rather they gladly became the employees of the State as gleaned from the pro-Government speeches of the leaders of the Nigerian Union of Teachers (NUT)[279]. Some even became polygamists as a way of expressing their "freedom" from the "yoke" of the expatriate manager of schools or from the Catholic priest[280].

This situation called for the reorganisation and modification of the ministry of the Catechist into three categories: the parish catechist who comes next after the parish priest, the full time station catechist, and the part time station catechist. They were trained not only to teach catechism but also to supplement where necessary the purely administrative and clerical work of parish

---

276 Cf. Anochie, Impact of Igbo Women, 75-81; CWO, Diocese of Orlu, 4-5; 8-9.
277 Cf. Vatican II, CD, 27;
278 Ozigbo, Igbo Catholicism.
279 Cf. Agu, op. cit., 320.
280 Cf. Eze, Catechist as a Model, 56.

priests. They were paid their little salary according to their grades and work-load[281]. Yet feedbacks indicated that most of them were devoted to duty as teachers of the faith[282].

10.7.7 Formation of Clergy and Religious.

Vocation explosion characterized the late 1970s in the Igbo Church[283]. In line with the instructions of *Optatam Totius* and *Ad Gentes*[284], the program of formation slowly began to de-emphasize Euro-Americanism and to emphasize the correlation of the christian message to the salvific aspects of the Igbo culture, customs and religious tradition.

The formation of the candidates by the native priests and religious laid to rest the problem of *racial* prejudice in priestly or religious formation. This supports the Igbo proverb which says that "*Diala ma ibe ya*" (the free borns or natives know each other). The common culture and background easily created mutual understanding between staff and students. Moreover the honour and respect accorded to the clergy attracted the youth to priestly and religious life[285].

During the long vacations Seminarians are sent to live among the people and acquire some practical experience. They help as much as they can in preparing candidates for the sacraments, teach songs, visit the old, the sick, the poor, the weak in faith, participate in various forms of lay apostolate and make recommendations to the parish priest[286].

Although the Junior Seminary formation is more costly than State education and even lasts longer than before (*6-8 years*), and although the candidates are strictly scrutinised, the Seminaries are still over-crowded with enthusiastic prospective candidates for the priesthood[287]. Of course many enter solely to profit from the high quality of intellectual, religious, moral, cultural and even basic technical education[288].

---

281 Cf. Kalu, Administrative Duties, 114-118; Eze, Parish Records, 104-106; Nwosu, Laity, 117-124.
282 Cf. Eze, Catechist as a Model, 55-58.
283 In the political scene the East-Central State was divided into two: Anambra and Imo States.
284 Cf. Vatican II, Opt. Tot., 19-21; AG, 16.
285 Ozigbo, Igbo Catholicism, 40ff.
286 Cf. Aniagwu, Priestly Formation, 42-44; Okere, Theological Canonical Admnistrative Issues, 53-54.
287 Okere, op. cit. 54-55; Aniagwu, op. cit., 36-39.
288 Aniagwu, op. cit., 44-46.

The result is a yearly turn out of picked young men ready to proceed to the already over-crowded Provincial Bigard Memorial Seminary, Enugu. The vocation boom necessitated the opening in 1976 of a separate Philosophy campus at Ikot Ekpene[289] while Bigard served as Theology campus. The story is the same in the Juniorates, Postulates and Novitiates of the Religious Congregations[290].

Within this period, the creation of the dioceses of Awka (1976) from Onitsha, Orlu (1980) from Owerri, Okigwe (1981) from Umuahia[291], was a testimony to the apostolic zeal of the laity, to the miracle of priestly and religious vocations, and to the rapid growth of the Church east of the Niger. From 1970 to 1981, the number of dioceses rose from four to eight.

Commenting on the "vocation miracle", the retired Irish Bishop Whelan said in my interview with him during the dedication of the imposing Owerri Assumpta Cathedral in 1980:

> ...we (the white missionaries) have achieved our purpose by creating an Igbo clergy and Hierarchy ... to take over the administration of the Church in the 'Igbo country'. That the white man will leave today and the Igbos take over tomorrow without the smallest hitch is a miracle that could have happened nowhere else in the whole missionary world[292].

I was elated at such a profuse eulogy of the Igbo clergy and religious by the respected first Bishop of Owerri. But the Laity, the parents or guradians, noted for their sacrifice and dedication to the cause of the Church are also entitled to so much praise for the *vocation boom*[293].

10.7.8 Igbo Theologians (1970-1981).

At this time, the trend or emphasis was on the Church's need of African contribution to her theology[294]. Shorter affirms:

---

289 Ikot-Ekpene is an Ibibio diocesan town in the Cross-River State, the former South-Eastern State.
290 Cf. Eke, Priestly and Religious Vocations, in: Obi et alii, Hundred Years, 327-330.
291 The Bishops of the dioceses are A. K. Obiefuna (Awka), G. O. Ochiagha (Orlu), A. Ilonu (Okigwe). In 1977 Bishop M. N. Okoro was consecrated the Auxiliary Bishop of Abakaliki, and in 1978 M. U. Eneja succeeded (Enugu) the late Bishop G. M. P. Okoye, founder of the young D.D.L. Congregation (cf. Annuario Pontificio 1982).
292 The Leader, Owerri, January 25-February 7, 1981. This time the writer was already a priest and also the EDITOR of this important catholic organ from 1980 to 1981.
293 Cf. Aniagwu, Priestly Formation, 38-39.
294 Shorter, African Christian theology, 27-33.

Christianity has to come to terms with the theologies and systems of beliefs of the religion-based cultures of Africa, if it is to be Africanised at all. Without such a dialogue Christianity would simply be living in a vacuum. Christianity, therefore, cannot afford to neglect African theology[295].

Hence in accordance with the directives of the Church[296], some Igbo theologians and pastors began to search for the way of professing the faith in Christ without losing their "*Igboness*" or cultural identity just as the Jews and the Euro-Americans did not simply lose theirs by embracing the christian faith[297]. It was an effort at integrating sound cultural heritage with christian theologizing[298].

This logically led to the research into the possibility of using African/Igbo products, arts and symbols, (fruit of the earth and work of Igbo hands) for the celebration of the Liturgy and the Sacraments. Without prejudice to the teachings of the Church[299], some began to question constructively the absolute necessity of using imported materials for liturgical and sacramental celebrations[300].

10.7.9 Evaluation of Adaptation Method (1970-1981).

This method helped to some extent in adapting the christian message to the people and in accomodating some healthy cultural values within christian life and worship[301]. This was especially true of the use of religiously symbolic Igbo names for baptism, confirmation and religious profession[302], the celebration of most of the liturgies in the mother tongue or in a foreign language intelligible to a particular worshipping community.

Indigenous music and instruments gradually began to replace the songs from the English "*West Minster Hymnal*" and the Euro-American organ or piano. As the people sing and accompany the music with graceful bodily move-

---

295 Id., 27.
296 Cf. Paul VI, To SECAM. AAS (1969) 573-578; cf. 32 Articles, 32-36; Vatican II, SC, 1; AG, 10-14; 20-21.
297 Cf. Uzukwu, Blessing and Thanksgiving, 17-22.
298 Cf. PACT, Statement, 121ff; Kraft, Christianity in Culture, 304-310.
299 Cf. Canons 880; 847; 924; 926; 999.
300 Okolo, Christ, 'Emmanuel', 130-139; Uzukwu, Food and Drink in Africa, 370-385; 398; Cf. Geoghegan, African Sculpture, 218-220; Wermter, African Art, 235-240; Carroll, African Textiles, 241-248.
301 Cf. Kraft, Christianity in Culture, 38; 358f.
302 Cf. Ezeanya, Handbook of Igbo Christian Names, Port Harcourt (Nigeria) 1967, passim.

ments, one can feel how the use of the local musical instruments is catching up with the people's psyche and is helping in vivifying and incarnating the liturgy in their souls[303]. But there was also "adulation of latin"[304] by those who were impervious to the liturgical reforms and changes of the SVC.

While problems and anxiety of the post war era gave rise to a diminished faith and practice among the people, many more were also being converted to the faith in gratitude to God's protection during the hard times[305]. In terms of quantitative achievement, Igbo pastoral workers convincingly demonstrated that they effectively took over and continued the ministry from where the expatriates stopped.

The hallmark of this period was the Church's gradual assumption of a typical Igbo nature, the active participation of the Laity in the Church's daily ministry, the steady rise of indigenous priestly and religious vocations and the founding of new Congregations.

In 1973 Bishop Okoye's Congregation of the Daughters of Divine Love had its first professions. In the same year the Claretian Congregation came into being. The women Carmelites established in Owerri in 1974. By 1975 Bishop Nwedo's Mercy Congregation was showing signs of rapid growth, while the older Immaculate Heart of Mary (IHM) had waxed strong and was already sending out missionaries[306]. In the same year Archbishop Arinze founded the Congregation of the Brothers of St Stephen (BSS)[307].

The gradual progress of Igbo monasticism led to the erection of two Benedictine and three Cistercian monasteries in the Archdiocese of Onitsha and the diocese of Enugu between 1971 and 1978[308]. Other new Congregations were also springing up leading to what Fr. R. Ozigbo described as "over-multiplication of Religious Congregations"[309].

The publication of the inter-denominational translation of the New Testament in Igbo (1981) was a landmark in the movement of the Igbo Church towards the insertion of the Good News in the thought and lives of the people. By the end of 1981 the Igbo Church has fully recovered from the traumatic experiences of the civil war and has become, in response to the earlier call of Pope Paul VI[310], a local Church endowed with zealous men and women ministering to their own people in their language and culture and also missioning to

---

303 Cf. Echezona, Use of Local Musical Instruments, 84-87.
304 Cf. Ozigbo, Igbo Catholicism, 35ff.
305 Cf. Nwosu, Laity, in: Obi, Hundred Years, 360-374.
306 Cf. Eke, Priestly and Religious Vocations, in: Obi et al., Hundred Years, 320-327.
307 Cf. Ozigbo, op. cit., 42.
308 Ozigbo, op. cit., 55-56; Obi, op. cit., 394.
309 Ozigbo, op. cit., 50.
310 Cf. Paul VI, To SECAM, Kampala (Uganda) 1969. AAS 61 (1969) 573-578.

other peoples of Nigeria, Africa, Europe, America and Asia in the official languages of their audiences[311].

*10.7.10 Main Areas of Faith-Culture Conflict in Igbo Evangelism (1970-
1981).*

The State had only cashed in at an auspiscious moment and, with a stroke of
the pen robbed the legitimate proprietors of their educational and health centres, thereby executing its age-old plan to secularize Church schools and institutes[312]. This renewed the Church-State conflict over the education question
of the 1950s (10.6.6).

In a Joint Pastoral Letter of 1971, the Bishops of ECS tersely protested
against the State's confiscation of Church schools, some hospitals and welfare
centres[313]. All their efforts to dialogue with the State were "frustrated again
and again"[314]. Some of the clergy and religious who resisted the Edict were
either intimidated or molested or forcefully ejected from the State's "new
school premises". Some suffered real religious persecutions like the apostolic
people[315]. But they were undaunted in their witnessing to the faith (cf. Ac
4,20).

The pastoral ministry continued to face faith-culture conflicts comparable to
those between the Christian message and the idolatrous practices of the devotees of the Graeco-Roman Religions[316]. Fr. Ejizu reports that

> estimates of Igbo Christian population that still shop from one mushroom, faith-healing
> and prayer house to another and patronise traditional religious experts in search of one kind
> of material benefit or the other, average 60%[317].

And Prof. Afigbo affirms that

> an Igbo attends communion at the same time as he believes in the potency of traditional
> magic; he ties up in the same handkerchief the rosary and the traditional talisman and

---

311 An admirable quality of the Igbo missionaries is that they try to know much about the
cultures and languages of their future audience before they embark on their mission.
312 Cf. Agu, Secularization, 310-324.
313 Cf. ECS, "Public Education Act of 1970, No 2 of 1971".
314 Education: 1971 Easter Joint Pastoral Letter, 5
315 Cf. Ac 4,1ff; 5,17ff; 9,1ff; 12,1ff etc; Anochie, Impact of Igbo Women, 59-62.
316 Cf. Ac 13,4ff; 14,11ff; 16,16ff; 19,11ff; 19,23ff. For more on these, cf. Wildhaber,
Paganisme Populaire, 75-79; 88-100; 101-111; 112-124; 125-137.
317 Ejizu, Endurance of Conviction, 131.

plants side by side in the garden round his new cement and pan-roofed home the hibiscus of 'civilisation' and the *ogirisi* tree of the pagan family rites[318].

Generalizations may require qualifications to back them up, but the depositions of these Igbo scholars just reveal the gravity of the problem of the "rift" between the christian faith and Igbo culture within this period marked by a gradual exodus of some Catholics from the Church[319].

Add to this the fact that some of the numerous social clubs were notorious either for their squandermania or laxity in religion. Thus a people admired for their religiousity were becoming secularised by the impact of modernity and material comfort. Isichei observes that

> the religious situation in Igboland now is very similar to that in Europe: most people have been baptized, but secularism is widespread, and intense religious conviction probably rare... Secularization in Igboland is partly the product of the same underlying factors as the phenomenon elsewhere, but it is often the result of an ecounter with European secularism, in Africa or in Europe[320].

This was the situation as Pope John Paul II prepared to visit Nigeria in 1982.

10.8 The NEE and Inculturation Method (1982-1994).

Just as inculturation is a more adequate word[321] than adaptation or incarnation, so also is the inculturation method a refined form of adaptation or incarnation method[322]. Inculturated evangelisation was initiated in Nigeria by Pope John Paul II during his pastoral visit from 12th to 17th February 1982. It aims at deepening the faith of the people by giving adequate pastoral attention to their traditions and cultural heritage. In terms of degree and intensity, the method may correspond to the intensive literary educational evangelism of the white missionary era (10.6).

---

318 Afigbo, Education, 130.
319 Cf. Ndiokwere, Prophecy, 19-23.
320 Isichei, Seven Varieties, 220-221.
321 Cf. Schineller, Handbook, 21-24.
322 "Synod of Bishops from Africa Issue Declaration", (1974) 2. In 1974, the SECAM preferred the incarnation method to the adaptation.

10.8.1 Papal Message: Inculturate Your Faith.

The Pope's address to the Bishops at the Apostolic Nunciature in Lagos on 15th February[323] depicts the situation of the National Church and sets the tone for the challenges of a new era of évangelisation (NEE)[324] in a local Church in which the Igbo are the majority. Excerpts from the address reads:

Your people are enthusiastic, hospitable, full of faith. They understand the immense treasury of grace that is theirs in our Lord Jesus Christ... Your seminaries are full, your religious congregations have a steady flow of candidates and your lay apostolate organisations are dynamic... You promote orthodox doctrine and approved liturgical practices, and you encourage priestly discipline[325]... In anticipation of this pastoral visit, I expressed the hope that it would initiate "a new era of evangelization"[326].

By NEE the Pope means the era of *evangelisation of culture*[327] or the era of evangelisation through *inculturation*[328]. It is an era of effective mutual ecounter between the Good News and the Nigerian cultures for their regeneration and transformation[329]. It is an era of naturalizing the Church in all the strata of the Nigerian society[330]. It is for Nigeria "a new pentecost"[331] in which the Church seeks to consolidate and intensify her pastoral gains and attunes her praxis to the people's life situations[332].

It is the era in which the old imported methods of evangelisation should give way to the new inculturation method[333]. The new era is urgent because the Nigerian Church must develop her own liturgical arts, architecture, texts, symbols and rites, songs and dance, etc. and should depend less on imported forms[334].

---

323 As a member of the diocesan committee for the papal visit, I was privileged to be present at this meeting with the Bishops.
324 Paul VI, EN, no. 2. Here the Pope talks about a new and more frutiful era of evangelisation".
325 To Bishops, in: Papal Message To Nigeria, 37.
326 Id., 38.
327 Id., 39. Cf. CT, no. 53.
328 Cf. CBCN, Nigerian Church, 8.
329 Cf. John Paul II, CT, 53; Paul VI, EN, 20; Carrier, Evangelisation, 88.
330 Cf. Carrier, op. cit., 87-88.
331 Cf. Onaiyekan, Why A New Era, 43-44.
332 Cf. Okoye, Special Assembly, 178-182.
333 Cf. for example: John Paull II, To Bishops of Zaire on *Inculturation*, 3rd May 1980, in: AFER, 22 no.4 (1980) 222-228.
334 Cf. Uzukwu, Liturgical Celebration, 53-56.

10.8.2 Impact of Inculturation Call on Nigeria.

The Pope's message was well received at diocesan and national levels. It aroused the local Church from her long years of cultural slumber[335].

In 1983 the Bishops issued a Joint Pastoral Letter[336] reminding all about the demands and expectations of the NEE. This was followed in 1984 by a national seminar[337] focusing on the *what*[338], the *why*[339] and *how*[340] of the NEE.

The *what* or substance of the NEE as pointed by Fr. James Okoye is the evangelization and development of Nigerian peoples and cultures according to the teachings and instructions of the conciliar and post-conciliar documents[341].

Bishop Onayekan stressed that the *why* for the NEE is the need for pastoral readjustment (*aggiornamento*) to the new socio-political and cultural changes in the pluralistic modern Nigeria[342]. "A new era is called for, not because the old era has failed, but because it has so succeeded that we are now being called to higher things[343]".

The *how* or method according to Fr. M. Cullen is the involvement of every Nigerian Christian in the incarnation or inculturation of the christian message in oneself and in all the strata and contexts of the Nigerian society: among atheists, non-christians, uncommitted and committed christians, the youth, adults, intellectuals, schools, institutions, social groups, towns, villages, families and individuals[344].

The three papers were followed by group discussions and reports by the participants on the import and implication of the NEE for the whole local Church. Their recommendations required each Christian to contribute to the new or "secondary" evangelization which should in principle excel and deepen the "old" or "primary" evangelization.

All are expected to deepen their faith and engage in fruitful dialogues with Christians and non-Christians. Major Seminaries, Pastoral Institutes and the

---

335 Cf. *Gaudium et Spes*, nos. 53-62.
336 Cf. CBCN, Holy Father, Pope John Paul II Ushers In A New Era Of Evangelization (1983).
337 Cf. CBCN, New Era of Evangelisation (1984), passim.
338 Cf. Okoye, New era, in: CBCN, Seminar, 9-38
339 Cf. Onaiyekan, Why A New Era, in: CBCN, op. cit., 39-55.
340 Cf. Cullen, How Will We Initiate, in: CBCN, op. cit., 56-73.
341 Cf. Okoye, New era, 9-38
342 Cf. Onayekan, Why A New Era, 39-55.
343 Id. 48.
344 Cf. Cullen, How Will We Initiate, op.cit., 56-73.

Catholic Institute of West Africa (CIWA) are tipped as centres for inculturated theological research and for the training of personnel for the NEE[345].

The results of the national seminar and the Bishops' study session[346] in response to the Pope's exhortation to an inculturated evangelisation[347] form the basis for the current effort at inculturated ministry in the Igbo Church.

10.8.3 The NEE and Centinary Celebration (1984-1985).

As the NEE was exercising its impact on the whole nation, the centinary celebration of the Catholic missionary enterprise in Eastern Nigeria (1885-1985) providentially drew near. The festivities were particularly significant for the Igbo Church with 9 out of the 13 dioceses of the Onitsha Ecclesiastical Province. The programme for the celebrations was based on the papal call to a NEE. The activities at the parish and diocesan levels showed that the papal message reached every sector of the Igbo community.

Committees made up of priests, religious lay persons and experts were set up to coordinate inculturation activities in the parishes and dioceses[348]. They organised seminars, workshops, symposia, discussions, lectures and publications at the parish and diocesan levels to deepen the knowledge of the faith in preparation for the centinary[349]. Intense theological debates focused on how to inculturate the faith among the people after celebrating the glories of the "old era" of evangelisation.

The "Joint Centinary Pastoral Letter" of the Catholic Bishops of the Province provided the guideline for studies and pastoral action in the centinary period and beyond[350]. The Letter first looks retrospectively and gratefully at the "old" white missionary era, then makes a critical evaluation of the new era of the local Church that is becoming self-supporting and is already sending out missionaries to needy Churches.

Hence those who celebrate the centinary should do well to "*Put Out Into Deep Water*" and scoop out a faith better in quality than the "old" quantitative

---

345 Cf. CBCN, New Era, 75-135, where the group reports are given in details.
346 Cf. CSN, Inculturation in Nigeria (proceedings of catholic Bishops' study session, 1988).
347 Cf. CBCN, Evangelisation through Inculturation (1991 Joint Patoral Letter).
348 Cf. CSN, Inculturation, 97-98; 101-102; John Paul II, Christifideles Laici (CL) 44.
349 Ojo, Laity and the New Era, 27-32.
350 CBOEP, Centinary Pastoral Letter, "Put Out Into Deep Water", passim.

and shallow faith in a "Century-Old Faith"[351]. All these make it obligatory for the faithful to be fully committed to the NEE via inculturation.

Three years after the centenary, the Bishops of Nigeria organised a special study session on inculturation[352]. They studied the relevance of inculturation to the Nigerian Church[353], the use of inculturation as a modern approach to evangelisation[354] and reviewed the extent of liturgical inculturation by the Nigerian Hierarchy[355]. The Bishops also listened to the Ghanaian Bishop P. Sarpong tell of his country's inculturation experience[356] and heard the English Fr. K Carroll give his own testimony of practical inculturation since 1936[357].

10.8.4 Impact of Inculturation on the Igbo.

Though at its preliminary stages, the NEE through inculturation is already bearing some visible fruit. The Laity in their various states of life increased their laudable spontaneous response to personal formation in the faith, to the material welfare of the local Church and to the evangelisation of the local culture[358]. The Knights of St John and St Mulumba strive to represent the political interests of the Church[359]. The women no longer content themselves with their vocation as mothers (10.7.4) but some move forward to philosophical and theological studies while others take active part in party politics[360].

The reorganised catechist system creates the opportunity for the Catechists to receive periodic intensive courses on basic thelogical and doctrinal matters in order to cope up with the new demands of their ministry in a fast growing literate society[361]. "Imbued with the apostolic spirit, they make a singular and

---

351 Cf. Obiefuna, Idolatory (1985), passim; Ejizu, Endurance of Convictions, 126; Nwosu, Evangelisation, 338.
352 Cf. CSN, Inculturation in Nigeria (1988), passim.
353 Cf. Okure, Inculturation, in: CSN, Inculturation, 39-62.
354 Cf. Carrier, Inculturation, in: Id., 4-25.
355 Cf. Nwazojie, Nigerian Hierarchy, in: Id., 63-78.
356 Cf. Sarpong, Inculturation, in: Id., 29-38.
357 Cf. Carroll, Practical Inculturation, in: Id., 79-91.
358 Cf. John Paul II, CL, op. cit., 56-63; 42-44.
359 Cf. Obi, Hundred Years, 344-345.
360 Cf. Anochie, Impact of Igbo Women, 43-49; Idem, Inculturation, 174-177; Njoku, Mother the Centrepiece, 21ff; 41ff; 94ff; Ojo, Laity, 57-63; Odudoye - Kanyoro, Talitha, qumi!. This book is a compilation of the theological essays by some African Women Theologians in 1989. (For some reflections on Women's role in the Church, cf. Tzabedze, 76-79; Materu, 139-144; Tetteh, 155-164; Ada James, 173-179).
361 Cf. Okoye, Bible Knowledge, 6-8; Nwosu, Laity, 123.

absolutely necessary contribution to the spread of the faith and the Church by their strenuous efforts"[362].

Seminary studies and formation increased the emphasis on African traditional religion, thought and culture[363]. Seminarians are encouraged and guided to make research into the areas of faith-culture conflict in their localities. Institutes of theology like CIWA[364] take inculturation studies as their main area of specialization[365].

Parishes are multiplying through the zealous apostolate of the Laity who are ever ready to give in their best for the good of their communities[366]. There is a deeper penetration of the Gospel among the people through the Bible study groups, charismatic renewal movements[367], and various forms of apostolate which cater for the needs of believers and unbelievers in their communities[368]. Some have joined human rights movements to combat social and political injustice[369].

Moreover the elevation of Archbishop F. Arinze to the Cardinalate[370] in April 1984 was seen by the Igbo as a papal acknowledgment of the maturation of their Church[371]. Meanwhile three more dioceses, Ahiara (1987) and Nsukka (1990), Aba (1991)[372] were created to bring the faith closer to the thousands of the faithful.

---

362 SVC II, AG, 17. Cf. John Pau II, Redemptoris Mission (RM), 73.
363 Cf. Onwubiko, African Thought, Religion and Culture (1991). This book is the fruit of his lectures in the Seat of Wisdom Major Seminary, Owerri.
364 CIWA or the Catholic Institute of West Africa was established in 1981 for English-speaking West African countries. Its first Rector was Msgr. Prof. now Archbishop S. Ezeanya. I was in the department of Biblical Studies of this Institute from 1989 to 1991.
365 Cf. CBCN, New Era, 147-148.
366 An example is the diocese of Orlu created in 1981 with 23 parishes. By 1993 it has 56 parishes (cf. statistics below).
367 Cf. CBCN, Guidelines, 14-16.
368 Cf. Idem, E., op. cit., 154-164; Ojo, Laity, 27-31.
369 Uka, Justice, 50-55.
370 Dominic Cardinal Ekandem, the first Ibibio Bishop of Ikot-Ekpene, and now the retired Bishop of Abuja, was nominated the first Nigerian Cardinal in May 1976 by Pope Paul VI. Francis Cardinal Arinze is the second Nigerian Cardinal, but the first Igbo Archbishop and Cardinal.
371 The Cardinal heads the "Sacred Congregation for Non-Christians" or for Interreligious Dialogue. He was succeeded at Onitsha by Archbishop S. Ezeanya, a retired Professor of Religious Studies.
372 The Bishops are: Mgsr. Victor Chikwe (Ahiara); Mgsr. Francis Okobo (Nsukka); Msgr. Vincent Ezeonyia (Aba); In 1991, Mgsr. Lucius Ugorji succeeded the retired Bishop A. Nwedo in Umuahia. In 1993 Msgr. Anthony Obinna suceeded the retired Bishop Mark Unegbu in Owerri.

In the language of the Acts, the word of God continued to increase and multiply among the people in the NEE and the Lord daily opened "the door of faith" to Igbo Gentiles (cf. Ac 14,27). It was logical then that within this period, a third regional Major Seminary, the "Seat of Wisdom Owerri"[373], was opened in 1990 in response to the miraculous vocation boom in an era when most of the ethnic groups in Nigeria, Africa and other continents are lamenting the dearth of vocations. Also the Spiritans and Claretians have their own Major Seminaries to take special care of their needs.

The Igbo Church today is a missionary and a missioning Church to Africa, U.S.A., Asia and Europe (Austria, Belgium, England, France, Germany, Italy)[374]. At present, the total number of the purely Igbo Catholic dioceses are *twelve*: *eleven* east of the Niger in the former Onitsha Ecclesiastical Province and *Issele-Uku* on the west bank in the former Lagos Province[375]. The diocese of Port Harcourt in the East is partly Igbo. Below are selected data about the stand of the dioceses in 1992/1993 as found in the *Pontificio Annuario*.

---

373 In the 1991/1992 academic year, Nigeria's ten Major Seminaries had 2,783 seminarians, the great majority of whom are the Igbo studying in all the Seminaries. Five of these are located in Igboland alone, namely: in Attakwu, Enugu, Isienu, Nekedi, Owerri respectively. Those at Attakwu and Isienu belong to the Spiritan Congregation. The one at Nekedi belongs to the Claretians (cf. Association of Nigerian Priests and Religious in Rome, Encounter, 137).

374 These missionaries are mainly drawn for the indigenous Congregations of the Holy Rosary Sisters, the Daughters of Mary Mother of Mercy, the Daughters of Divine Love, the Sisters of Immaculate Heart of Mary, and Sisters of the Handmaid of the Child Jesus. The missionary Priests are the Igbo Spiritans, the Dominicans, the Claretians, and Priests of the National Missionary Seminary of St Paul. The Brothers of St. Peter Claver work in Africa. (cf. Obi, Hundred Years, 315-326; 376-377;394).

375 Although in the former Lagos Province, Issele-Uku is an Igbo diocese. What is said of the other eleven dioceses can be applied to it. Let us recall that on March 31, 1994, the Onitsha Ecclesiastical Province was divided into Onitsha and Owerri Provinces. Lagos and Kaduna Provinces were subdivided into three Provinces respectively (cf. 1.8.2).

Dio	TP	CP	Pa	DPr	MS	MR	FR
ABA	1,073,000	268,211	26	51	95	7	40
ABAKALIKI	1,260,000	166,000	31	30	46	12	55
AHIARA	500,000	404,117	29	54	132	2	26
AWKA	855,000	460,824	74	127	182	7	91
ENUGU	998,998	567,620	44	90	138	328	197
Issele-Uku	*376,000*	*177,020*	*22*	*29*	*63*	*11*	*43*
NSUKKA	1,000,000	250,000	27	54	61	89	39
OKIGWE	1,187,490	363,778	37	98	109	30	43
ORLU	668,109	510,715	56	94	180	32	67
ONITSHA**	1,225,290	804,312	73	127	465	79	268
OWERRI*	1,187,490	466,826	53	69	121	113	120
UMUAHIA	882,000	96,000	24	37	100	55	49

KEY to the Data Culled from Pontificio Annuario 1993: Dio = diocese; TP = total population; CP = catholic population; Pa = Parishes; DPr = Diocesan Priests; MS = Major Seminarians; MR = Male Religious; FR = Female Religious. ** Archdiocese in 1950; * Archdiocese in 1994.

Except in Abakaliki and Issele-Uku, where expatriate priests are still ministering, all the diocesan priests are Igbo[376]. There is a also good number of indigenous regular priests working in all the dioceses. All the twelve Bishops are Igbo. Yet it must be pointed out that despite the several million believers, Catholics are in the minority in seven of the twelve dioceses[377]. But when one recalls that there was not a single Igbo Catholic before the arrival of Fr. Lutz and companions at Onitsha in December 1885, then one must rejoice at the rapid growth, expansion and strength of the Igbo Catholic Church within a century[378].

Recently theological meetings and researches have been stepped up in preparation for the African Synod of Bishops[379]. With her force of indigenous personnel of active and contemplative life, structures and infrastructures gradually built up since 1970, it is not an exaggeration to say that the Igbo

---

376 As already pointed out, there are also Igbo priests in the multi ethnic diocese of Port Harcourt.
377 Catholics are the majority in the dioceses of Ahiara, Awka, Enugu, Onitsha, Orlu.
378 Cf. Onaiyekan, Church in Africa, 24. Synod of Bishops, Lineamenta, 9: "The area of the Church's fastest growth, at present, is Africa where the increase has been 50% in the last 10 years".
379 Cf. Okoye, Special Assembly for Africa, 173.

Church remains one of the most virile *ecclesia* in Africa today. Thanks to the sacrifices of all the evangelisers, the Igbo can joyfully say that the Lord has done marvels for them and "holy is his name" (cf. Lk 1,49). "This is Yahweh's doing and we marvel at it" (Ps 118,23).

10.8.5 Unresolved Problems and Challenges.

But despite the resounding success and external transformations of the local Church, there are still unresolved problems of faith and culture[380]. Christian faith and practice are in crisis[381]. It is in many ways superficial or skin-deep and fragile. Idolatory or religious syncretism is rife among "devout" Christians[382]. Messianic and religious sects are springing up daily[383]. The local theology is still incipient and to some extent dormant. The liturgy is timidly "local" and respectfully "Roman" and the sense of moral values is depreciating. Several millions are yet to be converted to Christianity[384]. "We are victims of our success"[385]. As years run by, older conflicts are either obliterated or give way to new ones or endure in newer forms. These are to be discussed in detail in the following section.

Section Three: Enduring Areas of Faith-Culture Conflict in Igbo Church Today.

10.9.1 Racial Prejudice and Cultural Revolution.

The enduring prejudice from the heralds of the message of love and peace is partly responsible for the rejection of Christianity by some Igbo today. Even Fr. Lutz, the first Prefect of the Lower Niger, advised his people that

all those who go to Africa as missionaries must be thoroughly penetrated with the thought that the Dark Continent is a cursed land, almost entirely in the power of the devil[386].

---

380 Cf. Arinze, Answering, 119; Ejizu, Dialogue at Depth Level, 32.
381 Cf. Adibe, Crisis of Faith and Morality (1992) passim.
382 Ejizu, Endurance of Conviction, 126f; 130f.
383 Cf. Id. 30; 32.
384 Cf. John Paul II, RM, 31.
385 So says Archbishop Arinze cited by Onaiyekan, in: op. cit., 25.
386 Cf. Holy Ghost Fathers' Archive (Paris), 191/A/5, 335.

And inspite of the missionaries' "holy devotion" to evangelise the Igbo searching for God in shadows and images[387], the racial prejudice continues today in new forms and shapes. As the early evangelisers could not easily overcome their prejudice and culture-shock, so do many modern Euro-Americans find it hard to overcome their inherited racial prejudice.

This is very evident in the language and expression of the white man. The God-given *black* colour of the African is simply associated with some *evils* (black sheep, black market, black money, black magic, blackmail, black list, black spot etc)[388]. But the tendency is to associate the "*good*" with the *white* man (white lie, white magic, white garment, white goods, white paper, white-wash, etc)[389] as if the "good" is coterminous with the "white". As Fr. Hastings testifies,

> there can be no question but that Europeans in general and European missionaries in particular, with some few exceptions, admitted little if any culture of value in Africa just as many had denied that it really had any religion - other than fearful superstitions[390].

Consequently with the cultural revolution[391] of the 1970s some Igbo have abandoned their Euro-American (baptismal) names or refused "to have their children baptised with other than African ones - generally names with deep religious meaning"[392]. The people's growing awareness of their cultural heritage discredited by the early evangelisation has equally given rise to unchristian forms of cultural revival[393]. Hence the local Church is confronted with a resurgence of traditional but non-christian practices[394].

---

387 Cf.Vatican II, LG, no. 16.
388 Cf. Sinclair, Dictionary, 134-136.
389 Cf. Id., 1665.
390 Hastings, African Christianity, 37.
391 Cf. Kato, African Cultural Revolution, 32f; 42f; Aguwa, Christianity, 27-34.
392 Hastings, op. cit., 37.
393 Cf. Usanga, Cultural Revival, 7-26, here: 5f; 22f. An example of this was the All Blacks' "Festival of Arts and Culture" (FESTAC) held in Lagos (Nigeria) in 1975 in which some participants made a show of nudity and some forms of obscenity in the name of "cultural revival". Cf. Mbefo, Towards a Mature, 13-16.
394 Cf. Ejizu, Endurance of Convictions, 125-135.

10.9.2 Scandalised by Dechristianized White World.

The French Philosopher Voltaire once observed that

> Europeans have preached their religion from Chile to Japan only to make men serve their avarice. There is reason to believe that the heart of Africa conceals a great deal of the metal that makes the universe go - the gold sand that rolls in her rivers is a sign of a mine in the mountains[395].

Such sarcastic remarks coming from the white intellectuals do alienate the contemporary Igbo audience of the Christian message, especially the students, the *intelligentia* and the elite[396]. Many Igbo are now apathetic to Christianity or even dereligionized because of the appalling and scandalous news or experiences from a *dechristianized* white world. The former "Christian world" of the missionaries has lost the "awareness of the originality of Gospel morality" and is suffering from "an eclipse of fundamental and ethical values"[397].

> Dechristianization, which weighs heavily upon entire peoples and communities once rich in faith and Christian life, involves not only the loss of faith or in any event its becoming irrelevant for everday life, but also, and of necessity, *a decline or obscuring of the moral sense*[398].

Euro-American news papers, radio and television report daily on how Christians in these "highly civilized" cultures freely legalize abortion; use contraceptives; practise divorce, sexual promiscuity and rape even children and infants[399]; they cheat, bribe, rob, kidnap and murder; practise racism, hate foreigners or burn some of them or their possessions - and other violent crimes[400] - as if they had not for once heard of the Gospel of love and mercy. Other examples of a *dechristianized* white world include the frequent shootings and murders on the streets of the U.S.A, the current wave of hatred for foreigners in Germany, the continued fratricidal violence in Northern Ireland and the gruesome war in the former Yugoslavia.

---

395 Voltaire, Essai sur les Moeurs, Garnier edition 12:376. Cited in Ela, African Cry, 14.

396 Cf. Sarpong, Emphasis on Africanizing, 106-107; Agu, Secularization, 299-302.

397 John Paul II, Veritatis Splendor (VS), no. 106.

398 Ibid.

399 These evils are also the subjects of scholarly reflections in some magazines and periodicals. Cf. for example, the informations contained in the periodical: *Concepte, Zeitschrift für ethische Orientrierung, Heft 11-12 (1990)* 1-33; Rheinland-Pfalz/Panorama, Madchen trotz Bitten, in: Rhein Zeitung, NR 47 (25 Februar 1994), 4.

400 Cf. Foitzik, Die Allgegenwart von Gewalt, 31-35; Nientiedt, "Armut Spielt eine Zentrale Rolle". Ein Gespräch zur Kriminalitätsentwicklung mit Professor Christian Pfeiffer, 79-89.

Worse still, the Igbo in close contact with the white man are dismayed at seeing them rapturously celebrating carnivals with some measure of obscenities (because it is their "cultural heritage") while similar Igbo cultural celebrations were condemned by the early missionaries as "primitive, savage, barbaric, superstitious, fetish"[401].

Even the artefacts and objects of the traditional religion condemned as dreadful African "black devils" were carted away by some colonialists and missionaries and are now exihibited either in the secular or "christian" museums[402] without any fear of reprisals from those "black devils". Back home, the long years of tyranny and brutality of the apatheid white regime in South Africa makes the Igbo even more skeptical of the white man's trumpeted christian love and holiness[403]. Here Chief Osadebay picturesquely speaks the mind of many Africans today:

> Old men in Africa... shake their heads for the days that used to be, when a man was a man... The missionaries condemned their weapons and enjoined them to be like "gentle Jesus, meek and mild" and, meanwhile, fellow-country men of some of the missionaries came with guns and overpowered them... We must desecrate the memory of our ancestors in order to qualify for the 'City with Golden Gates?'" Some young people have complaints too: "the missionaries came with the Bible and asked us to kneel down and close our eyes in prayer. While we knelt and prayed, race-fellows of missionaries came with swords and guns and planted flags... When we rose up in prayer, our land was gone... The missionary tells us that good people must go to church. We have been to his country. His countrymen hardly go to Church..."[404].

All these sad experiences have brought about a large measure of disillusionment and disenchantment with the Christian (Catholic) religion[405]. Some have totally rejected it as a foreign, colonialistic imposition on the black man[406]. As they quit, they accuse preachers of this "foreign religion"[407] of having dedivinized and desacralised the Igbo traditional shrines, beliefs, morals, and medicine[408]. They are no longer interested in an "imported religion"

401 Ejizu, Decolonizing, 220; Cf. Kalilombe, Salvific Value, 133; 141.

402 Cf. Uzukwu, Liturgical celebration, 53-54

403 Ndiokwere, Prophecy, 17-18.

404 Osadebay, Easter Reflection, 289. For similar sad observations, cf. Kenyatta, Facing Mount Kenya, 269-270; Ngugi, Homecoming, 31f.

405 Onaiyekan, Christianity: Foreign Religion, 1-15.

406 Cf. Iwe, Christianity, 75-80.

407 Cf. Onaiyekan, Christianity: A Foreign Religion, 9-12.

408 Cf. Boulaga, Christianity Without Fetishes, 56-57; Sarpong, Emphasis on Africanizing, 106; Agu, Secularization, 264-268.

that has condemned even the *salvific values* of their traditional religious culture (1.12)[409].

10.9.3 Backsliding into Superstition and Idolatory.

Apostasy or backsliding into idolatory is one of the dynamic movements on the "religious arena in Africa". Rejection of Christianity paves the way for the regression into the superstitious practices of the traditional religion or to "religious concubinage" or even to "de-religionization"[410]. In search of new values and security, or in an effort to fill up the *spiritual vacuum* in their lives as Catholics or in moments of crisis, many have recourse to the new indigenous "*life-giving*" sects[411]. Others prefer to employ the services of diviners, oracles, and local medicine men (*Ndi dibia*).

Even some considered as "very convinced" Catholics do apostasize in secret. For these, the usually "powerful Holy Mass and blessings of the catholic priest" are no longer as salutary as the traditional sacrifices to personal deities or the ancestral spirits. Nothing today poses a greater challenge to the Igbo pastor than the frequent relapse of the faithful into various forms of superstition and idolatory[412].

Although Ayandele has triumphalistically proclaimed "the collapse of 'Pagandom' in Igboland"[413], yet the collapse of the *official pagandom* has only paved the way for an *unofficial pagandom*. This tallies with the observation of Bishop Obiefuna in a "Century-old Church" that

> Christianity has made an impact on our people. There is no gainsaying it. Thousands come to our churches. Many also avail themselves of the Sacraments. But times without number the remark reaches us that our christians are worshipping 'idols', false gods. They swear on idols. They erect shrines in their homes, in their compounds. They hide fetishes in their shades in the market places and in their workshops... We cannot simple deny they obtain[414].

This strong evidence reveals the shallowness of the faith of modern Catholics and the inner tension between their traditional beliefs and the Christian

---

409 Cf. Arinze/Fitzgerald, Pastoral Attention, 49.
410 Mbiti, African Religions, 264-266.
411 Cf. Ela, My Faith, 140; Ndiokwere, Prophecy, 274-278; Ikeobi, Healing Ministry, 191.
412 Cf. Ejizu, Endurance of Conviction, 125-127; 133-135; Mbiti, op. cit., 264.
413 Ayandele, Collapse, 125f.
414 Obiefuna, Idolatory, 11.

life. It is comparable to the relapses of the OT Israel into idolatory[415]. They are indicators that the local Church has not yet to come to terms with the traditional religious convictions of some of her people. It also calls into question the extent of the salutary credibility of the Igbo Church among her faithful[416].

The taking of traditional titles (*Igwe, Owelle, Ogbu-ehi, Ogbu-agu, Ozo, Owelle*, etc) and the enstoolment of chiefs also ignite faith-culture conflict in the Church. This is because the candidate, whether Christian or not, is required to perform traditional rituals that are not inseparable from idolatory and superstition. The *Ozo* title is a special example. To take it is a sign of nobilty in the society, but it is intimately bound with idolatory and superstition[417].

Although every one who takes the title promises never to bring in non-christian practices[418], yet since "old habits never die" and since the traditional convictions are more often than not brought into Christianity, one cannot rule out completely the constant intrusion of religious syncretism in the lives of the Catholics who take those titles. In the early 1970s such Catholics were banned from receiving Holy Communion until they perfomed the prescribed public penance.

10.9.4 Unjust Social Structures.

A special case in point is the *Osu caste* system and its allied *Ume* and *Mgbeke-Mgbafo* taboo groups[419] which are impervious to the billowing and uprooting waves of westernisation, christianisation and state legislation (10.1.12). Although it was an area of pristine conflict with Christianity, the *Osu* system did not and does not exist in all Igbo communities. The Government legally abolished the system in 1956 with civil punishments prescribed for the offenders[420]. But it has proved to be an enduring, silent and resilient form of idolatory among the Igbo[421].

Today there may no longer be an open denigration of the *Osu* or an open rejection of social intercourse with them, but even the "pious Christian" *Diala* still refuses to be married to an *Osu* man or woman. Indeed the Good News with all its inculturation thrusts has been incapabale of wiping off the vestiges

---

415 Cf. Ex 32; Dt 13; Jg 7,33f; I Kg 18,16ff, etc.
416 Ela, op. cit., 133-134.
417 Cf. Arazu, A Cultural Model for Christian Prayer, in: Shorter, African Christian Spirituality, 114-115.
418 Cf. Arinze, Church, 24-25; Usanga, Cultural Revival, 7.
419 Cf. Ezeala, Can The Igboman, 27.
420 Atado, op., cit., 25.
421 Cf. Onwubiko, Facing the Osu, 35ff.

of this evil system to the chagrin of some who continue to question whether the Igboman can ever be a Christian in view of this unjust system[422]. The total abolition of the *Osu* system remains one of the principal tasks of the contemporary Igbo Church.

10.9.5 Imported Theology, Liturgy and Materials.

Igbo theological thinking and prophetic role are still very much influenced by western philosphical and theological categories. Indigenous theologians and pastors are still reeling from the slavery and wounds of the western forms of thought and "talk about God" and from the devastating experiences of colonial cultural imperialism. In this respect Fr. L. Mbefo observes that

> even today, the fears induced by slavery... and the leaving of initiative to the white man... are still evident in the timidity with which we approach and propose our cultural viewpoints even in the church[423]. The slave mentality is still discernible in the "worship" we accord the white man and every thing "foreign" or "imported"... the fear deriving from experienced slavery still has its effects on us - even on churchmen and theologians.

These morbid fears and enslaved mentality are very evident in the liturgical celebrations of the local Church still under the yoke of imported forms of worship whose sacramental symbolisms often escape the grasp of the faithful.

> The liturgy, its rites, books, vestments, bread and wine for the Eucharist, etc are all Western. A few sprinklings of Africanism or should we say "Nigerianism" consist of translations... of Western prayers and hymns, in addition to superficial adaptation of the ceremonies[424].

It is a fact that a cross-section of the Nigerian society is permanently allergic to local materials while it is hopelessly addicted to anything foreign. Therefore, besides canonical regulations and ecclesial usage, the Igbo's avid adulation of imported but not necessarily superior materials is partly responsible for the lack of the "Igbonization" of Christian liturgical celebrations up till now. As "the indigenization process of the clergy and hierarchy was going on at a rapid speed", Bishop B. Usanga reported that someone asked boldly "if 'palm wine' cannot be used in Masses and Communion Services instead of

---

422 Cf. Ezeala, op. cit., passim. This is the theme of the whole book; Unegbu, Osu/Diala Scandal, passim.
423 Mbefo, Theology And Inculturation, 58.
424 Okolo, Nigerian Church, 46.

Wine from Grape"[425]. That question is yet to be answered by the Nigerian Church.

In 1650 the *Propaganda Fide* had asked the missionaries to the far East: "what is more absurd than to bring France, Spain or Italy or any other part of Europe into China"[426]? In the same way I continue to ask today: what meaning have Christmas songs that describe the "white snow" and the "*wintery wind*" that "*blows cold and dreary*" for the millions of Igbo who have never been to the temperate regions? Should the products of Christians of certain countries be made "absolutes" for divine worship by the Christians of other countries? Are the imported "matter and form" of the Holy Sacraments really *necessary* for the salvation of the Igbo? Are these products and symbols exactly and absolutely the ones used by the Lord Jesus in Jerusalem or Israel of his time or are they "inspired fabrications" of the Graeco-Roman and Euro-American Churches?

Furthermore, why do the richer "*First World*" Churches[427] not import, for example, palm fronds from the poor "*Third World*" Churches for the Palm Sunday celebrations? Why should a poor Igbo or African Church spend her little income to import materials from the very rich Churches in order to worship the one God and Christ?. Is that not an example of the exploitation of the poor by the rich ? Is that not a typical case of imposition of an unbearable yoke (*zugon*, Ac 15,10; cf. Mt 23,4) and unnecessary burden (*baros*, 15,28) on the young Church? Would the Lord Jesus sanction such oppressive practices if he were to incarnate Himself again among us today?

10.9.6 Imported Marriage Forms.

This theme requires a separate treatment because of its special importance to the local people. Aylward Shorter has summarised for us the main areas of conflict between the Igbo (African) marriage and western marriage forms[428] :

Western marriage is oriented to nuclear family, contractual and synchronic. It requires only the consent of partners, emphasizes monogamy and indissolubility (at least theoretically if not practically) and more equality between partners. Children are not essential to the survival of the union which assumes

---

425 Usanga, Cultural Revival, 12.

426 SCPF, Collectanea, 1, no. 135, p. 42.

427 Here one must note that Christianity established its presence in some parts of Africa long before it reached the present "First World" countries. (Cf. Synod of Bishops, Lineamenta, 2-3).

428 Cf. Shorter, African Culture, 156-195, here 181-182.

absolute stability from the beginning. Children of extra-marital unions are faced with problems of parental care.

But African marriage is oriented to the lineal family, dynamic and dia-chronic. It requires consent of partners as members of a group, permits polyg-amy, accepts less equality between partners and recognises solubility of union. Stability of union grows gradually because children are essential to the union otherwise polgamy or dissolution ensues. Customary law caters for children of extra-marital unions.

Also the canonical form is always in tension and conflict with the dynamic process of the traditional marriage which takes place in stages and which is the "*real*" marriage for the people[429]. After performing the long and expensive customary marital ceremonies, a couple is validly and licitly married[430]. In fact without the traditional marriage process, the canonical christian form can never take place.

Hence some Igbo are becoming less and less convinced that they should perform the short, canonical and even less expensive form of marriage. Why should they marry three times - first in the traditional manner, then in the court, and finally in the Church?[431] Is that a necessary (*epanankes*, Ac 15,28) triplication of marriage for the salvation of Igbo couple?

Therefore some couples perform the canonical form as a mere ritual to please their parents or brethren. Others perform it as a formal ritual to avoid exclusion from the Holy Eucahrist[432]. For others still, it is financially cumber-some to perform an additional "europeanised" marriage rite. These latter may defiantly delay or postpone the canonical form indefinitely[433]. But that is not the whole story.

While financial insolvency may be a genuine excuse for some couples, the main reason for their postponement or avoidance of the canonical form is the man's fear of consumating a monogamous indissoluble union without an as-surance that such a union will be blessed with children, especially sons[434].

10.9.7 Childnessness and Polygamy.

Even if the problem of the imported forms of marriage is resolved, the contin-ued practice of polygamy by a negligible minority of the Igbo remains a

---

429 Cf. Shorter, African Culture, 192-194.
430 Cf. Atado, African Marriage, 7-8; 28-42.
431 Cf. Okoye, Special Assembly, 179.
432 Cf. Kisembo et al., African Christian Marriage, 192f.
433 Cf. Atado, op. cit., 112-114.
434 Cf. Id,. 113.

teething pastoral problem for the Church[435]. The question of the indissolubility of a childless or a maleless marriage continues to be a serious existential problem to some affected couples and families. It is a source of constant pastoral anxiety in a patrilineal society[436] which still lays emphasis on lineage and progeny. The interventions of African Bishops in the 1980 Synod on the Family focused on the different nuances of this problem in Africa[437].

10.9.8 Use of Foreign Language in Worship.

The production of the "official" Igbo translations of the NT and some liturgical and paraliturgical texts[438] is so far the best effort made in the provision of the *Roman liturgy* in the native tongue. While it may be admitted that many pastors are making sincere efforts in ministering with the Igbo language, certain *westernised* Igbo pastors are yet to attune themselves to the reality of evangelisation through inculturation[439].

It is true that some older Christians still cherish the latin liturgy. But is it not strange and absurd to hear a local pastor preaching or singing away in English or Latin language among an illiterate, monolingual brothers in Christ just because there happened to be an English or Italian person in the Church? Will that ever happen in Europe or America? Is that *unnecessary burden* not against the JC theology and the centuries-old teaching of the Catholic Church?[440].

It is left to anybody's guess to imagine how deeply involved are the people in such a liturgy, and how spiritually they are nourished by such a worship in which they are entertained only by the strange but sonorous chants of Confirmation or Ordination rites in non-pentecostal languages (cf. Ac 2,5f).

---

435 Cf. Trobisch, My Wife Made Me a Polgygamist, passim.
436 Cf. Kisembo et al., African Christian Marriage, 63-78 Uka, African Family, 189-200.
437 Cf. Synod of Bishops, Selected Interventions, 96-108.
438 There are official transaltions of only some portion of the "Order of the Mass" of Paul VI and the Five Sacraments (the texts for Confimation and Holy Orders are yet to be translated into Igbo). The transalation of NT Bible is out while the OT is yet to be finished.
439 Cf. Ozigbo, Igbo Catholicism, 62f.
440 Id., 66f.

10.9.9 Internal Rivalry, Divisions and Conflicts.

But even if the imported forms of Church life are consigned to the "limbo of the Patriarchs", the local Church will not yet be free from internal divisions and rivalry as was the case in the apostolic Church (cf. Ac 6,1; 15,1.5.39). Some of these intractable disputes are carried over from the traditional society into the Church, while some are the unhappy legacies of the white missionary past[441].

There is also a certain measure of religious bigotry that breeds unhealthy rivalry which splits some ecclesial communities into parties (*haireses*, Ac 15,5). Internal divisions and open quarrels also arise from: sharp disgreement between ecclesial ministers (cf. Ac 15,2.7.39), faith-culture questions like the participation of christians in the traditional rites and festivals, fraudulent management of church finances and property (cf. Ac 5,1-11) power-tussle in the parish community, unhealthy priest-people relationship, human frailty and injustice (cf. Ac 15,1-2)[442]

Sub-ethnic prejudice have sometimes blown up into unedifying conflicts in some dioceses. There is equally the problem of different Christian groups and sects in rivalry and conflict with the themselves and with the Catholic Church[443]. And finally the problem of Islamic fundamentalists causing divisions, instigating open conflicts and persecution of the Christian minorities in the North as they carry their "Jihad" to the South of Nigeria[444]. Of course the Church-State conflict over schools and christian education is stiil on[445].

10.9.10 Religionless Education and Indiscipline.

Tepidity, lack of faith, materialism, greed, examination malpractices, sexual immorality, armed robbery and general absence of discipline are common experiences among the youth and adults brought up without the knowledge of basic doctrines of Christianity[446]. Despite the efforts being made to teach and

---

441 Cf. Okolo, Justice in the Nigerian Church, 9. In a certain parish, I spent several years trying to settle such intractable village disputes brought into the ecclesial community by the factious groups similar to those in Corinth of Paul's era (cf. 1 Co 1,10ff).

442 Cf. Id., 11; 15-16.

443 Cf. CBCN, New Era, 134; Synod of Bishops, Lineamenta, 57-59; Ihejiofor, Christian Inter-denominational Relationship, 58-59.

444 Cf. Synod of Bishops, op. cit., 60. Onotu, Christian Muslim Relationship, 7-9; 20-24; 34-35.

445 CBN, Listen: The Church Speaks, 7.

446 Cf. Achebe, Trouble With Nigeria, 27-43; Sarpong, Emphasis on Africanizing, 106.

instruct the youth in the parish or station centres, a good number are still suffering from the unhealthy aftermath of secularised State schools[447]. Their neo-atheistic lifestyle diametrically opposed to the christian faith and practice creates a lot of crisis in the family and society and presents more problems to all pastoral agents[448].

Gross indiscpline is not only the effect of religionless education. Some regular "Church-goers" are also indisciplined. The Nigerian Hierarchy has taken pains to diagnose the aspects of indiscipline: "unfair competition, bribery, corruption, raising costs, brigandage, embezzlement"[449]. But their cures are yet to come. At a certain point the indiscipline was so much that even the *indisciplined* military coup leaders had to wage "a war against indiscipline". There is at present

> conspicuous consumption, indiscipline, plain cheating in business deals, nepotism, irresponsibility by public officials, abuse of power and authority, etc. These ills are by no means superficial. They have formed part of our social structures since they generate all sorts of social injustice in the lives of the individual as well as the nation and of course the Church[450].

Nigerian "nobles" behave like neo-colonialists. The Christian soldiers join in the violent seizure of power, impose inhuman dictatorship and with the co-operation of blatant corrupt politicians and government officials, they rob the nation of millions of petro-dollar. Some Christians who communicate daily at the Holy Mass behave like "Anti-Christ" and betray the Church by scandalous lifestyle (cf. Lk 21,8.16-18). These are certainly opposed to the Gospel precepts.

10.9.11 *Dichotomy and Hypocrisy.*

The intrusion of the white man's culture, civilization, and Christian message has generated various forms of dichotomy. To the "indigenous" Osu/Diala controversial dichotomy are added new dichotomies: literate and non-literate, catholic and non-catholic, Christian and non-Christian, Church and State, sacred and profane, and so on. This is also actualised in the conflicts between christian and traditional marriages, monogamy and polygamy, christian and traditional burial rites, etc. (cf.10.1.13).

---

447 Cf. Ochiagha, Emerging Nigerian, 5.
448 Cf. Arinze, Christian and the Family, 47-48.
449 C.S.N., The Nigerian Hierarchy, 7.
450 Okolo, Nigerian Church, 61. Cf. Achebe, Trouble With Nigeria, 27-36.

Sometimes the dichotomy exists in the form of hypocrisy. For example, Some of those who readily point accusing fingers at the "sins" or "misdemanours" of a pastor or religious are among the least examplary[451]. They commit heinous crimes while at the same time offering "long prayers of love" from a "Child of Blessed Mary's" booklet or pray the "chaplet of mercy". Others who loudly decry Christianity as a "foreign religion" through which the white man deceived them and looted the treasures of the land are the very ones living in a manner more deceitful than those they are condemning[452].

10.9.12 Medieval Style of Leadership.

Some members of the Hierarchy seem to have forgotten that all believers in Christ, irrrespective of their ecclesial positions, are simply brothers (adephoi) in the Christian community (cf. Ac 15,1.3.23.32). Some pastors are yet to be initiated into an inculturated leadership style commensurate with the democratic nature of Igbo society. Others are still very much influenced by their Euro-American brand of education and upbringing. Occasionally they behave as if they were 19th century colonial administrators and missionaries.

Some behave like authoritarian, medieval monarchs with all the divine rights of kings vested solely on their mortal bodies.

One sees many Bishops acting as if the Vatican Council never happened, many priests imitating everything coming from Europe and, in fact going to Europe and North America and staying there longer than needed by their studies. Worst of all one detects a fear of making mistakes, maybe of being brought to task, resulting in stagnation...[453].

Nowadays Church leaders are being sharply criticized for stifling the prophetic, pastoral and liturgical initiatives of their fellow adelphoi. These inspired "lay" initiatives are rejected because they do not probably emanate from the "wisdom of the hierarchy". Some leaders spend more time on mere externals and stagnating protocols than on the actualisation of the "salus animarum, suprema lex".

It sounds incredible and absurd but it is true that some "chief pastors" live in palaces and use several big cars concurrently while some "subordinate" pastors (Kaplan) are even denied the privilege of roadworthy mini cars to

---

451 Cf. Okere, Theological Canonical, 45.
452 Cf. Achebe, Trouble With Nigeria, 19-38.
453 Salvoldi, An Interview with Bishop Bernard Agre (of the Diocese of Man, Ivory Coast), 342.

minister to their flock scattered over a large area of a diocese. Another example is the incredible use of *motorcades* and *sirens* by a Bishop to go and open new parishes built with "widows' mites" (Lk 21,1f) and with the sweat of poor rural farmers who are later heavily taxed by the parish council in order to pay up the "parish debt" to the "Diocese". Éla aptly notes that

> a certain number of bishops cling to Roman tradition as drowning persons might cling to a plank. In some regions (dioceses), we simply have a pre-Vatican II Church, despite the Council's daring overtures. It is not easy to rid oneself of the habit of submitting to dogmatized practices that one has been taught to identify with tradition. No wonder, then, new generations continually return to a series of faith problems in the African context that have been with us for many years now[454].

So the strange behaviour of the ecclesial leadership alienates the afflicted people and tends to turn the Good News into a "sad news" for them. All these weaknesses, problems and conflicts of the missionary enterprise[455] demand serious pastoral attention and solutions.

Section Four: Suggestions and Recommendations for the Resolution of Faith-Culture Conflict in Igbo Church Today.

The following suggestions and recommendations in the light of the JC theology are based on two basic principles of inculturation: firstly, on the catholicity of the "*Church founded upon the identical, essential, constitutional patrimony of the self-same teaching of Christ, as professed by the authentic and authoritative tradition of the one true Church*"[456]; secondly, on the fact that the expression of the catholic Faith "*may be original, suited to the tongue, the style, the character, the genius and the culture of the one who professes this one Faith*"[457]. To actualise these principles intimately bound with the JC theology, the Igbo Church should do as follows:

---

454 Ela, African Cry, 121-122.
455 Cf. Ejizu, *Ofo*, Igbo Ritual Symbol, 148; Osadebay, Easter Reflection, 289; Azikiwe, Renascent Africa, 178-192; Achebe, Arrow of God, 36-37; Cf. Nyerere, Church, 221-222; Agu, Secularization, 247-276, etc.
456 Paul VI, To the Inaugural 1969 SECAM, no. 2.
457 Ibid.

350

10.10.1 Decolonize and Dewesternise the Local Church.

Decolonization or dewesternization proceeds from the perennial teaching of the Church that faith and salvation are universal, transcultural and supracultural[458]. It is an acknowledgement of the fact that

> many customs and rites, once considered to be strange, are seen today, in the light of ethnological science, as integral parts of various social systems, worthy of study and commanding respect[459].

Just as the JC theology did not require the Graeco-Roman peoples to be *judaized* and the Jews to be *graecized* or *hellenised* in order to be saved, so also should the Igbo not be europeanised or americanised by the missionary message in order to be saved. Although the white missionaries did not set out to preach the necessity of the Euro-American *ethos* for salvation[460], yet their actions and attitudes at times pointed to that direction[461] because

> more than commerce and colonial adminstration, Christian missions constituted the highest single factor that domesticated Western culture and civilisation and that waged a sustained war against the Igbo religious culture and society[462].

Such Western *ethos* can no longer be the norm for the Igbo in this new era of cultural pluralism, tolerance and evangelisation through inculturation[463]. If indeed salvation depends on circumcision (Ac 15,1.5), then most of the uncircumcised Euro-Americans - even their holy men and women - will not be saved while most of the Igbo (Christians and non-Christians, holy and unholy) are already saved because as infants most of the males are usually circumcised while the females undergo the corresponding ritual of clitoridectomy[464].

---

458 Cf. Justin Martyr, Ad Diognetum, 5-6; Apologia, 1,44 & 46; St., Augustine, De civitate Dei, 10,29; Gregory the Great, Ad Mellitum, 1215-1217; Collectanea SCPF, vol. 1, no. 2, pp. 1-2; Rouleau, Matteo Ricci, 470-472; Pius XII, EP, AAS 43 (1951) 521-524; Paul VI, Africae Terrarum. AAS 59 (1967) 1073-1097; Id., To SECAM. AAS 61 (1969) 573-578; Id., EN. AAS (1976) 1-96; Vatican II, AG, 10-22; John Paul II, CT. AAS 71 (1979) 1277-1340; Id., SA. AAS 77 (1985) 779-813. These are only selections from the inculturation teachings of the Church from the first to the twenty century.

459 Paul VI, Africae Terrarum, op. cit., no. 7.

460 Cf. Id., nos. 23-24.

461 Cf. Isichei, History, 123; 212; Achebe, Arrow of God, 45-46; 189-190; No Longer at Ease, 115.

462 Ejizu, Religion and Social Change, 115. Cf. Id., Ofo: Igbo Ritual, 148.

463 Cf. Carrier, Church, 146-151.

464 Cf. Mbiti, Introduction to African Religion, 91-92.

Such a tenet would only reduce the christian teaching on salvation to absurdity. Therefore in this era of inculturation, the first step to an effective evangelisation should be dewesternisation and/or decolonization[465].

Decolonization is a call to do away with the old colonial missionary ways of life. It is an invitation to obliterate every modicum of missionary ethnocentric prejudice against the Igbo [466]. It is a call to remove every obstacle (*baros*, Ac 15,28) to the people's practice of the Christian faith[467].

Dewesternization is like late Mazi Mbonu Ojike's clarion call to Nigerians to "boycott all boycottables" from foreign countries[468]. Dewesternization demands that strange rituals, forms of worship and the outmoded medieval social structure of the Church[469] be replaced with the authentic indigenous socioreligious elements and structures (10.1.5 & 11)[470]. This is because in the light of the JC theology, all things European and American may be permissible for the Igbo but not all may be *necessary for their salvation* (cf. 1 Co 10,23f).

For the Igbo Church, it means divesting her of anything that is in no way necessary for the salvation of the people. It means doing away with the strange Euro-American cultural accretions that have gradually displaced the salvific elements of Igbo way of life (10.1.11). It implies communicating Christ to the people through their own philosophy[471] but not through the confusing philosophical categories like the Kantian idealism and the communist theory of Karl Marx. It means the use of Igbo metaphysics (10.1.5)[472] to teach the knowledge of the true God rather than the employment of the western metaphysical categories of being that confuse rather than help the people understand the nature and attributes of the Supreme Being[473]. It means the abandonment of non-helpful scholastic theological categories and thought-patterns that burden the minds of the faithful for whom such knowldege is neither meaningful *nor necessary (epanankes) for their salvation.*

While every culture admits of reciprocal borrowing and mutual enrichment, the Igbo should no longer continue to ape too much of the foreign ways of

---

465 Cf. Okolo, Nigerian Church, 44-46; Ejizu, Decolonizing, 211-223; Shorter, African Christian Theology, 21-23; Mbefo, Reshaping, 60-64.
466 Cf. Shorter, op. cit., 130-132.
467 Cf. Waliggo et al., Inculturation, 19.
468 Cf. Metuh, African Traditional Religion, 15. Here Metuh cites Mbonu Ojike who lament's the people's penchant for anything foreign.
469 Okolo, Nigerian Church, 46; Ejizu, Decolonizing, 223-224.
470 Okolo, op. cit., 56-6; Ejizu, op. cit., 224-226; Metuh, Theological Basis, 79f.
471 Cf. Shorter, African Christian Theology, 23-26.
472 Cf. Edeh, Igbo Metaphysics, 69ff.
473 Cf. Id., 113ff.

eating, dressing and worshipping etc.[474]. It is time to cure the mania for "made in Britain/American" goods and liturgical tensils[475] as a "sign of social prestige".

Concretely put, the oil from the Mediterranean olives do not necessarily possess a greater healing power than the "rich" Igbo palm oil. Wine from Italy is not more alcoholic or more nourishing than the naturally sweet and medicinal Igbo "palm wines". Unleavend bread from Europe or from the Holy Cities of Jerusalem and Bethelehem (Israel) is as good as unleavened bread from Igboland. Moreover some of these plants and crops were cultivated in the African belt long before they found their way into the other continents[476].

Dewesternising the imported forms of Christian life and practice shall no doubt help the Igbo recover the salvific elements of their pristine, cultural and cultic identity[477] and will immensely contribute in minimizing the "shibboleth"[478] of dichotomies in their present society. Here the "apostolate of the pen" is also very essential for dispelling the superiority complex and prejudice of the western ecclesial culture[479].

10.10.2 No More Foreign Tongues in Community Worship.

Just as the Graeco-Roman Gentiles learnt the Good News through Peter the Jew in a language intelligible to them (cf. Ac 15,7; 10,34ff) so should the Igbo Gentiles learn the Good News in the language they can understand. Just as the apostolic missionaries addressed their audience in the language comprehensible to them[480], so must the Igbo pastor address his Igbo audience in a language intelligible to them.

And just as God through his Holy Spirit approved of the Graeco-Roman Gentiles through the ministry of Jews and Gentiles (cf. 15,7-8.12.22.40.), so has he approved of the Igbo Gentiles through the ministry of white and black pastoral workers. Just as salvation is for the Jewish and Gentiles alike (cf. Ac 11,18; 15,11), so is salvation for both white and Igbo (black) Gentiles. Hence each race is entitled to serve God, praise him and hear his marvels in their own native tongues (cf. Ac 2,6.8.11).

---

474 Cf. Fagun, Evangelisation, 12.
475 Cf. Nwahaghi, Contextualization, 124-125.
476 Cf. Uzukwu, Food and Drinks, 371-374; Okigbo, Plants and Food, 10-18.
477 Cf. Agu, Secularization, 406; cf. 385-390.
478 Cf. Ojukwu, Because I am Involved, 1-2.
479 Cf. Onwubiko, Theory and Practice, 190-193, 196f.
480 Cf. Ac 14,1-18; 22,1-23.

Since the liturgy is one of the primary places for the Igbo to demonstrate that they have totally rejected the colonial logic that "*Africans must evolve from their frozen state to the dynamism of Western civilization*"[481], the Igbo must get rid of the *unnecessary* use of foreign language in their liturgical worship. Can a pastor who speaks to his own people in a foreign language command their attention and respect?.

While it is indisputable that the "Gospel message cannot be purely and simply isolated"[482] from its original Jewish roots (cf. Ac 15,1.5.29) and Graeco-Roman cultures (cf. Ac 13-28) or from the Euro-American cultures and forms of worship through which it reached the Igbo, and while it is true that this message "does not spring spontaneously from any cultural soil", but has "always been transmitted by means of an apostolic dialogue of cultures"[483], is it then proper and right for a caring pastor to continue singing the songs of Yahweh in foreign tones (cf. Ps 137,4) unknown to *his own People of God*?

Perhaps the protesting voice of the African scholar, J. S. Mbiti, can act as a corrective measure to the pastors who are still unable to divest themselves of the vanity of the "glorious liturgies" in foreign tongues and tones:

> For too long we have sung borrowed hymns from Europe and America. Now we are beginning to realise that these imported hymns have nearly all become theologically extinct. The more we continue to sing them, the nearer we draw to extinguishing the freshness of the Christian faith[484].

While it may look like an act of pastoral charity to celebrate in a language intelligible to a foreigner in a worshipping community, it may be against pastoral love and common sense to sacrifice the welfare of the "many" for the good of the "one".

10.10.3 Pastoral Attention to Igbo Religious Values.

The JC theology indicates that the apostles and elders of the Church gathered to give pastoral attention to Jewish traditional religion in conflict with Christian religion (Ac 15,2.6f). In the same way the Igbo or African traditional religion should be pastorally studied in order to uncover those elements that

---

481 Mudimbe, Invention of Africa, 76; Cf. Uzukwu, African Cultures, 75.
482 John Paul II, CT, no. 53.
483 Ibid.
484 Mbiti, Christianity, 438.

continue to exercise a powerful magnetic influence on the people. This is because

African Traditional Religion (ATR) is the religious and cultural context from which most Christians in Africa come, and in which many of them still live to a great extent, and many Christians, at the critical moments of their lives, have recourse to practices of the traditional religion... where they feel that certain elements of their culture are more respected[485],

Such an intelligent dialogue with the traditional religion should be geared to highlighting the salvific values (10.1.11) of the religion[486] for the resolution of the people's socio-religious problems[487] because

unless the Church becomes conscious at one and the same moment of the demands of both Christianity and the African Religions, Christianity in Africa is inviting syncretism[488].

So then the proposed Bishops' commission of serious theologians and researchers[489] on the ATR should not forget to consult and cooperate with the traditional priests of the shrines and deities, the holders of the *Ofo*, the titled men (*Ndi echichi*), the Town Union leaders and of course, the traditional rulers (*Ndi eze*) and all those much attached to the ATR[490].

Futhermore the scientific study of ATR should be made compulsory in all the "seminaries, ecclesiastical institutes and houses of formation in Igboland"[491]. Hence the research into the symbols and values of the ATR and its points of dialogal contact with the Christian religion, may serve as a *hermeneutical* bastion for an authentic inculturation of the faith in the lives of the Igbo[492].

---

485 Cf. Arinze/Fitzgerald, Pastoral Attention, 47-51; Synod of Bishops, Lineamenta, 64-66.
486 Cf. Kalilombe, Salvific Value, 141-143.
487 Cf. Shorter, African Christian Theology, 5-18;
488 Shorter, African Christian Theology, 17.
489 Synod of Bishops, Lineamenta, no. 72.
490 Cf. Nwosu, Laity, 142-143; Kalilombe, op. cit., 129-132; 141-143.
491 Arinze/Fitzgerald, Pastoral Attention, 51.
492 Cf. Id., Pastoral Attention, 48-50; Arinze, Meeting Other Believers, 17-22; Lineamenta, op. cit., 64-65; Hillman, Missionary Approach, 155-158.

may confer special favours on certain peoples from different races (cf. Lk 1,28f; Ac 10,1f) yet he has no favourites (Ac 10,34-35; Rm 2,11) because "*his faithful love extends age after age to those who fear him*" (Lk 1,50). Even if God may love someone more than the rest, that in no way means that he loves the *white* person more than the *black* and vice-versa (Ac 15,8-9). In this context, it would be against the divine salvific will to make the theology of the "white world" *the "absolute theology"* for the "black world".

God is one but the plurality of ways of thinking and talking about him and of approaching him requires a *theological pluralism* and hence "theologies" of the same God. As L. Magesa aptly observes, "*there is not only one theology in the universal Church, but a pluriformity of theologies. These should share and enrich one another*"[493]. This must have encouraged the All-Africa Conference of Churches (AACC, 1969) to a description of "African Theology". It

> is a theology based on the Biblical faith of Africans, and which speaks to the African soul. It is expressed in categories of thought which arise out of the philosphy of the African people. This does not mean it is narrow in outlook (syncretistic). To speak of African Theology involves formulating clearly a Christian attitude to other religions...[494].

Also in 1974, the SECAM Bishops stressed that there must be an African theological thinking which

> must remain faithful to the tradition of the Church and, at the same time, attentive to the life of our communities and respectful of our traditions and languages, that is of our philosophy of life[495].

Since then it is exhilarating to note that a threefold trend of "African theologies"[496] has emerged: a critical theology based on biblical revelation and open to African realities and in dialogue with non-African theologies; a black theology inspired by the biblical faith in facing the experience of domination and oppression and in struggling for liberation; an African inculturation theology which is based on the Bible and uses the salvific elements of the African Traditional Religion (ATR) in theologising[497].

---

493 Magesa, Authentic African Christianity, 113.

494 AACC (1969) Engagement, Nairobi. Cited in Shorter, African Christian Theology, 23.

495 SECAM, Synod Bishops from Africa, 2.

496 Cf. Ukpong, African Theologies Now - A Profile, Spearhead no. 80 (1984) 4-64. This booklet reviews the three main streams of African theology today.

497 Cf. PACT, Statement, 124-125.

ogy which is based on the Bible and uses the salvific elements of the African Traditional Religion (ATR) in theologising[497].

In the Nigerian scene, inculturated African theology, as Bishop Onaiyekan observes, is still on its preliminary stages[498] even though it is doubtful "if any country in Africa has as many experts in theology and the sacred sciences as we have in Nigeria"[499]. And I add that the majority of these *Nigerian experts* are from the Igbo Church who should now desist from importing theologies *in toto* but should rather continue to develop and deepen their own incipient theology, compare it with the Western theologies and reappraise it in the light of biblical revelation[500].

Though contact with theologies emanating from sister churches is helpful, yet the Nigerian (Igbo) theologian may not allow the agenda for the theological reflection in the Nigerian Church to be established from outside this local Church. The moment is opportune; one must pass to action[501].

I follow the many others in calling for and insisting on an African theology that takes African culture as a point of departure[502] but bases its reflection on the critical use of the inspired word[503]. Such a theological reflection should integrate the positive or salvific values of the traditional religion (10.1.11), anthropology and daily experiences in the family and society[504].

Since many of the African universities have already "incorporated the study of religion and philosophy into their body of courses"[505], an African theology should also be enriched with the points of contact between Christianity and "the big religious cauldron" of African Independent Churches (AIC) and Islam[506] not merely out of the spirit of ecumensism and dialogue[507] but as a recongition of the varied operations of the Spirit who breathes where he wills (Ac 15,28; cf. Jn 3,8; 1 Co 14,1ff). No African religious element is to be re-

---

497 Cf. PACT, Statement, 124-125.
498 Cf. Onaiyekan, Nigerian Theology, 1.
499 Cf. Id., 10.
500 Cf. Shorter, African Christian Theology, 27-29; Ogbu, Church, Mission and Moratorium, in: Id., History of Christianity, 372.
501 Uzukwu, Service of the Theologian, 15.
502 Ukpong, African Theologies, 4-7; 59-61.
503 It is noteworthy that besides the Catholic Institute of West Africa (CIWA), there are now some associations and journals that promote inculturated theological research, e.g., BTS; CATHAN, NJT; NACATHS; WAJES; Shalom; The Catholic Elite, etc.
504 Cf. Magesa, Authentic African Christianity, 117-118; PACT, Statement, 124; Kalilombe, Salvific Value, 141-143; Ejizu, Dialogue at Depth Level, 31-48.
505 Mbiti, African Religions, 261.
506 Cf. Id., 229-261; here: 246; 252f; 257 and 261.
507 Cf. Synod of Bishops, Lineamenta, nos. 60-68; Vatican II, UR, nos. 1; 5; 9.

jected if it is compatible with the Christian message[508] because no one who really drives out devils in the name of Jesus is against his disciples (cf. Lk 9,49f).

Igbo theologians must continue to study and make theology open to the aspirations of the people if they are to incarnate Christianity in the lives of the people[509]. They must stop depending on the imported Western Theology whose questions and answers no longer address the religious problems of the people. They should seek to communicate the Good News through the authentic values of their socio-religious background for the salvation of the people (cf. 10.1.0 & 10.10.3)[510].

10.10.5 Integrate Theologically Authentic Local Elements into Christian Liturgy.

Certainly the JC theology recognises that all Christians "are not marked off from the rest of men either by country, by language, or by political institutions"[511]. Hence all "should live for God and Christ according to the usages of their race..."[512]. This *living* for God is especially celebrated in the Church liturgy. This makes it imperative for the Igbo Church to develop her own christian liturgy[513] celebrated with her local salvific products.

It is time for the Igbo to rethink the importation of "canonically and valid" materials, rites and forms of worship that are not *necessary* for salvation but are rather like yokes and burdens on the people (Ac 15,10.19.28). The praiseworthy Zairean rite[514] provides an imitative example for the Igbo Church. The *salvific elements* of the traditional religion - initiation rites, forms of prayer, sacrifice, friendship, community, commensality, relationship between the living and the dead etc (10.1.12) - should be integrated with the native Chrisitian liturgy. In Jean-Marc Éla's words,

the total sacramental nature of the Christian mystery and its basic symbolism need also to be rediscovered from our own cultural rooting... We cannnot think of the basic elements

---

508 Cf. Nyamiti, The Theological Value of African Tradition, in: Shorter, African Christian Spirituality, 104.
509 Cf. SECAM, Synod Bishops from Africa, 2.
510 Cf. Arinze/Fitzgerald, Pastoral Attention, 49f; Uzukwu, Service of the Theologian, 13-14. Adibe, Crisis of Faith, 159f.
511 Ad Diognetum, 5. PG, 1173; Vatican II, LG, 38; Ac 15,7.11.13f; 17,24-29.
512 Vatican II, AG, 15.
513 Cf. Agu, op. cit., 399-400.
514 Cf. Probst, Inkulturation, 109-121.

of Christian worship as manufactured goods exported throughout the world according to invariable and uniform standards[515].

However the use of the fruits of the Igbo (African) earth and work of their hands for worshipping God does not mean that the Igbo Church would introduce any type of local food, drink or materials into the celebration of the Church's sacraments and liturgy. Rather the emphasis is on the use of theologically valid and licit local products found in abundance in Igboland and Africa. As Uzukwu the Spiritan liturgist suggests,

> any part of the African *ethos* being proposed for adoption should be examined, related to its counterpart in the Jewish Christian tradition, and conclusions can only be drawn from frank mutual dialogue and criticism between both traditions[516].

Therefore the local Church should courageously and sensibly introduce without further delay the authentic local products into her liturgical worship. This is consonant with the Igbo saying: "*what the humans eat they give to the spirits*".

> Christ "for us" is our centre, our head; and he does not find it repugnant to eat what we eat, drink what we drink. In other words, he would find African food and drink more adequate to convey the memorial of his passion, death, and resurrection celebrated in the context of a meal on the continent, than imported material[517].

In the concrete, the Eucharistic food and drink should be celebrated with maize or millet bread and palm wine or banana wine found in abundance in Igboland and in Africa[518]. Follwing *canon 847*, the symbolic and healing palm oil should be processed and employed for the anointings in Baptism, Confirmation, Holy Orders, and for anointing the Sick.

Biblically is the palm not as "holy" as the olive since both are products of the Holy Land of the Lord Jesus? If the Lord Jesus is *the vine* (of Israel) and Christians are his branches (Jn 15,1.5), so also shall *the just "flourish like the palm tree"* (Ps 92,12) of Israel (and Igboland). And if Jesus had instituted the Sacraments in Igboland, would he not have used the local products and materials for their celebration just as he did in Israel?[519]. Hence Sanon asks:

---

515 Ela, My Faith, 114.
516 Uzukwu, Food and Drink, 370. Cf. Shorter, African Christian Theology, 15-17.
517 Uzukwu, Food and Drink, 381-382; Cf. Okolo, Christ, Emmanuel, 133-134.
518 Cf. Uzukwu, op. cit., 382-383; Okolo, Nigerian Church, 57.
519 Cf. Uzukwu, op. cit., 382-383.

Does not the implantation of worship in a culture include the use of the fruits of the earth and human labour? How far is the use by Jesus of the fruits of wheat and the vine normative to the end of time?[520].

Outside canonical regulations, there may be no other justifying reason for the poor Igbo Church to continue to import materials from the rich Churches of Europe and America[521] in order to worship God in Igboland. This also tallies with the theology of the JC[522] which prohibits the imposition of any form of legal, cultural or religious burden on the Christian *adelphoi* (Ac 15,10.19.28).

Furthermore justice and fairplay demand that the richer Churches who do not produce palms and olives should import from the African Churches such products as *palm fronds* for Palm Sunday, *palm wine* for the Eucharist, and *palm oil* for anointing, in order to help finance the administration of the poorer local Churches (cf. 2 Co 8,1ff).

10.10.6 Away with Oppressive Social Structures.

The Igbo brethren or *adelphoi* in Christ Jesus must no longer allow certain modes of living that dehumanize their fellow brethren in Christ. Such is the vicious *Osu* caste system[523] which subjects to indignities people of unquestionable probity and denies them honours accorded even to the *Diala* of questionable character. The "*Osu*" must also try to liberate themselves from the oppression which questions their freedom as children of God and brethren in Christ[524].

Since in Christ there is no room for distinction between the *Osu* or the free born (cf. Ga 3,27f, Col 3,11), the Igbo Church must practically do away with the *Osu* taboo system[525]. Also she must make no compromise with any form of apartheid and oppressive structures opposed not only to the letter and spirit of the JC theology of equal love for the *adelphoi* but also to the very Christian law of love and freedom.

Is it not a grave sin for brethren to oppress the brethren who eat the body and drink the blood of the same Saviour Jesus Christ? Therefore "the bishops, priests and people in Igboland must unite and speak out in one voice against

---

520 Sanon, Universal Message, 91.
521 Cf. John Paul II, Sollicitudo, nos. 18.32-33.37; Iwe, Christianity, 126-127.
522 Cf. Vatican II, SC, nos 37-39.
523 Cf. Ezeala, Can the Igboman, 24; 26-29.
524 Cf. Unegbu, Osu/Diala Scandal, 7; Onwubiko, Facing the Osu Issue, 7-8.
525 Cf. Jinehu, Osu Caste, 49-53; Ezeala, op. cit., 35-37.

the Osu Caste System"[526] Nothing beyond what is essential (Ac 15,28) shall be required from *Osu* as christian brethren. Any form of unnecessary imposition from within or without should be resisted in exactly the same way as the Antiochian Church resisted the imposition of Jewish *ethos* on the Christian community (Ac 15,2f).

10.10.7 Merge Canonical and Igbo Marriage Forms.

The Council of Trent cited verbatim by the Second Vatican Council teaches that

> certain regions traditionally use other praiseworthy customs and ceremonies, when celebrating the Sacrament of Matrimony; the Sacred Synod earnestly desires that these, by all means, be retained[527].

So more than four hundred years ago, permission was given to all the Churches to "inculturate" marriage celebrations[528]. Yet the "Tridentine" Igbo Church failed to carry out this pastoral instruction and continued to place marriage yokes on the couples.

Recently, however, three options have been propsed in order to take away the human burden of the triplication of marriage consent and ceremony (10.9.6): there should be either the suppression of the canonical form in favour of the native form; or the extension of the powers of the Local Ordinary to dispense from the canonical form for couples who so desire it; or the incorporation of the ritual celebration of the canonical form of marriage within the process of the traditional form[529]. For this reason

> SECAM requires the Episcopal Conferences to see how the African marriage process "could be celebrated in a Christian way and find at what exact moment the canonical form could be inserted, in such a way as to eliminate the present dichotomy between the liturgical and traditional forms..."[530].

---

526 Onwubiko, op. cit., 66.
527 Council of Trent, Session 24, 11 November 1563, "On Reform", chapter 1; Vatican II, SC, 77.
528 Cf. Ozigbo, Igbo Catholicism, 80.
529 Cf. SECAM, Recommendations, 370-376; Synod of Bishops, Selected Interventions, 57-61; Mbiti, Introduction to African Religion, 100-107.; Id., African Religions, 133-143, Atado, op. cit., 112-117.
530 SECAM, Recommendations, 373.

I propose that the Igbo Church should merge the canonical and traditional forms of marriage[531] so as to avoid unnecessary triplication of the sacramental union among couples. It is left to the Igbo Church to carry out without delay this marriage instruction of the Magisterium since 1563.

10.10.8 Organise Pastoral Care for Childless and Maleless Couples.

If the grief and sorrow of infertile or childless Igbo couples may be incomprehensible to the non-Igbo who choose not to marry or to couples who from the outset exclude child-bearing from their marital union, the depression of Igbo couples over the absence of a *male* child may still appear more prostesterous to the non-Igbo. But from pastoral experience[532], I am quite aware of the sufferings of the childless or maleless couples or/and of women who could not conceive and bear children within the first two or three years of their church wedding. This innate existential problem cannot be easily brushed aside or resolved simply by citing for the affected couples some consolatory biblical pericopes on the acceptance of God's *will* (cf. Lk 22,42) in order to be the brother of Jesus (Lk 8,21) or on taking up one's *cross* daily to follow Jesus (Lk 9,23).

It is also true that some childless or maleless couples have heroically adjusted themselves to their marital situation and are very good practising catholics. It is also a fact that some have adopted children to supplement for their childlessness. But it is also a fact that some infertile or sonless couples are still unable to come to grips with their difficult situation. At the moment, private efforts are being made to provide psychical and spiritual assistance to those so affected (cf. CIC, 1063).

But I think that in this inculturation era, the Igbo Church should develop through her pastoral and medical experts a *special* form of marriage apostolate to advise intending partners on how to forestall the problem of infertility and malelessness. In this regard, each of the diocesan marriage tribunals should handle not only the judicial matters but should also be a forum for counselling engaged couples on how to live when faced with the crisis of childlessnees or sonlessless (cf. CIC. 1063).

---

531 Cf. "Introduction", nos.17-18, in: The Rites, pp. 537-538; cc. 1112-1113; 1120.

532 Besides pastoral experience, "Igbo childless Marriage and the Christian Church" was the title of my unpublished BD thesis (1979) passim. My research and conclusions profited from, and are similar to, Kisembo-Magesa-Shorter's "African Christian Marriage" in this order of reflection: 72-74 (on polygamy, care of widows and childlessnes); 86-88 (on childless marriages); 22-31 and 88-93 (on models for pastoral action).

Each parish can also establish a functioning *"marriage catechetical forum"*. Such a forum can be composed of respresentatives of the Women Religious, some happy and examplary couples, some from the Mary League Girls and the Catholic Youth under the direction of the pastor. In accord with the JC theology, such a forum should emphasize that bad Christian couples cannot be saved by their children or sons but through their active and living faith in the saving grace of Jesus (cf. Ac 15,11).

This forum should help the couples discover "a Christian significance of their situation"[533] by stressing to them that they should not allow childleness or malelessness lead them into feelings of guilt and mutual reproach, that a childless union is also an authentic married love, and that oneness in love is the principal end of marriage[534].

10.10.9 Pastoral Attention to Polygamy.

Like the Universal Church, the Igbo Church may not accept traditional polygamy as a legitimate form of marriage. The arguments from the OT theology of "holy polygamists" like Abraham, Jacob, David, etc[535] may not easily replace the OT Genesis theology on monogamy (Gen 1,27f; 2,18f) or even that of the NT (Mt 19,4f; Mk 10,6f). But since polygamy continues to pose a big challenge to both the canonical form of marriage and to the Gospel message itself, there is need to set up a permanent commission to find possible remedies for polygamy in the light of the JC teachings.

This body should continue to teach the faithful that polygamy due to divorce or to a frivolous search for social prestige should be discouraged as an aberration from the original union of "one man one wife" (Gen 1,27f; 2,18f)[536]. Jesus himself also taught and upheld the *Genesis* ideal of monogamy (cf. Mt 19,5f). By way of analogy with the moral stance of the JC theology which forbids "illicit marriages" (Ac 15,20.29), polygamy for social prestige[537] cannot be allowed among the followers of Jesus[538] today.

Furthermore, according to popular wisdom, in an alliance with three, one of the partners is victimised. The great traditional sorcerers are either monogamous or celibate. They are

---

533 Kisembo et al., op. cit., 92.
534 Cf. Id., 92-93.
535 Cf. Gen 16,1f; 29,15f; 2 Sm 16,20f.
536 Cf. Synod of Bishops, Selected Interventions, 97-98.
537 Cf. Id., 107-108.
538 Cf. Clement et al., Cross-Cultural Christianty, 26-29. Kisembo et al., African Christian Marriage, 67-76; 81-84.

never polygamous. Their state of life would reveal a will of total offering to the Godhead and service to the clan community. Very probably this would bring out the original image of the conjugal union[539].

Polygamy due to infertility or malelessness may not receive the Church's blessing and approval but does require sustained pastoral love for the couple in view of the great importance which the Igbo attach to progeny and lineage. Although the Church may not sanction polygamy, the same Church may not declare that no christian polygamist will be saved. For if a repentant thief (cf. Lk 23,39-43), tax-collectors, publicans and prostitutes are fit for the kingdom of heaven (cf. Mt 21,31-32), "good" christian polygamists like the "good" OT polygamists may not be excluded from it. So pastoral effort should focus on what can be done for the ultimate salvation of every polygamist[540].

10.10.10 Eschew Divisions, Conflicts and Rivalry.

In an "*ecclesia*" of people with group or personal interests and world views, misunderstandings or controversies are bound to arise from time to time[541]. The JC theology shows that sharp disagreements do not only disrupt pastoral work but also endanger the unity and spiritual fibre of the community or local Church (Ac 15,2.6.24). Therefore such dissensions among the brethren (*adelphoi*) in Christ should be looked into and settled as quickly as possible (15,2.6ff; 11,4-18).

Though the Igbo Church has so far done well in trying to settle controversies among her faithful, she should not only rest content with only settling disputes but must do something more to check the root causes of the unhealthy rivalry, divisions and conflicts[542]. To this effect I propose the setting up of a "*social affairs forum*" in each community. The forum should steadily monitor the areas and causes of conflicts among all the categories and levels of people[543] in order to ensure social justice and equity.

At the same time priests and pastoral workers should not cease to stress that christian life is service and not a position of honour and prestige in the community so that no personal ambitions may constitute an obstacle to another's spiritual growth or welfare (Ac 15,1.5.19.28). Pastors should continue to teach

---

539 Synod of Bishops, op. cit., 102.
540 Cf. Id., 98; 101-102; 105f; 108..
541 Cf. Ac 6,1; 11,2-3; 15,1.5-6.39, etc.
542 Cf. Anyanwu, Catholic Social Teaching, 11-18.
543 Cf. Id., 18-19.

the christian virtue of mercy and forgiveness[544] and lay great emphasis on the supreme eminence of the virtue of love which overcomes a multitude of divisions and contentions[545] and fulfils the whole Christian Law[546].

On the political scene, I think that the Church-State conflict can be settled if only the State is prepared for a humble dialogue with the Church(es) and is ready to recognize and respect the civic rights and duties of her citizens as regularly demanded by the Catholic Church in Nigeria[547]. Meanwhile pious Christians should no longer hesitate to join the various human rights movements in defence of the rights of the Church as is currently promoted by the Catholic Institute for Development, Justice and Peace (CIDJAP) in Enugu[548]. This is also in harmony with the JC theology which defends and respects the religious cultures and rights of peoples (Ac 15,10.19.28).

10.10.11 Check Proliferation of Sects and Islam.

In relation to the "Churches and ecclesial communities separated from the Roman Apostolic See"[549], I do not think that the ecumenical movement and religious dialogue have done much for the restoration of the unity of Christians in Igboland. Rather ecumenism seems to be an excuse for more disunity and upsurge of new sects among the already divided and scattered people of God. This is because

the religions and religious systems of Africa are largely self-isolated and incapsulated... they are still in competition with one another. At worst there is a completely closed situation; at best, a certain degree of syncretism[550].

Although in accord with the JC theology everyone has a right to worship God according to ones situation (Ac 15,19) and although the Church upholds religious freedom[551], yet the Igbo Church must give serious pastoral attention (Ac 15,6f) to the root causes of the rise of splinter groups within the Christian fold[552].

---

544 Cf. Ac 7,60; Lk 23,34; Rm 12,14ff; Col 3,12f; Ph 2,1f, etc.
545 Cf. Lk 10, 25-28; 1 Co 13,1-13; Ga 6,1-10; Col 3,14; I Jn 4,7-21 etc.
546 Cf. Lk 10,25f; Rm 13,8f; Ga 5,13f.22f.
547 Cf. CBCN, Civic and Political Responsibility of the Christian, 4f; 9f; Id., Listen: The Catholic Shurch Speaks 4ff; Anyanwu, Catholic Social Teaching, 41-46.
548 Cf. Ike, CIDJAP, African Charter, 6-14; Anyanwu, op. cit., 47f.
549 Vatican II, UR, nos. 13-23.
550 Shorter, African Christian Theology, 15.
551 Cf. Vatican II, DH, no. 1-2.
552 Cf. Ndiowkere, Prophecy, op. cit., 19-22.

To help the Igbo Christians showing signs of disenchantment with the Catholic Church, I propose the practical application of the accommodation JC theology to the native genius of the Igbo in the service of God (cf. Ac 15,19).

Since it is accepted that the people are "almost a nation of dancers, musicians and poets" and their "manners are simple" and their "luxuries are few[553]", and since the numerous indegenous Independent Churches or Faith Healing Missions, Sects and Centres[554] are noted for their application of this native genius to their forms of prayer and worship[555], Igbo pastors should also seek to introduce such authentic elements and forms of the native genius into the "Catholic" liturgy[556]. This may help in restoring unity of life to the chequered lives of many and stem the mounting tide of the annual exodus of Catholics to the local "christian sects".

At the same time, patrons or clients of the schismatic religious sects[557] should be encouraged to emulate the examples of the Early Christians in holding fast unanimously (*homothymadon*) to the loving God who has called them as a "people for his name" (Ac 15,14). In union with the Holy Spirit received at Baptism and Confirmation, the weak should be constantly exhorted to adher only to the essentials for their salvation (v.28) and stop running helter skelter to the numerous cauldrons of messianic cults and religious sects[558] in the midst of God's "*chosen race, a kingdom of priests, a holy nation...* called out of darkness into his wonderful light" (1 Pt 2,9).

Furthermore, organised prayer groups and meetings can give the weak and suffering a rare opportunity to express their problems of life, release internal or suppressed tensions and foster the unity of mind and heart among the participants. The native Church should also develop and promote more of the ministries of healing and prayer patterned on the successful forms currently carried out at *Elele* and *Onitsha* by Frs. Edeh and Ikeobi respectively[559].

Also, the Igbo Church as the "stronghold" of the Catholic Church in Nigeria should in no way take for granted the onslaught of Islam from the North and West of the country. The *AECAWA* studies on Christianity and Islam in Dialogue (1987) and the enlightenment seminar by the *ANIM* on "Muslims Master Plan and Method (1988)" are already right steps in the right direction. But

553 Nwoga, Focus of Igbo, 1984 Ahiajoku Lecture, 2. Here Prof. Nwoga is citing OLAUDAH EQUIANO, an Igbo ex-slave as far back as 1789.

554 Cf. Ochiagha, Emerging Healing Centres, 7-8.

555 Cf. Arinze/Fitzgerald, Pastoral Attention, 48; Ochiagha, op. cit., 9-15.

556 Cf. Ndiokwere, Prophecy, 273-275; 279-281.

557 Cf. Ochiagha, op. cit., 8-9.

558 Cf. John Paul II, RM, 32.

559 Uzukwu, Liturgical Celebration, 55-56; Ikeobi, Healing Ministry, 190-201; Ejizu, Dialogue at the Depth Level, 36; Ndiokwere, op. cit, 274.

there is need for a more concerted monitoring, vigilance and action especially at the political level to check the proselytizing activities and political manoeuvres of the Islamic fundamentalists[560].

10.10.12 Forestall Resurgence of "Neopaganism".

Neopaganism or religious syncretism or religionlessness is a sad fact in the present society. To forestall or diminish the problem, I propose the *narrative* pastoral approach of recalling the wonderful deeds of the Lord for his people as is evident from the JC theology. The recalling of the Lord's wonderful and saving deeds (or *terata kai semeia*) in order to exhort the people to fidelity to Him, is one of the meeting points of the teachings of the OT theology[561] and the JC or NT theology[562].

This is equally true of the traditional Igbo who never ceases to recall and thank God for his favours. No Igbo may deny that God who gave him/her *life* is not working *semeia kai terata* for the one as he did for the Jews and Gentiles of the apostolic times (Ac 15,13). Even the modern Igbo who claims to be religionless or indifferently says that "all religion is the same", invokes "Yahweh" at the sight or experience of the least obstacle because he/she knows that "Yahweh saves".

Using this traditional contact-point with Christianity, Igbo pastors should exhort and encourage the people to persevere in their christian vocation: Let all of them keep the word of the covenant, put them into practice and they will thrive in everything they do (cf. Dt 29,8). This is especially necessary for those who are still weak in faith or flagging in zeal or are on the verge of backsliding into some form of neopaganism or religious syncretism. The experience of the past divine favours should be used to strengthen them in their daily trials, tell them that all is not lost but that the good Lord is still alive and able (cf. Lk 1,37).

10.10.13 Lord it Not over the Brethren.

In our times, Igbo Gentile Church leaders should accept the fact of socio-religious change, invent new forms of communication, rethink the concrete

---

560 Cf. Onotu, Christian Muslim-Relationship in Nigeria, 39-45; Onaiyekan, Strategies for Islamic Expansion, 25ff; Mbiti, African Religions, 243; 252f.
561 Cf. Ex 19,3-6; Dt 4,34; 29,1-8.
562 Cf. Ac 2,11.27f; 14,27; 15,3-4.7f.13f. etc.

structures of authority, decentralise the exercise of power, redefine the concrete objectives of our vocation, help to discover new forms of religious freedom in order to reduce tension, foster unity and promote justice and peace in the local Church[563].

The *lordly* Church leaders should begin to put into practice the true spirit of the "*adelphoi* theology" of the JC that has no place for uncritical "Generals", "Monsignori", "Lordships", "Graces", "Excellencies", "Eminences", etc[564] in the brotherhood and sisterhood of Christ. Led by the Holy Spirit, they should stop putting God to test by making their *lordly* authority and powers felt like a yoke or burden on the common brethren's shoulders (cf. Ac 15,10.19.28).

It is very edifying to note that some Igbo pastors and religious brought up in the Euro-American ecclesial tradition are courageously urging for the dismantling of the non-salutary "absolute monarchical" structure of the Igbo Church[565].

If one recalls the 'supra democratic' character of pre-colonial Igbo political culture... this type of absolute monarchy fits into their community and mentality exactly like a square peg in a round hole. Among the Igbo who have no tradition of kings, queens, or monarchs of any type to follow and who acknowledge no king (absolute authority and dictator) over them, ecclesiastical structures inherited from medieval Europe should be considered unsuitable[566].

So let the Igbo Gentile ecclesial *overlords* remember every second of their lives that love, and not power and titles, is "the fulfilment of the Law" (Rm 13,19; cf. Lk 10,25f), and that without love they are *nothing* (cf. 1 Co 13,1ff) inspite of the wonders and signs they may be working, and despite the heavy ornamentation of their mortal bodies with golden purple honours. Let them always recall and put into practice the democratic and communal aspects of Igbo culture which tally very well with the democratic and communal life of the Early Christians and of the JC theology of *adelphoi*[567].

It is a truism that the most suitable title for each member of the Hierarchy is "*pastor*" (cf. Jn 10,1ff) and the second best is *adelphos* or brother (Ac 15,22-23.32). Here one ought to learn from some men and women religious who address each other as "brother" or "sister". As I once wrote in a protest four-page letter to an elder brother in Christ,

563 Cf. Carrier, Evangelisation, 129-132; 136ff.
564 Cf. Ozigbo, Igbo Catholicism, 4.
565 Cf. Mbefo, Reshaping, 60-64; Ejizu, Decolonizing, 212-226.
566 Agu, Secularization, 407.
567 Cf. Ac 1,15ff; 2,42ff; 4,32ff; 5,12ff; 13,3f; 15,23-24.32, etc; John Paul II, CFL, nos. 19-25; Weiser, Gemeinde und Amt, 312-320; Id., Basis und Führung, 66-71, especially 71.

no Igbo or any one else goes to heaven just because the one is a Christian or a Chief or King, Doctor, Professor, Rector, Religious, Bishop, Cardinal, Pope, etc. or because the one is an American, African or European, etc. or because the one is a German, Italian, English, French, Nigerian or Zairean, etc. but because the one is a **good Christian** who does what is right and pleases God. (Letter to Elder Brother, January 10, 1993, p. 3).

This agrees with the teaching of Peter the Apostle who is the fundament of the Church of Christ (Mt 16,18): "'I now really understand that God has no favourites, but anybody of any nationality who fears him and does what is right is acceptable to him' (Ac 10,34-35). This is the basic inculturation of our faith" (*Letter*, 4).

So then the Igbo Church leadership should eschew those *lordly* titles and honours which are never *necessary* for salvation (cf. Ac 15,28) but are rather opposed to the humble life of our model, God-man Jesus (Ph 2,5ff), our master yet our servant (cf. Lk 22,24f; Jn 13,12f)) and brother (cf. Heb 2,11f.17) anointed to bring the Good News to the poor and the afflicted (cf. Lk 4,18-19)[568].

We, the clergy and leaders of our people in different capacities, should not allow Christianity to be the opium of the masses by blessing the status quo... We must not "sleep on" and occassionally "talk in the sleep" (or worse "bark" in sleep) but be vigilant and critically outspoken in and with Truth. This is the essence of not being of the world, that is to say of warring against sinful social structures of the Nigerian society[569].

Here for example, one must bodly speak out against the unnecessary regulations over protocols and absurd rules for adults on *when and how to move or travel from one town to another and whom to befriend or not to befriend*. The time wasted in making such empty regulations in this NEE should have been fruitfully used for the practice of the weightier matters of the Law such as pastoral love, justice, mercy and good faith (cf. Lk 5,29f; Mt 23,,23)[570].

Again, the strenuous diocesan enforcement of the law of abstinence from meat on Fridays (cf. CIC 1250-1252) for poor people who hardly find meat to eat from Sundays to Thursdays of the week should be substituted with the *brotherly* and more salutary yet *canonical* counsel to abstain from *imperfections* and *habitual* sins on Fridays (CIC 1253). Is it not better for the poor and hungry to avoid sin than to fast and quarrel on fridays? (cf. Is 58,3f). Is the fasting or abstinence that pleases God not "to break unjust fetters, to undo the thongs of the yoke, to let the oppressed go free and to break all yokes"? (58,6). Is it not taking adequate care of the poor by the Church leaders? (cf. 58,7f).

---

568 Cf. Vatican II, CD, 15-16; PO, 15.
569 Okolo, Nigerian Church, 62.
570 Cf. Okolo, Justice in the Nigerian Church, 18-19.

One also wonders whether the "Igbo daughters of Sion" will ever be happy to see some of the powerful representatives of their meek King Jesus (cf. Mt 11,28f) living magnificently (cf. Lk 16,19f) at the expense of their "widows' mites" (cf. 21,1f) instead of using a modern equivalent of the "humble ass" (Lk 19,28ff; Mt 21,1ff) for their ministry to the poor. The Igbo Hierarchy should

> learn and accept in practice to demythologise authority and to sacramentalise humanity... Power is given for service and not for domination; the symbol of that power, the "crozier" or staff is given to gather the flock and not to knock or scatter them[571].

So like good shepherds (Jn 10,14f; 1 Pt 5,2f) the Igbo Church leaders should learn to *lead* and not to *dominate*, to serve and not to be served[572]. Church leaders "born in stables" should learn to live like the Master and Saviour born in Bethlehem's manger (cf. Lk 2,12). Perhaps, a deep reflection on the "brotherliness" of the *apostles* and *elders* (Ac 15,23) may serve as a corrective measure to the lordly show of authority and might by some Church leaders.

Perhaps, borrowing a leaf from the constructive evangelical opposition of Paul and Barnabas to the Judaizers in Antioch (Ac 15,2-4) and Paul's confrontation with the dissimulating Peter, the head of the Apostles (Ga 2,11-14), a similar constructive opposition to a defaulting local Church leader may be considered necessary (*epanankes*, 15,28) for the salvation of the people in our times.

10.10.14 Live in Spirit and Truth.

The JC theology of the operation of the Holy Spirit on the faithful (Ac 15,28) is a big challenge to sincere and honest living in every facet of Igbo life. The Splendour of truth should shine[573] in the lives of a people who are the temples of God and the Spirit of truth (cf. 1 Co 3,16). People led by the Spirit of truth should live like the Spirit. Duplicity or hypocrisy is a betrayal of the indwelling Spirit in Christians. Hence God despises hypocrites as anti Spirit (cf. Ac 5,3). The local Church must try to overcome duplicity with truth and honesty. Deceit, lies and falsehood should yield to reliability and sincerity of heart.

Emphasis should be laid on the fact that duplicity as a way of life is coterminous with possession by Satan (Ac 5,3) the "father of lies". More recogni-

---

571 Nwazojie, Nigerian Hierarchy, 71.
572 Cf. Lk 22,24-27; Mt 20, 24-28; Mk 10,42-45; Vatican II, CD, 15-16; PO, 15.
573 Cf. John Paul II, Veritatis Splendor (1993) passim.

tion should be given to honest living and not just for donating money good or bad for the "upkeep" of the Church. Christians should develop the courage to call a spade a spade and stop hobbling up and down with half truths even in the most insignificant matters. Since "God is Spirit, those who worship (him) must worship in spirit and truth" (Jn 4,24). This liberating truth can free the Igbo Church from hypocritical life (Jn 8,32)[574].

10.10.15 Focus on What is Necessary for Salvation.

The provision of remedies for faith-culture conflicts should be crowned with the focus on what is necessary for salvation. No one contests that food and drink are necessary (*epanankes*, Ac 15,28) to sustain sacred human life. It is undeniable that traditional titles and honours are recognitions of human achievement. The Church is generally very much concerned with "an authentic development of man and society which would respect all the dimensions of the human person"[575]. Civilisation, technology, wealth, titles, honour, prestige, cultural values, etc are all good things of life. But the effort to possess the goods of life should not blind our Christian vision of eternal life. For "what benefit is it to anyone to win the whole world and forfeit or lose his very self?" (Lk 9,25). Since "life does not consist in possessions" (Lk 12,15) and "life is more than food" (v.23), and since faith is above all human values and is the norm for all of them[576], all these values, when necessary (*epanankes*, Ac 15,28), must give way to one's faith in Christ.

Therefore what must worry every Igbo Christian should not be the high or low level of one's state in life, but rather one's fidelity to the christian call, depth of faith and grace acquired for the peace and salvation of one's soul[577]. The principal task of the local Church should be to set the people's heart on God's kingdom (Lk 12,31), to give light to *those who live in the shadow dark as death*" (Lk 1,79), to give them "knowledge of salvation through the forgiveness of their sins (v.77), and to guide them "*into the way of peace*" (v.79).

All efforts by the Igbo to improve the living human condition notwithstanding, the Church's main focus should be on what is necessary (*epanankes*) for the people's salvation. This focus can not be realised without much prayer and fasting in union with the Holy Spirit (Ac 15,28).

---

574 Cf. VS, op. cit., 31-34; Merecki-Styczen, Splendour of Human Freedom, 10.
575 John Paul II, Solicitudo Rei Socialis (SRS), 1.
576 Cf. Vatican II, GS, nos. 58-62.
577 Cf. Ac 3,16; 4,8-12; 15,9.11; 16,31; Lk 7,9-10; 8,47-48; 18,8; etc.

General Summary And Conclusion.

Now comes the end of this long study, moving slowly but steadily from the exposition of terms to a brief review of Acts-research, then to the exegesis and theology of the faith-culture conflict of the JC, and finally to the *hermeneutical* correlation of its theology with the faith-culture conflicts in an indigenized Igbo Church.

In the late 19th century, the white evangelisers came, "planted" the seed of the divine word among the Igbo and left them in peace (*met' eirenes*, cf. Ac 15,33) in the later part of the 20th century. Now through the wonders and signs (*semeia kai terata*, cf. 15,12) of God the local Church, structures and infrastructures are almost solely in the hands of Igbo pastoral workers. It is therefore left to these native evangelisers to "water" the seed of the divine word sown among them so that God may give the increase (cf. 1 Co 3,6f). In other words, it is the duty of the Igbo Church to inculturate the faith among her people. So had the Church Magisterium taught from of old (*aph' hemeron archaion*, cf. 15,7) and continues to teach all peoples and the Igbo who are now enthusiastically responding to the ecclesial call to insert the faith in all the strata of their community.

At this point it is appropriate to restate and respond to my *thesis* or *status questionis*: *Can the inspired inculturation theology of the JC really act as a basic guide for inculturation in the modern Igbo Church? Can it really inspire this Church in resolving her faith-culture conflicts?*

Having demonstrated in many ways that Acts 15 is "the basic text for inculturation" and hence the JC theology can be regarded as a "fundamental theology" for inculturation, my contention is that the Igbo Church can learn much from the JC theology for her inculturated evangelisation. This theology can help the Igbo Church if she faithfully follows the course and counsels of the JC and meticulously studies every faith-culture conflict in the local Church in the light and context of the JC proceedings and directives.

My response is a "*big yes*" if the Church leadership and all the faithful should avail themselves of the provisions and regulations of the JC in making the Christian message relevant to their way of life. My response is in the affirmative if the Igbo Church should seriously consider the suggestions and recomendations for the resolution of her faith-culture conflicts in the light of the JC.

Following the teachings of the JC, the Igbo Christians can salutarily live the Christian Gospel in their socio-cultural milieu which is their God-given situation. My position is that the *inculturation elements* latent or patent in the proceedings and instructions of the JC can act as an inspiration and encouragement for an authentic inculturation of the Good News in the lives of the Igbo today.

If the JC teaching fails to inspire the local Church in inculturating her faith, the problem lies with the Igbo people and their leaders and not with the nearly two thousand year-old teaching of the Church.

But by no means will the assimilation and application of the JC theology be an easy task for the present *colonised* and *westernised* Igbo Church as it was not easy for the initially *judaized* Apostolic Church (Ac 15,1-2.5-6).

However with patience and steadfastness demanded by the slow process of inculturation which would require an incubation[578] of the JC message in the genius of the Igbo people[579], and above all with the help of the overshadowing Spirit of God (cf. Lk 1,35) who oversees the pastoral activities of every local Church (cf. Ac 1,8; 15,28), an inculturated evangelisation according to the JC theology will not be impossible (cf. Lk 1,37) for the contemporary Igbo Church.

But the ever recurring and nagging question is: When the Son of Man visits Igboland again (*episkeptesthai*, Ac 15,14), will he really find his Igbo Gentile Church ready and willing to draw inspiration from the JC mission theology and message for an inculturated faith and practice? (cf. Lk 18,8b).

Let the Igbo Gentile Church, through the JC inculturated mission theology, strive to make it possible for each faithful to say at the end of one's earthly life:

Now, Master, you are letting your servant go in peace as you promised; for my eyes have seen the salvation which you have made ready in the sight of the nations; a light for the revelation of the gentiles and the glory of your people Israel (Lk 2,29-32).

This is also my earnest prayer and hope!

---

578 Cf. John Paul II, RM, nos. 52-54.
579 Cf. Paul VI, To SECAM (1969), no. 2.

Appendix

1. Some Loan or Rare Words in Acts 15.

Alisgema	v.20
Anaskeuazein	v.24
Anaginoskein	v.31
Baros	v.28
Diakrinein	v.9
Diastellesthai	v.24
Diaterein	v.29
Diatribein	v.35
Eidolothuton	v.29
Eirene	v.33
Epanankes	v.28
Epistellein	v.20
Episterizein	v.32
Epistrophe	v.3
Homothymadon	v.25
Kardiognostes	v.8
Katharizein	v.9
Paraklesis	v.31
Peirazein	v.10
Propempein	v.3
Parenochlein	v.19
Stasis	v.4
Symphonein	v.15
Zetema	v.6
Zugos	v.10

2. Some Eulogies of Acts 15.

Bruce, F. F: Acts 15 is "an event to which Luke attaches highest importance" [Book of Acts, 282].

   Crowe, J: Acts 15 is the "heart of his (Luke's) second volume" [Acts, 111].

Haenchen, E: Acts "chapter 15 is the turning-point, the 'centrepiece' and the 'watershed' of the book, the episode which rounds off and justifies the past developments, and makes those to come intrinsically possible" [Acts, 461].

Kee, H. C: Acts 15 "is literally, conceptually and theologically the midpoint of the book" [Good News, 57].

Marchesi, G: "The decisions of the Council are put (styled) in a form of written document. This shall remain a memorable event for the future of the Church" [My translation from the *Italian*, in: Il Vangelo, 180)].

Mbachu, H: "Although in the OT and NT...there are many biblical texts with inculturation value, but Acts 15 surpasses them because it contains the collective authoritative inculturation teaching of the apostolic people and special witnesses of Jesus (Ac 1,8)" [Inculturation Theology, 53].

Pasinya, M: Acts 15 is "a basic text on inculturation" [*le text fondamental sur l'inculturation* (L'Inculturation, 126)].

Pervo, R. I: "Acts 15 is indisputably Luke's most compelling account of a Church meeting" [Profit with Delight, 41].

Weiser, A: "The report about the 'Apostolic Council' occupies a central place in the Acts of the Apostles". [My translation from the *German*, in: Apostelkonzil, 185)].

Wilson, G: "Acts 15 is of central importance both for Luke's attitude to the Gentiles and for assessing his reliability as a historian" [Gentiles, 178].

Id., "Luke clearly sees the Apostolic Council as a confirmation of the momentous turning point in chs. 10-11 when Gentiles are accepted as equal members of the Church... Ch. 15 forms a watershed in the book of Acts. It is a, if not the, turning point in the whole narrative" [Gentiles 192-193].

3. Some Eulogies of Acts In General.

Bruce F. F: Luke-Acts combined is "the most literary part of the NT" [Acts ([2]1952), 26].

Gasque, W. W.: "Scholars do not usually agree: they have opinions. Nowhere is this more true than in connection with the Acts of the Apostles... With the exception of the question of ultimate Christian origins, there is probably no other area of the New Testament research in which scholarly opinion is so divided" [Historical Value, 68-69].

Ghidelli, C: "The Acts of the Apostles is a unique book in its type and a crucial inexhaustible source of informations and an object of reflection never yet sufficiently explored" [My translation from the *Italian*, in: Studi Sugli Atti, 390].

Mbachu, H: "The study of the inculturation theology of Acts continues to bring the early apostolic mission of the Acts narrative into the limelight of the contemporary missiology, pastoral theology and inculturated evangelisation especially in the 'young Churches' of Africa" [Inculturation Theology, 2-3].

Van Unnik, W. C.: Luke-Acts is a "storm-centre in contemporary scholarship" [Luke-Acts, 15].

Von Harnack, A: Acts is the "weightiest and best book of the New Testament" [Lucas der Arzt, 87. Also cited in *Mcgiffert, A. C.*, Historical Criticism, 390].

Bibliography.

1. TEXTS, CONCORDANCES, DICTIONARIES, ENCYCLOPEDIAS LEXICONS AND TEXTUAL AIDS.

Aland, K. et al., Vollständige Konkordanz zum Griechischen Neuen Testament, vols. 1-3, Berlin-New York 1978-1983.

Balz, H. - Schneider, G., Exegetisches Wörterbuch zum Neuen Testament (EWNT), Band/Vol. 3, Stuttgart-Berlin-Köln-Mainz 1983.

Botterweck G. J. - Ringgren, H. et al. (Ed.), Theologisches Wörterbuch zum Alten Testament, Band/Vols. 3 & 4, Stuttgart-Berlin-Köln-Mainz 1982 & 1984.

Brown E. R. et al. (Ed.), The New Jerome Biblical Commentary, Englewood Cliffs, NJ 1990.

Coenen, L. et al. (Ed.), Theologisches Begriffslexikon zum Neuen Testament, Band/vol. 3, Wuppertal 1972.

Di Berardino, A., (diretto da), Dizionario Patristico e di Antichità Cristiane, vols. 1 & 2, Casale Monteferrato, 1983.

Eliade, M (Ed.), The Encyclopedia of Religion, vol. 2, New York-London 1987.

Ellinger, K. - Rudolph, W (Ed.), Biblia Hebraica Stuttgartensia, Stuttgart 1977.

Hastings, J. et al. (Ed.) Encyclopedia of Religion and Ethics, vol. 9, Edinburgh 1980

Hatch, E. - Redpath, H. A., A Concordance to the Septuagint and other Greek Versions of the Old Testament (Including the Apocryphal Books), Vols. 1-3, Oxford 1898-1906; reprint: Graz 1975.

Kittel, G. - Friedrich, G (Ed.), Theologisches Wörterbuch zum Neuen Testament, 3. Band. (1933), 6. Band (1959), 7. Band (1964), Stuttgart.

Koehler, L. - Baumgartner, W., Lexicon in Veteris Testamenti Libros, Leiden ²1958. On "Qahal", p. 829.

Koehler, L., Baumgartner, W. et al., Hebräisches und Aramäisches Lexikon zum Alten Testament, Lieferung II & III Leiden 1974 & 1983.

Lampe, G. W. H. (Ed.), A Patristic Greek Lexicon, Oxford 1961.

Lenfant, F. D., Concordantiae Augustinae, vols. 1 & 2, Bruxelles 1982.

Lisowsky, G., Konkordanz zum Hebräischen Alten Testament, Stuttgart 1958.

Metzger, B. M., A Textual Commentary on the Greek New Testament, London 1971.

Mills, W. E., A Bibliography of the Periodical Literature on the Acts of the Apostles 1962-1984, Supplements to Novum Testamentum, vol. 58, Leiden 1986.

Morgenthaler, R., Statistik des neutestamentlichen Wortschatzes, Zürich - Frankfurt a. M. 1958.

Moulton, W. F. - Geden, A. S (Ed.), A Concordance to the Greek New Testament, Edinburgh 1957.

Nestle, E. - Aland, K. et al., Novum Testamentum Graece Stuttgart 26\ 1979; 7. revidierter Druck: 1983.

Newman, B. M. (Jr.), A Concise Greek - English Dictionary of the New Testament, UBS, Stuttgart 1971.

Pontificia Commissio Pro Nova Vulgata Bibliorum Editione, Novum Testamentum, Typis Polglottis Vaticanis 1971.

Quasten, J., Patrologia, vol. 1 (traduzione italiana del De. Nello Beghin) Marietti 1980.

Rahlfs, A. (Ed.), Septuaginta, Id est Vetus Testamentum Graece iuxta LXX Interpretes, Stuttgart 1935; reprinted: 1979.

Sinclair, J. - Hanks, P. et al. (Ed.), PONS Collins Cobuild English Language Dictionary, London-Glasgow-Stuttgart 1987 (1992 reprint).

Stier, F. - Lang, B. et al., Internationale Zeitschriftenschau für Bibelwissenschaft und Genzgebiet (IZBG), Düsseldorf 1951-1993.

The Catholic University of America, New Catholic Encyclopedia (NCE), vols. 1-14, New York 1967.

Wansbrough, H. (genl. Ed.), The New Jerusalem Bible, New York-London 1985.

Vermes, G., The Dead Sea Scrolls in English, Third Edition, Sheffield 1987.

Zerwick, M. - Grosvenor, M., A Grammatical Analysis of the Greek New Testament, Rome 1981.

2. PAPAL AND ECCLESIAL DOCUMENTS RELEVANT TOCULTURE AND INCULTURATION.

Benedict XV, Pope, Apostolic Letter, Maximum Illud, November 30, 1919. AAS 11 (1919) 444-496.

Collectanea Sacrae Congregationis de Propaganda Fide (SCPF), Constitutio Gregorii PP. XV: De Erectione S. C. de Propaganda Fide, Romae 22 Iunii 1622, pp. 2-4.

Id., Instructio SPCF 1659-: Ad Vicarios Apostolicos Societatis Missionis ad Exteros, vol. 1, 135, p. 42.

Id., Collectanea SCPF seu Decreta Instructionibus rescripta pro apostolicis Missionibus, second edition, vol. 1 (1622-1866) nos.1-1299: vol. 2 (1867-1906) nos. 1300-2317, Romae 1906 (=MCMVII).

Congregation du Saint-Esprit, Holy Ghost Fathers' Archive, Paris, 191/A/5 (Manuscript Biography of Fr. Joseph Lutz by Fr. Ebenerecht).

Flannery, A (genl. Ed.), Vatican Council II: The Conciliar and Post Conciliar Documents (Vatican Collection, vol. 1), Northport, New York 1975 (revised edition 1988).

Id., Vatican Council II, More Post Conciliar Documents (Vatican Collection, vol. 2), Northport, New York 1982.

John XXIII., Encyclical Letter, Princeps Pastorum, November 28, 1959. AAS 51 (1959) 833-864.

Id., Allocutio iis qui interfuerunt Conventui II "des Ecrivains et Artistes Noirs" Romam indicto a "Sociéte Africaine de Culture" April 1, 1959. AAS 51 (1959) 259-260. Cf. AFER 2/4 (1960) 331.

John Paul II, Address to Bishops of Zaire, in: AFER 22/4 (1980) 222-230. Cf. Okure, van Thiel, et alii, 32 Articles, 40-45.

Id., Address to Cardinals, November 9, 1979. AAS 71 (1979) 1447-1461.

Id., Ad eos qui Plenario Coetui Pontifici Consilii pro Hominum Cultura interfuerunt coram admissos. AAS 76 (1984) 592-596 (here 594).

Id., Address to the College of Cardinals, November 23, 1982. AAS 75 (1983) 135-146.

Id., Address to the Members of the Diplomatic Corps Accredited to the Holy See, January 12, 1981. AAS 73 (1981) 185-196.

Id., Address to the Members of the Pontifical Biblical Commission. AAS 71 (1979) 606-609.

Id., Address to Men of Culture in Rio de Janeiro, July 1, 1980. AAS 72 (1980) 847-852.

Id., Address to Nigerian Bishops. AAS 74 (1982) 611-618.

Id., Address to the Participants at the Gregorian University on the Occasion of the 400th Anniversary of the Arrival of Fr. Matthew Ricci in China, October 25 1982, in: Acta Romana Societas Iesu (Curia of the General of the Society of Jesus 1983) vol. 18/3, pp. 740-747.

Id., Address to the United Nations Educational, Scientific and Cultural Organisation (UNESCO), June 2, 1980. AAS (1980) 735-752.

Id., Address to the Vatican Curia, June 28, 1982. AAS 74 (1982) 1024-1039.

Id., Apostolic Constitution, Sapientia Christiana, April 15, 1979. AAS 71 (1971) 469-499.

Id., Apostolic Exhortation, Familiaris Consortio, November 22, 1981. AAS 74 (1982) 81-191.

Id., Apostolic Exhortation, Catechesi Tradendae, October 16, 1979. AAS 71 (1979) 1277-1340.

Id., Apostolic Letter. Mulieris Dignitatem, Libreria Editrice Vaticana, August 1988. AAS 80/2 (1988) 1653-1729.

Id., Encyclical Letter. Redemptor Hominis, March 4, 1979. AAS 71 (1979) 257-324.

Id., Encyclical Letter. Redemptoris Missio, December 7, 1990. AAS 83 (1991), Libreria Editrice Vaticana, Vatican City,

Id., Encyclical Letter. Solicitudo Rei Socialis, Liberia Editrice Vaticana, Vatican City, December 1987. AAS 80/1 (1988) 513-586.

Id., Encyclical Letter, Veritatis Splendor, Libreria Editrice Vaticana 1993. AAS 85 (1994) 1133-1228.

Id., Epistula. Pontificium Consilium pro Hominum Cultura Instituitur, May 20, 1982. AAS 74 (1982) 683-688.

Id., Hiroshimae, ad Mathematicarum et Naturalium Scientiarum Cultores Habita. AAS 73 (1981) 422-428.

Id., Homiliam, (lingua italica) October 22, 1978. AAS 70 (1978) 944-950.

Id., The Special Assembly for Africa of the Synod of Bishops. Instrumentum Laboris, Kampala (Uganda) 1993.

Id., Post-Synodal Apostolic Exhortation. Christifideles Laici, Libreria Editrice Vaticana, December 1988. AAS 81/1 (1989) 393-521.

Metzler, J. (Ed.), Sacrae Cogregationis de Propaganda Fide, Memoria Rerum 1622-1972, vols. 1/1 and 3/2, Rom-Freiburg-Wien 1971 & 1976.

Id., Foundation of the Congregation "de Propaganda Fide" by Greogory XV. Translation from German by G. F. Heinzmann, in: Metzler, Memoria Rerum. vol. 1/1, 79-111.

Id., La Situazione della Chiesa Missionaria, in: Metzler, Memoria Rerum, vol. 1/1, 15-37.

Id., Orientation, Programme et Premières Décisions (1622-1649). Traduit de l'Allemand par Auguste Ehrhard, in: Metzler, Memoria Rerum, 146-196.

Id., Pope John Paul II Speaks on Africa and to Africans, in: AFER 22/4 (1980) 207-231.

NECN (now CBCN), Papal Message to Nigeria: A Collection of Speeches by Pope John Paul II on the Occasion of His Visit to Nigeria from 12th to 17th February 1982, Lagos 1982. [See. AAS 74 (1982) 608-624].

Paul VI, Address to SECAM), Kampala (Uganda) July, 31, 1969. AAS (1969) 573-578. Cf. 32 Articles Evaluating Inculturation, 32-39.

Id., Encyclical Letter, Ecclesiam Suam, August 6, 1964. AAS 56 (1964) 609-659.

Id., Apostolic Exhortation, Evangelii, Nuntiandi, December 8, 1975. AAS 68 (1976) 1-96. Cf. A. Flannery, Vatican II, 711-761.

Id., Address in Gregorian University, March 12, 1964. AAS 56 (1964) 365.

Id., Address to Non-Christian Leaders, Bombay, India December 3, 1964. AAS 57 (1965) 132-133.

Id., Africae Terrarum, October 29, 1967. AAS 59 (1967) 1073-1097. Cf. 32 Articles Evaluating Inculturation, 14-31.

Id., Allocution to 6th International Thomistic Congress, September 10,1965. AAS 57 (1965) 788-792.

PCID, Bulletin 82 (1993) XXVIII/1.

Id., Bulletin 84 (1993) XXVIII/3.

Pius XI, Encyclical Letter, Rerum Ecclesiae, February 28 1926. AAS 18 (1926) 65-83.

Pius XII, Address to the Directors of Pontifical Mission Work, June 24, 1944. AAS 26 (1944) 207-211.

Id., Christimas Message, 1945. AAS 38 (1946) 15-25.

Id., Encyclical Letter, Evangelii Praecones, June 2, 1951. AAS 43 (1951) 497-528.

Id., Encyclical Letter, Fidei Donum, January 15, 1957. AAS 49 (1957) 225-248.

Id., Encyclical Letter, Summi Pontificatus, October 20, 1939. AAS 31 (1939) 413-453 (here, 429).

Id., Sermon to Seminarians, June 24, 1939. AAS 31 (1939) 245-252 (here, 247).

SCCE, Catholic Schools (Malgré les Déclarations), June 24, 1977. Cf. A. Flannery, Vatican II, vol. 2, 606-661.

SCC, Catechetical Directory (Ad Normam Decreti), April 11, 1971. AAS 64 (1972) 97-176. Cf. A. Flannery, Vatican Council II, vol. 2, 529-604.

SCPF, Instruction Vicarium Apostolicorum ad Regna Sinarum, Tonchini et Cocincinae Proficiscentium, 1659, in: Metzler, Memoria Rerum, 697-704.

Second Vatican Council, Ad Gentes Divinitus, December 7, 1965. AAS 58 (1966) 947-990. (Note: The English citation of the Council's documents follow that of A. Flannery, Vatican II, vol. 1).

Id., Apostolicam Actuositatem, November 18, 1965. AAS 58 (1966) 837-864.

Id., Christus Dominus, October 28, 1965. AAS 58 (1966) 673-696.

Id., Dignitatis Humanae, December 7, 1965. AAS 58 (1966) 929-941.

Id., Gaudium et Spes, December 7, 1965. AAS 58 (1966) 1035-1115.

Id., Gravissimum Educationis. 28 October 1965. AAS (1966) 728-739.

Id., Lumen Gentium, November 21, 1964. AAS 57 (1965) 5-75.

Id., Nostra Aetate, October 28, 1965. AAS 58 (1966) 740-744.

Id., Optatam Totius, October 28, 1965. AAS 58 (1966) 713-727.

Id., Perfectae Caritatis, 28 October, 1965. AAS (1966) 702-712.

Id., Presbyterorum Ordinis, December 7, 1965. AAS 58 (1966) 991-1021.

Id., Sacrosanctum Concilium, December 4, 1963. AAS 56 (1964) 97-134.

Id., Unitatis Redintegratio, November 21, 1964. AAS 57 (1965) 90-107.

Second Extraordinary Assembly of Synod of Bishops (1985), Ecclesia sub Verbo Dei Mysteria Christi Celebrans pro Salute Mundi. RELATIO FINALIS, II, D, 4.

SECAM, Synod Bishops from Africa Isssue Declaration, in: AMECEA Documentation Service, 11/2 (1974) 2-3.

SPUC, Spiritus Domini, April 16, 1970. AAS 62 (1970) 715-724.

Synod of Bishops, Convenientes ex Universo (On Justice in the World) 30 November 1971, in: Enchiridion Vaticanum, 4, nos. 1238-1308. Citation from A. Flannery, Vatican Council II, More Post Conciliar Documents, New York 1982, pp. 695-710.

Synod of Bishops 1980, Selected Interventions on Marriage, in: Special Double Issue, AFER 23/1-2 (1981) 15-117.

Synod of Bishops, Special Assembly for Africa: The Church in Africa and her Evangelising Mission towards the Year 2000, "You Shall Be My Witnesses" (Acts 1:8). LINEAMENTA, Vatican City 1990.

The Canon Law Society Trust, The Code of Canon Law in English Translation. Prepared by the Canon Law Society of Great Britain and Ireland, etc. (with index) London-Dublin-Sydney 1984.

Vatican Bulletin, Ecclesiastical Provinces, in: L'Osservatore Romano, Weekly Edition in English, [N. 14 (1335), 6 April 1994) p. 8.

3.   THE FATHERS OF THE CHURCH AND INCULTURATION.

Anonymi Viri Apostolici Ad Diognetum, Capitulum 5, in: Migne, PG, 2, p. 1174.

Augustine, St., Epistola 118.4.23, in: Migne, PL 33, 442-443.

Id., De Civitate Dei, 10.29, in: Migne, PL 41, 307-309.

Id., De Trinitate, 13.19.24, in: Migne, PL 42, 1033-1034.

Id., Sermo, 165,3, in: PL 38, 946.

Id., Sermones 266-269, in: PL, 38, 225-1237.

Id., Ennaratio in Psalmum 130.9-12, in: Migne, PL, 36-37, 1710-1711.

Clement of Alexandria, St., Stromata 1-4; 6, in: Migne, PG, 8-9, 685-1582; 207-402.

Chrysostom, St., In Epistola I ad Corinthios, Homilia 35, in Migne, PG 61, 295-306.

Eusebius of Caesarea, Ekklesiastikes Historias, in: Migne, PG, 20, 29-905.

Id., Apodeiseos Euangelikes , Liber 1-10, in: Migne, PG, 22, 14-794.
Id., Proparskeues Euangelikes , Liber 1-15, in: Migne, PG, 21, 91-1407.
Fulgentius, St., Sermon 8,2-3, PL 65, 743f.
Gregory the Great, St., Liber 11, Epistola 76, Ad Mellitum Abbatem, in: Migne, PL, 77, 1215-1217.
Irenaeus, St., Adversus Haereses, Book 3: 18,1; Book 4: 6,7; 20,6-7, in: Migne, PL, 932; 990; 1037.
Justin Martyr, Apologia 1 & 2, in: Migne, PG, 6, 327-470.
Leo the Great, St., Sermo 76, PL 54, 404-411.
Migne, J. P., Patrologiae Graecae (**PG**), 161 volumes, Paris 1857-1865, (here "Apologetae", vol. 6). (Note: Relevant Works by Greek Fathers are taken from these volumes).
Id., Patrologiae Latinae (**PL**), 217 volumes, Paris 1878-1890. (Relevant works from the Latin Fathers are cited from these volumes).
Tertullian, Apologetics, 27, in: Migne, PL, 1, 377 A.

4.   NIGERIAN BISHOPS' PASTORAL LETTERS.

Arinze, F. A., The Church and Nigerian Culture, 1973 Lenten Pastoral, Onitsha 1973.
Catholic Bishops of Onitsha Ecclesiatical Province, Put into Deep Water, Onitsha 1985.
Catholic Bishops: Joint Circular Letter on Education, Onitsha (Nigeria) 1953.
Catholic Bishops of East Central State of Nigeria, Education: 1971 Easter Joint Pastoral Letter, Onitsha 1971.
Catholic Bishops of Nigeria, His Holiness, Pope John Paul II Ushers in a new Era of Evangelization in Nigeria, Joint Pastoral Letter, February 1983.
Id., The Nigerian Church: Evangelization Through Inculturation. Pastoral Letter, Lagos 1991.
Id., Guidelines for the Catholic Charismatic Renewal of Nigeria, Lagos 1991.
Id., Listen: The Church Speaks, Joint Pastoral Letter, Lagos (Nigeria) 1985.
Nwedo, A. G., Christinity Among Us. Its Survival? Pastoral Letter, Umuahia (Nigeria) 1990.
Ochiagha, G. O., Lenten Pastoral: Faith Transforms Culture, Lenten Pastoral Orlu (Nigeria) 1992.
Id., The Emerging Nigerian, Lenten Pastoral, Orlu (Nigeria) 1983.
Id., The Emerging Healing Centres: Their Potential for Good And/Or Evil, Lenten Pastoral, Orlu 1993.
Unegbu, M., The Osu/Diala Scandal, Lenten Pastoral, Owerri 1977.

5. BOOKS ON INCULTURATION.

Abd - Ul - Masih, Islam and Christianity,. Ninety Questions and Answers, Ibadan (Nigeria) 1965.

Adibe, G. E. M., The Crisis of Faith and Morality of the Igbo Christians of Nigeria, Onitsha 1992.

AECAWA, Christianity and Islam in Dialogue, Cape Coast (Ghana) 1987.

Agu, C. C., Secularization in Igboland: Socio-Religious Change and its Challenges to the Church among the Igbo, Frankfurt am Main 1989.

Aguwa, J. U. C., The Anthropological Challenges of Christianity in the Changing African Culture: the Nigerian Case, Rome 1987.

Aniagwu, J. K. A., Priestly Formation in the AECAWA Seminaries Past and Present, in: WAJES 1 (1989) 33-53.

Anochie, R. C., The Impact of Igbo Women on the Church in Igboland, Roma 1979.

Arinze, F. A., Answering God's Call, London 1983.

Id., The Christian and the Family, Onitsha (Nigeria) 1983.

Azorji, E. E., Faith and Culture in Dialogue (The African Experience), Enugu 1991.

Bosch, D. J (Ed.), Church and Culture Change in Africa, LUX MUNDI 3, Pretoria 1971.

Bosch D, T., Transforming Mission, Maryknoll, New York 1991.

Botkin, J. W. et alii, No Limits to Learning: Bridging the Human Gap, "A Report of the club of Rome", Oxford 1979.

Cannon K. G. - Fiorenza E. S (Ed.), Semeia 47: Interpretation for Liberation, Atlanta, Ga 1989.

Carbon, A (Ed.), Notes et Documents relatifs à la Vie et l'Oeuvre du Vénérable Francois-Marie Paul Libermann, vols. 9 & 10, Paris 1949.

Carrier, H., Évangélisation et Développement des Cultures, Roma 1990.

Catholic Secretariat of Nigeria (Ed.), Inculturation in Nigeria. Proceedings of Catholic Bishop's Study Session (November 1988) Lagos 1989.

Clement, A. H. et al. Cross-Cultural Christianity. A Textbook in Cross-Cultural Communication, Jos (Nigeria) 1989.

Crollius, A. A. R (Ed.), Inculturation. Working Papers on Living Faith and Cultures, Rome, vol. 1 (1982); vols. 2 & 3 (1983); vol. 4 (1984) in French Language; vol. 8 (1986); vols. 9 & 10 (1987).

CBCN, New Era of Evangelization. Seminar Proceedings, Ibadan (Nigeria) 1984.

Dorr, D., Integral Spirituality, Dublin 1990.

Eboussi-Boulaga, F., Christianity Without Fetishes, New York 1984.

Echiegu, A. O. U., Translating the Collects of the Solemnities of the Lord in the Language of the African: Volume Three, Sacral Igbo and Its Rhetoric.

Ekandem, D. I., The Church in the Rise of Nigeria, Enugu (Nigeria) 1974.

Ekechi, F. K., Missionary Enterprise and Rivalry in Igboland 1857-1914, London 1972.

Ela, Jean-Marc, African Cry, Maryknoll, New York 1986. (Translated from the French by Robert R. Barr).

Id., My Faith as an African, Maryknoll, New York 1988; London 1989. (Translated from the French by John Pairman Brown and Susan Perry).

Ezeanya, S. N. (Ed.), Apostolate in Nigeria Today and Tomorrow (with Special Reference to Catechists and Choir masters), Enugu (Nigeria) 1977.

Id., A Handbook of Igbo Christian Names, Port Harcourt, (Nigeria) 1967.

Id., The Church Speaks to Africa: Some Aspects of Christianity in Nigeria, Enugu 1976.

FABC, First Plenary Assembly (Tapei, 22-27 April 1974). His Gospel to Our Peoples..., Vol. 2, Manila 1976.

Fabella, V. - Torres, S., Irruption of the Third World: Challenge to Theology, Maryknoll, New York 1983.

Fashole-Luke, E. et al. (Ed.), Chritianity in Independent Africa, London 1978.

Fitzpatrick, J. P., One Church Many Cultures: The Challenge of Diversity, Kansas City 1987.

Galilea, S., The Beatitudes: To Evangelise as Jesus Did, New York 1984.

Gritti, J., L'expression de la Foi dans les Cultures Humaines, Paris 1975.

Hastings, A., African Christianity. An Essay in Interpretation, London 1976.

Hering, W (Hrsg.), Aspekete der Evangelisierung. Erfahrungen und Aufgaben, Limburg 1989.

Id., Christus in Africa. Zur Inkulturation des Glaubens im Schwarzen Kontinent, Limburg 1991.

Hesselgrave, D. J., Communicating Christ Cross-Culturally: An Introduction to Missionary Communication, Grand Rapids Michigan.

Idem, M. E. O., Inculturation of leadership in the Nigerian Situation (Focus n the Laity), Rome 1988.

Ilogu, E., Christianity and Igbo Culture, New York 1976.

Ilonu, L. O., Priest and People, Okigwe (Nigeria) 1990.

Isichei, E. (Ed.) Varieties of Christian Experience in Nigeria, London-Basingstoke 1982.

Id., Entirely for God. The Life of Michael Iwene Tansi, Ibadan 1980.

Iwe, N. S. S., Christianity, Culture and Colonialism in Africa, Port Harcourt (Nigeria) no date.

Jinehu, E. D., The Osu Caste in Our Society, Enugu (Nigeria) no date.

Kisembo, B. et alii, African Christian Marriage, London-Dublin 1977.

Kraft, C. H., Christianity in Culture. A Study in Dynamic Biblical Theologizing in Cross-cultural Perspective, Maryknoll, New York 1979 (ninth printing).

Lohfink, N. F., Option for the Poor - The Basic Principle of Liberation Theology in the Light of the Bible, Berkeley, California 1987.

Luzbetak, L. J., The Church and Cultures. New Perspectives in Missiological Anthropology, Maryknoll, New York 1989.

Mayers, M. K., Christianity Confronts Culture: A Strategy for Cross-Cultural Evangelism, Grand Rapids 1974, [2]1987.

Mbah, C. S., Building Up African Christian Families, Enugu (Nigeria) 1985.

Mbefo, L. N., John Paul II and the Nigerian Catholicism, Enugu (Nigeria) 1982.

Id., The Reshaping of African Traditions, Enugu (Nigeria) 1988.

Id., Towards A Mature African Chritianity, Enugu 1989.

Nida, E. A., Religion Across Culture, New York 1968.

Ndiokwere, N. I., Prophecy and Revolution - The Role of Prophets in the Independent African Churches and in Biblical Tradition, London 1981.

Id., Message And Mission: The Communication of the Christian Faith, New York 1960, especially, pp. 33-58.

Nwosu, V. A., The Laity and the Growth of Catholic Church in Nigeria. The Onitsha Story 1903-1983, Onitsha 1990.

Nwosu, C. U., Evangelization in Igboland - Evangelii Nuntiandi Applied to a Nigerian Ecclesiastical Province, München 1992.

Obi, C. A (Ed.), A Hundred Years of the Catholic Church in Nigeria, Onitsha 1985.

Obiefuna, A. K., Idolatory in a Century-old Faith, Enugu (Nigeria) 1985.

Odudoye, M. A. - Kanyoro, M (Ed.), Talitha, qumi! Proceedings of the Convocation of African Women Theologians 1989, Ibadan (Nigeria) 1990.

Ogbu, K (Ed.), The History of Christianity in West Africa. London 1980.

Onyeocha, A. E (Ed.), Faith and Practice. The Reflections, Acts and Declarations of Owerri Diocesan Catholic Synod, Owerri 1984.

Ojo, G. A., The Laity and The New Era of Evangelisation, Kaduna (Nigeria) 1987.

Ojo, G. A. - Dodo, D. D (Ed.), Activities of the Laity in a Parish, Kaduna, 1986.

Id., The Role of the Layperson in the Church in Nigeria, Kaduna 1985.

Okoye, C. J (Ed.), Bishop Shanahan, Papers of Uwani Symposium, Onitsha (Nigeria) 1971.

Okure, T - van Thiel, P. et alii, 32 Articles Evaluating Inculturation of Christianity in Africa, Spearhead Nos. 112-114, Eldoret (Kenya) 1990. (Note: For easier references, articles in this antology appearing in the AFER shall be cited according to the pages of this antology).

Oliver, R., The Missionary Factor in East Africa, London 1952.

Onyenemegam, J. O, Pastoral Care of the Sick in Igbo Community - Nigeria, Rome 1985.

Onwubiko, O. A., Theory and Practice of Inculturation (African Perspective), Enugu (Nigeria) 1992.

Id., Facing the Osu Issue in the African Synod (A Personal Response), Enugu (Nigeria) 1993.

Osuji, C. C., The Concept of Salvation in Igbo Traditional Religion, Roma 1977.

Schineller, P., A Handbook on Inculturation, New York 1990.

Schreiter, R. J., Constructing Local Theologies, Maryknoll, New York 1985.

Shorter, A., African Christian Theology - Adaptation or Incarnation, London 1975.

Id., African Culture and the Christian Church. An Introduction to Social and Pastoral Anthropology, London 1973.

Id., Toward A Theology of Inculturation, Maryknoll, New York 1988.

Tracy, D., Blessed Rage for Order: New Pluralism in Theology, New York 1975.

Trigault, N., The China That Was. (Translated from the Latin by L. J. Gallagher), Milwaukee 1942.

Uka, L (Ed.), "Justice", the Foundation of Peace in Nigeria, Lagos (Nigeria) 1988.

Ukpong, J. S., African Theologies Now - A Profile, Spearhead no. 80, Eldoret (Kenya) 1984.

Ukpong et al. (Ed.), Evangelization in the Third Millenium: Challenges and Prospects, Port Harcourt (Nigeria) 1992.

Usanga, B. D., Seminar on Cultural Revival: The Church in the Era of Cultural Revival, Calabar (Nigeria) no date.

Uzukwu, E. E., Church and Inculturation: A Century of Roman Catholicism in Eastern Nigeria, Obosi 1985.

Uzukwu, E. E. Litrugy, Truly Christian, Truly African, Gaba Publications, Eldoret (Kenya), Spearhead No. 74, December 1982.

Id., (Ed.), Religion and African Culture, 1. Inculturation - A Nigerian Perspective, Enugu (Nigeria) 1988.

6. ARTICLES ON INCULTURATION.

Agré, B., Bericht eines Teilnehmers an den Vorbereitungen zur Afrikanischen Synode, in: Concilium 28. Jahrgang, Heft 1 (1992) 71-74.

Aguwa, J., Christianity and the Development of Igbo Culture Today, in: BTS 10/1 (1990) 26-37.

Ahmadu, I. M., Peace and Stability in Nigeria: The Role of the Church, in: BET 2/2 (1989) - 3/1 (1990) 44-59.

Akwue, F. A., A Growing African Vision of the Church's Mission, in: AFER 23/3 (1981) 148-161.

Anyanwu, S., The Church in Africa: Our Way to the Third Christian Millenium, in: BTS 10/1 (1990) 12-18.

Id., Catholic Social Teaching in Africa: A Hundred Years After "Rerum Novarum", in: BTS 11/2 (1991) 34-52.

Anyika, F., The Beginnings of the Bishopric in Roman Catholicism in Igboland, in: BTS 12/1 (1992) 29-42.

Id., Military Force and Evangelism in Southern Nigeria: The 1901/02 Aro Expedition, in: ATJ 20/1 (1991) 28-41.

Id., The Missionary Enterprise of the Rev. Fr. Alexander Leo Lejeune in Eastern Nigeria 1900-1905, in: BTS 14/1 (1994) 50-69.

Aquinas, T., In Decem Libros Ethicorum Expositio, in: Ethic., 1.2-3.

Id., Summa Theologiae 1a, 3.4 ad 2; 1a 2ae, 94.2.

Arinze, F., Meeting Other Believers: Introductory Speech to the Work of the Plenary Assembly of the PCID in: Bulletin 82 (1993) XXVIII/1, pp. 17-22.

Arinze, F. - Fitzgerald, M. L., Pastoral Attention to African Traditional Religion (ATR), in: AFER 30/3 (1988) 131-134. Cf. 32 Articles Evaluating Inculturation, 47-51.

Arrupe, P. (S.J.), Message to the Interdisciplinary Seminar on Inculturation, in: Crollius, Inculturation, 1 (1982) XI-XII.

Id., Letter to the Whole Society on Inculturation, in: Studies in the International Apostolate of Jesuits (SIAJ) 7 (June 1978) 9-10.

Azevedo, M. De C., Inculturation and the Challenges of Modernity, in: Crollius, Inculturation 1 (1982) 1-63.

Barney, G. L., The Supercultural and the Cultural: Implications for Frontier Missions, in: R. P. Beaver (Ed.), The Gospel and Frontier Peoples, Pasadena 1973.

Beauchamp, P., The Role of the Old Testament in the Process of Building up Local Churches, in: Crollius, Inculturation 3 (1983) 1-16.

Biernatzki, W. E., Intercultual Communication, in: SEDOS Bulletin 21/7 (1989) 219-227.

Blaser, K., Multicultural Christianity: A Project for Liberation. The Meaning of the Conflict North-South for Theology and our Churches, in: IRM 82/326 (1993) 201-223.

Blomjous, J., Development in Mission Thinking and Practice 1959-1980: Inculturation and Interculturation, in: AFER 22/6 (1980) 393-398.

Bujo, B., Mehr als ein Vertrag - Ehe als dynamischer Prozeß in Afrika, in: Hering, Christus, 94-106.

Id., Sexualverhalten in Afrika und Naturrechtsethik, in: Theologie der Gegenwart 36 (1993) 209-218.

Buswell (III), J. O., Contextualization: Theory, Tradition, and Method, in: Theology and Missions, D. J. Hesselgrave (Ed.), Grand Rapids 1978.

Carrier, H., Inculturation: A Modern Approach to Evangelization, in: CSN, Inculturation, 4-28.

Id., Les Universités Catholiques face au Pluralisme Culturel, in: Gregorianum 58 (1977) 607-640.

Carroll, K., practical Inculturation in Nigeria - a Testi-mony, in: CSN, Inculturation,

Chepkwony, Adam K. A., Theological Trends in Africa, in: AFER 34/1 (1992) 4-17.

Congar, Y. (O.P.), Christianisme come Foi et comme Culture, in: Evangelizzazione e Culture. Atti del Congresso Internazionale Scientifico di Missiologia, (Roma 5-12 Ottobre 1975), vol. 1, Roma 1976, pp. 83-103.

Courth, F., Warum bringen wir Christus nach Afrika, in : Hering, Christus, 67-78.

Crilly, W. H., Scholastic Philosophy, in: NCE, 12, 1146-1147.

Crollius, A. A. R., Inculturation: From Babel to Pentecost, in: Crollius, Inculturation 8 (1986) 1-7.

Id., Inculturation and Incarnation. On Speaking of the Christian Faith and the Culture of Humanity, in: Bulletin, Secretariatus pro Non-Christianus, 13 (1978) 134-140.

Id., Inculturation and the Meaning of Culture, in: Gregorianum 61 (1980) 253-275.

Id., What is so New about Inculturation? A Concept and Implications, in: Gregorianum 59 (1978) 721-737.

Cronin, V., Nobili, Roberto De, in: NCE, 10, 477-479.

Crossan, D. M., Logos, in: NCE, 8, 967-968.

Cullenm M., How Will We Initiate The New Era of Evangelisation, in: CBCN, New Era, 56-73.

Curtin, P. D., Scientific Racism and the British Theory of Empire, in: The Journal of the Historical Society of Nigeria 2/1 (1960) 40-51.

De Gasperis, F. R., Continuity and Newness in the Faith of the Mother Church of Jerusalem, in: Crollius, Inculturation 3 (1983) 19-69.

De Napoli, G. A., Inculturation As Communication, in: Crollius, Inculturation, 9 (1987) 69-98.

Devos, P., Cyril (Constantine) and Methodius, SS., in: NCE, 4, 579-581.

Du Roy, O. J.-B., Augustine, St., in: NCE, 1, 1041-1058.

Dwan, S., Taking the Exotic out of Inculturation, in: SEDOS Bulletin 20/7 (1988) 240-244.

Eboussi-Boulaga, F., Christianity Without Fetiches, New York, 1984.

Echezona, W. W., Use of Local Musical Instruments in the Liturgy, in: Ezeanya, Apostolate, 84-87.

Edet, R. N., The Nigerian Theologian at the Service of the Church, in: NJT (1985) 43-53.

Ejizu, C. I., Dialogue at the Depth-Level. Inculturation Prayer in the Nigerian Church, in: NZMw = NRSM 46/1 (1990) 31-48.

Id., Decolonizing the Nigerian Church: A Challenge to Theologians, in: Présence Africaine, Revue Culturelle du Monde Noir, Nos. 137-138 (1986) 212-226.

Id., Endurance of Conviction: The Persistence of the Traditional World-View in Igbo Christian Converts, in: NZMw 43/2 (1987) 125-135.

Id., Religion and Social Change. The Case of the Igbo of Nigeria, in: NZMw 45/2 (1989) 110-119.

Ekechukwu, A., Religious Intolerance or Ecumenical Dialogue: Roman Catholic and Anglican Case, in: Uzukwu, Religion and African Culture, 102-121.

Id., Theology of Religions and the Theological Problematic of Inculturation, in: Uzukwu, Religion and African Culture, 123-145.

Eneja, M. U., The Catechist as 'Public Relations Officer' in the Church, in: Ezeanya, Apostolate, 46-54.

Engel, A., Die Missionsmethode der Missionare vom Heiligen Geist auf dem Afrikanischen Festland, Knechtsteden 1932.

Eyt, P., L'Assemblée Speciale du Synode des Éveques pour l'Europe, in NRT 114 (1992) 481-499.

Eze, A., Parish Records for Sacred Returns, in: Ezeanya, Apostolate, 104-106.

Eze, R., The Catechist According to Second Vatican Council, in: Ezeanya, Apostolate, 19-21.

Eze, S., A Catechist As A Model for Christians to Imitate, in: Ezeanya, Apostolate, 55-58.

Ezeala, J. O. L., Can the Igbo Man be a Christian in View of the Osu Caste System? Orlu (Nigeria) no date.

Ezeanya, S. N., Adaptation of the Gospel in Africa: Principles and Methods, in: Ezeanya, Apostolate, 34-45.

Faciola, P. G., Inculturation According to the Teaching of John Paul II, in: Omnis Terra 18 (1984) 135-143, Engl. ed.

Fagun, M. O., Evangelization and the Changing West African Scene, in: WA-JES, 1 (1989) 3-13.

Glanville, J. J., Aristotelianism, in: NCE, 1, 1799-808, esp. 805 & 807.

Griffiths, B., Vedanta, in: NCE 14, 584.

Id., Vedas, in: NCE 14, 584.

Hadot, P., Neo-platonism, in : NCE 11, 334-336.

Hearne, B., Christology and Inculturation, in: AFER 22/6 (1980) 335-341. Cf. 32 Articles Evaluating Inculturation, 89-96.

Id., Missio ad Gentes, in: AFER 35/1 (1993) 2-12.

Hering, W. Die Evangelisierung der Kulturen, in: Hering, Aspekte der Evangelisierung, Limburg 1989, pp. 11-34.

Id., Interreligioser Dialog und Inkulturation, in: Lebendiges Zeugnis, Heft 3, 44 (1989) 204-214.

Hillman E., Missionary Approach to African Cultures, in: AFER 22/6 (1980) 342-356. Cf. 32 Articles Evaluating Inculturation, 147-162.

Hinfelaar, H., Evangelization and Inculturation, in: AFER 36/1 (1994) 2-18.

Igboko, P. M., Teaching methods, Including the Use of Audio-Visual Aids, in: Ezeanya, Apostolate, 98-103.

Ihejiofor, T., Christian Inter-denominational Relationship - Assessment and Prospects, in: Anim Seminar Paper, Muslim Master Plan and Method, Onitsha (Nigeria) 1988, pp. 46-63.

Ikeme, C., Cordination between the Priest, the Catechist, the Committee and the Choirmaster, in Ezeanya, Apostolate, 60-71.

Ikeobi, G., The Healing Ministry and Igbo Christianity, in: Uzukwu, Religion and African Culture, 191-201.

Isichei, E., Seven Varieties of Ambiguity: Some Patterns of Igbo Response to Christian Missions, in: JRA 3 (1970) 209-227.

Isichei, E. - McCarron, M. M., Method of Evangelisation in African Cultures, in: NJT 1/4 (1988) 91-104.

Kaigama, I., The Role of the Catholic Youth in the Parish Lay Apostolate, in: Ojo - Dodo, Activities, 82-95.

Kalilombe, P., The Salvific Value of African Religions, in AFER 21/3 (1979) 143-57. Cf. 32 Articles Evaluating Inculturation, 129-143.

Kalu, O. U., Missionaries, Colonial Government and Secret Societies in Southern-Eastern Igboland, 1920-1950, in: Journal of the Historical Society of Nigeria, 1/1 (1977) 73-79.

Kalu, M., Administrative Duties of a Catechist in General, in: Ezeanya, Apostolate, 114-118.

Id., The Gods in Retreat: Models for Interpreting Religious Change in Africa, in: Nigerian Journal of Humanities 1/1 (1977) 49-55.

Kato, B. H., African Cultural Revolution and the Christian Faith, Jos (Nigeria) 1976.

Kealy, Sean P., The End of the Missions, in: AFER 53/1 (1993) 20-26.

Köster, F., Ansätze zu einer afrikanischen Theologie, in: Hering, Christus, 79-93.

Kroeger, J. H., Cruciform Dialogue in Mission, in: AFER 35/1 (1993) 13-19.

Langan, T., Accomodating Cultures without Dissolving the Unity of Faith, in: Crollius, Inculturation, 8 (1986) 43-53.

Legaspi, L. Z., Evangelization and Culture, in: Seminarium 25 (1985) 104-114.

Long, H. S., Neo-pythagoreanism, in: NCE, 11, 336-337.

Legrand, H., Évangelisation de l'Europe, in: NRT 114 (1992) 500-518.

Lourdusamy, D. S., Paul VI and the Encounter with the Cultures, in: Omnis Terra 18 (1984) 119-134, Engl. ed.

L'Osservatore Romano, Message of the Synod of Bishops to the People of God, (November 3, 1977) 5, Engl. ed.

Id., Holy See and Israel Sign Historic Agreement in an Atmosphere of Great Cordiality and Goodwill (January 5, 1994) 9, Engl. ed.

Magesa, C. L., Authentic African Christianity, in: AFER 15/2 (1973) 110-117. Cf. 32 Articles Evaluating Inculturation, 112-120.

Id., Some Critical Theological and Pastoral Issues Facing the Church in East Africa Today, in: SEDOS Bulletin 21 (1989) 236-245.

Manus, C., Contextualization: Theology and the Nigerian Social Reality, in: NJT 1/1 (1985) 21-42.

Mante, G. A. B., Christian and Traditional Values and Priestly Formation, in: WAJES 1 (1989) 54-70.

Masson, J. , L'Église ouverte sur le Monde , in: NRT 84 (1962) 1032-1043.

Maurer, E., Inculturation or Transculturation among the Indians, in: Crollius, 9 (1987) 99-128.

Mbah, A. U. D., Group Laity Activities at the Parish Level, in: Ojo - Dodo, Activities, 73-81.

Mbefo, L. N., Theology and Inculturation: Prospects and Problems - The Nigerian Experience, in: NJT 1/1 (1985) 54-69.

Mbiti, J. S., Christianity and Traditional Religion in Africa, in: IRM 60 (1970) 430-439.

Mejia, R., Foreign Missionaries at the Eve of the African Synod, in: AFER 35/3 (1993) 144-152.

Merecki, J - Styczen, T., The Splendour of Human Freedom Must be Seen in Relation to Truth. Reflections on the Encylical Letter 'Veritatis Splendour' - 6.

Merten, A., The Missionary Dilemma: A Ghanaian Experience, in: SEDOS Bulletin 22 (1990) 303-343.

Metuh, E. I., African Traditional Religion and the Challenges of the Renaissance of African Culture, in: BARC 1/1 (1987) 11-18.

Id., Contextualization: A Missiological Imperative for the Church in Africa in the third Millenium, in: SEDOS Bulletin 22/5 (1990) 144-151.

Id., Theological Basis for Christianising African Forms of Worship of God: A Case Study of the Igbo, in: NJT 1/1 (1985) 70-90.

Meze, P., The Catechist as a Promoter of Vocations, Ezeanya, Apostolate, 25-32.

Müller, K., Accomodation and Inculturation in the Papal Documents, in: VERBUM SVD 24 (1983) 347-360.

Njoku, R. A., Mother, the Centrepiece. A Collection of Articles and Lectures, Owerri (Nigeria), no date

Nthamburi, Z., The Church in Africa: Its Background and Present Situation, in: African Theological Journal 20/2 (1991) 89-100.

Nubuasah, F., The African Missionary to Africa, in: SEDOS Bulletin 22/6 (1990) 170-172.

Nwahaghi, F. N., Contextualization of Christian Liturgy in Igboland: a Pragmatic Approach to African Christian Theology, in: ATJ 20/2 (1991) 123-135.

Nwatu, F., Africa and the Return of Priestcraft, in: AFER 35/3 (1993) 240-251.

Nwazojie, B. K., The Nigerian Hierarchy and Liturgical Inculturation in the Nigerian Church, in: CSN, Inculturation, 63-78.

Nwosu, V., Doctrinal Formation of Catechists, in: Ezeanya, Apostolate, 11-18.

Nyamiti, C., African Sense of God's Motherhood, in: AFER 23/5 (1981) 269-274. Cf. 32 Articles Evaluating Inculturation, 97-102.

Nyerere, J. K., The Church and Socio-Economic Development in the Context of African Socialism, in: AFER 23/4 (1981) 221-231.

Oger, L., Inculturation: To Evangelize as Christ Did, Can This Be Done Without Compromising Ourselves? in: AFER 36/1 (1994) 19-31.

Ohaeri, C., Study of the Local Religious and Cultural Heritage, in: Ezeanya, Apostolate, 107-112.

Ojo, G. A., Laity Participation in the Mission of the Church in West Africa, in: WAJES 1 (1989) 71-100.

Id., The Significance of the Parish as the Basic Forum of Laity Activities, in: Ojo - Dodo, Activities, 22-50.

Okafor, F. U., Legal Positivism and African Legal Experience, in: Uzukwu, Religion and African Culture, 46-58.

Okere, T., The Theological, Canonical and Administrative Issues Posed by Priestly Formation Today, in: WAJES 2/1 (1990) 39-57.

Okereke, G., Some Reflections on the Maintenance and Support of the Clergy: Towards a More Effective Pastoral Functionality, in: BTS 10/1 (1990) 4-25.

Okolo, C. B., Christ, Emmanuel: An African Inquiry, in: AFER 20/3 (1978) 130-139.

Id., Justice in the Nigerian Church: A Theological Prologomenon to the Forthcoming African Synod, in: BTS 11/2 (1991) 4-20.

Id., The African Synod: A Forum to Discuss Major Issues Facing African Christians, in: AFER 35/3 (1993) 153-169.

Id., The Church and 'the New African', in: AFER 23/6 (1981) 358-365.

Id., The Nigerian Church and Leadership: A Critique, in: NJT 1/5 (1990) 39-70.

Okoye, C. J., Bible Knowledge for the Catechist and Choirmaster, in: Ezeanya, Apostolate, 3-11.

Id., The Special Assembly for Africa of the Synod of Bishops - Commentary on the Instrumentum Laboris, in: AFER 35/3 (1993) 170-191.

Id., The Synod of Bishops, Special Assembly for Africa. The Church, Universal and Particular, in: Encounter 2 (1993) 4-15.

Id., What Will Be New About the New Era of Evangelisation, in: CBCN, New Era, 9-46.

Okoye, M., The Catechist in a Station Without a Resident Priest, in Ezeanya, Apostolate, 67-71.

Okure, T., Inculturation, Biblical/theological Bases, in: 32 Articles Evaluating Inculturation, 55-88.

Onaiyekan, J., Christianity: A Foreign Religion, in: The Catholic Elite, Premier Edition, Ibadan (Nigeria, 1980) 4-15.

Id., Nigerian Theology: Preliminary Questions, in: NJT 1/1 (1985) 1-20.

Id., Strategies for Islamic Expansion in Nigeria - A Christian Response: Notes and Reflections, in: BET 2/2 (1989) - 3/1 (1990) 16-30.

Id., The Church in Africa: A Theological Reflection, in: The Catholic Elite, Ibadan (Nigeria, 1981) 23-32.

Id., Why Do We Need A New Era of Evangelisation? in: CBCN, New Era, 39-55.

O'Neill, W. H., Plotinus, in: NCE 11, 443-444.

Onotu, J. J., Christian-Muslim Relation in Nigeria, in: Anim Seminar Paper, Muslim Master Plan and Method, Onitsha (Nigeria) 1988, pp. 6-45.

Id., Individual Activities of the Laity at the Parish Level: Spiritual Build-up for the Laity, in: OJo-Dodo, Activities, 51-72.

Onwubiko, O. A., Inculturation as a New Vision of Evangelisation in the Light of the Lineamenta of the Special Synod on Africa: the Thological Implications, in: BTS 11/2 (1991) 21-32.

Osadebay, D. C., Easter Reflection: The Missionary in West Africa, in: West Africa (April 5, 1947) 289-291, London 1947.

Otunga, M. M., African Culture and Life-Centred Catechesis, in: AFER 20/1 (1978) 27-28. Cf. 32 Articles Evaluating Inculturation, 144-146.

PACT, Statement of the Accra Meeting (1977), in: AFER 20/3 (1978) 175-182.

Payeur, J. A., Inculturation through Small Christian Communities, in: AFER 37/1 (1993) 37-42.

Penoukou, E-J., The Churches of Africa: Their Identity? Their Mission, in: SEDOS Bulletin (1990) 119-125.

Peter, C. J., Logos, Theology of, in: NCE, 8, 968-972.

Probst, M., Inkulturation der katholischen Liturgie in Schwarzafrika, in: Hering, W (Ed.), Christus in Afrika, Limburg 1991, pp. 107-123.

Poupard, P., Statements on Church and Culture by John Paul II, 1978-82, in: Gremillion, Church and Culture, 223-231.

Richard, L. et alii (Ed.), Vatican II: the Unfinished Agenda. A Look to the Future, New York-Mahwah 1987.

Richard, L., Mission and Inculturation: The Church in the World, in: Richard et alii, Vatican II, 93-112.

Riedl, J. O., Platonism, in: NCE, 11, 433-435.

Rosso, A. S., Confucius (K-ung Fu-Tzu) and Confucianism, in: NCE, 4, 156-165.

Rouleau, F. A., Ricci, Matteo, in: NCE, 12, 470-472.

Russel, R. P., Augustinianism, in: NCE, 1, 1063-1068.

Id., Augustinianism, Theological School of, in: NCE, 1, 1069-1071.

Salvoldi, V., African Synod: An Interview with Bishop Agré, in: SEDOS Bulletin 22 (1990) 342-343.

Sanon, A. T., The Universal Message in Cultural Plurality, in: Concilium 135 (1980) 87-93.

Sarpong, P. K., Emphasis on African Christianity, in AFER 17/6 (1975) 322-328. Cf. 32 Articles Evaluating Inculturation, 105-111.

Id., Inculturation: The Ghana Experience, in: CSN, Inculturation, 29-38.

Schneider, G., First Evangelisation - Its Circumstance and Theological Basis in the New Testament, in: VERBUM SVD 26 (1985) 18-30.

Schineller, P., Inculturation and Modernity, in: SEDOS Bulletin, 20/2 (1988) 43-47.

Id., The Life and Teaching of St. Thomas Aquinas, A Challenge for the African Church Today, in: AFER 34/1 (1922) 18-33.

SECAM, Sixth Plenary Assembly: Recommendations and Conclusions on Christian Family Life and Marriage in Africa Today, in: AFER 23/6 (1981) 370-376.

SEDOS, Research Seminar on Mission, March 1981, in: AFER 23/6 (1981) 377-382.

Sesana, R. K., An African Synod without Africa? in: AFER 35/3 (1993) 134-143

Shannon, A. C., Augustinians, in: NCE, 1, 1071-1076.

Stockmeier, P., Die Inkulturation des Christentums, in: LS 39 (1988) 99-103.

Surlis, P., The Relation between Social Justice and Inculturation in the Papal Magisterium, in: Crollius, Inculturation, 8 (1986) 3-40.

Uchendu, V. C., Missionary Problems in Nigerian Society, in: Practical Anthropology 9 (1964) 105-117.

Ugwu, S., Liturgical Formation of Catechists, in: Ezeanya, Apostolate, 75-83.

Uka, E. M., The African Family and Issues of Women's Infertility,, in: ATJ 20/3 (1991) 189-200.

Uzukwu, E. E., African Cultures and the Christian Liturgy, in: WAJES 2/1 (1990) 59-83.

Id., African Personality and the Christian Liturgy, in: NJT 1/3 (1987) 24-36.

Id., Blessing and Thanksgiving Among the Igbo (Nigeria): Towards an African Eucharistic Prayer, in: AFER 22/1 (1980) 17-22.

Id., Church-State Relations in the Early Church and the Crisis Facing the Christian Church in Nigeria, in: BET 2/1 (1989) 31-45.

Id., Food and Drink in Africa, and the Christian Eucharist, in: AFER 22/6 (1980) 370-392; 398.

Id., Liturgical Celebration and Inculturation in Igbo Christian Communities 20 Years After Vatican II, in: NJT 1/2 (1986) 46-60.

Id., Missiology Today: The African Situation, in: Id., Religion and Culture, 146-172.

Id., The Service of the Theologian in the Nigerian Local Church, in: NJT 1/5 (1990) 4-17.

Wallace, W. A. - Weisheipl, J. A., Thomas Aquinas, St., in: NCE, 14, 102-115.

Id., Thomism, in. NCE, 14, 126-135.

Wilfred, F., A Power Draws - Reflections on the Church and the Exercise of Power, in: SEDOS Bulletin (1989) 287-297.

Id., Christian Inculturation and World Religions, in: SEDOS Bulletin, 21/1 (1989) 37-44.

Id., Inculturation: Reflections in the Asian Context, in: SEDOS Bulletin 21/6 (1989) 185-194.

Id., Local Church: Practices and Theologies, Reflections from Asian Context, in: SEDOS Bulletin (1990) 87-103.

Zvarevashe, I. M., Racist Missionaries to Evangelization in Africa, in: AFER 35/2 (1993) 115-131.

7. ON CULTURE AND CULTURAL ANTHROPOLGY.

Adelakun, O. A., The Concept of Culture, in: Metuh-Ojoade, Nigerian Cultural Heritage, 5-12.

Carrier, H., "Culture" in the Discourses of John Paul II,1983-84, in: Gremillion, Church and Culture, 232-234.

Id., Understanding Culture: The Ultimate Challenge of the World-Church? in: Gremillion, The Church and Culture, Notre Dame, Indiana 1985.

Geertz, C., The Interpretation of Culture: Selected Essays, New York 1973.

Gremillion, J (Ed.), The Church and Culture Since Vatican II - The Experience of North and South America, Notre Dame Indiana 1985.

Grunlan, S. A. - Marvin, K. M., Cultural Anthropology. A Christian Perspective, Grand Rapids, Michigan 1979.

Herskovits, M. J., Man and His Works: The Science of Cultural Anthropology, New York 1952.

Hoebel, E. A., Anthropology: The Study of Man, New York [4]1972.

Imo, C., The Concept and Ramifications of Culture, in: Metuh-Ojoade, Nigerian Cultural Heritage, 13-22.

Keesing, F. M., Cultural Anthropology: The Science of Custom, New York 1958.

Kluckhohn, C. - Kelly W. H., The Concept of Culture, in: R. Linton (Ed.), The Science of Man in the World Crisis, new York 1945, pp. 78-106.

Kluckhohn, C., Mirror of Man: The Relation of Anthroplogy to Modern Life, New York-Toronto 1949.

Kroeber, A. L., Anthropology: Race, Language, Culture,Psychology, Prehistory, New York 1948.

Kroeber, A. L. - Kluckhohn, C., Culture: A Critical Review of Concepts and Definitions, New York 1952.

Lang, G. O., Culture, in: New Catholic Encyclopedia, vol. 4, pp. 522-532.

Linton, R., The Study of man: An Introduction. The Century Social Science Series. Student's Edition, New York 1936.

Lowie, R. H., The History of Ethnological Theory, New York 1937.

Nida, E. A., Customs and Cultures, Pasadena 1954.

Pellegrino, M., Cristianesimo e Cultura Classica, in: Di Berardino, Dizionario, vol. 1, 839-847.

Tylor, E. B., Primitive Culture, London 1871, I, p. 1.

UNESCO, Mexico City Declaration: Final Report, in: World Conference on Cultural Policies, Mexico City, July 26 to August 6, 1982.

8. ON THE IGBO AND NIGERIA AND AFRICA.

Abernethy, D. B., Church and State in Nigerian Education, Ibadan (Nigeria) 1966.

Id., The Political Dilemma of Popular Education, California 1969.

Achebe, C., Things Fall Apart, London 1962.

Id., No Longer at Ease, London 1963.

Id., The Trouble With Nigeria, Enugu (Nigeria) 1983.

Adigwe, H. A., Nigeria Joins the Organization of Islamic Conference, O.I.C. The Implications for Nigeria, Onitsha 1986.

Afigbo, A. E., An Investigation of the Relationship between Christian Missions and Secular Authorities in Southeastern Nigeria from Colonial Times, in: Oduma 1 (1973) 16-19, Port Harcourt (Nigeria)

Id., Education, Urbanization and Social Change in Colonial Africa, in: Kalu, O. U (Ed.), African Cultural Development - Readings in African Humanities, Enugu (Nigeria) 1978.

Id., Prolegomena to the Study of the Culture History of the Igbo Speaking People of Nigeria, in: Ogbalu, Igbo Language and Culture, 28-50.

Id., The Aro Expedition of 1901-1902 in the British Occupation of Iboland, in: Odu, Journal of West African Studies 7 (1972) 3-27.

Id., The Background to the Southern Nigeria Education Code of 1903, in: Journal of the Historical Society of Nigeria 4/2 (1968) 197-225.

Id., The Mission, the State and Education in Southeastern Nigeria, in: Fashole-Luke, Christianity, London 1978.

Aluko. T. M., One Man One Wife, London 1967.

Anigbo, Osmund, A. C., Commenasality and Human Relationship Among the Igbo - An Ethnographical Study of Ibagwa Aka, Igboeze L. G. A., Anambra State, Nigeria, Nsukka 1987.

Animalu, A. O. E., "UCHEAKONAM" - A Way of Life in the Modern Scientific Age, 1990 Ahiajoku Lecture, Owerri (Nigeria) 1990.

Arinze, F. A., Sacrifice in Ibo Religion, Ibadan (Nigeria) 1970.

Azikiwe, N., Renascent Africa, London 1944 (reprinted 1968).

Basden, G. T., Among the Ibos of Nigeria, London 1966.

Id., Niger Ibos, London, 1966.

CIDJAP, The African Charter on Human and People's Rights, Enugu (Nigeria) 1990.

Coleman, J. S., Nigeria: Background to Nationalism, Berkeley-London-Los Angeles 1958 (reprinted 1971).

CWO, Our Women Today, Diocese of Orlu (Nigeria), no date.

ECSN, Public Education Edict 1970 (Edict No. 2 of 1971), Enugu, Government Printer.

Echeruo, A., Matter of Identity, 1979 Ahiajoku Lecture, ISMIC, Owerri (Nigeria), 1979.

Edeh, E. M. P., Towards an Igbo Metaphysics, Chicago, Illinois 1985.

Ejiofor, P. N. O., Cultural Revival in Igboland, Onitsha (Nigeria) 1984.

Ejizu, C. I., **Ofo**: Igbo Ritual Symbol, Enugu (Nigeria) 1986.

Ezekwugo, C. U. M., Chi, the True God in Igbo Religion, Alwaye, Kerala, India 1987.

Forde, D. - Jones, G. I., The Ibo and Ibibio-Speaking Peoples of Nigeria, London 1950.

Forsyth, F., Emeka, Ibadan (Nigeria) 1982.

Gbulie, B., The Fall of Biafra, Onitsha (Nigeria) 1989.

Green, M. M., Igbo Village Affairs, Chiefly with Reference to the Village of Umueke, Agbaja, London [2]1964.

Idowu, E. B., African Traditional Religion - A Definition, London 1973.

Ifemesia, C. C., Southeastern Nigeria in the Nineteenth Century. an Introductory Analysis, New York 1976.

Ifesieh, E. I., Prayer in Igbo Religion: Some Traditional Models, in: Uzukwu, Religion and African Culture, 73-91.

Imo State Ministry of Information and Culture (ISMIC): Ahiajoku Lecture 1979-1991, Owerri (Nigeria).

Isichei, E. A History of the Igbo People, London-New York 1976.

Id., The Ibo People and the Europeans, London 1973.

Jordan, J. P., Bishop Shanahan of Southern Nigeria, Dublin 1949 (reprinted 1971).

Kenyatta, J., Facing Mount Kenya, London 1979.

Leonard, A. G., The Lower Niger and Its Peoples, London, 1968.

Madiebo, A. A., The Nigerian Revolution and the Biafran War, Enugu (Nigeria) 1980.

Mbefo, L. N., The Reshaping of African Traditions, Enugu (Nigeria) 1988.

Mbiti, J. S., African Religions and Philosophy, London-Ibadan-Nairobi 1969 (reprinted 1982).

Id., Introduction to African Religion, London-Ibadan-Nairobi-Lusaka 1975 (reprinted 1977).

Meek, C. K., Law and Authority in a Nigerian Tribe, New York [2]1970.

Metuh, I. E., Comparative Studies of African Traditional Religions, Onitsha (Nigeria) 1987.

Id., God and Man in African Religion, London, 1981.

Metuh, E. I. - Ojoade, O (Ed.), Nigerian Cultural Heritage, Jos (Nigeria) 1990.

Munonye, J., The Only Son, London 1977.

Newswatch, Nigeria's Weekly Magazine, Ikeja, March 20, 1989.

Nnabuife, F. C., The History of the Catholic Church in Eastern Nigeria, vol. 1: The Foundation Period (1885-1905), Rome 1983.

Ngugi, J. W., Homecoming, London 1972 (1982).

Njoku, R. A., The Advent of the Catholic Church in Nigeria: its Growth in Owerri Diocese, Owerri (Nigeria) 1980.

Nwabara, S. N., Iboland, London 1977.

Nwabueze, B. O., Igbos in the Context of Modern Government and Politics in Nigeria: A Call for Self-examination and Self-correction, 1985 Ahiajoku Lecture, Owerri (Nigeria) 1985.

Nwoga, D., The Focus of Igbo World View, 1984 Ahiajoku Lecture, ISMIC, Owerri (NIgeria) 1984.

Odumegwu-Ojukwu, E., Because I am Involved, Ibadan (Nigeria) 1989.

Ogbalu, F. C. - Emenanjo, E. N (Ed.), Igbo Language and Culture, Ibadan (Nigeria) 1975.

Ohickwu, J., The Abiding Anger of Islam: Will Nigeria Ever Enjoy Peace? Vol. No. 4 June 1991.

Ohuche, R. O., "**Ibu Anyi Danda**" - The Centrality of Education In Igbo Culture, 1991 Ahiajoku Lecture, Owerri (Nigeria) 1991.

Okafor, F. C., Africa at Crossroads, New York, 1974.

Okeke, P. U., Background to the Problems of Nigerian Education, in: Ikejiani, O (Ed.) Nigerian Education, Longman, Nigeria 1964; 1971.

Okigbo, B. N., Plants and Food in Igbo Culture, 1980 Ahiajoku Lecture, Owerri (Nigeria) 1980.

Okigbo, P. N. C., Towards a Reconstruction of the Political Economy of the Igbo Civilization, 1986 Ahiajoku Lecture, Owerri (Nigeria) 1986.

Onwubiko, O. A., African Thought, Religion & Culture, Enugu (Nigeria) 1991.

Onwuejeogwu, M. A., Evolutionary Trends in the History of the Development of the Igbo Civilization in the Culture Theatre of Igboland in Southern Nigeria, ISMIC, Ahiajoku Lecture (1987).

Parrinder, G., West African Religion. A Study of the Beliefs and Practices of Akan, Yoruba, Ibo and Kindred Peoples, London 1969 (reprinted 1975).

Perham, M., The British Problem in Africa, in: Foreign Affairs 29 (1950/1951) 637-650.

Talbot, P. A., Peoples of Southern Nigeria, Oxford 1926.

Uchendu, V. C., The Igbo of Southeast Nigeria, London 1965.

Von Rosen, C. G., Le Ghetto Biafrais, Paris 1969.
Zahan, D., The Religion, Spirituality and Thought of Traditional Africa 1979.

9. COMMENTARIES ON ACTS.

Arrington, F. L., The Acts of the Apostles. An Introduction and Commentary, Peabody Massachussets 1988.

Barclay, W., The Acts of the Apostles (The Daily Study Bible), Revised Edition, Edinburgh 1976 (1990 reprint).

Bruce, F. F., The Acts of the Apostles. The Greek Text with Introduction and Commentary (3rd Revised & Enlarged Edition) Grand Rapids, Michigan 1990.

Id., The Acts of the Apostles, London ²1952.

Id., The Book of the Acts (Revised Edition), Grand Rapids, Michigan 1988.

Conzelmann, H., Die Apostelgeschichte (Handbuch zum Neuen Testament 7) Tübingen ²1972.

Crowe, J., The Acts (New Testament Message, vol. 8), Wilmington, Delaware 1979.

Dillon, R. J., Acts of The Apostles, in: Brown et alii, NJBC, 44.722-767.

Foakes-Jackson, F. J. - Lake, K (Ed.), The Beginnings of Christianity. Part 1, The Acts of the Apostles, vols. 1-5, London 1922-1939.

Haenchen, E., The Acts of the Apostles, A Commentary, Oxford 1971 (reprinted 1982).

Kilgallen, J. J., A Brief Commentary on the Acts of the Apostles, New York-Mahwah 1988.

Loisy, A., Les Actes des Apotres, Paris 1920.

Marshall, I. H., The Acts of the Apostles, An Introduction and Commentary, (Tyndale New Testament Commentaries), Leicester, England-Grand Rapids, Michigan 1980 (reprinted) 1984.

Martini, C. M., Gli Atti degli Apostoli, Testo e Note a Cura di Carlo M. Martini, e di Nereo Venturini, Tipografia Poliglotta Vaticana 1967.

Munck, J., The Acts of the Apostles, Anchor Bible 31, New York 1967.

Neil, W., The Acts of the Apostles (New Century Bible), London 1973.

Pesch, R., Die Apostelgeschichte, Zürich-Einsiedeln-Köln 1986.

Phillips, J., Exploring Acts, Volume Two, Acts 13-28, Chicago 1986.

Roloff, J., Die Apostelgeschichte (Das Neue Testament Deutsch 5), 17th ed., Göttingen 1981.

Schmittals, W., Die Apostelgeschichte des Lukas, Zurich 1982.

Schneider, G., Die Apostelgeschichte, 2 Volumes, Herders Theologischer Kommentar zum Neuen Testament 5, Freiburg 1980 & 1982.

Schille, G., Die Apostelgeschichte des Lukas, Theologischer Handkommentar zum Neuen Testament 5, Berlin 1983.

Strack, H. - Billerbeck, P., Kommentar zum Neuen Testament aus Talmud und Midrasch, vol. 2, 1924; [7]1978.

Tannehill, R. C., The Narrative Unity of Luke-Acts, A Literary Interpretation. Volume 2: The Acts of the Apostles, Minneapolis 1990.

von Harnack, A., The Acts of the Apostles 1909. (Translation from German: Die Apostelgeshichte: Beitrag zur Einleitung in das Neue Testament, vol. 3, Leipzig 1908).

Weiser, A., Die Apostelgeschichte (Ökumenischer Taschenbuch-Kommentar zum Neuen Testament 5), Volumes 1 & 2, Gütersloh 1981 & 1985.

Williams, C. S. C., The Acts of the Apostles (Black's New Testament Commentaries), Second Edition, London [2]1964 (reprinted 1985).

10. STUDIES ON ACTS 15, 1-35.

Bammel, E., Der Text von Apostelgeschichte 15, in: Kremer, Les Actes, 439-446.

Barrett, C. K., Apostles in Council and in Conflict, in: ABR 31 (1983) 14-32.

Boismard, M - E., Le "Concile" de Jerusalem (Act 15,1-33). Essai de Critique Litteraire, in: ETL 64 (1988) 433-440.

Boman, T., Das Textkritische Problem des Sogennanten Aposteldekrets, in: NT 6 (1963) 26-36.

Brown, R. E. et al. (Ed.), Petrus beim "Konzil" zu Jerusalem (Apg 15), in: Brown, Der Petrus, 48-53.

Catchpole, D. R. Paul, James and the Apostolic Decree, in: NTS 23 (1976/77) 428-444.

Dahl, N. A., A People for his Name, in: New Tesatment Studies 4 (1957-58) 319-327.

Dupont, J., Un Peuple d'entres les Nations (Acts 15,14), in: NTS 31 (1985) 321-335.

Fahy, T., The Council of Jerusalem, in: IrTQ 30/3 (1963) 232-261.

Haenchen, E., Quellenanalyse und Kompositionsanalyse in Apg 15, in: BZNW 26 (1960) 153-164.

Hoerber, R. G., A Review of the Apostolic Council after 1925 Years, in: CJ 2/4 (1976) 155-159.

Holtz, T., Die Bedeutung des Apostelkonzils für Paulus, in: NT 1 (1974) 110-133.

Kaiser, W. C., Jr., The Davidic Promise and the Inclusion of the Gentiles (Amos 9:9-15 and Acts 15,13-18): A Test Passage for Theological Systems, in: JETS 20/2 (1977) 97-111.

Kaye, B. N., Acts Protrait of Silas, in: NT 21 (1979) 13-26.

Klijn, A. F. J., The Pseudo-Clementines and the Apostolic Decree, in: NT 10 (1968) 305-312.

Kümmel, W. G., Die älteste Form des Aposteldekretes (Acts 15,20.29), in: Marbuger Theologischen Studien (Mar) 3 (1965) 278-288

Nolland, J., A Fresh Look at Acts 15,10, in: NTS (1980/81) 105-115.

Pasinya, M., L'Inculturation dans les Actes des Apotres, in: Amewowo et alii, Les Acts, 120-133 (here: 126-133).

Radl, W., La Legge in Atti 15, in: Kertelge, La Legge, 161-166.

Richard, E., The Divine Purpose: The Jews and the Gentile Mission (Acts 15), in: SBL Seminar Papers (1980) 267-282.

Squillaci, D., Nel XIX Centenario Paolino - Il Primo Concilio e San Paolo (Atti 15,1-34), in: PalCl 40 (1961) 829-834.

Schwartz, D. R., The Futility of Preaching Moses (Acts 15,21), in: Bib 67 (1986) 276-281.

Weiser, A., Das "Apostelkonzil", in: Weiser, Studien zu Christsein und Kirche, 185-210.

11. LITERATURE ON ACTS AND LUKE.

Amewowo, W. et al. (Ed.), Les Actes des Apotres et les jeunes Eglises, Kinshasa (Zaire) 1990.

Amewowo, W., The Christian Community in the Acts of the Apostles: Model for Our Days, in: Amewowo et al., Les Actes, 105-116.

Arowele, P. J., Mission and Evangelisation in Acts and the African Experience, in: Amewowo et alii, Les Actes, 219-240.

Balch, David, L., Comments on the Genre and Political Theme of Luke-Acts: A Preliminary Comparison of two Hellenistic Historians, in: Lull, SBL Seminar Paper 28 (1989), pp. 343-361.

Barbi, A., La Missione Universale negli Atti, in: Parola, Spirito e Vita 16 (1987) 171-186.

Barclay, W., The Gospel of Luke (The Daily Study Bible), Revised Edition, Edinburgh 1975 (1990 reprint).

Barrett, C. K., The Third Gospel as a Preface to Acts? Some Reflections, in: F. van Segbroeck et al., The Four Gospels 1992, BETL C, 1451-1466.

Bassey, M. E., Witnessing in the Acts of the Apostles, Rome 1988.

Beck, B. E., The Common Authorship of Luke and Acts, in: NTS 23 (1977) 346-352.

Benoit, P., La deuxième Visite de Saint Paul à Jérusalem, in: Bib 40 (1959) 778-796.

Bock, Darrell, L., The Use of the Old Testament in Luke-Acts, in: SBL Seminar Paper 29 (1990) 494-511.

Bovon, F., Luc le Theologien. Vingt-cinq Ans de Recherches (1950-1975), Neuchatel-Paris 1978.

Id., Tradition et Redaction en Acts 10,1-11,18, in: TZ (1970) 22-45.

Bowker, J. W., Speeches in Acts: A Study in Proem and Yelammedenu Form, in: NTS 14 (1967-68) 96-111.

Brown, S., The Role of the Prologue in Determining the Purpose of Luke-Acts, in: Talbert, Perspectives in Luke-Acts, 99-111.

Bruce, F. F., Commentaries on the Acts, in: EpR 3/3 (1981) 82-87.

Id., The Acts of the Apostles Today, in: BJRUL 65 (1982/83) 36-56.

Id., The Holy Spirit in the Acts of the Apostles, in: Interpretation 27/2 (1973) 166-183.

Bruno, W., Paganisme Populaire et Prédication Apostolique, Genève 1987.

Buetubela, B., L'Autonomie des jeunes Églises et les Actes, in: Amewowo et alii, Les Actes, 77-104.

Bultmann, R., Zur Frage nach den Quellen der Apostelgeschichte, in: Exegetica. Aufsätze zur Erforschung des Neuen Testaments, Hrsg. von E. Dinkler, Tübingen 1967, pp. 412-423.

Burini, C., Gli Studi dal 1950 ad oggi sul Numero e sulla Classificazione del Discorsi degli "Atti degli Apostoli" - un contributo d'individuazione, in: Laurentianum 15/3 (1974) 349-365.

Id., Gli Studi dal 1950 (Part 2), in: Laurentianum 16/1-2 (1975) 191-207.

Cadbury, H. J., The Making of the Acts, London 1968 (reprinted edition).

Id., Speeches in Acts, in: Jackson - Lake, The Beginnings of Christianity, vol. 5, pp. 402-427.

Id., The Tradition, in: Jackson - Lake, The Beginnings of Christianity, vol. 2, pp. 209-264.

Id., "We and I" Passages in Luke-Acts, in: NTS 3 (1957) 128-131.

Campbell, R. A., The Elders of the Jerusalem Church, in: JTS 44/2 (1993) 511-528.

Carroll, J. T., Response to the End of History: Eschatology and Situation in Luke-Acts, SBL Dissertation Series 92, Atlanta, GA 1988.

Id., The Use of Scripture in Acts, in: SBL Seminar Paper 29 (1990) 512-528.

Cassidy, R. J., Society and Politics in the Acts of the Apostles, Maryknoll, New York 1987.

Conzelmann, H., The Theology of St. Luke, New York-London 1960.

Cook, M. J., The Mission to the Jews in Acts: Unravelling Luke's "Myth of the Myriads", in: Tyson, Luke-Acts, pp. 102-123.

Culpepper, R. A., Paul's Mission to the Gentile World: Acts 13-19, in: REx 71/4 (1974) 487-497.

Danielou, J., La Chiesa degli Apostoli, Roma 1991. (Translation from French: L'Église des Apotres, Paris 1970).

Dawsey, James, M., Characteristics of Folk-Epic in Acts, in: SBL Seminar Paper (1989), pp.317-325.

Id., The Literary Unity of Luke-Acts: Questions of Style - A Task for Literary Critics, in: NTS 35 (1989) 48-66.

Derrett, J. D. M, Clean and Unclean Animals (Acts 10,15; 11,9): Peter's Pronouncing Power Observed, in: HeyJ 29 (1988) 205-221.

Dibelius, M., Studies in the Acts of the Apostles, London 1956. (Translation from German: Aufsätze zur Apostelgeschichte, Hrsg. von H. Greeven, Göttingen 1951).

Dillon, R. J., The Prophecy of Christ and his Witnesses According to the Discourses of Acts, in: NTS 32 (1986) 544-556.

Downey, J., The Early Jerusalem Christians, in: Bible Today 91 (1977) 1295-1303.

Dumais, M., The Church of the Acts of Apostles: a Model of Inculturation? in: Crollius, Inculturation, 10 (1987) 3-24.

Id., Le Langage des Discours d'Évangelisation des Actes: une Forme de Langage Symbolique, in: Kremer et alii, Les Actes, 467-474.

Du Plooy, G. P. V., The Author in Luke-ACts, in: Scriptura 32 (1990) 28-35.

Id., The Design of God in Luke-Acts, in: Scriptura 25 (1988) 1-6.

Dupont, J., Etudes sur les Actes des Apotres, Lectio Divina 45, Paris 1967.

Id., J., Le Salut des Gentiles et la Signification Théologique du Livre des Actes, in: NTS 6 (1960) 132-155.

Id., Les sources du Livres des Actes. État de la Question, Brugge 1960.

Edward, Douglas, E., Acts of the Apostles and the Graeco-Roman World: Narrative Communication in Social Contexts, in: SBL Seminar Paper (1989), 362-377.

Elliot, J. K., The Text of Acts in the Light of two Recent Studies, in: NTS 34 (1988) 250-258.

Id., Jerusalem in Acts and the Gospels, in: NTS 23 (1977) 462-469.

Emmet, C. W., The Case for the Tradition, in: Jackson-Lake, The Beginnings of Christianity, vol. 2, 265-297.

Fackre, G., An Acts Theology of Evangelism, in: Religion in Life 44 (1975) 73-89.

Fahy, T., A Phenomenon of Literary Style in Acts of the Apostles, in: IrTQ 29/4 (1962) 314-318.

Ferguson, E., The Hellenists in the Book of Acts, in: RQ 12/4 (1969) 159-180.

Id., Apologetics in the NT (Acts), in: RQ 6 (1962) 189-196.

Fitzmyer, J. A., The Gospel According to Luke (I-IX). Introduction, Translation and Notes, Anchor Bible 28, Garden City, New York 1981.

Gager, J. G., Jews, Gentiles, and Synagogues in the Books of Acts, in: HarvTR 79/1-3 (1986) 91-99.

Gasque, W. W., A Fruitful Field: Recent Study of the Acts of the Apostles, in: Interpretation 42/2 (1988) 117-131.

Gaventa, B. R., 'You will be my Witnesses': Aspects of Mission in the Acts of the Apostles, in: Missiology 10/4 (1982) 413-425.

Id., Toward a Theology of Acts. Reading and Reading, in: Interpretation 42/2 (1988) 146-157.

Ghidelli, C., Gli Atti degli Apostoli nella Chiesa oggi. Bollettino Bibligrafico, in: RCI 53 (1972) 220-227.

Id., Studi sugli Atti degli Apostoli, in: Scuola Catholica 93/Supp. 3 (1965) 390-398.

Gräßer, E., Die Apostelgeschichte in der Forschung der Gegenwart, in: TRu 26 (1960) 93-167.

Id., Acta-Forschung seit 1960, in: TRu 41/2 (1976) 141-193.

Id., Acta-Forschung seit 1960 (Fortsetzung), in: TRu 41/3 (1976) 259-290.

Id., Acta-Forschung seit 1960 (Fortsetzung und Schluß), in: TRu 42 (1977) 1-68.

Green, M., Evangelism in the Early Church, Grand Rapids, 1975.

Gunther, J. J., The Fate of the Jerusalem Church, in: TZ 29 (1973) 81-94.

Guthrie, D., Recent Literature on the Acts of the Apostles, in: Vox Evangelica 2 (1963) 33-49.

Guy, C., The Missionary Message of Acts, in: (SWJT) 17 (1974) 49-64.

Haenchen, E., Acts as Source Material, in: Keck, Studies in Luke-Acts, Nashville 1966.

Id., Judentum und Christentum in der Apostelgeschichte, in: ZNW 54/3-4 (1963) 155-187.

Haenchen, E. - Weigandt, P., The Original Text of Acts? in: NTS 14/4 (1968) 469-481.

Harrisville, R. A., Acts 22,6-21, in: Interpretation 42/2 (1988) 181-185.

Hengel, M., Der Historiker Lukas und die Geographie Palästinas in der Apostelgeschichte, in: ZDP 99 (1983) 147-183.

Id., Zwischen Jesus und Paulus. Die 'Hellenisten', die 'Sieben' und Stephanus (Apg 6,1-15; 7,54-8,3), in: ZTK 72/2 (1975) 151-206.

Hoerber, R. G., Evangelism in Acts, in: CJ 7/3 (1981) 89-90.

Id., Several Classics Reprinted: On Language of the New Testament and the Reliability of Acts, in: CJ 5/2 (1979) 63-65.

Horsley, G. H. R., Speeches and Dialogues in Acts, in: NTS 32/4 (1986) 609-614.

House, C., Defilement by Association: Some Insights from the Usage of koinós/koinóo in Acts 10 and 11, in: AUSS 21/2 81983) 143-153.

Hoyt, H. A., The Frantic Future and the Christian Directive: Acts 1:8, in: Grace Theological Journal 10/1 (1969) 36-41.

Hubbard, B. J., Commissioning Stories in Luke-Acts: A Study of their Antecedents, Form and Content, in: Semeia 8 (1977) 103-106.

Id., The Role of Commissioning Accounts in Acts, in: PRS 5 (1978) 187-98.

Hunkin, J. W., British Work on the Acts, in: Jackson-Lake, The Beginnings of Christianity, vol. 2, pp. 396-433.

Jefford, Clayton, N., An Ancient Witness to the Apostolic Decree, in: Proceedings. Eastern Great Lakes and Midwest Biblical Societies; vol. 10 (1990) 204-213.

Jervell, J., Luke and the People of God: A New Luke at Luke-Acts, Minneapolis, Minnesota 1972.

Id., Paul in the Acts of the Apostles: Tradition, History, Theology, in: Kremer et alii, Les Actes, 297-306.

Id., Paulus in der Apostelgeschichte und die Geschichte des Urchristentums, in: NTS 32 (1986) 378-392.

Id., The Acts of the Apostles and the History of Early Christianity, in: ST 37/1 (1983) 17-32.

Id., The Church of Jews and Godfearers, in: Tyson, Luke-Acts, 11-19.

Johnson, Luke, T., The Literary Function of Possessions in Luke-Acts, SBL Dissertation Series 39, Atlanta, GA 1977.

Jones, D. L., Luke's Unique Interest in Historical Chronology, in: SBL Seminar Paper (1989), 378-387.

Karris, R. J., The Gospel According to Luke, in: Brown et alii, NJBC, 43: 1-198, pp. 675-721.

Keck, L. E. - Martyn, J. L (Ed.), Studies in Luke-Acts, Festschrift for Paul Schubert New York-Nashville, 1966.

Kee, Howard, C., Good News to the Ends of the Earth - The Theology of the Acts, London-Philadelphia 1990.

Id., The Changing Role of Women in Early Christianity, in: Theology Today (1992) 225-242.

Kilgallen, J. J., A Brief Commentary on the Gospel of Luke, New York-Mahwah 1988.

Id., Acts 13,38-39: Culmination of Paul's Speech in Pisidia, in: Bib 69 (1988) 481-506.

Id., Acts: Literary and Theological Turning Points, in: BTB 7 (1977) 177-180.

Kingsbury, J. D., The Pharisees in Luke-Acts, in: F. van Segbroeck et al., The Four Gospels 1992, BETL C, 1497-1511.

Koet, B. J., Simeons Worte (Lk 2,29-32.34c-35) und Israels Geschick, in: Van Segbroeck, F. et al. (Ed.), The Four Gospels 1992, Festschrift Frans Neirynck, vol. 2, pp. 1549-1569, Leuven 1992.

Kremer J. - Barrett, C. K. et al., Les Actes des Apotres: Traditions, Rédaction, Théologie, BETL 48, Gembloux-Leuven 1979.

Lachs, S. T., A Rabbinic Commentary on the New Testament. The Gospels of Matthew, Mark, and Luke, Hoboken-New Jersey-New York 1987.

Lake, K., Proselytes and Godfearers, in: The Beginning of Christianity, vol. 5, 74-96.

Legrand, L., The Church in the Acts of the Apostles, in: Bhash 4/2 (1978) 83-97.

Id., Local Church and Universal Church in the Acts of the Apostles, in: Vidyajoti 40/7 (1976) 290-298.

Lukasz C., Evangelizzazione et Conflitto; Indagine sulla Coerenza Letteraria e Tematica della Pericope di Cornelio (Atti 10,1-11,18), Frankfurt am Main 1993.

Lull, D. J (Ed.), Society of Biblical Literature, 1989 Seminar Papers 28, Atlanta, GA 1989.

Maddox, R., The Purpose of Luke-Acts (Studies of the New Testament and its World), Edinburgh 1982.

Mangatt, G., The Acts of the Apostles - An Introduction, in: Bhash 4/2 (1978) 75-82.

Manus, C., The Areopagus Speech (Acts 17,16-34): Study of Luke's Approach to Evangelism and its Significance in the African Context, in: Amewowo et alii, Les Actes, 197-218.

Marshall, I. H., Luke - Historian and Theologian, Exeter [3]1988.

Id., La Communicazione dell' Evvangelo al Mondo non-Cristiano nel NT, in: STE 2/3 (1979) 37-76.

Id., Recent Study of the Acts of the Apostles, in: ET 80/10 (1969) 292-296.

Id., The Present State of Lucan Studies, in: Themelios 14 (1989) 52-56.

Marchesi, G., Il Vangelo da Gerusalemme a Roma - L'Origine del Cristianesimo negli Atti degli Apostoli, Milano 1991.

Martini, C. M., La Tradition Textuelle des Actes des Apotres et les Tendances de l'Église Ancienne, in: Kremer et alii, Les Actes, 21-25.

Menoud, Ph. H., Le Plan des Actes des Apotres, in: NTS 1 (1954) 44-51.

Miesner, D. R., The Missionary Journeys Narrative: Patterns and Implications, in: Talbert, Perspectives on Luke-Acts, 199-214.

Moessner, D. P., The Ironic Fulfilment of Israel's Glory, in: Tyson, Luke-Acts, 35-49.

Mussner, F., La Vita Secondo la Tora nell'Interpretazione Ebraica, in: Kertelge, La Legge, 24-40.

Neirynck, F., Le Livre des Actes dans les Recents Commentaires, in: ETL 59 (1983) 338-349.

Id., The Miracle Stories in the Acts of the Apostles, in: F. van Segbroeck (Ed.), Evangelica, Collected Essays by Frans Neirynck, BETL 50, 835-880.

Omanson, R. L., A Gentile Palaver, in: UBS Monograph Series. Issues in Bible Translation, Stine, P. C (Ed.), London 1988, pp. 274-286.

O'Neil, J. C., The Theology of Acts in its Historical Setting, London [2]1970.

O'Toole, Robert, F., The Unity of Luke's Theology, An Analysis of Luke-Acts, Good News Studies 9, Wilmington, Delaware 1984.

Id., Why did Luke write Acts (Lk-Acts)? in: BTB 7/2 (1977) 66-76.

Palmer, D. W., Literary Background of Acts 1,1-14, in: NTS 33 (1987) 427-438.

Parker, P., Once More, Acts and Galatians, in: JBL 86 (1967) 175-182.

Id., The "Former Treatise" and the Date of Acts, in: JBL (1965) 52-58.

Pathrapankal, J., The Church of the Acts of the Apostles: A Model for our Times, in: TDig 34/1 (1987) 19-24.

Id., The Hellenists and their Missionary Dynamism in the Early Church and its Message for our Times, in: Bhash 8 (1982) 216-226.

Pervo, R. I., Profit with Delight: The Literary Genre of the Acts of the Apostles, Philadelphia 1987.

Id., Must Luke and Acts Belong to the Same Genre? in Lull, SBL Seminar Paper (1989) 309-316.

Plumacher, E., Acta-Forschung 1974-1982, in: TRu 48/1 (1983) 1-56.

Id., Acta-Forschung (Fortsetzung und Schluß), in: TRu 49/1 (1984) 105-169.

Id., Die Apostelgeschichte als historische Monographie, in: Kremer et alii, Les Actes, 457-466.

Polhill, J. B., The Hellenist Breakthrough: Acts 6-12, in: Rex 71/4 (1974) 475-486

Praeder, S. M., The Problem of First Person Narration in Acts, in: NT 29/3 (1987) 193-218.

Ravassi, G. F. et al., Fede e Cultura dagli Atti degli Apostoli. Ciclo di Conversazioni Organizzato dal Centro Culturale San Fedele, Milano, Bologna (Italia) 1988.

Ravassi, G. F., Studi sugli Atti degli Apostoli - Un bilancio bibliografico e teologico, in: Ravassi et alii, Fede e Cultura, 7-26.

Richard, E., Luke - Writer, Theologian, Historian: Research and Orientation of the 1970's, in: BTB 13 (1983) 3-15.

Id., The Creative Use of Amos by the Author of Acts, in: NT 24/1 (1982) 37-53.

Robbins, V. K., By Land and By Sea Voyages, in: Talbert, Perspectives in Luke-Acts, 215-242.

Rutledge, A. B., Evangelistic Methods in Acts, in: SWJT 17 (1974) 35-47.

Salmon, M., Insider or Outsider? Luke's Relationship with Judaism, in: Tyson, Luke-Acts, 76-101.

Sanders, J. N., Peter and Paul in the Acts, in: NTS 2 (1955/56) 133-143.

Sanders, J. T., The Jewish People in Luke-Acts, in: Tyson, Luke-Acts, 51-75.

Id., Who is a Jew and Who is a Gentile in the Book of Acts? in: NTS 37 (1991) 434-455.

Schmidt, Darly, D., Syntactical Style in the "We" Sections of Acts: How Lukan is it? in: SBL Seminar Paper (1989), 300-308.

Slingerland, D., The "Jews" in the Pauline Portion of Acts, in: JAAR 54/2 (1986) 395-321.

Sheeley, S. M., Narrative Asides and Narrative Authority in Luke-Acts, in: BTB 18/3 (1988) 102-107.

Sterling, G. E., Luke-Acts and Apologetic Historiography, in: SBL Seminar Paper (1989), 326-342.

Stuehrenberg, P. F., The Study of Acts Before the Reformation - A Bibligraphic introduction, in: NT 29/2 (1987) 100-136.

Sugirtharajah, R. S., Luke's Second Volume and the Gentiles, in: ET 100 (1989) 178-181.

Talbert, Charles, H (Ed.), Perspectives on Luke-Acts Perspectives in Religious Studies (Special Studies Series No. 5), Danville-Edinburgh 1978.

Id., Literary Patterns, Theological Themes and the Genre of Luke Acts, SBL Monograph Series 20, Missoula (Montana) 1974.

Tannehil, R. C., Rejection by Jews and Turning to Gentiles. The Pattern of Paul's Mission in Acts, in: Tyson, Luke-Acts, 83-101.

Id., The Function of Peter's Mission Speeches in the Narrative of Acts, in: NTS (1991) 400-414.

Id., The Narrative Unity of Luke-Acts, A Literary Interpretation. Volume 1: The Gospel According to Luke, Philadelphia 1986.

Taylor, J., The Making of Acts: A New Account, in: RB 97/4 (1990) 504-524.

Tiede, D. L. Acts 11:1-18, in: Interpretation 42/2 (1988) 175-180.

Id., "Glory to thy People Israel": Luke-Acts and the Jews, in: Tyson, Luke-Acts, 21-33.

Tyson, J. B., The Death of Jesus in Luke-Acts, Columbia 1986.

Id., The Emerging Church and the Problem of Authority in Acts, in: Interpretation 42/2 (1988) 132-145.

Id., The Problem of Jewish Rejection in Acts, in: Tyson, Luke-Acts, 124-137.

Trocmé, E., Le "Livres des Actes" et l'histoire, Paris 1957.

Van de Sandt, H., The Quotations in Acts 13,32-52 as a Reflection of of Luke's LXX Interpretation, in: Bib 75 (1994) 26-57.

Van der Horst, P. W., Hellenistic Parallels to the Acts of the Apostles: 1,1-26, in: ZNW 74/1-2 (1983) 17-26.

Van Unnik, W. C., Die Apostelgeschichte und die Häresien, in: ZNW 58/3-4 (1967) 240-246.

Id., Luke's Second Book and the Rules of Hellenistic Historiography, in: Kremer et alii, Les Actes, 37-60.

Id., Sparsa Collecta, vol. 1, Leiden 1973.

Id., Luke-Acts, A Storm Centre in Contemporary Scholarship, in: Keck, Studies in Luke-Acts, 15-32.

Veltman, F., The Defense Speeches of Paul in Luke-Acts, in: Talbert, Perspectives in Luke-Acts, 243-256.

Von Harnack, A., Luke the Physician, London 1907. (Translation from German: Lucas der Arzt, der Verfasser des dritten Evangeliums und der Apostelgeschichte: Beiträge zur Einleitung in das Neue Testament, vol. 1, Leipzig 1906.

Waliggo, J. M., Acts of the Apostles and a Hundred Years of Catholic Evangelization in Africa, in: Amewowo et alii, Les Actes, 25-46.

Wall, Robert, W., The Acts of the Apostles in Canonical Context, in: BTB 18 (1988) 16-24.

Weiser, A., Critica della Legge e del Tempio da Parte degli "Ellenisti", in: Kertelge, La Legge, 139-160.

Id., Gemeinde und Amt nach dem Zeugnis der Apostelgeschichte, in: Id., Studien zu Christsein, 305-320.

Id.., Studien zu Christsein und Kirche (Stuttgarter Biblische Aufsatzbände 9, Neues Testament) Gerhard Dautzenberg und Norbert Lofink (Hrsg.), Stuttgart 1990.

Wenham. D., The Paulinism of Acts Again: Two Historical Clues in 1 Thessalonians, in: Themelios 13 (1988) 53-55.

Wenham, G. J., The Theology of Unclean Food, in: EvQ 53/1 (1981) 6-15.

Wilcox, M., Luke and the Bezan Text of Acts, in: Kremer et alii, Les Actes, 447-455.

Wilkinson, T. L., Acts 17: The Gospel Related to paganism. Contemporary Relevance, in: Vox Reformata 35 (1980) 1-14.

Williams, R. B., Reflections on the Transmission of Tradition in the Early Church, in: Encounter 40 (1979) 273-285.

Willimon, W. H., Eyewitnesses and Ministers of the Word. Preaching in Acts, in: Interpretation 42/2 (1988) 158-170.

Wilson, S. G., The Gentiles and the Gentile Mission in Luke-Acts, London-New York.

Windisch, H., The Case Against the Tradition, in: Jackson-Lake, The Beginnings of Christianity, vol. 2, 298-348.

12. LITERATURE AKIN TO THEMES OF LUKE-ACTS.

Benhayim, M., Jews, Gentiles and the New Testament Scriptures (Alleged Antisemitism in the New Testament), Jerusalem 1985.

Betz, O., Peritome, in: Balz, Wörterbuch, vol.3, Stuttgart-Mainz 1983. pp. 186-189.

Box, G. H., Pharisees, in: Hastings et alii, Encyclopedia, vol. 9, 831-836.

Brown, R. E., Biblical Exegesis and Church Doctrine, New York-Mahwah 1985.

Id., The Churches the Apostles Left Behind, New York-Ramsey 1984.

Brown, R. E. et al. (Hrsg.), Der Petrus der Bibel - Eine ökumenische Untersuchung, Stuttgart 1976.

Brown, R. E. - Osiek, C. - Perkins, P., Early Church, in: Brown et al., NJBC, 80:1-82, pp. 1338-1353.

Brown, R. E. - Meier, J. P., Antioch & Rome, New Testament Cradles of Catholic Christianity, New York-Ramscy 1984.

Cannon, K. G. - Fiorenza, E. S., Interpretation for Liberation, Semeia 47, Atlanta, GA (USA) 1989.

Castelot, J. J. - Cody, A., Religious Institutions of Israel, in: Brown et al., NJBC, 76: 1-157, pp. 1253-1283.

Douglas, M., Purity and Danger, London 1966.

Faley, R. J., Leviticus, in: NJBC, 4: 1-55, pp. 61-79.

Foerster, K. L., Iesous, in: Kittel - Friedrich, TWNT, 3, 284-294.

Fitzmyer, J. A., A History of Israel: From Pompey to Bar Cochba, in: Brown et alii, NJBC, 75:145-193, pp.1243-1252.

Id., The Letter to the Galatians, in: NJBC, 47:1-32, pp. 780-790.

Id., Paul, in: NJBC, 79: 1-54, pp. 1329-1337.

Id., Pauline Theology, in: Brown et alii, NJBC, 82:1-152, pp. 1382-1416.

Foley, R. L., Circumcision of Our Lord, in: NCE, 879-880.

Gray, Louis H., Custom, in: Hastings et alii, Encyclopedia, vol. 4, pp. 374-377.

Kertelge, K (Ed.), Saggi Esegetici su La Legge nel Nuovo Testamento, Milano 1990. (DEUTSCH: Das Gesetz im Neuen Testament, Freiburg im Breisgau 1986).

Küng, H., The Church, London and Tunbridge Wells 1968. Eight Impression.

Lüdemann, G., Paul, Apostle to the Gentiles, Philadelphia 1984.

Lull, David, J (Ed.) Society of Biblical Literature (SBL), Seminar Papers 1989, Atlanta, Georgia (GA) 1989.

Macdonald, D. R (Ed.), The Apocryphal Acts of Apostles, Semeia 38, An Experimental Journal for Biblical Criticism (by SBL), Decatur, GA (USA) 1986.

Marcus, J., The Circumcision and the Uncircumcision in Rome, in NTS 35 (1989) 67-81.

Mckenzie, J. L., Aspects of Old Testament Thought, in Brown et al., NJBC, 77:140-178, pp. 1308-1315.

Müller, D., Pharisäer, in: Coenen et alii, Theologisches Begriffslexikon, vol. 3, pp. 1001-1003.

Osborne, R. E., St Paul's Silent Years, in: JBL (1965) 59-65.

Panagopoulos, J., Zur Theologie der Apostelgeschichte, in: NT 14 (1972) 437-159.

Pathrapankal, J., Critical and Creative. Studies in Bible and Theology, Bangalore 1986.

Polan, S. M., Circumcision, in: NCE, 3, 878-879.

Rivkin, E., Pharisees, in: Eliade, Encyclopdeia, vol. 11, pp. 269-272.

Roloff, J., Die Kirche im Neuen Testament, Göttingen 1993.

Schmidt, K. L., Ekklesia, in: Kittel - Friedrich, TWNT, 3, 502-539.

Schweizer, E., Pneuma, Pneumatikos, in: Kittel - Friedrich, TWNT, 6, 394-449.

Schoeps, H. J., Jewish Christianity: Factional Disputes in the Early Church, Philadelphia 1969.

Id., Theologie und Geschichte des Judenchristentums, Tübingen 1949.

Smallwood, M. E., The Jews under Roman Rule: From Pompey to Diocletian. Studies in Judaism in Late Antiquity 20, Leiden 1976.

Stauffer, E., Theos, in: Kittel - Friedrich, TWNT, 3, 95-122, especially, 107-109.

Strathmann, H., Martus, in: Kittel - Friedrich, TWNT, 4, 477-510.

Verseput, D. J., Paul's Gentile Mission and the Jewish Christian Community. A Study of the Narrative in Galatians 1 and 2, in: NTS 39 (1993) 38-58.

Weiser, A., Basis und Führung in kirchlicher Communio, in: BiKi 45 (1990) 65-71.

Id., Die Kirche in den Pastoralbriefen, in: BiKi 46 (1991) 107-113.

Whitakker, M., Jews and Christians: Graeco-Roman Views (Cambridge Commentaries on Writings of the Jewish and Christian World 200 BC to AD 200, no. 6), New York 1984.

Wong, J.H. P., The Holy Spirit in the Life of Jesus and the Christian, in: Gregorianum 73 (1992) 57-95.

13. LITERATURE ON BIBLICAL CRITICISM AND METHOD.

Abrams, M. H., A Glossary of Literary Terms, New York 1985.

Alter, R., The Art of Biblical Narrative, New York 1981.

Bar-Efrat, Narrative Art in the Bible, JSOTS 70, Sheffield 1989

Best, O. F., Handbuch Literalischer Begriffe, Frankfurt 1982.

Boot, W. C., A Rhetoric of irony, Chicago-London 1974.

Id., The Rhetoric of Fiction, Chicago 1983.

Brown, R. E. - Schneiders, S. M., Hermeneutics, in: Brown et al., NJBC, 71, pp. 1146-1165.

Cannon, K. T. - Fiorenza, E. S., Semeia 47: Interpretation for Liberation, SBL 1989, Atlanta, GA.

Chatman, S., Story and Discourse. Narrative Structure in Fiction and Film, Ithaca-London 1978.

Cordesse, G., Narration and Focalisation, in: Poetique 76 (1988) 487-498.

Crane, R. S., The Concept of Plot, in: Stevick, P (Ed.), The Theory of the Novel, New York-London 1967, pp. 141-145.

Culler, J., Defining Narrative Units, Style and Structure in Literature: Essays in the New Stylistics, Ithaca, New York 1975.

Dipple, E., Plot, London 1970.

Egan, K., What is Plot? in New Literary History 9 (1978) 455-473.

Freytag, G., Technique of the Drama, Chicago 1908. (German: Technik des Dramas, Lepzig 1886).

Gasque, W. W., A History of the Criticism of the Acts of the Apostles, Tübingen and Grand Rapids 1975.

Id., The Historical Value of the Book of Acts: An Essay in the History of New Testament Criticism, in: EvQ 41/2 (1969) 68-88.

Genette, G., Figures III, Poetique, Paris 1972. (English: Narrative Discourse, Ithaca-London-Oxford, 1980).

Hierbert, P. G., Critical Contextualization, in: SEDOS Bulletin 19/9 (1987) 337-345.

Kselman, J. S. - Witherup, R. D., Modern New Testament Criticism, in: Brown et alii, NJBC, 70, pp. 130-1145.

Kwok Pui Lan, Discovering the Bible in the Non-Biblical World, in: Cannon - Fiorenza, Semeia 47 (1989) 25-42.

Licht, J. Storytelling in the Bible, Jerusalem 1978.

McGiffert, A. C., The Historical Criticism of Acts in Germany, in: Jackson-Lake, The Beginnings of Christianity, vol. 2, 363-395.

Mlakuzhyil, G., The Christocenrtic Structure of the Fourth Gospel (Analecta Biblica 177), Rome 1987.

Müller, G., Die Bedeutung der Zeit in der Erzählkunst; Erzählzeit und erzählte Zeit (Festschrift P. Kluckhorn und H. Schneider) Tübingen 1948 = Morphologische Poetik, Tübingen 1968.

Parrat, J., Theological Methodologies in Africa, in: Verbum SVD 24 (1983) 47-62.

Petersen, N., Literary Criticism for New Testament Critics, Philadeplhia 1978.

Pistaky, K., The Process of Contextualization and its Limits, in: VERBUM SVD 24 (1983) 163-171.

Powell, M. A., What is Narrative Criticism? Guides to Biblical Scholarship, Minneapolis 1990.

Scholes, R. - Kellog, R., The Nature of Narrative, New York 1966.

Ska, J. L., "Our Fathers Have Told Us". Introduction to the Analysis of Hebrew Narratives. Subsidia Biblica 13, Roma 1990.

Suezler, A. - Kselman, J. S., Modern Old Testament Criticism, in Brown et alii, NJBC, 69, pp. 1113-1129.

Sternberg, M., Expositional Modes and Temporal Ordering in Fiction, Baltimore-London 1978.

Id., The Poetics of Biblical Narratives, Bloomington 1985.

Id., What is Exposition, in: Halperin, J (Ed.), Theory of the Novel, New York 1974, pp. 25-70.

Vorster, W. S., The Reader in the Text: Narrative Material, in: Semeia 48 (1989) 21-39.

Welch, J. W (Ed.), Chiasmus in Antiquity - Structures, Analyses, Exegesis, Hildesheim 1981.

Wilder, A. N., Early Christian Rhetoric, London 1964.

Wimbush, V. L., Historical/Cultural Criticism as Liberation: A Proposal for an African American Biblical Hermeneutic, in: Cannon - Fiorenza, Semeia 47 (1989) 43-55.

14. MISCELLANEOUS.

Bruce, V., Introduction to Prophetic Literature, in: Brown et al., NJBC, 11, pp. 186-200.

Carpenter, D., Inspiration, in: Eliade, The Encyclopedia of Religion, vol.7, pp. 256-259.

Collins, R. F., Inspiration, in: NJBC, 65: 1-72, pp. 1023-1033.

Concepte, Zeitschrift für ethische Orientierung, Heft 11-12 (Köln, Germany 1990), 1-33.

Deutsche Tagespost. Katholische Zeitung für Deutschland, Nummer 14, 47. Jahrgang, Würzburg, Donnerstag, 3. Februar 1994.

Foitzik, A., Die Allgegenwart von Gewalt. Neue Veröffentlichungen untersuchen deren Ursachen, in: Herder Korrespondenz, Monatshefte für Gesellschaft und Religion, Heft 1 (48. Jahrgang 1994) 31b-35.

Pegon, J., Inspirations of the Holy Spirit, in: NCE, vol. 7, pp. 545-546.

Rheinland-Pfalz/Panorama, Mädchen trotz Bitten und Flehen brutal vergewaltigt, in: Rhein-Zeitung. Unabhängige Westdeutsche Landeszeitung. Nr. 47 (Freitag, 25. Februar 1994. 49. Jahrgang. Ausgabe B - Koblenz) p. 4.

Maps/Illustrations

FEDERAL REPUBLIC OF NIGERIA

Map of Present-Day Nigeria showing the 30 States of Nigeria and their Capitals. Abuja is the Federal Capital Territory.
(Courtesy of the Embassy of Nigeria, Bonn, Germany)

419

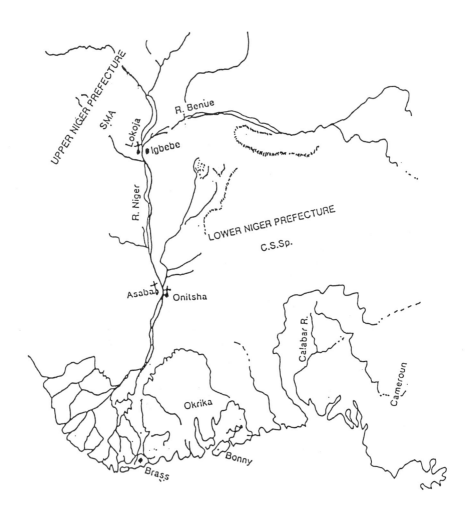

Territories of the Prefectures of Upper and Lower Niger
(Courtesy of Nnabuife, F., History, 89)

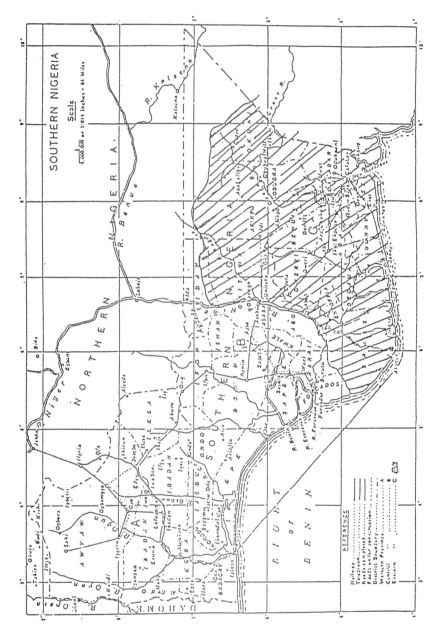

Southern Nigeria after the Almagamation
(Courtesy of Nnabuife, History, 7)

421

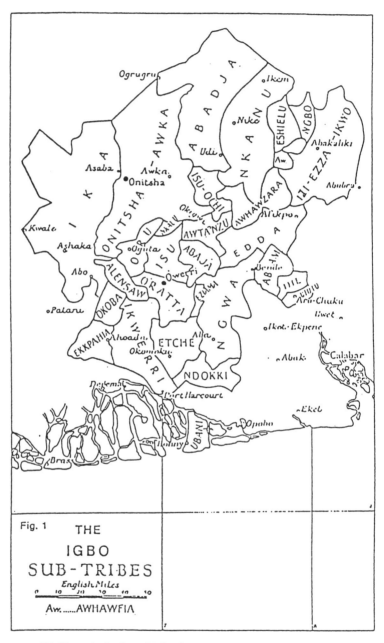

(Courtesy of Echiegu, A. O., Sacral Igbo, 8)

422

The Ecology and dialect zones of Igbo culture area

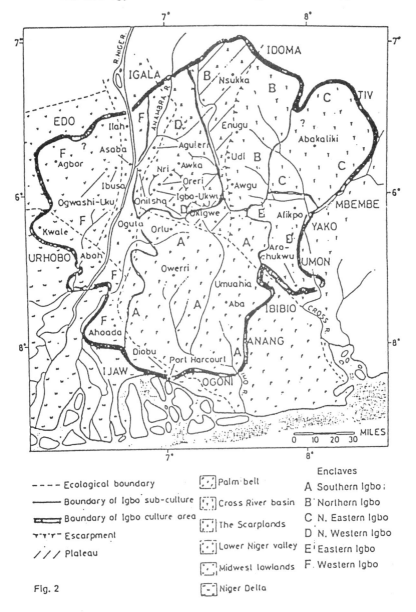

Fig. 2

Legend	
– – – – Ecological boundary	Palm belt
——— Boundary of Igbo sub-culture	Cross River basin
▭▭▭ Boundary of Igbo culture area	The Scarplands
ⲧⲧⲧ Escarpment	Lower Niger valley
/ / / Plateau	Midwest lowlands
	Niger Delta

Enclaves

A Southern Igbo;
B Northern Igbo
C N. Eastern Igbo
D N. Western Igbo
E Eastern Igbo
F Western Igbo

(Courtesy of Echiegu, A. O., Sacral Igbo, 9)

423

Charles Ok. Onuh

Christianity and the Igbo Rites of Passage
The Prospects of Inculturation

Frankfurt/M., Berlin, Bern, New York, Paris, Wien, 1992. XVIII, 263 pp.
European University Studies: Series 23, Theology. Vol. 462
ISBN 3-631-44974-7   pb. DM 79.--*

Owing to their value and strategic importance in the people's mentality and culture, this work proposes the Igbo Rites of Passage as a necessary parameter and a transmitting wave-length for a firm rooting of the christian faith among the Igbos.
"Culture, in relation to a people, can be compared to a radio and its 'frequency'. And just as a radio picks up every sound which is attuned to its frequency perfectly and with ease, and transmits the same clearly and strongly, so also can a people absorb the christian message and make it a part of themselves, provided this message is properly brought to them through the radio frequency of their culture."
(Paul C. Ekowa)

Contents: Incarnating christianity · Making the faith feel at home · Solidarity of the Igbos · Inculturation · Rites of Passage · Dialogue with the traditional rites · The birth rites · Strategy of the Igbo traditional headship and other values

Peter Lang ≋ **Europäischer Verlag der Wissenschaften**
Frankfurt a.M. • Berlin • Bern • New York • Paris • Wien
Auslieferung: Verlag Peter Lang AG, Jupiterstr. 15, CH-3000 Bern 15
Telefon (004131) 9411122, Telefax (004131) 941.1131
- Preisänderungen vorbehalten - *inklusive Mehrwertsteuer